CHASING
A FLAWED
SUN

CHASING A FLAWED SUN

DANIEL MCGHEE

Authors Note: The events in this story are all true as far as my memory and perception of them have interpreted. Names and minor details have been changed to protect the rights of those involved. It is not my wish to include anyone else unwillingly in my tale of transparency. We are all at different stages in our own journeys.

The Library of Congress has catalogued the paperback edition as follows:
Phoenix rising publishing:
McGhee, Daniel, 2019.
Chasing a flawed sun/ Daniel McGhee
Library of congress control number: 2019939069

ISBN 978-1-7339485-0-0
ISBN 978-1-7229485-1-7 (ebook)

Published by Phoenix Rising Publishing.

www.chasingaflawedsun.com

ACKNOWLEDGEMENTS

This book is dedicated to Wendy, Adele, and all the other angels
who saw something in me
when I wasn't able to see it in myself.

…and of course, to my God, Who has stood by me
every single step of the way.
With You beside me, no one nor anything
could ever drag me down.

"We build our castles in the sky and in the sand.
Design a whole world, can't nobody understand.
I found myself alive in the palm of your hand.
As long as we are flying, oh this world ain't got no end.
…no, this world ain't got no end."

-Paul Kalkbrenner, "Sky and Sand"

BEFORE YOU READ THIS BOOK

Chasing a Flawed Sun is a story from a very critical piece of my life. The names of the people and a few of the places have been altered to protect identities. Other than that, the story is completely true. From the beginning, transparency has been essential to me in relaying my experiences. Along with transparency though, comes brutal honesty. Because of that, there are some very graphic scenes, as well as vulgar language, contained within. I have chosen not to jeopardize the integrity of the stories by watering down the language or vividness of the events that occurred. While reading, keep in mind that there is a happy ending, eventually.

When we, as a human race, first desired to understand the inner workings of the human body, it was necessary for us to open up some unlucky volunteers in order to study the inside of their bodies. I believe there are too many people who do not understand the mind or reasonings of those who struggle with addiction. So, I have written an autopsy into my own mind, heart, and soul during active addiction and my mental state leading up to it. My hope is that other addicts (recovering or still using), as well as their families and loved ones, will get a glimpse into why we do what we do (or did what we did), what goes on in our minds, and how the addiction controls us. This is a no-holds-barred journey into my soul, heart, and mind, when I was a lost young man in the midst of my dark struggle with addiction. While my story is unique, it is not special. There are millions of stories out there just like mine. I only have the blessing of conveying it so vividly.

Don't give up before the story unfolds. I struggled whether to include the First Season in this book or omit it. I concluded that it was a necessary evil, as it shows my progression from the early stages of my life to the madness that eventually took me down into the subculture of heroin. Be patient and open-minded, as there are children making these same mistakes all across the world every day. Hopefully there are clues in my experiences here that can help to stop it out there.

Interestingly, one characteristic of my book is that the writing matures as the narrator matures. As I wrote the book, I purpose-fully revisited the state of mind I was in back when the events unfolded. I tapped into, not only those experiences, but the thoughts and emotions I felt as they transpired. Much of the writing carried me to such dark places, that I fell into a series of depression and anxiety as I relived some of the most difficult moments of my life. The writing reflects that and grows with the narrator as time elapses through the Seasons.

Lastly, this book is meant to be read from front to back in its entirety to truly grasp the meaning and message of my story. It is a saga of pain, guilt, shame, and a never-ending series of mistakes that ultimately lead to a powerful and unforgettable breakthrough. I look forward to meeting you at the end, where I will introduce you to the "me" of today.

INTRODUCTION

There is nothing magical about a crystal ball. The ball itself does nothing of its own accord. It is not until the beholder focuses his gaze upon the crystal and falls into a trancelike state that images begin to appear. Even then, images do not appear inside the crystal ball, but rather they surface in a person's mind as he stares into the ball. The crystal is only a medium, a tool, for reaching deep inside oneself.

The murky water, shallow in my spoon, is my medium. It's where I come to reflect. It's where the demon dissolves just before the water begins to boil into a soft chorus of crackling, and the bottom of the spoon turns black from the lighter's faithful flame. I bite a small chunk of cotton from the filter of my Newport and roll it into a tight little ball between my thumb and forefinger, only to drop it into the solution and watch it expand. I feel the soft bite and watch the mushroom cloud of blood that grows in the neck of the needle that tells me I'm coming home.

The familiar kick hits the back of my throat, my skin flushes warm, my eyes rest heavily in their sockets, and I am here again. I'm back where I swore I'd never come, but where I've always wanted to be. I come back here to reflect, and even though the spoon is not real, nor the needle, the dope, nor the murky water... still, I can almost taste it.

Eighteen years out of its grip, and my stomach still drops at the mere thought of it. Butterflies flitter inside my belly, and my pulse quickens when I think about dumping a vial of soft, scaly coke into the back of that same syringe…and I crave. I crave it all. I'd give up everything to be on a dusty couch covered in cigarette burns or a mattress on the floor of a ghetto row home for one sweet embrace. To be numb again with no responsibility, no cares, no morals, no concerns. It's an easy vacation from the weight of this world. However, I know I've come too far. I have no choice but to carry this torch. I gaze into those murky waters, and they become my crystal ball. I come here to reflect and share with you. I risk my life to come here. I'm not being dramatic—it's as serious as it sounds. I risk my life to come here, to share these reflections with you, so let's not waste our time…

Danny Diamond McGhee

PROLOGUE

I instinctively thrust my right arm straight across the body next to me to keep her face from pounding into the dash as my left foot slammed the brakes. I cursed the car in front of me. Two more bodies bounced around in the back seat in a disheveled mess, one sprawled out on top of the other, a boy and a girl, leaning on each other in mock support. I didn't have time to check anyone's pulse at this point, I was moving through the city as fast as I could, praying no one noticed the bodies in the car with me and called the police. They danced in their seats as I swerved in and out of traffic ricocheting through the city's notorious potholes. The cold female in the front seat slid lifelessly onto my shoulder as I raced through the red light, tires spinning, trying to get anywhere less noticeable so I could try to work my magic on them. I had blown my high, but that could be regained. My freedom and my conscience could not. As long as I tried my best, then I could live with the repercussions. I skidded into the McDonald's parking lot at Highland and Orleans Street, pulled a needle from my pocket, and got ready to work a miracle. But first, here's how I got here...

That morning I was up early, drudgingly climbing into the car with my father. I had agreed to go with him to interview at an adult rehabilitation program on the outskirts of Washington

DC. It was about an hour drive, and I had promised to go. In my mind I had already made my decision not to enter into the program, but I had to appease my folks if I wanted to continue having a roof over my head. At twenty years of age, I wanted help, but I didn't actually want to take the measures required to get it. I wanted to stop shooting heroin almost from the time I started, but the alternative meant being sober and feeling all the hurt of the world, not to mention the mental and physical withdrawal. Those are things I was subconsciously willing to avoid at all costs, no matter how much my present mind told me I needed to quit.

We drove toward DC, most of the time in silence, as those car rides usually were. There's not much to talk about when you're a drug addict and a common street thug and have absolutely nothing in common with your old man. In fact, there's not much to say when you feel like a complete and utter disappointment to him, when you know you've wrought hell upon his life and become nothing but a nuisance. Yet here he was, taking me to a rehab interview, on a two-hour round-trip drive when I'm sure there were many other things he'd rather be doing.

We pulled into an unfamiliar town in unknown territory. The building looked old and hard, just unadorned red brick, more like a cold prison than a warm, inviting rehab facility. I made up my mind instantly that I wasn't going in. I hopped out of the car and lit up a cigarette in an effort to prolong our entrance as long as possible. I knew my father was growing impatient, so I eventually stubbed it out, and we walked in. The man in charge explained to us that it was more like a halfway house in which we would have a lot of Christ-centered meetings and Bible studies. He made it clear that I needed to detox before I came in, and that I wasn't allowed to smoke while I was here. I shifted around in my seat. My father sensed my anxiety and disappointment, and in a rare moment I could tell that he empathized with my feelings.

After the brief introduction, we went outside to talk about it.

I explained to him that there was no way I could give up drugs and cigarettes at the same time, that I still needed to detox, and that the whole place made me uncomfortable. I felt like an utter failure for letting him down again, but he didn't express any anger. Strangely enough, he agreed to get in the car and leave without a fight. It just didn't feel right to either of us. My reasons were only inner-excuses to protect my habit. I'm not sure where his feelings of discomfort with the facility stemmed from.

The drive back to Baltimore was just as silent as the drive down had been. The closer we got to Baltimore, the more I started formulating a plan in my mind to get high. I had to stop him from taking me all the way to the county. Once I was out there, I would have to go through the painstaking task of getting all the way back downtown. I only had $25 on me, nowhere near enough to pay a ride to get me downtown. I mustered up the courage to bluntly ask something I'd never asked of him before.

We were passing one of the Eastside exits on I-95 when I blurted out, "Can you pull over right here and let me out?"

He looked surprised, but pulled over. "What's wrong?" he asked.

I told my father, "Look, I'm sick. I need to get well. You can take me all the way back to the county, but I'm just going to have to come back down here."

He wasn't sure what to do at this point, but he reluctantly relented, "Fine. Go. But don't ever ask me for a ride back down here again."

"I wasn't. We were just passing by," I explained to him as I got out of the car. I shut the door, hopped the double median, and ran across the four-lane highway to my freedom.

Once on the other side, I ran up the embankment and onto the exit. I walked into East Baltimore like a man on a mission. I had a couple of miles to walk to get over to the west side of the city. It didn't matter how I felt before I started walking, once I knew I had all the pieces of the puzzle together, I felt almost superhuman. This meant I had money, a plan, and a destination in mind. I hadn't had time to feel the early pangs of full withdrawal yet, only the anxiety and gloom of knowing that sickness was impending. Once I started walking, I couldn't stop. I was moving like a man with a bus to catch. But there was no bus—only a high. Speed walking through the side streets toward Lafayette, I passed two people, but I wasn't paying them any attention when I heard a crackly voice call out my full name from behind me. Surprised, I spun around.

"Motherfucker!" she exclaimed happily as she dropped her hoodie so I could see her.

My heart sank when I saw it was Crystal. We were best friends as early teenagers. She was the most beautiful girl in Edgewood High School. She remained a virgin until she was twenty years old, which was unheard of, especially in our circles. She dated a couple of my friends, but I never got romantically involved with her. We were beyond that. We had been best friends. We had a lot of memories together as teenagers, from staying up all night for hours talking on the phone, to prank calling people, to beating people up together. We had each other's backs, and when I went to jail, she was one of the only people who ever made time to write me. She would send scolding letters, saying she believed in me and never thought I'd get involved in heroin. She would tell me how I was so different and better than everyone else, and she always told me she loved me. She was the last person I ever expected would try heroin.

I looked at her now in disbelief. It had been years since I'd seen her. I'd heard a few rumors about her using, but she hadn't been around to confirm. I could plainly see that the rumors were true. Her face was busted up, she looked like she had just climbed out of a dumpster, and she was quick to tell me that she was out there tricking. The same beautiful girl, once a virgin who nobody could crack, a smart girl who lectured everyone else about using hard drugs, and once my best friend, was now down here selling her body for drugs. I couldn't believe it, and I didn't have time to believe it. I'd think about it after I got high. I told her I had to get to Westside, and I turned to keep moving, as she started asking for money.

"I'm in the same boat you are," I shouted over my shoulder with my back to her, hustling up the street. I pushed all of those thoughts out of my mind.

The walk took me all the way through downtown, across Martin Luther King and up Franklin. Now I was out of my element. I walked with my hand in my pocket, balled up around my cash, to make sure it hadn't disappeared. This is how important money becomes to you when you need your next fix. I'd have irrational thoughts about it disappearing before I was able to cop my dope with it. I was deep in the hood now for the next twenty blocks or so, and my white skin stood out like a billboard, revealing that I didn't belong there. I made a right onto Arlington, praying not to get hassled by the police or stick-up boys as I kept my eyes low and kept moving. I made it several blocks to Mosher and turned left down the hill.

People called out to me trying to hustle me to buy their coke and other brands of heroin, or maybe even drywall or soap. I wasn't taking my chances. Because I was caught off guard this morning, I didn't have my works on me. I needed to get a needle, and a place with water and a cooker to get high. But I knew exactly where to go. Once I got to the corner of Calhoun and Mosher, the strip was jumping. There were touts and lookouts on every corner.

"DOA out! DOA out y'all!" they hollered.

The entrance to "the hole" was in the middle of the block on the left. I'd been in a lot of dope holes, but the DOA hole on Calhoun and Mosher was unforgettable. See, a dope strip was set up like this: You have corner boys who oversee their dope operation. Then there are touts and lookouts standing on the corners of the block to let passersby know what shops are open and what brand of dope is being sold. They also keep a watchful eye out for the police. The hole itself is an alley in which a buyer enters into, deep inside so his transaction remains out of sight of the streets, primarily any form of law enforcement.

The particular brand of dope was called DOA (Dead On Arrival) and had become one of the city's most popular at the time due to its potency and the longevity at which it had been operating out of that same hole. The name didn't hurt either. If it sounded potent, you could expect it to be potent. Names like DOA, Flatline, Bodybag, Mike Tyson, and the like were often given to brand batches of dope to advertise their effectiveness. Once rumors got around that people were overdosing on a certain batch, then its sales would skyrocket. Everybody on the streets wants the strongest shit, and nobody expects that they will OD. They brush off the other overdoses as beginners. Some of us just didn't care about the risks.

Once in the hole, the buyer would give his money to a moneyman, who would then communicate with the hitter or pitcher how much he gave, and the hitter would piece him off with the right number of pills. The DOA hole was the perfect dope boy set up, but a nightmare for the junkies. It was an extremely thin long alley just wide enough to walk through that stretched about fifty feet into blackness. Once at the end of the alley, I handed my money to the moneyman, who in this case shouted out "Two!" because I had handed him a twenty. Now I was in a courtyard with trash and trees and rubble everywhere. It was extremely dark back there, and the majority of the homes that backed up there were boarded up and vacant. I wondered how many people got killed, beaten, raped, or robbed back here. It looked haunted.

"Here," a voice called out to me, and I walked back into a

dark corner where an invisible figure held out two pills from of a hole in one of the dilapidated concrete walls.

My heart beat out of my chest whenever I was back here, especially once I had the heroin in hand. If the police dared to come in, I was cornered. The thin alley was like a bottleneck. Once I popped out of it, I had no way of knowing what was waiting for me on the other side in the sunlit street. I half-jogged out of it, pills in hand, and headed across the street.

There was one, lone row home directly across the street from the hole. Both of the neighboring houses on each side had been torn down. I walked right up the front steps and banged on the door. I had never done this before, but I knew the residents were cool. I'd heard many stories about them helping people out. Pearl answered the door. She was blacker than midnight, probably around forty years old, and a full-fledged junkie. She and her husband Paul had worked as touts for the DOA dope boys at various times, and I knew they both got high.

"Look, I've got five bucks. I just need a pin and a place to get well. Let me come in, and I won't stay long," I said through the crack in the door.

It opened further, and I walked in. I crashed down on the couch and waited while Paul fetched me a "new one" from underneath the kitchen sink where he kept a stock of them. "New one" was common slang for a clean syringe. You could often hear people on drug corners or around the city's various markets shouting out "New ones!" where they would sell individual needles for a dollar apiece. Paul brought me a needle and a bottle cap and asked that I just tap him out a third of one of my pills. I wondered what Pearl got out of the deal, although they both looked contentedly high. I cooked up, tied off, shot half a pill, and sank into comfort on their couch.

"Give me about fifteen minutes," I said.

I wanted to make sure I didn't go out (overdose) before I

shot the other half. Better to be safe than sorry. I wasn't worried about death, but an overdose would put an unnecessary burden on Pearl and Paul, and possibly land me in central booking if I survived. I lit up a cigarette and embraced the warmth that surrounded me. It was good, almost perfect. It was good enough that it wouldn't warrant me taking another shot for a while—DOA dope always was. But you never knew, sometimes dope fell off, either because it expired or because the market dried up and they were cutting it down more. One thing was certain, it rarely ever stayed consistent in quality, which is why an addict never knew what they were really getting and often overdosed.

When a new brand is introduced on the street, initially it is very potent. "Testers," free samples handed out to local junkies, are intentionally made strong in order to promote the new brand. Word spreads like wildfire through the inner-city heroin community. When a new brand is hitting, everyone knows about it. DOA was my go-to brand that month, and I had shown it to many others, just as it had been shown to me. Carloads of kids drove into this hot zone to get their morning fix from all directions including Harford, Anne Arundel, Howard, and Baltimore counties, some coming from as far as West Virginia. Most of them had a local guy like myself who was street savvy, someone who knew the street life inside and out, someone who could get out and cop for them while they waited safely around a corner.

My high had settled in, and now I had to figure out how to get home. I was in a different world right now. I didn't belong in this house. Nor did I belong outside in gangland. I had to get out safely. I thanked Paul and Pearl, stepped out onto their front stoop, and looked up and down the block for police. I started my fast walk up the sidewalk out of there. I didn't get forty feet up the street before I recognized a car with a familiar face riding shotgun. Three white faces in a car down here only meant one thing, but I knew these jokers. I waved them down, laughing in relief. They rolled down a window looking sketchy as hell, like they were afraid I was either going to ask them for money or try to rob them.

"I already copped. I just need a ride to get the fuck out of here," I told them.

They told me they hadn't copped yet, and I knew they were scared.

I said, "Look, let me hop in, and I can grab it for you."

I didn't know who the driver was, but my guy Mick in the passenger seat had the biggest afro I'd ever seen on a white boy. He pointed toward the back. As soon as I heard the locks click, I slid into the backseat and said "Hi" to his girlfriend, Cori. I told them to make a U-turn and park on the corner out of sight of the hole. Without saying so, it was evident they didn't want to hand me their money. They were afraid I wouldn't come back with it, and I didn't blame them. We were all friends, and I had never been in a position to steal from them before. I was well now, so I definitely wasn't going to today. However, I understood that giving someone your money to cop heroin when you are sick is like giving someone your entire life savings to gamble on a hand of blackjack. You never felt safe once it was out of sight. They said that if I'd take Cori up in the hole with me to cop, they would give me a ride home with them. Cori was the smallest, most innocent looking white girl. She didn't look like a typical addict, if there is an actual look, but she was definitely the bravest one of the three. I walked into the hole with her as she got their pills, and we got back into the car without an issue.

She divvied up the pills among them, and we headed off. They were eager to get high, but we stuck out like a sore thumb in this area. There were way too many pitfalls here to be avoided. They were discussing where to safely go to get high. I told them that I knew the perfect place. There was a Park and Ride five minutes from here at Franklin and Pulaski where we could go and not be noticed.

"You sure?" they asked.

"Yes, I'm sure!" I said.

Cori told them to chill, that I knew this city like it was my own backyard, and we pressed on. I guided them into the Park and Ride, and we sandwiched ourselves in a spot surrounded by empty cars. It was midday on a weekday, so I knew there would be little traffic there. The girl who was driving, the only one I didn't know, asked me to hop into the driver's seat and keep watch while they got high. So, I took the driver's seat, and she hopped into the passenger seat. Mick got into the backseat with his girl. They all started cooking up immediately, so I joined them.

"Dude, what the fuck? You're supposed to be looking out!" Mick griped.

"Don't worry, I got you." I said, "There's nobody here. Chill."

I wasn't about to let them have all the fun without joining in. I didn't need it, but I couldn't stop myself either. I dumped the other half of my pill into the bottle cap I brought with me from Paul's house, got even higher and drifted into a daze. I lit a cigarette and started nodding out behind the wheel of the parked car. As far as I was concerned, I was alone in there. The rest of the world ceased to exist, except for me and my cigarette.

I was floating blissfully head first into the steering wheel, when I was abruptly awakened by a smack to the back of my head.

"Are you okay?"

"Yeah, what the fuck?" I moaned.

It was Cori. She said in a half-high, half-worried voice, "Mick is out! He won't wake up!"

Shit! I turned around in the seat. The girl next to me was nodding. Mick was in the back, eyes rolled up in his head. The only reason I knew he was alive was because he was giving off a snoring sound, commonly referred to as a "death rattle." *We could lose him at any minute*, I thought, and Cori knew enough to know the same.

"Hey, hey, hey!" I shouted loudly into the car trying to startle both Mick and the female passenger into waking up. I reached back and slapped him across the face, but nothing. "Cori, she's going out too!" I said in reference to the chick next to me. "We need to get out of here fast and get somewhere safe. Keep working on him!"

I took the keys out of the girl's pocket next to me and tried to shake her a few times before giving up and starting her car. *She couldn't possibly be mad at me, a stranger, driving her car while she and another person were dying in it,* I rationalized to myself. I backed out of the spot and headed to I-40 East (a brief expressway through the inner-city). I was high as hell myself, so I wasn't thinking clearly. I had set my mind on going to a McDonald's way over on the Eastside where the community was mixed black and white, and we wouldn't attract nearly as much attention. We would pass several hospitals and service stations on the way, but this is what my heroin-fueled instinct told me to do. As I bounced through the intersections and stoplight after stoplight, I looked over at the girl next to me. She was slumped over with her forehead bouncing on the dash.

"Do you see this? Is he okay?" I shouted back to Cori, but got no reply. Panicked, I looked up in the rearview mirror and saw what I was afraid of. Cori was out, falling into Mick in the backseat, as her mouth hung open and her skin flushed.

"Wake the fuck up!" I yelled into the car, but nobody heard me. If the cops pulled me over, I was doomed. I had a car full of heroin pills and potentially three dead bodies. I sped through the city streets, keeping a watchful eye out for them, knowing that at this point I may just make them chase me. At every stoplight I took turns slapping and shaking each of them in the car. I took the water bottle that we used to cook the heroin and threw it in their faces. Still nothing.

That car ride was like something out of a movie, and enough to give an average person a heart attack, but I was gently embraced in a pillow of heroin where nothing was that serious, except running out. I did what I could to wake them, and when I finally pulled into the McDonald's parking lot, I knew exactly what I had to do as a last-ditch effort to save them. I yelled to wake them up, and I shook each of them one more time before running inside the McDonald's. Sweaty and frantic, I ran to the counter and asked for a large cup of ice water. I then went over to the condiments section and grabbed a huge handful of salt packets. I busted back out of the McDonald's doors on a mission, praying I hadn't sparked anyone's interest enough that I might be watched. When I got to the car, I was relieved to see the passenger door cracked halfway open. The girl in the passenger seat had started to wake up on her own. She had the door cracked because she felt the need to vomit.

I sat down in the driver's seat and said, "Listen, I need you to wake up. You almost died, and I have two people in the back of your car ready to die too. I need your help!"

She sat there nodding in shame.

"Wake the fuck up!" I said.

I sat the cup of ice water between my legs and started ripping the salt packets open and dumping them into the water. I wasn't sure why this worked, but it was old junkie lore, and it had worked on me a few times. Once I stirred in the salt with the straw, I took a syringe full, got out, and opened the back door.

"I need you to grab a handful of ice out of that cup and put it down Mick's pants. He needs ice on his balls. I'm not kidding!" I yelled out to her. She seemed to take me seriously. "Don't dump the water. We still need it," I followed.

With the back door open right there in the McDonald's parking lot, without a care of who might be watching, I began searching Cori's arm for a vein. I plunged the needle in, drew blood, and pushed the salt water back in.

"Here, give me the cup," I said.

She handed it to me across the two bodies after she hesitantly finished reaching into Mick's pants, putting ice on his testicles. I think she felt like I was pranking her, and I would have felt that way too, if someone hadn't saved my life before using this same process.

I drew up another syringe of the cold saltwater, unbuttoned the front of Cori's jeans, and dumped the rest of the ice water into the front of her panties. I had no idea if this was effective on women because I had only heard of it being done on men, but I figured it couldn't hurt to try anything at this point. I passed the needle of saltwater across the car to the sick, timid girl on the other side, instructing her to inject it into Mick's vein and to make sure she was on one before pushing it in. I grasped Cori's face tightly in my hand and shook it.

"Come on, come on, come on!" I pleaded.

I could feel that she wasn't dead. I prayed, as I continued to shake her lightly, and eventually I heard her gasp. She was confused and thought she had wet herself. Then she immediately turned to Mick next to her, and I saw life spring into her.

"No, no, no, no, no," was all she could say, but it wasn't long before his eyes cracked open too.

I fell into the driver's seat relieved, but aggravated that my high was blown. All three of these fools were alive, and now I could get the ride home that I had wanted.

In my junkie mind, all I could think and say was, "You guys owe me for that one."

After they had finished getting sick, and I was pretty sure they weren't going to fall back into unconsciousness, I started up the car and drove us all back to the county. The day was still young, and it was time to figure out how to get some money so I could get well and do it all again tomorrow.

SPRING RACES
TOWARD SUMMER

"Tell me something boy,
Are you happy trying to fill that void?
Or do you need more?
Ain't it hard keeping it so hardcore?"

~Lady Gaga, "Shallow"

I.

I've often heard people argue that pop culture doesn't affect our youth. People will vehemently defend violence in video games, music, and movies, claiming that it in no way impresses upon a young fragile mind. It impressed upon mine. I'm not blaming pop culture for making me into the young person I once was, but it became a conduit for me without question. The evil desire to defy every societal standard of conventionalism was already inside of me—and building. Pop culture fueled me with ideas to devise and shape it. It gave me role models and goals. As an eleven- or twelve-year-old boy, there was nothing more I wanted to be than an LA gang member or a New York drug kingpin. I envied the respect they garnered, the power they held, their utter lack of concern for consequences, and most of all their apathy. I set out to be a gun-toting, rag-wearing Compton Crip, or an Italian high-rolling crime lord in the Bronx.

Before any of that could take shape, I actually started out as a lover, a poet, and a fragile little child from a middle-class family in the suburbs of Baltimore. My parents were still married, unlike all of my friends' parents who had divorced. They weren't drug addicts. They weren't alcoholics. They weren't even smokers. As a matter of fact, no one in my entire family had ever been a drug addict. My parents were just two young people in love endeavoring to start a family and live the American dream. I wasn't an average child. Early on, it became apparent that I was intellectually advanced. I was reading by age two and quickly elevated to gifted and advanced courses at school. I loved nature, reading, writing, and girls. I spent my childhood building forts, throwing rocks, and playing different hide and seek games that my friends and I created. I was passionate about nature and God's creations, but there was another side to me.

I began smoking at an early age. By the time I was in the fifth grade, my friends and I had what we called "The Tobacco Club." We would go up to the neighborhood shopping center and either hit the deli or the 7-Eleven and steal as much tobacco as we could, then come to school and show it off and trade it with those in our inner circle who we could trust. We also formed a "Graffiti Team," spray painting trees and culvert pipes with curse words. It wasn't long before we climbed on top of our elementary school and spray painted "fuck you pussy" across the top of it like a billboard sign, and then basked in our glory as a school bus full of our peers roared with laughter as they pulled up to our school.

My friends were outgrowing me physically, and I hated it. I was the youngest and a late bloomer. I hated the fact that the girls thought I was cute, but wanted to date my friends. I hated that I was smaller and had a higher pitched voice. I hated that they all had older brothers who had hardened them, and that they had a type of anger and toughness that didn't come naturally to me at the time. My friends were like little grown men, and I was always trying to catch up. I overcompensated, not only by being the smartest, but also the craziest. I would do the wildest things and come up with all of the plans. I wasn't the physical leader of the crew, but I was the leader of our schemes, so it made me laugh inside when my parents accused me of being "such a follower" and "hanging around the wrong crowd." Almost all of the devious stunts we got involved in were of my own creation.

By the time I was twelve years old, my friends had girlfriends. We would go over to their houses to hang out, or meet them at the park or in the woods. They would make out with their girlfriends and even have sex with them. I was way too timid around females for that. I could be friends with them, and I affectionately thought about them all of the time, but if there was any inclination that it was more than friends, I would clam up. I would literally shake, and my thoughts and fears would drive me crazy. Most of my friends lost their virginity in sixth grade, but I hadn't even kissed a girl yet. There were quite a few that I passed notes with, but if it came down to talking in person, or touching, I shut down. I was obsessed with females and loved them all, but I got too nervous when I got close to them.

There was another major difference between the boys my age and myself. They all seemed to have no conscience when it came to animals and to each other. I distinctly remember going to a friend's house whose family was having a pool built. In the construction pond were hundreds of frogs. My buddies thought it was funny to play baseball with the frogs, picking them up and smashing them in the air with a bat. I tried my best to stop them, and to talk sense into them, but only ended up walking home physically sick and crying as they continued slaughtering the frogs. I had the same reaction when kids in the neighborhood smashed a turtle or skinned a snake alive. I couldn't believe the sickness in other people, and it made me severely depressed and physically nauseous until the feelings passed. Many fights throughout my teenage years were because of this kind of ignorance. I punched the son of a family friend for squeezing minnows until their eyes popped out and beat up another kid for killing a praying mantis for no reason.

I took the same attitude toward people who bullied children. I was a weaker child, but I never got bullied because I ran with the worst crowd and was considered "cool." I couldn't stand to see other people hurt or taken advantage of.

I hated this about myself. Not the fact that I stood up for what was right, but that I wasn't tough enough to overlook these things. I hated that I was too weak to stop them. I didn't like the shy, timid, tiny little guy that I was, and I resented my parents for creating me that way. I tried to force myself to be outgoing, to be hard and calloused, and to be noticed. I disliked myself from the very first time I realized that I could have feelings about my own self. And although I came from a family who loved me, I despised it all and did my best to get away from it.

I was drawn to negativity, hence my love affair with pop culture. My first favorite band as a child was Guns-n-Roses. Mr. Brownstone was the favorite song of my youth, unbeknownst to me at the time the song was about heroin. When I heard Eazy-E, I instantly fell in love. I knew every word to every song on his first album and would recite the vulgar lyrics in school or soccer practice to entertain and shock the children around me. I was obsessed with heavy metal and rap, and I was heavily influenced by it. I wanted to be a drug dealer and a gangbanger. It all enticed me and became a dream of mine.

I spent years writing poetry, which opened the doors for me to awards and advanced classes. In my first year of high school I submitted poetry to the high school poetry magazine and won first place out of the entire high school for best poem of the year, only I wasn't there to collect it because I had been expelled for selling drugs. In the first month of high school, my group of friends and I found a drug connect and determined we were going to get rich. We all chipped in and bought a bunch of LSD. My best friend Chris met the connect and divvied up the LSD to us. I came to school like a boss, ready to pursue my life-long dream of being a drug lord, and I didn't even make it to second period.

I was in the back of my typing class setting up sales when

the police came into the classroom calling out my name. My heart dropped to the floor as they walked me to the principal's office. Once there, I saw all of my co-conspirator friends lined up on chairs under police supervision. *Who had dimed me out?* I kept wondering. They called me into the office and asked me to empty my pockets. I was cornered, so I reached inside and tossed all of the tabs of LSD, individually wrapped in tinfoil, onto the principal's desk. My parents had been called, and soon all of the parents of my friends were showing up. My best friend Chris had been observed in the purchase because apparently the connect he was dealing with was already under surveillance. When they came to search his locker, this fool had a black book with everyone's name in it, and exactly how many tabs of acid we had purchased, so it was nothing for the police to come track each person in their classroom and pull us out.

I was scared to death, but secretly glad I wasn't alone. The fact that there was a large group of us fourteen- and fifteen-year-olds softened the blow and made it more tolerable. During questioning, Chris and another guy, who were deemed to be the ringleaders out of the crew, decided to climb out of the school window of the room they had been locked into. They got into the other boy's car and took off for Mexico. They even left a note on the desk of the school office that they escaped from. They didn't make it twenty miles before they were pulled over, arrested, and brought back to school. *Whew!* I thought, *that made me look better.*

"At I least I didn't do *that*!" I could try to rationalize to my parents later. The incident made the local newspaper headlines three weeks in a row: "Bel Air High School Acid Ring Busted."

Throughout the next year I shifted away from that group of friends. I ate acid with them a few times and tried marijuana, but didn't like it. They were all hippies, growing their hair out in dreads, wearing tie-dye, and reeking of patchouli. My best friend Chris had a full-grown beard and dreadlocks to the middle of his back by age fifteen. He was like a freak of nature. People, including my family, joked and called him Jesus, because of his appearance. Our crew's lives began to revolve around smoking weed, and I just couldn't get with it. Instead, I watched mobster movies to get my adrenaline going. I watched every single mobster and gangster movie I could find. I dreamed of being in the mafia. I read all of the books and worshipped those guys. I knew as an Irishman that I stood no real chance, so that fantasy was short-lived.

I learned from the likes of *Scarface*, *Colors*, and *New Jack City*. These movies quickly became my stepping-stone toward the life I wanted for myself. I wasn't black, but I always loved black culture. I relished the music and the dress, and just the vibe of black folks in general. I slowly started changing my ways. I listened to hip-hop full-time and dressed in baggy clothes, bucket hats, and visors. My old friends hated it, and they rejected me. At one point, I came around to hang with them, and my much bigger best friend Chris snatched my bucket hat off of my head and lit it on fire in an act of defiance toward the culture I was embracing.

No longer fitting in with my old crew, I began hanging with different crews, mixed groups from rougher areas. I sought out the people with the toughest reputations and hung out with them. We would ride around drinking all night and fighting, jumping people almost every single night. Ironically, I didn't like watching people get hurt when I was sober, but I disliked that softer side of me. I wanted to be a tough guy, so I would get drunk and beat people half to death and revel in the war stories the next day. A lot of innocent guys got punched in the mouth for things like looking at me wrong or giving me an attitude. I wasn't so much a bully because I didn't prey on the weak, I was just a little guy with something to prove. More than anything, I wanted a reputation for being hard.

I was allowed back into Bel Air High School in the tenth grade and quickly got expelled for lighting a fire in the classroom in an attempt to be funny. From there, I went to night school where I was expelled for my involvement in a fight in the high school lobby that left a kid with seven of his teeth knocked out. I, for once, wasn't in the actual fight. I had been with the assailant and instigated him though. Honestly, I didn't think he would take it that far. I quickly regretted my decision after I saw the damage that was done, and as we ran across the school field in different directions while ambulances and police flooded the high school parking lot. I was no longer welcome at Harford County Public Schools after that, so I abandoned my education for good at age fifteen. It was too far for my parents to take me anywhere else, and pretty much useless anyway given my track record. Whenever I was at school, I'd just sneak out and ask a homeless person to buy me forties of malt liquor, then show up at the school hill after dismissal, drunk.

I was home one night around the age of fourteen. My parents were out of town, and we had a babysitter. I got a telephone call from two boys that I knew of, but had never met. Once they confirmed it was me on the phone, they said they had an opportunity to make some money and wanted to know if I was interested. They had heard that I was thorough enough to do the job and that they could trust me. I said I had to know details. They told me they couldn't discuss it over the phone. I had to meet up with them at a certain intersection at 1:00 am, and they would tell me at that moment. They assured me that I could change my mind. I considered the fact that they could be setting me up, but I was only fourteen. My intrigue got the best of me, and I told them I'd be there.

When 1:00am came, I dressed in all black with a hoodie on like they'd instructed me. My bike had recently been stolen from my front yard, so I stole my little sister's Strawberry Shortcake bike with the tassels and took it for a ride. I pedaled out of the neighborhood and two miles up the highway to the rendezvous point where we were to meet, and sure enough they were there waiting on me.

They relayed their solid plan to break into the Subway at the shopping center. They were certain they knew exactly where the safe was and that there would be at least $1,000 in it that we could split between us. Apparently, one of the boys was friends with the manager there. All I had to do was be the look out. We all pedaled our bikes to a group of trees, where each of us took our socks off under cover and put them over our hands. We then made our way around the back of the shopping center. The back was lined with pine trees, which blocked the view from the main road. They told me that earlier in the day they had stashed a brick under one of the trees, and that they would lie low while I threw the brick through the glass door. Then, I was to keep lookout while they went in, and whistle if I saw any sign of police.

I grabbed the brick from under the pine tree while they laid in wait, and I crept down to the glass backdoor. I launched the brick at it with full force. *Boom!* It bounced back off, and the sound ricocheted through the quiet night air. Adrenaline surging, I picked it up and hurled it again with full force. Another loud boom echoed through the air as the brick bounced back off of the door yet again.

"Shit," I said, as I ran back for cover under the trees. "There's no way," I whispered to them in the darkness as we lay in the pine needles.

A car drove by, so we laid there for maybe two minutes, which felt like an eternity, waiting to hear police sirens.

"You're too far away. You've got to get right up on it," one of them said.

"You do it then!" I replied, "I'll keep an eye out."

They both went down to the door. Seconds later I heard a crash, and they were in. Ten, fifteen, twenty, thirty seconds—it wasn't even a full minute, and they were back out carrying a metal box under one of their arms. I hopped on my bike and followed them, hoping they weren't trying to ditch me at this point. They very well could have. I didn't do much, and they may not have known it, but I'd never snitch. I kept right on their heels as we went through a neighborhood just across the street from the shopping center, and down a small hill and dropped our bikes at a townhome back door.

We walked inside, and they sat on a bed counting the money, while I sat on the floor smoking a cigarette and watching in anticipation. We didn't have to argue much about the money. They did the most work and set the whole thing up, but I was taking the most risk at this point. I had to ride my bike two miles to get home with the stolen money, right back past the scene of the crime. There was eight hundred and some change in the box, and we split it evenly. However, since I did the least, I got stuck with almost a hundred of it in rolled coins. What the hell was I supposed to do with five pounds of rolled change? Oh well...I was lucky I got this much, especially since I didn't even know these guys. I hopped back on that Strawberry Shortcake bike and pedaled my little ass off that night. I pedaled two miles home without stopping, pink and red tassels on the handlebars blowing in the wind and five pounds of rolled coins in my hood pulling me backward. When I finally made it home, I felt like it was all a dream—except the money was real. For a fourteen-year-old I was rich, and it was easy earnings. I hoped more opportunities like this one would arise.

The Subway wasn't discovered burglarized until the next morning when the workers arrived. Who would have a glass backdoor and no alarm? *I bet they'll never do that again*, I rationalized to myself, as if they deserved it. I chuckled inside every time as a teenager that I would drive by and see the stainless-steel door they had installed afterward.

II.

When I was fourteen, I was a fighter. I used pool sticks, bats, crowbars, bottles, beer mugs, bricks—anything I could get ahold of. I learned about breaking into cars. It was another get rich scheme. I would sneak out on a nightly basis after my parents went to sleep, meet up with friends, and collect as many Kenwood and Pioneer stereo systems as we could in the middle of the night and resell them. Eventually, the police came to my high school in my tenth grade year and pulled me out of class to search my locker, piled from bottom to top with amps, speakers and head units, and also an ounce of weed at the top that I had found in a car and planned to sell.

I was sentenced to house arrest at the age of fifteen. Once I was released from house arrest, I returned to drinking. It became a nightly ordeal. I met an older girl, Sabrina, who had moved to Bel Air from the projects in Chicago. She was old enough to buy us liquor, so we would hang out with her overnight, and she would tell stories about living in the Chicago projects and the different gangs out there. That was the kind of stuff that intrigued me. I learned about gangster disciples, and vice lords, and their hand signs, and culture. She was thorough and quick to fight a guy or girl, so I liked having her on the team. She lived in an apartment complex a few miles from where I lived, so I would

Chasing A Flawed Sun

either catch a ride or walk the few miles there and back every night. I ended up meeting a lot of people who lived there, and it was my home base to hang out for a year or two. One night, we were up drinking until 3:00am at a party in the complex when one of the guys started arguing over the phone with another guy at a party across town. They were threatening and taunting each other until we finally decided to go over there and fight. Three carloads of us piled in and headed over, guys and girls from the ages of fifteen to thirty. I rode with an older black dude, Gotti, from Edgewood.

Before we left, he said, "Hey, I got something to show you. We gonna light their asses up when we get there."

He popped the trunk, and there were all kinds of guns like I'd never seen. They looked like high-powered assault rifles in the dark. I got excited! The whole ride over my adrenaline was surging. We were set to do some real gangster shit, and I loved it. We pulled up on the main highway, left the cars on the shoulder, and snuck down the long wooded gravel driveway in the dark to the house where they were. When we got there, everyone looked at each other puzzled. There was supposed to be a house party going on here, yet the house was as dark and quiet as it could be. KJ, the biggest black dude in the group went up and beat on the door. Nothing.

He beat again, and yelled, "Come out bitches! We know you're home."

Still nothing.

Then I heard my friend Bird say, "Fuck this shit!"

I watched as he sailed a forty-ounce bottle right through their front window. Suddenly everyone started throwing shit at the house, and KJ kicked the front door wide-open. Through all the madness, everyone heard a distinct "click-click" in the darkness.

A voice from the roof said, "Back the fuck up. Now."

We could barely make out a group of figures standing on

top of the house in the dark. Somebody from our group yelled, "Fuck you!" and tossed a stick up at them.

It was returned with gunfire. Two shots rang out in the dark, and we all scattered up the driveway ten times faster than we had come down it. Just as we got to the highway where the cars were parked, we heard sirens and saw red and blue lights coming toward us. Everyone split off in different directions at that point. The drivers didn't want to leave their cars. A girl and I hopped the guardrail and headed straight into the woods in the dark. I thought about all of those assault rifles, and I ran with everything in me. We would be going to jail for a long time, I thought. I ran full force through dark woods, through brush and trees and thorns, spotlights dancing behind me. An officer announced that he was releasing a dog and ordered us to stop. The girl running beside me stopped, but I kept on trucking. I ran, and ran, and ran. I got through the woods and ran across car lots and down side streets, ducking every time I saw car lights. Twelve miles through the county I ran. I stopped to vomit a few times, but I made it home safe.

The next day I learned that everyone was released without being taken to jail, and that the guns in the trunk were only paintball guns. The joke was on me. I assume charges weren't pressed because the guys at the house we had gone to had drugs and guns there as well.

Not long after that, I got a call from another friend who asked if I wanted to rob some drug dealers they knew of downtown. I was too trusting that people knew what they were talking about, and I was blinded by the chance to make some money and do something I could brag about to build my rep. They picked me up, and we went to a hotel to pregame. I drank a forty or two of malt liquor until the ride arrived and we headed out. There were five of us: my friend Crystal and her boyfriend, my other friend John, and some older dude in his forties who they referred to as a "crackhead," who was our getaway driver. He pulled up in a purple mustang. Crystal took shotgun, and the rest of us guys got in the back. Crystal's man showed off a gun that he brought with him and then stuck it under the seat. We also had two baseball bats lying on the floorboard.

This was the plan: there would be two guys on the corner hustling in Greektown in East Baltimore. They would have at least two grand in cash on them because they were due to re-up from their connect that night. We had to get there before the connect would arrive. Crystal received this information from one of the guy's girlfriends who, for whatever reason, wanted to see him get robbed. He must've done her dirty, I assumed. I didn't much care, I just wanted to continue to prove to everyone how much of a gangster I was and make some bread in the process. On the drive down I drank as much of my forty ounce as I could to build my courage.

"Put on some gangster shit!" I yelled up front, getting myself hyped.

The mood in the car was pretty somber. Were these guys even up to it? As we got to the city, I tensed up, ready to hop out and go. We rolled into Greektown, and everything was quiet. Crystal gave out directions, and we turned down some dark backstreets. We rounded a corner, then pulled off for a second.

"Okay," I said, "Are you guys ready? They'll be up on this next corner."

Everybody nodded an affirmative, so I picked up a bat and clutched it in my sweaty palms.

As we rolled slowly up the street and approached the corner, a large group of people rose up off of the front steps of the houses, and one of them yelled out, "There they are!"

We rolled right into an ambush. The girl had set Crystal up. We thought we were going to rob them, but they were waiting for us.

"Pull the fuck over!" I yelled.

Someone threw something that bounced off our car as we rolled past.

"Are you fucking crazy?" Crystal screamed. "There's more of them than us."

"Who gives a fuck!" I yelled back. "We've got bats and a gun! Let me out!"

I was dying to show off how brave and crazy I could be. There was no argument from the guys in the back, but Crystal and the driver weren't having it. They were both terrified, as he sped around the block and through the city streets. Suddenly headlights started flashing behind us. They were chasing us, but we couldn't tell how many carloads. The driver of our purple Mustang floored it out onto Eastern Avenue, but there were two cars right on our tail.

I was still running my mouth, "Pull over, pull over!" I repeated.

"Danny, shut the fuck up!" Crystal yelled.

She was the mastermind behind the whole thing and was probably embarrassed and confused as to how she let herself get betrayed. Somebody obviously wanted her hurt, and we were casualties in the game. We hit the exit onto I-95, and at least one car followed us onto the highway.

This is perfect, I thought. "Pull over on the shoulder. We can fuck them up there."

Neither of the guys in the back said much. I wondered if they were scared, or if they just didn't care. The driver was tired of my mouth and not sure what to do. He started playing games with them, switching lanes, slowing down, and speeding up. Finally, he took my advice and pulled off to the shoulder, and I got ready to hop out.

As they slowed to follow us, Crystal's boyfriend said, "Watch this!" and hung out the window with the pistol firing shots at them. He blew out their windshield with a bullet.

Holy shit! I thought. The car stopped moving and didn't follow. He may have just killed one of them. One, or all of them, could be dead or severely hurt. This was not good. Our driver gunned it, and we hopped off onto 695, then onto Bel Air Road North heading into the county and hoping to get as far away from the scene of the crime as possible. We didn't make it a mile up Bel Air Road before we were surrounded by police. We pulled off into the parking lot of the Putty Hill Skating Rink. Cops surrounded our car with weapons drawn and slowly ordered us out one at a time.

They handcuffed the four of us and loaded us into the paddy wagon. The driver was taken away separately in handcuffs because he was an adult. We were in serious trouble, but we didn't act like it. We were fooling around in the back of the paddy wagon. Being minors, we were handcuffed in front, so we used our hands to pull cigarettes and lighters out of each other's pockets and put them in each other's mouths and light them. I had to pee so badly that I pulled the front of my pants down and pissed in the wagon as it was transporting us through the city. When we got to our destination, it was something I never knew existed. We were at a police station over top of the Baltimore Harbor Tunnel, home to the Maryland Transportation Authority. They brought us in and tossed us into separate cells to await our fate.

We were positioned in adjacent cells, but we couldn't quite speak to each other to corroborate our stories because we were all within earshot of the police. I heard cell doors open one at a time, as each of the other guys were brought out to talk to the police interviewers. When it was my turn, I had a solid plan, and that was to play dumb. When the detective asked me what my version of the events was, I told him I was asleep. I said I drank too much and passed out in the back seat and didn't see or hear anything.

"So, you mean to tell me that you slept through gunshots going off right next to your ears?" he inquired.

Oh shit. He had me, but I continued my charade. "Yes sir. I didn't hear anything. I was out cold."

He continued to tell me that they had possession of the gun from under the seat, and they could tell it had been fired. He explained that they would get the fingerprints off of it. I played dumb and stuck to my story, and frustrated with me, they placed me back in the cell.

An hour or two later, they pulled me back out and said, "Okay, we know what happened. We just need to hear you say it."

"Okay then, what happened?" I said coyly.

"We know that the guy next to you fired the gun. Your other buddies already told us."

"Well, then you don't need me anymore. You got your answer," I responded.

"We know what happened. Your buddy told us. We're willing to let you go tonight. You just have to tell us your version," he pressed.

"He already told you apparently. From what I know, he didn't lie," I said, trying to get out of there without telling.

Finally, exasperated, he asked for my parents' phone number. I reluctantly gave it to him, but only after trying to be released on my own. I was a minor, and I was lucky to be getting released from custody without incident, so I'd take what I could get.

The phone call that woke my parents up at 4:00 that morning from the police went something like this, "Mr. McGhee?"

"Yes sir?"

"Hello, this is officer so-and-so from the Maryland Transportation Authority. We have your son Daniel down here. He's been involved in a shooting."

"Oh my God, is he okay?"

"Sir, he was not a victim. He was with the party that was doing the shooting," replied the officer.

I can only imagine the thoughts going through my father's

head as he drove twenty miles into the city to pick up his fifteen-year-old son. This was a man who never committed a crime, who never touched a drug, who set the best example he could, and struggled to provide. What did he do to deserve me?

We were all eventually released that night except for Crystal's boyfriend, who did the shooting, and the adult driver. They were both held overnight to be transported to the city jail, where the shooter would be charged as an adult for attempted murder, and the driver would be charged as an accessory. The next morning the driver was found dead in his cell. He hung himself with a bed sheet. I never even knew his name, only that he was referred to as the "crackhead."

III.

I was never home during the summertime. Even before my birth, my family would go to a campground called Cherrystone on the Eastern Shore of Virginia. My grandparents stayed all summer long, and my parents would bring us for a two-week vacation during their stay. Once I started my troublesome ways, my parents decided it would be much easier to leave me with my grandparents all summer, while they did their best to raise my two normal siblings.

My Nana loved me and spoiled me, and I loved her as well. I loved camping, I loved fishing, and most importantly I loved the attention I received. We would go out to eat every morning, and then I would go fishing with my Pop-Pop on good weathered days. I loved the nature trail and bird watching, fishing, and meeting new friends there. My Nana encouraged my style and would take me to buy matching outfits from the hats down to the shoes. When I was fourteen, I earned the nickname "Trip" down there from my exploits back home of being kicked out of school for selling acid. The nickname spread like wildfire and soon everybody including the campground staff and friends of the family were referring to me as Trip.

I got a two-dollar allowance every day from my Nana and learned how to flip it in the arcade gambling at pool. I was a great pool player and could hustle anyone in the campground. Just like at home, I befriended the older kids, especially those over twenty-one so they could buy me alcohol and introduce me into their world. As I aged, sadly enough, I stopped playing cards with my Nana and fishing with my Pop-Pop, and instead hung out at the arcade more and more, or took trips out of the campground with the older kids who worked and lived there.

Throughout the years, I had my first alcoholic drink at the campground, smoked my first joint, tried crack for the first time, and even lost my virginity there. Every night at the entrance to the nature trail, there were huge bonfire parties where all the young people gathered illegally to drink and party. If you couldn't afford alcohol you had to sneak through the campsites at night and steal it out of people's coolers. I always managed to pay for mine.

One of the things I liked most about camping there was that I got to stay the whole summer, but every week or two some people left and new people would come in. It was sad, yet exciting at the same time. Year after year, I'd grow accustomed to seeing mostly the same faces. It was possible for me to have four or five crushes in one summer because they were only there for a week at a time, and I was girl-crazy. I'd cry when each one of them left, and then I'd cry at the end of summer every year when I had to leave my dreamland and return to my harsh reality.

I met a girl down there when I was fourteen and felt like I'd hit the jackpot. She was a beautiful blonde sixteen-year-old cheerleader named Alicia, and she took an immediate liking to me. We walked around and held hands and made out all day long, and she told me that she was going to take my virginity before she left. I was scared, but extremely excited. I would finally get to do what all of my other friends had already done. I could finally be a real man now, and she was making it so easy on me. She told me on her last full day there that at the bonfire that night, we were going to have sex. I prepared for it all day, working hard to calm my nerves, but I was so nervous I could have thrown up.

When evening came, we walked to the party hand-in-hand and sat on the rocks overlooking the bay. Many of the older guys were after her and were confused as to why she was with a young guy like me. Luckily, I was friends with most of the main guys who hosted the party, so they would back me up or threaten them if they started honing in on me or her. I grabbed one beer, then two, then three out of the cooler as I sat next to her. My nerves were so frazzled, I had no idea how I was going to pull this off. Five beers in, she was hugging on my arm.

"Are you ready?" she asked.

I literally replied, "Hold up, just one more beer."

She sat back and sighed. I was so worried about how it would turn out that I secretly wished something catastrophic would happen to interrupt the plan.

Finally, she grabbed my arm and said, "Let's go," and led me back into the woods. We walked about one hundred feet down the trail to where we were out of sight of the light of the party, and she looked at me and said, "Well?"

I looked back at her in the dark and repeated, "Well?"

I had no clue what to do. I mean, I had seen porn magazines, and I knew what to do, I was just timid and frozen in place. Finally, I leaned forward and kissed her. We kissed for a while, lowering ourselves down to the ground. Laying on the dirt on the side of a small wooded embankment in the dark, we made out for a long time because I was so scared to move forward. She moved my hand to her jeans button. I undid it, and she slipped her jeans off in the dark and sat them beside her. She then took off her panties. I didn't know what to do. I couldn't have sex with her because my nerves wouldn't allow me to get an erection. I tried to force one in my mind.

I immediately lowered my face down to her crotch and she said, "uh-uh..." and pulled me back up.

"I thought you might like that," I said.

"No, just put it in," she replied.

I couldn't go this far toward losing my virginity and fall short here, I didn't know when I'd get the chance again. My nervousness was going to cause me to blow it as usual. All the alcohol didn't help. I lowered my pants and started to grind myself up against her as I kissed her until I finally got some semblance of an erection. I pushed it into her and within a minute it was soft again because I couldn't stay out of my own head. I kissed her several times, stroking her hair out of her face, and I apologized profusely in my own embarrassment. I somewhat expected her to snap at me and say something like, "You're pathetic!" But she didn't.

She got up, put her clothes back on silently, then grabbed my hand and kissed my cheek and said, "It's okay."

We walked back out of the darkness of that nature trail hand-in hand and back into the brightness of the bonfire and the crowd surrounding it. As we came out of the woods, a few people clapped and cheered.

Somebody yelled, "Hey Trip, did you hit that?"

Before I could formulate a response, she put her hand over my mouth and said proudly, "He sure did!"

It was one of the sweetest things anyone had ever done for me, and it broke my heart in a million pieces when I lost her phone number and address. I never saw or heard from her again.

The next year, I was thrown out of the campground for robbing another kid at knifepoint, and setting fires in the bathhouses. I almost cost my entire family their ability to stay there as well—a family tradition for decades, almost ruined by my ignorance. I eventually returned to the campground to be with my family twelve years later using an alias. I came back as a changed man, but things had changed at the campground as well. My childhood was lost, the best times of my life were ruined and gone forever because I wanted to grow up too fast and be someone I wasn't.

Summers at the campground had been my favorite part of the year. Most of my fondest memories were here, and yet again I destroyed what I loved with my own foolishness.

IV.

Back at home, I was tired of everyone else having fresh clothes and all of the latest brands that my family couldn't afford. They had name brand skateboards, bikes, everything. For the most part, my parents bought off-brand things for us. I needed a remedy to that problem. There was a Merry-Go-Round warehouse near our home, and a lot of cool kids worked there. In the early 1990s, they were the hottest clothing store of the time, carrying all the brands that were in style—and that I longed to wear—such as Cross Colours, IOU, Boss, Skidz, Karl Kani.

I got a job working there through a temp agency. The place was huge, and everyone I knew from the hood worked there. I got to know the layout within a week and figured out how to steal the coolest clothes. I would spend all of my time on the clock dodging work, and instead shopping within the warehouse for new leather jackets and jeans to smuggle home. Once my wardrobe was intact, some of the crew and I figured out how to beat the system even further. Since the place was so huge, and there were several temp companies supplying employees there, it was easy to disappear without being noticed. We would clock in at 9:00am, then sneak out the door and go out drinking all day, only to sneak back into the warehouse and clock out at 5:30pm, or have someone we trusted do it for us.

My friend Sabrina had gotten food stamps and moved into a row home in the projects in Edgewood, which made for a new party house in the hood. One of the first nights she was there, a bunch of my friends were there partying and decided that they were going to pull an armed robbery at a Kentucky Fried Chicken in Edgewood. They ran in at about 10:00pm with a sawed-off shotgun and made everyone lay down on the floor except the cashier, who handed them a few hundred dollars. I was sad that I missed out on the action until I heard that they got busted within the next couple of days. That night they gave the gun to a friend of mine to get rid of. He picked me up, and we stashed it in the woods. It wasn't long before I went back into the woods to get it.

A few weeks later one of my friends had a problem with some Crips from Aberdeen, so we invited them to the school hill after dismissal at Bel Air High School. None of us were in school anymore. Most of us had already been kicked out, except the one who had the issue with the Crips. We showed up after school to have his back. With red bandanas, red flannel shirts, and red shoelaces, we played the part of Blood members just to invoke a fight with the other crew. As an afterthought, I stuffed the sawed-off shotgun down the front of my pants, and we headed up to the school when it let out. We hopped out of our vehicles and made our presence known as the crowds were dispersing from the school. None of the so-called Crip members were from that school either, so I can't imagine the shock to the school administrators and the police when they arrived and saw us all milling around the high school hill. The police showed up almost immediately and ordered us on their bullhorns to leave the area. We didn't hesitate to listen, knowing that I had a shotgun down the front of my pants. That would have definitely landed me another newspaper headline.

It wasn't long before I basically lived at Sabrina's house in Edgewood. I was the only white boy there most of the time, and I relished it. I started learning about crack cocaine, how to cut it up, weight it, and bag it appropriately. Nights were filled with tons of drinking. I spent my days and nights there drinking forty-bottle after forty-bottle of malt liquor, and going out at night to fight. I would set out into the neighborhood late at night, completely drunk, with the intention to strong-arm rob people. At one point I hit a woman in the head with a bottle as she got home from work. Another time, I stabbed a man in the shoulder with a screwdriver. I thought this was cool and that it made me thorough. All the money I made at the warehouse, and other warehouses after I lost that job, was spent on trivial things. I had to have a gold chain and gold caps on my teeth. I had to have the freshest clothes, even though I was sure to ruin them fighting when I was drunk or falling asleep with a cigarette in my hand. I was a menace, and I kept myself drunk at all times to bury the feelings that threatened to surface about what a waste my life had become.

I had a couple of homeboys living in Sabrina's house, and a couple more in the neighborhood who hung out there, who were selling crack out the backdoor of her house. One Friday night when I got paid, I asked to be put on. They took me over to the Village (another project neighborhood in Edgewood) to meet their connect. I bought a quarter ounce of cooked coke. I chipped it off into $20 and $50 bags of rock and started my new passion of hustling.

I loved it! I thrilled at the feeling of importance it gave me, of making money and supplying a need. In that neighborhood most of my clientele were older black folks, and they adored me. I was a fifteen-year-old white boy with gold teeth, matching denim cross colors suits, and bandanas tied in the front like Tupac, selling them work. I was almost like a caricature standing on the side of that row home cutting off clients as they headed for the backdoor. I'd usually have a Newport in my mouth and a sixty-four-ounce jug of Colt 45 in my hand (because a forty was no longer enough). I had a big Gucci gold ring and a Nike three-finger ring, even a gold tooth that had a Nike symbol on it. At that time, you couldn't tell me anything.

Sometimes my friends from outside the neighborhood would scoop me up, and we'd go out drinking to a house party or club. One night on the way home, a horrible hobby was born.

I'm not sure how it came up, but one of the guys said, "Let's jump somebody and take their money."

We drove around until we saw a grown man walking down Hanson Road on the way home from the store. We parked in a neighborhood about an eighth of a mile up the street and hid behind some trees until he got close. There were three of us, and we told the driver to wait in the car and keep it running. We ran down on him. He towered over all three of us. He had to be about forty-years-old and in decent shape. We surrounded him.

My friend Joe said, "What's up, Mike?"

We didn't know his name. We were just trying to catch him off guard and have a motive other than robbery if things went sour.

He turned and said, "My name's not Mike," just in time to catch a blow to the jaw.

As soon as he got hit, he dropped his bag, jumped back, and did some karate stance and kicked in the air. We all paused, and looked at each other thinking that we had just made a huge mistake. My other friend Billy decided he had no choice but to hit him again from the other side, and we all pummeled into him. Billy held him on the ground as I kicked and stomped his head, and Joe worked his body. Cars sped past us on the busy road.

"Grab his wallet, Billy!" I yelled, not even thinking.

Once we had his wallet out of his pocket, we jumped up and sprinted back to the car and got the hell out of there. We split the sixty some dollars among us and took the credit cards to fill up with gas and buy cartons of cigarettes, then almost immediately disposed of the cards. It wasn't until we were in the car on the way out that Billy pointed out that I had said his name during the beating. We never did get caught though.

I'm so ashamed about stories like these that it makes me wince to even tell them. Once a week we would do the same; it was sick. It was easy back then because the alcohol kept me hardened. I could drink away any feelings of shame or remorse and keep drinking so they'd never arise. When I finally got sober, I had a lot of guilt and shame to deal with, and still do.

We went out to the city and Baltimore County and caught people out walking home from stores and did the same. It was always men, and always men bigger than us. One night after dropping everyone off but me, the driver, Steve, said he was tired of feeling like a pussy and that he wanted to give it a try. We were driving through a neighborhood in a town called Riverside, and we spotted a thick black bodybuilder-looking dude jogging through the neighborhood.

"Who the hell jogs at 2am?" I said.

"Come on, let's go," was all he said.

He gunned the truck up next to him and slammed on the brakes so it spun sideways in the street, threw it in park, and hopped out.

"What's up?" he said, and he hit the guy in the face before I could even make it around the truck.

The guy looked like he could have easily taken the both of us, but I think he was in such shock that his only response was to run. He turned and took off, and I dove and tackled him. Then Steve was on him too. I hopped up. I actually felt bad. Clearly, he was terrified, and I was trying to spare him an unnecessary beating.

"Give me your wallet before I stomp on your fucking face," I stood over him yelling, as Steve kneeled into his midsection.

He reached into his pocket and handed it up to me. It was empty. I started pretending that I was in disbelief looking at his driver's license.

"Holy shit, it's the wrong guy," I said, slapping Steve on the shoulder. "It's the wrong guy!" I repeated.

Steve got up and extended an arm, helping him up off the ground.

"Sorry about that," I said as I handed his wallet back.

The guy actually said, "No problem," brushed himself off, and headed out jogging back down the street like we had just accidentally bumped into him or something.

I got back in the truck, and Steve looked over at me and said, "That was fun!" as we drove off down the road.

I lectured him on the ride home about how I didn't want him getting involved in stuff like that with us, how it wasn't like him, and how I wanted him to maintain his nonviolent disposition. I felt bad myself. I had to stop this stuff and do something more legitimate. It made me ill afterward to think about the pain I inflicted on innocent people.

The whole neighborhood was getting extremely hot. It was so bad that they built a police station right in the middle of the neighborhood in one of the row homes. I found out the hard way when I slipped out the backdoor of one of the houses with my arms full of electronics that had just been traded to me. I had just made a sale for some crack rocks, and I had more crack in my pocket, when I looked up and saw the Harford County Sheriff's symbol staring back at me. It was on the front and back of the row home, and until that moment I had no idea that they had put it in just two days prior. I flipped out on the people who made me leave through their backdoor with all the hot Rent-A-Center merchandise, thinking they were trying to set me up.

Most of my electronics back then had Rent-A-Center stickers on them. There was a location right there in Edgewood, and most of the addicts would rent equipment with good intentions, but then end up selling it for drugs when they started fiending. I had no qualms about this. My morals were obviously non-existent at the time, so I welcomed it all.

A beautiful, dark-skinned woman named Candy lived next door to us. She would come over and buy rocks occasionally, but she also did a little hustling of her own. Everyone knew she was sleeping with one of the white, married patrol cops in the area, named Sonny. One night Candy came over. Frantic, she explained that she was holding a stash for someone, and that she had misplaced it in her house and couldn't remember where. She trusted us because she knew we didn't get high, so she asked if we would help her look through her house for it. A couple of us went over to help. I mainly went because I thought Candy was beautiful, but something about the whole scene seemed sketchy. I assumed she smoked it all and wanted whoever she got it from to think that she had misplaced it or it was stolen, so the repercussions wouldn't be as harsh. What blew my mind though, was that halfway through the search, Sonny pulls up in his patrol car and comes in the house in full uniform. I tensed up immediately.

"No, he's cool," she said.

Then he asked her details about what the package looked like.

"It was a clear baggy full of little pink baggies with $50 rocks inside," she explained to him.

Then he joined in the search, looking under couch cushions and pillows. I couldn't believe what I was seeing. Eventually, Candy found the bag later that night and half the rocks were missing. Of course, accusations were thrown around about who could have stolen it. I didn't pay it any mind. I just wondered if Sonny also smoked it with her.

A couple of nights later, another woman named Regina, who was always buying from us, came over and asked if she could have a twenty rock. Out of her mind and wound up tight, she was saying she was going to smoke the rock to "gas up," then go over and fight Candy. She claimed Candy owed her $50 and wouldn't pay her back.

She slightly lifted her shirt on the way out the door to show us a pair of scissors tucked into her waistband and said, "I got something for that bitch," as she walked out the door.

It wasn't twenty minutes later we could hear screaming and beating on the door next to ours.

"Candy, come out! Don't be scared now, bitch! I want my money!" Regina screamed in her horrible voice.

What I saw next, I'll never forget. The door flew open and Candy came rushing out like a bull in her bra and panties. She barreled into Regina—the poor old lady didn't stand a chance. Flailing wildly at each other, Candy came down swinging on top of Regina. She landed blow after blow to Regina's face. As Regina swung her hands trying to block them, she pulled Candy's bra down and her breasts fell out. The whole neighborhood had gathered around by now watching a naked Candy pummel this poor old lady with her huge boobs swinging around wildly.

Candy got a puzzled look on her face all of a sudden, and reached down to Regina's waistband, and said, "What's this, bitch? You were gonna stab me?" With fury in her eyes, Candy grabbed the scissors and rammed them right into the side of Regina's head.

"Oh shit!" somebody yelled, and suddenly men from the crowd rushed in to pull them apart. I had mixed emotions. I felt sorry for Regina because she tried to stand up for herself and didn't stand a chance, yet I adored Candy because she was both sexy and thorough.

"We don't need the cops here. Nobody call the police," someone said, and the crowd pretty much agreed. Nobody wanted that kind of drama or police presence in the neighborhood. An older, bigger black man stepped up and introduced himself as Rick, a friend of Regina's. He volunteered to drive her to the hospital and anyone else who wanted to come. Regina's wounds weren't deep enough to kill her, but scissors in the side of the head and blood coming out from where they poked her was deep enough to warrant concern. Rick and a couple of others loaded her into the back of his Lincoln Town Car and off they went. I hoped for her sake, and Candy's, that she wouldn't die.

I continued selling crack out of that house in Edgewood using all of the money to re-up, buy bling, and drink excessive amounts of alcohol. One night, the same guy, Rick, came over to buy some crack from me.

He said, "Hey, if you want, I can take you around and get the rest of that shit you got sold. It's fire."

I agreed because there was nothing going on around the house where I was staying. His Lincoln Town Car was parked out front. I hopped in, and he drove me around like a boss. We went to various projects, and he introduced me to people and bought me beer from the store. I made a ton of sales and broke him off a little rock here and there for driving me around and helping me sell it all so quickly. We hung out at different apartments with different women, drinking and hustling, until everything I had ran dry. I got on the phone to try to get more, but my guy's phone was off. I tried another guy I knew from a neighborhood next to mine, still nothing. For an hour or two, I plugged away trying to call connects so we could both get hooked up. I could get money, and he could get high. Still nothing. It was around 2:00am now, and nobody was answering. We were driving around in the dark through Edgewood, smoking and drinking and making phone calls, when he pulled into an empty parking lot, then into a field. Something wasn't right. His hand hit the power locks, as his other arm quickly came up holding a knife tight against my Adam's apple, pinning my head against the headrest.

"Give me everything you got in your socks, not your pockets, your socks," he demanded.

Apparently, he had been watching me all night. I had maybe $70 in my pocket, but damn near $500 in my sock. I reached down and took it out.

"Everything!" he said. The knife drew a bead of blood at my throat from the pressure, I felt it run down my neck.

"I gave you everything!" I said, and flipped the tops of my socks inside out.

He must not have seen me cuff the other money in my pocket earlier, or he was being nice and letting me keep it.

"Okay, here's what's going to happen," he continued in a serious voice. "I'm going to take you back to the house where I got you from. You're going to go in and go to sleep and pretend like this never happened. And you're not going to tell anyone."

"Okay" I replied, knowing I was lying.

He was so much bigger than me, I felt eerie parked back in that field, like maybe he really had further intentions, but I was relieved when he started the car back up and began driving.

On the way back, he taunted me, "I bet you wish you had this right now, don't you?" as he waved the knife in front of me.

I snatched it quickly from his hand, but instead of stabbing him with it, I hit the power window and tried to throw it out. He intercepted me and grabbed it back. I hated myself for not stabbing him, but I was terrified that after being stabbed he would still overpower me, and it would be my demise. It was better this way, the only thing I lost was my pride, and that hurt enough. He pulled up on the side of the highway where it ran alongside the projects. There was a half-mile long chain link fence separating the neighborhood from the highway.

"Up there," he pointed up toward the fence, "there's a hole in the fence. You're going to run through that hole, and go home, and not tell anyone about this."

I got out of the car and ran up the small dirt path. Sure enough, at the top there was a hole big enough for me. I looked back and he was gone. That was the last time I ever saw him. When I got home, the house was locked, and everyone was asleep. I had no key, so I banged and banged until I woke up Sabrina's new boyfriend. He was aggravated and didn't want me staying there, but he let me in, and I told him what happened.

"He'll be dealt with," I was told.

I don't know if he ever was, but I knew one thing, if I was going to continue to hustle, I needed to get even tougher and smarter. Rick was like a ghost, he showed up for a week, and after the robbery he just disappeared. Nobody seemed to know him or where to find him in order to enact revenge. Dynamics began changing at Sabrina's house. I started feeling unwelcome there the more that her new boyfriend started coming around and eventually living there. I imagine I was a nuisance in his eyes. I was like Sabrina's little brother, but I was also a drunken loose cannon who took up room and brought nothing positive into the house. I started feeling completely out of place, as the usual crew stopped coming around and new guys started hanging around the house.

One night, two guys I had never met came knocking at the backdoor, out of breath. They were running from the cops and needed a place to hide out, so I let them in. They were friends with some of the other people who were hanging out in the house that night. I sat in the living room, smoking and drinking, and listening to all the strangers talk. I felt out of place, but extremely intrigued by their stories. They had apparently just done a robbery and the cops chased them through the courts, but they were sure they had lost them. One of them was about 6' 4" and went by "Bushwick." He reached into his waistband and set a big, heavy silver gun on the coffee table. I admired it from a distance. I was too uninformed about guns to know what kind it was. It just looked shiny and silver, and big and heavy.

Finally, I mustered up the courage to ask the stranger, "You mind if I check it out?"

"Naw, go ahead, Shorty," he replied.

I could feel Sabrina's boyfriend behind me rolling his eyes, or so I thought. I reached out with timid hands and knocked his can of grape soda over, and it poured all over the gun. I half-expected to get my ass beat over my clumsiness, but he was cool. Embarrassed, I ran to the kitchen and grabbed handfuls of paper towels, and hands trembling, I cleaned up the mess. I had made it clear to everyone that I was a fool. I didn't come back into the room for the rest of the night.

Two guys from the neighborhood who were hustling with us got locked up for dealing. Shortly after, my connect in the village got popped in a sting. I was still at the house drinking every night, but I had lost my job and my supplier, so I became somewhat of a joke. One night, I got blackout drunk and passed out on the living room recliner in a house full of people. Sabrina's boyfriend and his friends thought it would be comical to make cigarette burns in my new track pants while I was asleep. They eventually set them on fire and put them out before I woke up. I woke up with giant burn holes in my pants and people laughing at me. What could I do? It was me against the whole house, except for Sabrina. I did it to myself. I was a bum, and I made a fool of myself by getting so drunk every night. I knew I was unwanted there. The tides had changed. It was time for me to go.

A week or two later on Christmas Eve morning, Sonny showed up in uniform at Sabrina's door with a warning. The house was under surveillance for drug activity, and the neighborhood was notified that she had people living there unlawfully while she was on Section 8 and dealing drugs out of the house. If she got everyone out within twenty-four hours, she would be spared a house raid. Once again, I was shocked by the decency that was extended to her in spite of everything. I figured it was just the local police practicing some good old-fashioned Christmas spirit. I had already left, but I was sad that another chapter was over, and I would never be able to stay in that house again.

V.

I went back to my parents' house. I had left on my own accord; I wasn't forced out. Since I was only fifteen, I was technically still obligated to live there. So, even when they got frustrated enough to throw me out, legally they couldn't, and I used it to my advantage. My parents and I lived in two separate worlds. I despised theirs, and they dared not ask about mine. They were struggling to provide a normal life for the rest of our family. When it came to what I was up to, I believe, ignorance was bliss on their part.

I wasn't about to give up my illustrious career of selling cocaine either, so I sought out new resources. Now that I was back in the middle-class area, I knew crack wouldn't sell. My clientele would be kids who were more my age and up to their mid-twenties. I met an older guy named Nick who sold cocaine. He was also the only person I had ever heard of who used heroin. I would find rides for him to the city so he could cop his heroin and cocaine for the both of us.

I quickly became infatuated with the city. It was like a whole new layer of the world that I never knew existed. It became a ritual. I knew the exact drive down, and I knew once we crossed Bel Air Road on Sinclair Lane, we were in the hood. It was right alongside the biggest graveyard I had ever seen. The vibe changed once we entered this area. It felt almost haunted, like one could smell murder in the air. Dilapidated and boarded up row homes everywhere, crowds of people on the corners and in the streets, and not a single one of them white like us. There was an easy drive-through strip on North and Durham that I'll never forget. The row homes there have since been torn down, but there were always political posters pasted up on the boarded brick row home that signaled the entrance. On the narrow side street as we turned in, a young black kid on a bicycle would ask what we wanted.

Nick would say, "two boy and ten girl," or whatever the order was.

Boy meant heroin, and *girl* meant cocaine. Nick would hand him our money, then we'd roll down the street to an alley opening where someone would come running out and hand off the order through the car window. Just like that, within thirty seconds we were in and out of the drug strip. Nick would immediately dump some powder out onto a creased bill, and roll another one up to use as a straw. Then he would snort it and lay back in the seat. I would have to wait for this ritual to end before I could depend on him to divvy up our vials of cocaine.

The cocaine was chunky and came in small glass vials with brightly colored lids. Product was often known around the city by the color of the lids. For example, "Red tops!" "Purple tops!" Or, "Yellow tops!" would be shouted from various corners and alleyways in and out of the city. The vials were either $5 or $10 in the city, but in the county, they could easily go for $20 to $40. The cocaine was unlike anything that could be found in the county in quality or quantity. I would buy as many as I could with the sole intention of flipping it out in the county to triple my money.

Back in middle class suburbia, my parents would not let me smoke on the property, so I spent a good portion of my time on the street corner a couple doors down, smoking cigarettes and talking on the phone. Cordless phones were relatively new at the time, and this one's range was exceptional. I planted myself on that corner day and night in the middle of suburbia with my do-rag on, taking calls and selling coke to people who would come there to buy it from me. They'd pull up to the corner, I'd hop in their car, and we'd drive around the block while I made the transaction. Then they'd drop me back off so I could wait on the next car.

My parents had no idea what I was up to, and I tried to keep my misbehavior to a minimum. I was coming up on the end of my fifteenth year, and at fifteen years and eight months I could qualify for a learner's permit to drive. The only problem was that I needed a car. I hadn't saved any money from my illegal deeds. I basically sold drugs so I could stay drunk and look fresh. I barely had enough to buy more drugs when the time came to re-up.

Once I could drive, my folks bought me a red Dodge Daytona for cheap. I was working at a Roy Rogers restaurant at the time. It was one of my longer lasting jobs. I held that job for about a month. My parents thought they were buying the car for me to get back and forth to work and stop bugging them for rides. I was excited because this car was my ticket to the city whenever I wanted and without having to pay for a ride.

I would use the car to get in and out of the city every chance I got. I would even take other people at no cost. I loved the adventure of going down there and learning all of the neighborhoods. I would drive an hour to Reisterstown Road Plaza and Mondawmin Mall just to buy Baltimore Club mix tapes. I would also drive other county kids to a hot spot in Park Heights that was known for its weed. There was a weed drought in the county and everyone was driving to this same corner in the city to buy it. The Jamaicans ran that corner at Belvedere and Park Heights Avenue. I would drive down there for nothing more than gas money just for the experience of doing it. It was like exploring an uncharted part of the ocean or jungle to me. I would, of course, buy weed there and flip it in the county too. But it wasn't as easy. The weed down there was already overpriced since there was a drought. My only benefit was that I was the only person I knew who didn't smoke it.

One day, I didn't have my car for some reason, so my friend Guy and I talked this Asian kid Jin, who we were hanging out with, into taking us down to Park Heights. He started getting scared when he saw the neighborhood and refused to drive into it. We argued, but he stood his ground and would only park at Sinai Hospital. One of my friends was trying to buy an ounce of weed, but buying by weight in the hood was risky business. We had to walk a mile into Park Heights—two white teenagers—get an ounce of weed, and come back unscathed. I didn't smoke, so I wasn't pressed. I was just along for the show, but my buddy insisted we keep going. Once we made it in, there were no Jamaicans anywhere, but a car with two black men pulled up on us almost immediately.

"What do you need?" the driver shouted.

"You got any smoke?" my friend asked.

"Anything you want. How much you need?"

He told them an ounce. The driver instructed my friend to give him the money, and he'd be back in ten minutes.

"Absolutely not!" I told my friend, "He's not coming back once he gets that money, plus we can't stand here looking stupid and out of place for ten minutes."

We went back and forth. Finally, the driver told us to get in, and he would take us to his house. This was so stupid. We had driven forty-five minutes to get here, and my friend was too eager for common sense. We hopped in the car with two strangers and crisscrossed through the back neighborhoods until we pulled up on a street called Woodland. We hopped out of the car and walked up to the front porch of the house.

"Just give me the money and wait here," the passenger called out as we turned and saw the driver pull away.

My stomach dropped. We were stuck, just like I thought we would be.

He said, "Seriously, just sit here on the front steps. Let me run inside, and I'll be right back out."

My friend handed him the money, and he disappeared inside of the house. I knew it was over. That was the end of that. My friend's whole paycheck would be gone in the blink of an eye. We gave it about ten minutes before knocking on the door. We knocked and knocked.

Finally, an old black lady in a robe answered nastily, "What do you want?"

When we told her, she said, "Awww honey, that man gone. He don't live here. He went right out the back door." And she shut the door in our faces.

No point arguing, whatever the case may be, he just got beat for his money. Our bigger problem was figuring out where we were and how to get out of there. As we began to walk through the streets, my heart beat out of my chest. The looks we got from everyone in the neighborhood were like death glares. People shouted at us. Everyone tried to get our attention, probably to try to scam us out of whatever few dollars we had left. There was a Save-a-Lot grocery store ahead, so we headed in there to get change for the payphone. Hopefully Jin hadn't given up on us and left. Even more importantly, we hoped we could somehow get him to the Save-a-Lot to pick us up. The store was packed, and we were still the only white faces in sight. People scowled at us. We stood in line to get change, and people butted in front of us.

When we finally got to the cashier, she rolled her eyes and said, "Nope."

I said, "All we need is four quarters."

"Y'all best get out of here," a voice in line behind us warned.

My mind was reeling. I wanted to take his advice but had no idea how. We walked out to the main street again and stood at the curb trying to figure out which direction to head when finally, a cab came by. We waved at that cab like someone in the water being attacked by a shark. It must have been quite a sight to behold. When the cabbie dropped us off at Jin's car, I had never felt so relieved. Little did I know, I'd end up living and running around homeless in those same streets one day.

Not too long after that, some older friends of mine got the bright idea to go down there and rip off the Jamaicans. One of my friends, Kev, was one of the biggest bodybuilders in Bel Air High School. He was black and built like a young Ronnie Coleman. His father was our UPS man, and I would see him regularly around the neighborhood dropping off packages. Kev and another friend of mine, Brian, pulled up on the corner of Park Heights and Belvedere one night. They asked for a bunch of weed from the Jamaicans and tried to speed off in their Mustang without paying for it. A flurry of bullets went through the back windshield, through the back of the front seat, and lodged in Kev's back and stomach. Kev ended up living, but he'd never lift a weight again. I never knew of anyone from the county to go back down there and score successfully after that. We tried once or twice, but it was always a ghost town. I saw Kev many years later. Not long after that, he ended up dying from complications that stemmed from both the shooting and the many years of drug use that ensued. Brian eventually got addicted to heroin and killed himself. He was once the neighborhood bully, but the last time I saw him alive, he was sitting on a curb at a shopping center puking and falling over into it because he was so high.

VI.

I went down to the city a few times a week now with Nick. I
didn't understand heroin, so I didn't realize he had a daily
habit, or even how a habit worked. I just knew he liked it
and had money to pay me to go. The drug strip on North and
Durham had been shut down, so the routine changed slightly.
Now when we went down, Nick would have me park on a side
street while he disappeared around the corner for ten to twenty
minutes. I often grew antsy sitting there so long wondering what
was happening. The first time he had me do this, he disappeared
for ten minutes. Once he got into the car and we pulled to the
end of the block, there was a huge crowd in the middle of the
street. We looked so out of place, I was worried that they might
turn on us until I saw them all looking down at something.

"What the hell's going on?" I asked. I had never seen anything like it.

"Somebody either OD'd or got shot," Nick replied.

Oh damn, I thought, craning my head as we slowly rolled past
just in time to see a black man on his back seizing and flopping
around like a fish in the middle of the street. There was blood
everywhere on the hot asphalt, and it was evident that he'd been
shot. I wanted to help or stick around to see him get help, but it
was obvious this wasn't our place.

"Just get the fuck out of here quick! The shooters might still be out here," I heard Nick say just before he snorted a line of heroin.

I ran Nick back and forth to the city many times. Occasionally he'd get back in the car with a story about how he got robbed on the way back, or how he'd been stopped by the police and had to toss the drugs. I assumed he snorted his heroin in the alley before he came back to the car with these made-up stories, but I couldn't prove they were fabricated. I knew I had to start copping myself and cut him out of the equation, and eventually I did.

Once on the way down, I was feeling curious. Nick had often told me that I needed to stop buying cocaine and start buying heroin. I assumed that his advice was spoken merely to benefit him. There was no clientele for heroin in the county that I knew of except for him. I wanted to try it though…he had convinced me of that. His actions and his obsession made me curious about it. I told him to bring me back a pill of heroin one day along with my vials of coke. He got excited. He wanted to see how I liked it.

I fucking hated it. When I sniffed the pill of heroin that day, it was the nastiest, most bitter thing I had ever put in my nose. When it dripped into my throat after going through my sinuses, it made me ball up my face like I had just eaten a lemon. The taste was extremely medicinal, but the effect surely wasn't. It made me feel instantly sick like I had a stomach bug. I had to let Nick drive because I was nauseous and vomiting all the way home. I was angry at him for even talking me into trying that garbage. It was sheer misery. I would never touch heroin again, I was certain of that.

It was finally time to cut Nick loose. He was pinching my coke vials and coming back too frequently with stories about being robbed or chased by police. The last time I went with him, I ran into two guys at a 7-Eleven in Bel Air. They were in their late teens and told me that they were in town from Richmond,

VA visiting family. They asked if I could get them any weed. I told them I could, but we'd have to go all the way down to the city to do so. They agreed to pay me twenty bucks to take them down and get them an eighth of an ounce. I picked up Nick and told him the plan, and we scooped them up and headed down. When we went down, I gave Nick some cash to get a few vials of coke, and I gave him the twenty for their weed. They were in the backseat when we pulled up to the spot in the city. Nick got out and disappeared around the corner for the longest he ever had. We sat there, hot and losing patience, for almost a half an hour. They were getting restless. I know their adrenaline was elevated because not only were they in a new state, but we took them forty-five minutes from where they started and straight into one of the worst neighborhoods in Baltimore.

Nick came back much higher than when he left and claimed that the cops had chased him down the street, and that he had to ditch the coke and heroin, but managed to salvage the weed. He threw what looked to be a dime bag of weed to them in the backseat.

"This is it?" they asked flatly.

He told them that's what he had been given for $20. We all knew he was lying. He was as high as a kite. Halfway back to Bel Air, Nick asked to pull off at a gas station and went into the bathroom, most likely to sniff some more of his "invisible" heroin.

They asked me from the back, "You know he robbed you, right? Has he done this to you before?"

I felt like a fool having this conversation with total strangers. "Yeah," I replied, "once or twice. But this is it! I'm not fucking with him anymore. He's just got a way about him that almost makes me feel sorry for him."

They said, "Don't worry, we're gonna get him back for you."

I wondered what that even meant. When we got back to Bel Air, they directed us toward an apartment complex to drop them off. I pulled the car to a stop, Nick leaned forward to let the seat up to let them out, and we said our goodbyes. Just as Nick went to shake their hands, I saw their fists start flying. They pummeled him. One of them grabbed him and tried to drag him out of the car, while the other one stomped and punched his head through the open door. Once I felt like he'd had enough, I started drifting forward. He shut the door, and we sped off. Blood was running down his face and out of his nose.

"What the fuck? Why didn't you help me?" he whined.

"Fuck you! You're lucky I didn't help them," was my cold reply.

I never picked him up after that. It was time for me to go it alone. I had no problem copping coke by myself. Right away, I started exploring the city on my own and found even better places to score coke. I was going over to West Baltimore and buying bundles on Fayette and Monroe. I spent many nights over by the payphone on that infamous corner. I say infamous because years later there was a book written about that intersection that was aptly named *The Corner*, which also became a television show. I read the book and recognized many of the characters and places.

At the time, I usually kept a steady job. Every Friday after I got off, I would make the trek downtown, cop a few hundred dollars' worth of blow with my paycheck, and spend the weekend selling it, drinking, and fighting. I could usually take $300 down and cop thirty-five vials of "Red Top Shirley," as it was often referred to. I never knew why "Shirley" was the name given, but I knew coke was *girl* so that was the only rationale I could find for it.

Those thirty-five vials could net me about $700 to $800, but the problem was that I started sniffing half of it up on Fridays. It became my "treat" for finishing the work-week. I got butterflies in my stomach when I got off work at the end of the week, and as the time between clocking out and heading to the city got smaller and smaller. Frequently, I would take carloads of friends down with me because they weren't just friends, they were also customers. I started sniffing coke because everyone else in the car was, *so why not?* Sniffing coke meant drinking a lot more so I could fall asleep at night. It was a tricky game.

That Dodge Daytona saw many near-death collisions, spin-outs on the beltway into oncoming traffic, and more. I was so drunk and high one time driving up a backroad and arguing with a friend in the passenger seat that as I turned to yell at him, I could see sparks flying past the window. This went on for miles and miles as I rode against the guardrail the whole way up the road. That car looked like it had survived a war. Many times, I feel like I could have, and should have, died in that car, or potentially killed someone else. It baffles me to this day how I survived without injuring myself or another person while I drove drunk, sometimes blackout drunk…two times in particular.

The night I was riding along the guardrail, we were arguing because we were both severely intoxicated, yet my friend was insisting he should drive. His reasoning was that fifteen minutes prior, I had spun out on 695, ended up facing oncoming traffic, and almost killed us both and a handful of other people trying to turn the car around. Another time I was coming back from dropping Nick off after a city run. I was driving down a wet road in a State Park, drunk of course, and spun out about three times and somehow stopped just two feet shy of a telephone pole. I thanked God and kept driving. There was no other explanation for how I didn't die that night.

Unfortunately, my behavior didn't change. At one point, a couple of friends and I decided to head to the city after a night of drinking. We didn't make it three miles before I slid off the road and into someone's backyard and blew out three tires. How I didn't get a DWI that night is beyond me, but I got one shortly after. I was coming back from a party in Baltimore County one night and blew a 2.4 on a breathalyzer. When I went to court for the case, I'll never forget them reading off the statement of charges, and how embarrassed I felt in the courtroom full of people. It went something like this:

"Mr. McGhee could hardly keep his balance. We asked him to walk a straight line, and he was tripping over his own feet. He was emotionally distressed as well. At one point he was laughing, the next he was crying, and the next he was cursing out the officers."

I honestly didn't remember any of it. I was sixteen years old at the time and lost my license, and my parents sold the car. Getting to the city got a lot more complicated after that. But where there is a will, there is also a way. I paid friends and associates to take me down every Friday with the promise of free coke or money. A couple of friends in particular liked prostitutes or hanging out in the strip clubs. At the time there was a notorious hotel called The Marylander on Route 40 leaving East Baltimore. It was known for prostitution. The whole area was a gold mine for me because there was also a strip club called the Gold Club right up the street as well, and a lot of the prostitutes walked up and down the side of Route 40 between the two. The strippers and the prostitutes all liked coke and would happily pay the prices I was selling it for. It was an interesting little dynamic we had going every week. I would pay my friends to take me to the city, they would spend the money on the girls to get sex or blowjobs, then the girls would turn around and give the money right back to me for coke. I never had a desire to mess with the hookers or strippers. Not only was I still shy with women, but I tended to like girls who were for me and only me, not everyone else. I was different from all of my friends growing up in that way. I had to establish some sort of connection with a woman to have sex with her. Random sex did nothing for me.

This arrangement worked for a while. At one point, my friend Steve and I went down to the city. I copped a bundle of coke, and he went straight to the Route 40 strip to pick up a girl. She climbed into the backseat of the car, and we drove to a dead-end road in a warehouse park. He gave her money for a blowjob, and they both walked off around the corner of a building while I waited in the car as usual.

When they came back, she looked at me with bright eyes and said, "He told me you've got coke?"

I gladly took her money. She then told us we had to come back to her house to meet her husband because he would probably buy a lot more. I was immediately sketched out, but Steve liked that kind of crazy shit, so we headed over. It was a row home right up the street from the hotel where we had picked her up. When we walked inside, she introduced us to her husband by telling him that he had to try this "good-ass coke" that I had. I was afraid this was some kind of bizarre set up, but it wasn't. He asked to see a vial, and after looking at it, he handed me $60. Then they both did something I'd never seen before.

I cut out a line for Steve and I as we all sat around the kitchen table. They dumped the coke into spoons filled with water, then drew it into a needle and injected it. I had no idea that people did this, or that it was even possible. I was feeling weird and didn't want to be there. This wasn't the type of scene that I was into. I kept it cool though. I was there to make money.

We sat around sniffing an occasional line, smoking cigarettes and talking, until eventually I had to use the bathroom. She told me it was on the second floor, and I climbed the old, rickety staircase upstairs. I walked into the bathroom and flicked on the switch, and it was like something out of a horror movie. The paint was peeling off the walls, and the old claw-foot tub was full of grime and bugs. Roaches scurried across the bottom of the tub. I didn't want to touch anything. I didn't even close the bathroom door since clearly, nobody else was coming up the stairs. I didn't want the ghosts in this haunted house to lock me in there. I was standing there peeing as fast as I could when I look over and saw a little figure waving at me from the doorway.

There was a child, maybe three years old, standing there watching me curiously. I quickly finished and zipped up my pants. I didn't even know what to say.

"Hello," I muttered, almost in a whisper, with a slight wave back. "Are you okay?" I asked.

He nodded and walked away into a dark room.

I went downstairs, slightly paranoid from the coke and tipsy from drinking, and I asked, "Do you have a child here?" I wanted to be sure I wasn't seeing things or conversing with a ghost.

"Yes, two of them," the prostitute said.

I felt sick. This was disgusting. It wasn't my home, nor my place to say anything to her. After all, I was the one supplying her with drugs. I had to get out of there though.

I looked at Steve, "Okay, you ready?"

As we were getting up to leave, her husband asked me if I could float him another $60 of coke and come back to get the money in two days since I knew where they lived.

I told them, "No, I'm not doing all of that," and made my way to the door.

They began begging. The prostitute got up and followed us to the car begging for a loan. Then he came out behind her carrying a VCR and a record player. What was I going do with this stuff? The empath in me relented and gave them $40 of cocaine and a lecture about her children. I told her she needed to get her life together and do something for her children before they grow up to be like her. She nodded eagerly, acting like she was taking my words to heart and would start tomorrow. I knew she just wanted to get the coke and get back inside. My words were falling on deaf ears. We drove off into the night. I needed a drink to push that one deep down inside…and so I did.

VII.

A friend of mine, and his family, moved to a neighborhood in downtown Bel Air. One night when I was hanging out at their house, I ran down to the 7-Eleven to buy a pack of cigarettes. I saw a man outside of the store who appeared to be homeless, and I asked if he could buy alcohol for me. He went into the store and came out with a couple of forty-ounce bottles for me. I started talking to him, and it turned out that he lived only a block away on Archer Street, one street right in the middle of suburbia littered with houses that looked almost dilapidated and abandoned. The first house on the street was tall and grey and leaning to one side, almost as if it were straight out of an Edgar Allan Poe novel. It was his. Marcel was in his forties but lived there with his mother. She had the upstairs rented out to other people. I always thought the house was either abandoned or haunted. I quickly learned that there was a whole underground layer to the quaint little town that, as a child, I had no idea even existed. This particular street and another one called Lee Street were the central hubs for buying and selling drugs in the area.

Marcel suggested we go in and hit his vodka a few times, so we did. He led me into the front room, which served as his bedroom, and we drank vodka together, exchanged war-stories and smoked cigarettes. He professed his love for cocaine, and I professed my love for selling it. So, we quickly established the idea that he could supply customers to me there, and I could pay him for his service. We chatted for about thirty minutes before I let him know I had friends waiting. I walked back to my buddy's house and told my friends about Marcel, our new alcohol connect. I invited them back down there to meet him.

When we arrived at Marcel's rickety front porch, he opened the front door to let the four of us in. Marcel was a big, black guy, tall and heavy-set, almost 280 pounds. We were skinny, young white teenagers. All together, we made an awkward bunch. I had just come from living in a much harsher environment though, so I felt invincible and cocky. We sat in his room drinking, telling stories, and listening to NWA on his radio. There was something a bit off about him. I could tell he wasn't fully mentally equipped, and his stories about being a drug lord back in the day seemed questionable and a little far-fetched. Occasionally the fun would stop, and he would snap at one of the guys or me over nothing. I sensed there was trouble in the making. We continued drinking and having fun though.

At one point we were jamming out to an NWA song, and I said to him, "That's why you my nigga, Marcel."

He froze and said, "Don't say that to me."

"Huh, fuck that. You my nigga, Marcel."

He told me, "Don't say it again."

But I insisted. I had been saying it my whole teenage life, and it hadn't been a problem. "Naw bro, you my nigga," I repeated.

He reached out and slapped my face. My friend Guy and I jumped up simultaneously.

Guy said, "Come out front and do that shit to me!"

Instantly, it was out of my hands. We came spilling out the front door and onto the porch. Guy ran down the steps and turned up to face the porch.

"Come on, pussy," he yelled up at Marcel.

Marcel, twice his size, ran down the porch and straight at him.

For a minute I froze, not knowing how this was going to pan out. Guy wrapped his arm around Marcel's big head and fell backwards into the dirt with him. He got Marcel in a vice grip of a head-lock while pinned under him, as I came flying down the steps to the rescue. I began punching Marcel in the exposed parts of his head, taking turns stomping on his back.

"Let him go!" I yelled. "Trust me, just let him go!"

As soon as Guy loosened his grip, I rocked Marcel in the face and didn't let up, working him like a bag. I looked back and saw one of the other guys punt him right in the nuts. I was feeling bad for my new friend, but I couldn't risk him getting up and hurting one or all of us.

I kept going while asking Marcel, "Are you done yet?"

Finally, he yelled out, "Yeah, yeah. I'm done. I'm done!"

And I extended my hand to help him up. I'll never forget, in his own drunken eccentricity, he arose with two swollen eyes and blood pouring down his face, grabbed my hand, put it to his lips, and kissed it.

"Respect," he said. "Now, let's go back inside and finish our drinks."

I hung out at Marcel's house hundreds of times after that and never had another problem with him. That street became a cocaine and crack strip for the summer, another friend and I supplying all of the product. We would hang out there drinking day and night, selling to and hanging out with all of the older, less desirables of Bel Air. Most of them were homeless or disabled, alcoholics, drug addicts, or transients passing through. I would sit on Marcel's porch, drinking a mixture of grain alcohol and fruit punch, and sell coke to passersby on foot, bicycle, and vehicle. They would hold poker and domino games in the backyard, and there were often drunken fights, which usually involved my friend or me beating up on people three times our age. I felt pity for these people. They were full-grown men and women, ruled over by two teenagers.

I spent the majority of that summer on Marcel's porch, on his street, or in the second floor of his house, in the private apartment with the residents cutting up and bagging crack, and playing spades. One night, I was there partying and selling coke until late in the morning hours when my friend Guy said he was heading home to his house, several blocks away. Usually, I would crash there, but I wasn't ready to go home yet. So, I stayed up in the apartment drinking with a black guy, Julius, who lived there, and his roommate, Vicki. The guests started trickling out one-by-one until it was just the three of us. It was then that I realized that I had screwed myself by not going home with Guy. I had nowhere to sleep. Vicki and Julius said I could crash on the floor if I wanted to, so I planned on that. It would take a lot of alcohol to put me to sleep on the floor in this crack apartment, so I started drinking harder. Vicki then wandered off to bed. It was just Julius and I, drinking and smoking cigarettes, until around two or three in the morning. Julius was bald, black, and in his forties. He was a cook at Chili's, and was relatively new to the area. He was also about the size of Marcel and had a bull ring in the septum of his nose. We sat and drank and listened to music until something extremely awkward happened.

Julius asked me if he could give me a blowjob. My reaction was quick and over the top. I stood up and smashed my Saint Ides bottle across the top of his head.

"What? What the fuck did you just ask me?" I yelled.

His reaction was not what I expected. He began to howl like a wild animal that had just been trapped in a cage. It made me sad for a second, but I knew I had to keep up my image.

I continued shouting at him, "I don't know who the fuck you think I am!"

He was crying.

Vicki came flying out of the bedroom screaming, "What the hell did you do? Get out of my house!"

I didn't waste my time explaining. There was too much yelling. I opened the door and stepped out into the 3:00am rain. I staggered through the neighborhood and into the park that was central between Marcel's house and Guy's house, and I curled up on a picnic table in the rain. When I awoke the next day, I was at Guy's house, in his bed, and I had no clue how I got there. I woke up and crept through the house, but no one was home. I waited for Guy to get off work and found out he hadn't been the one to let me in. In fact, no one had. If I had slept all night on that picnic table in the rain, most likely I would have gotten hypothermia. I had no recollection of leaving the picnic table, and no one in Guy's house had let me in. So, I either sleep-walked my way there, or angels carried my corrupt body to that sanctuary. It wouldn't be the first or the last time I was miraculously kept alive.

One day on Archer Street, two friends of mine pulled up in a station wagon to pick up another friend and I to go to Ocean City Beach for the weekend. It was early afternoon, I was already drunk, and I still had a pocket full of coke to sell. We decided not to go, so we hugged our friends and told them goodbye. They were a brother and sister who we hung out with and drank with on occasion. The next day we got word that on their way to Ocean City, a drunk driver crossed over the median and hit them head on, instantly killing them both. The drunk driver was in a T-Top Camaro, and his passenger was the only person to survive the crash. The news crushed me and a lot of my friends. I couldn't imagine being a parent and losing both children at once. I went to the funeral for the sister, ended up selling cocaine in the parking lot at the viewing, and then dipped out early before the service. It was too hard for me to face real feelings. I had to find ways to avoid them. Plus, I had a gripping sense that I was supposed to be in that car when the accident occurred. My own life was spared because of my criminal and alcoholic behavior. I believed that the two kids who passed away in that car had a much brighter future than I did.

Twenty years later, I had a bail bonds company. I got a call one night to bail out a young lady in the Harford County Detention Center. The gentleman who wanted to bail her out lived in a house way out in the countryside and didn't have transportation, so I went to see him. When I arrived, I was taken back to a room to sit down with him and do the paperwork. He was a quadriplegic in a wheelchair, missing his feet, and he had deformities where his hands should be. His whole body was mangled. While he completed the paperwork, the topic of how all that had happened to him came up, and he proceeded to tell me that he was the passenger in a T-Top Camaro coming home from Ocean City one night twenty years ago, when the car he was in crossed the median and hit another car head on, instantly killing everyone but him. I lost my breath.

VIII.

One of the most horrible things I ever did was on Archer Street. We were sitting in Guy's house one night, stressing. We had each eaten a tab of LSD and had run out of cigarettes. Neither one of us had a dollar left to our name. It was late, we needed money for booze and cigarettes, and we were out of options. After some brainstorming, Guy told me that he had seen Vicki, the woman on the second floor of Marcel's house, with a carton of cigarettes. He said she always purchased them by the carton. We cooked up a devious plan to break into her house while she was asleep and steal some. We could justify these types of things in our minds because we looked at these people as second-class citizens. This was a woman who bought crack from me, drank day and night, lived off of food stamps, and was obnoxious and nasty. Whatever excuse we could create to justify our behavior and rationalize it with our conscience, or what was left of it, we did. Guy had a gorilla suit that he used for Halloween, and it sat folded up on his shelf year-round, until tonight. He decided to put the entire suit on from head to toe, so as to not be recognized. I put on a hat, keeping the brim low to cover my face, then pulled a hoodie on over that, and we stepped out into the night.

The acid was weak, but just strong enough to emit electricity to my cheeks as I laughed in the cool night. We chuckled all the way through the neighborhood as Guy darted in and out behind cars, trees, and bushes in his gorilla attire. We had about five blocks to cover and part of it cut through a park. We managed to make the entire trip undetected. When we arrived at the haunted-looking house on Archer Street, we made our way around to the back and hid in the shadows. Once inside, the plan was for me to keep an eye on Vicki as she slept. Meanwhile, Guy would go through her nightstand and purse. I could only imagine her rolling over in the middle of the night in her vodka-induced delirium and seeing a gorilla going through her belongings, then trying to relay the story to police.

There was a long wooden stairwell up the side of the house. We ascended it slowly, wincing at every little creak the steps made. Once at the stop, I pulled my ID card from my back pocket and shimmied the simple door lock open easily. We waited a few moments, then tiptoed inside to the bedroom. Vicki lay snoring in the bed as I approached her bedside, standing guard over her. Guy started going through nightstand drawers. I could tell he wasn't having any luck. He was frantically scurrying around shuffling through her things, when I saw him open a wardrobe across the room. As he was rifling through it, I heard Vicki's snores change.

Her voice started to crackle out the words, "What the…"

I cocked back and hammered down on her forehead with a closed fist as hard as I could while simultaneously saying, "Shut the fuck up, bitch."

I heard Guy say, "Holy shit!" from the other side of the room.

Vicki was dead silent, either knocked out or pretending to be. We took off out the door, down the steps, and back through the shadows the same way we came. A carton of cigarettes, an independence card (which was the welfare card of the time), and $20 were the rewards for one of the most heartless things I'd ever do.

There were a couple of times that my parents would go away on vacation and had no choice but to leave me home as a teenager. I did what every alcoholic teenager would do. I threw parties. On one occasion, I got so drunk I threw a chair through the window of my own house when people wouldn't listen to me, which caused a neighbor to call the cops and have me removed from the house. On another occasion, I had a few friends over, and I beat up one of my own friends in my living room over a disagreement. Afterward I felt bad, and somehow thought that by suggesting that we go beat or rob someone together it would make up for it. We left the house, and I let him drive my car. There were three of us in the car, and as we went down the highway, we saw an older, heavy-set white man jogging down the shoulder of the highway next to a graveyard. My friend and I hopped out to approach him in the dark night.

From a couple of feet back I yelled, "What's up bitch?" and threw my half-full forty-ounce bottle directly at his head as he turned to look at me. I have no idea how I missed from only a few feet away. My friend repeated my words and exact action, and from just a few feet away his forty-bottle sailed past the guy's head. *Holy shit!* This guy was bigger than both of us, and we were unarmed and basically just tried to maim him. He turned toward my friend and started chasing him down the street. I ran up into the graveyard and watched the scene on the street, as I pulled a big steel grave marker out of the ground.

"Hey you, over here!" I yelled from behind a tree to divert him from chasing my friend.

He turned and started walking my direction and shouted back, "Hey! What's your name?"

I blurted out the first thing that came to mind, "Satan, motherfucker!" and hurled the heavy iron grave marker at him.

He turned his back toward me and the metal stake arched through the air and bounced off his back, knocking him forward a few steps. He stumbled off clumsily in the other direction, then began his original trot out of there. A moment later, my friend pulled the car up on the street, and I hopped inside. In my heart, I was glad that neither of those bottles hit their mark. I didn't want to hurt anyone that badly. Hell, I didn't even know why I was doing what I was doing, but I wasn't ready to stop.

IX.

I continued to live recklessly and violently with no care for other people or their possessions. I was destructive and hurtful, but it wasn't who I really was. It was a monster I somehow created in order to bury the real me because I was embarrassed by the soft, empathetic, natural version of myself. I was unaware that I could be both tough and caring at the same time, or at least, I didn't think that I was capable of it.

I kept hanging out with different crews. I had my crew from the neighborhood, who I grew up with, that liked to drink and get high and relax; my crew of mostly black dudes from Edgewood and Aberdeen who sold drugs; and my crew of white boys who got drunk and fought every night of the week. I was exploring new areas in the city and found a place to get a fake ID near Lexington Market in downtown Baltimore. I quickly became everyone's alcohol connect. The youngest one in the group, but I could buy alcohol at age sixteen and seventeen. I always thought it was funny that I was banned from just about every bar in Harford County for fighting before I was even old enough to drink. We started going out to nightclubs in the city and its outskirts weekly.

One particular club was my favorite. Every Thursday we went to Club 101 in Baltimore County. It was a bring-your-own-beer nightclub, which was good for a bunch of broke kids like us. The

Daniel McGhee

eighteen-year-olds would get a stamp on their hand and the twenty-one-year-olds would get a bracelet to drink. I was neither, and the bouncers wouldn't accept my fake ID, so we had a foolproof plan every single week. We would go to the liquor store and pick up a case of forty-ounce bottles of malt liquor and head to the club. My friends would pull up in the alley behind the club and drop me off with the beer at the backdoor. I'd nervously wait back there for fifteen or twenty minutes until they got in and the bouncers weren't looking, then one of them would push the door open from the inside and let me in. Our scheme worked for over a year solid. Every Thursday my adrenaline would build in anticipation of heading down there. Everyone was there, kids from the projects of West Baltimore to the rich areas of the county. I could drink freely and was never bothered, out on the dance floor waving my forty-bottle around and dancing to Baltimore club music. Occasionally, I'd get drunk and get into a fight or hit someone with a bottle and get tossed out, but there were so many fights there that the police were never called. So, I could sneak back in the next week and lay low without being noticed. My last night inside the club, I got drunk and belligerent, and one of my friends instigated a bunch of drama between me and some other guys. They were trying to be funny and never expected my reaction when they told me that this other group of guys were saying things about me, which in fact they never said. I didn't know it was a joke, and I was out of my mind with alcohol, so I started picking up wooden chairs and throwing them into the crowd on the dance floor. I was literally hurling chairs into the crowd of people thinking it was funny.

Almost simultaneously, someone came running by me vomiting. Next, I saw other people gagging and choking and running. Suddenly all the lights came on in the club. It was immediately sobering. *What had I done?* The whole place was a mob scene of people choking and vomiting, and screaming. I had to hide, and quick. I was definitely getting my ass kicked by the bouncers or going to jail. Police flooded into the club yelling and screaming and ushering everybody out.

"Anyone still here in five minutes is going to jail!" they screamed over a bullhorn.

I felt a huge sigh of relief. We all poured out into the cold night air and ran to our cars. The club was being raided for the final time. That was the last night at Club 101 and the end of another era. That wasn't the last time I was in a Baltimore club that got raided, but the first of many.

It wasn't too long after that I found myself in trouble at another club called "The Spot." I was in the bathroom selling coke when a group of guys walked in. Just a week earlier, we had these same guys out of their car and beat them up at a 7-Eleven. They surrounded me in the bathroom and tried to rob me. I was able to duck between two of them and spin out from one of their grips.

On my way out of the bathroom door, I yelled, "Fuck you clowns! See me out here on your way out."

Once outside of the bathroom, I had to go find my boys to even the numbers. It's bad enough that I was tiny, but four-on-one definitely wouldn't work out for me. I rounded up the crew, and we walked through the club looking for them. We found them and started exchanging words and threats. It wasn't long before the bouncers intervened and threw them out. Two of the bouncers were from Edgewood and knew us, so that worked out in our favor. I hoped the guys would be waiting for us at the end of the night when the club let out, and we could get a little action in then.

It didn't quite work out that way though. Not even a half an hour later, the lights came on and the music stopped, and the club flooded with police officers. Everyone scattered for the doors and shoved their way out of them. I guess because I looked so young, an officer randomly stopped me and asked to see my identification. I nervously handed him my terrible fake ID, and to my surprise he looked at it intently, then handed it back to me and let me go. Once across the street and in the parking lot, it looked like a drunken riot scene. Cars were spinning their wheels as people tried to get out of the parking lot, banging on their horns. Police cars with their emergency lights were left empty and scattered everywhere. Before piling into our car and taking off, one of my boys had the bright idea to pick up a huge chunk of concrete and bounce it off of the hood of a police car. Never one to be outdone, I picked up a concrete block and caved in the hood. Across the parking lot we heard a boom, as someone imitated us.

We dove into the car and skidded out of the parking lot, screaming, "Fuck the police!" out of the open windows in our best NWA impressions.

It's amazing that no one went to jail that night. I discovered another new hangout right on the outskirts of the hood. This bar was aptly called "The New Spot" and was located on the corner of Bel Air and Moravia Road in East Baltimore. This wasn't a nightclub, but more of a bar, although they would bring in a DJ on certain nights. I loved it there because they never had a problem with my ID, drinks were extremely cheap, and the clientele loved cocaine. I would hang out there as often as possible, usually by myself at the bar drinking and hustling, but would sometimes find friends to show the place to.

One night, I was in there with one of the brothers who had been hustling out of Sabrina's house with me. We sat at the bar chilling and hitting sales, when apparently one of the customers called the police and reported that we were in there selling drugs. When the police showed up, the owner ushered us out the backdoor and down the fire escape in exchange for my promise that I would never sell drugs in there again. I darted up the alley to my car, and we headed back to the county.

Angry, drunk, and wanting to showoff, I pulled up to a stop-light, hopped out and challenged the guy next to me to get out of his car. I eventually punched him through the window when he refused to get out, all because of the way he looked at me.

His girl started screaming, "What the fuck is wrong with you?"

I told her to hop out, and I'd beat her up too. I was sick, and it was only getting worse. I went back to that bar on one other occasion, this time not to sell drugs, but to hang out for ladies night with a bunch of my friends. Three carloads of us went down there and started drinking and dancing and flirting with females. Some of the locals in the bar weren't too keen on us flirting with their home girls. Within an hour of being there, they were bumping and harassing one of my boys on the dance floor. Words were exchanged, and we found ourselves in a stand-off with some big boys. The bartenders squashed the fighting pretty quickly, and we were asked to leave. We left without a fuss. Out in the parking lot, we were trying to figure out where to go next, as we walked to our cars. My friend Kent put his key into the driver's side door of his yellow mustang. He turned it, but it didn't work. As he tried to figure out what was going on, the front door of the bar burst open, and the guys we were just arguing with came charging out.

They were yelling, "Get the fuck away from my car!"

As they walked in Kent's direction, Kent suddenly realized that it was the wrong yellow mustang. His was parked two cars down. It was an honest mistake. The rest of us were charged up and ready to fight, but Kent, being the biggest of us all by far, was extremely humble. He was not only huge, but he was a semi-pro kick boxer, and was well known in Edgewood for his fighting ability. These guys were huge as well, but had no idea what they were getting into. Even though most of us looked like toothpicks in comparison to them, we outnumbered them eight to five and were like a pack of wolves.

Kent apologized for putting his key in the wrong car and tried to talk his way out of trouble, but the guy continued yelling and bore down on him like a three-hundred-pound bull. Kent took two steps back and uppercut him, literally lifting him off of the ground. I saw the guy hit the ground like a giant sack of concrete and didn't think he would get back up, but he did. As he got to his feet, both sides rushed each other in a flurry of punches, and we took guys out one-by-one. The bartender and the DJ both came flying out the front door and into the mix. I busted the DJ's lip and stomped on his head when he went down. I looked over to see Kent and the bull square up out in the middle of Bel Air Road. As the bull charged, Kent jumped in the air and spin-kicked him in the side of the face. It was like something out of a movie, and if I hadn't been there to witness it, I'd probably have never believed it. We thrashed the entire bar that night, and it went down in the halls of teenage history as a story we could brag about for months, even years, to come.

Kent was older than the rest of us and wanted to go home, afraid that we would be getting locked up that night. The rest of us were charged up on alcohol and adrenaline and were out for blood. This night of terror was only beginning, and I seemed to be the catalyst behind everybody's excitement. "Let's go here," or, "let's go there," or, "let's go fuck someone up," I would say. Two carloads of us headed over to my buddy's house in the county projects called Maplecrest. We were looking for his sister and her friends, but they weren't home, so we sat on the picnic table outside of their building waiting to see if they'd arrive.

While sitting there, around 10:00pm we saw a lady pushing a baby stroller across the street, then a black man came up to her and started talking to her. We thought nothing of it and continued drinking until we heard her shrieking. I looked up to see the guy pulling her head back by the hair. That was the only incentive I needed. I grabbed a wine cooler bottle and ran toward them. My friends jumped up and trailed behind me. As I approached the two of them, I didn't ask a single question. I gripped the bottle in the palm of my hand and crushed it on the side of the guy's head.

"What, motherfucker?" I said and jumped back, squaring up, as he stumbled backward to the ground.

My buddies arrived and circled around him. He rose to his feet and darted between two of them and down the street.

"What happened? What was he doing?" I asked her.

She explained that he approached her on a bike trying to sell her crack, and when she said she didn't want any, he started harassing her and getting rough with her, asking for money. As soon as she mentioned that he had drugs on him, our eyes lit up. Without telling her our motive, we ran to our cars to go look for him. We drove around the apartment buildings for a good twenty minutes, keeping a watchful eye out for him, or anyone else looking like they were out hustling, that we could beat up and rob. Finally, we gave up and left for Harford County.

My hand was beginning to throb, and I couldn't figure out why, but by the time we got into Harford County it became apparent. Turning on the interior light in the car revealed that my right hand, the one that gripped the bottle, was extremely swollen. I had definitely broken something. As I drove the crew around, it was killing me. I continually tried to flex it, but couldn't even make a fist. When I hit the guy with the bottle, instead of holding it by its neck, I had wrapped my hand around the bottle itself and crushed it on his head with such force that I broke a bone in the side of my hand. I wondered if I had severely injured him and hoped not. I couldn't let that damper the mood though.

We drove through the Edgewood neighborhoods looking for victims until we came down a dark road in a low-income housing area called Harford Commons. There were two young guys walking down an unlit portion of the roadway. I flew up to the curb, and everyone piled out of the two cars and ran up on them. My hand was so swollen I couldn't make a fist, but in my drunkenness, I wanted to show off so much that I got to the tall one of the two first. Inspired by what I saw Kent do earlier, I jumped into the air and kicked this much taller man in his chin. I fell to the ground on my back, as the two guys took off running, probably having no idea what or why this was happening. Two of my friends took the tall one to the ground, while the other two chased the second guy into the bushes off the side of the road. We stripped the tall one down while he lay squirming on the ground and then whipped him with his own sweatpants out of disappointment for what little money we found in his pockets.

The other crew came back out of the bushes saying, "He didn't have nothing on him."

I had a feeling they let him go out of pity. I was disappointed in them for that. Something had taken over me, and it was sick. The guys in the cars with us were starting to get uncomfortable with how far things had gone, and I could sense it. I started yelling and arguing with them about being weak and sensitive. Half the group went home, but there was still one carload left of us. We drove around in the wee hours of the night and eventually parked behind a shopping center in my own neighborhood and waited for two guys to come out of the 7-Eleven. As soon as they rounded the corner and stepped into the light, my other boy and I were on them. I slammed one against the brick wall and smashed a bottle next to his head, holding the broken shard against his face until he emptied his pockets. I demanded him to run as fast as he could before I fucked him up. My friend got what little the other one had in his pockets, and we ran to the back of the shopping center, hopped in the car, and left.

I could have kept going all night, but they had had enough. It was like I was spiraling deeper and deeper. They sensed it and were getting sickened by it. I was even sickened by myself, but I didn't want to stop. My need for excitement and adrenaline and violence was insatiable, so insatiable that no one wanted any part of me, including myself. The alcohol brought out the demons that lay dormant deep within me, demons whose appetites could never be quenched. I'd find myself alone, nobody wanted to be around me when I got like that. As cool as I thought it was, they all thought I was a loose cannon. It was only a matter of time before I turned on them or did something to land us in jail for decades. But then something happened, something very strange and unforeseen happened. Heroin saved my life.

SEASON TWO

SUMMER DIES TO FALL

"She paints her eyes as black as night now,
She pulls those shades down tight.
She gives a smile when the pain comes,
the pain's gonna make everything alright."

-The Black Crowes,
"She Talks to Angels"

"I used to do a little but the little wouldn't do it
So the little got more and more
I just keep trying to get a little better
A little better than before."

-Guns N Roses
"Mr. Brownstone"

X.

"Ma'am, I really can't tell you what to do. I hope you understand that," I said into the phone apologetically. It had become a phrase I had grown accustomed to saying several times a day because my personal opinion would go against everything that was good for my business. Sometimes I felt so bad for the loved one on the other end of the line that I just laid it all out for them anyway.

"Okay listen, here's the question you need to ask yourself: If you bail your son out tonight, what changes? He's only been in there for a couple of hours. He hasn't even started to feel the pangs of withdrawal. I know he's crying to you and begging you. They all do. No junkie wants to sit in jail." I immediately realized what I had just said and instantly regretted it, but it was too late.

"My son's not a junkie," she snapped, cutting me off.

"Ma'am, listen, if someone is addicted to alcohol, they're an alcoholic. If someone is addicted to junk, they're a junkie. I was a junkie myself. It's a harsh reality. Like I was saying though, if nothing changes, then nothing changes. You can't expect him to come home and suddenly stop using. It's not going to happen. It never does. It's wishful thinking that an arrest will suddenly scare an addict straight—nothing can. My suggestion to you, if you insist on bailing him out, is to leave him in there for three days until the worst of the withdrawal is over. Turn your phone off, let him suffer, then let him have another go at it. Call me then."

I looked across my desk, out the huge plate glass windows of my office at the jurors emptying out of the courthouse and heading to their lunch destinations. Families crowded at sidewalk tables under umbrellas at the café across the street. The woman on the phone with me was still talking, but my attention drifted. I knew she would call me back within the hour to bail her son out. They almost always do. A child's incessant begging is most parents' kryptonite. They want to believe—they want to believe so strongly—that they ignore all of the obvious lies. *This time will be different*, but it never is. The son will come home on bail, and within the first twenty-four hours he will have a needle in his arm, sometimes within the first thirty minutes if he can escape from them that fast. They will call me, asking me to lock him back up, but it doesn't work that way.

The bail bonds profession can literally suck your soul away day by day. It's a never-ending series of heartbreaking disappointments, listening to lies and broken promises, and watching families and relationships be ripped apart. Many say I deal with the worst people, but I don't really see it that way. I like to think I just deal with the worst *in* people.

When I finally hang up the phone, I hear a car horn out front, someone impatiently letting the car in front of them know that the light turned green one second prior. As traffic moves on, I notice the Harford County Heroin Board across the street. So far this year, there have been 346 overdoses and 79 deaths, and it's early September. Harford is just one county out of twenty-four in Maryland, and only one out of 3,007 in the United States. The statistic has recently been thrown around that there are more opiate overdose deaths in the United States in one year than in the entire Vietnam War. While that fact alone is astounding, let's break it down: the Vietnam War lasted twenty years and took the lives of roughly 58,000 Americans. In 2016 alone, opiate overdoses claimed the lives of roughly 65,000. That is a lot of heartbreak, a lot of parentless children, a lot of families destroyed, and countless open emotional wounds.

Bel Air is a dot on the map, sitting about twenty miles north of Baltimore, still carrying its quaint small-town charm despite its rapid growth over the last thirty years. Antique shops, boutiques, and consignment shops litter Main Street, intermixed with the lawyers, a sheriff's office, the courthouse, and my bail bonds office right on the busiest corner in the town. Families have been flooding here in droves to escape the crime and drugs of Baltimore City. The further they can get from it, the safer they feel. But drugs are like water, they can find their way into any place. I witness transactions going down right there on the corner on a regular basis by the tenants who live above my office, which ironically sits right across from the sheriff's office. The Heroin Board tracks the number of overdoses in the county for the year and was put up in front of the sheriff's office in an effort to spread awareness of the opiate problem in our county. They replace the boards that used to announce the DWI fatalities for the year. The numbers aren't even comparable anymore. Despite the death reported on that board, poison is bought and sold right in front of it.

I should have been a number on that board, over and over again in fact. The number of overdoses or near-death experiences I walked away from is staggering. Now I sit behind a big oak desk in my own office with employees who work for me, in a company I own, and I look out at that sign everyday as a constant reminder of what my fate could have been. Life is full of surprises. Life is full of beautiful irony and dark poetry intertwining into a fabric of experience that can only be lived and not explained. One of those ironies is right out in front of my office window.

Jessie—my lady in black, my soul mate, my dark mystery,

my black magic fantasy. Her face is ashy pale, and her long black hair hangs lazily at her sides. Her brown eyes squint as she bends over and scans the ash cans on my office steps for any unfinished cigarette butts. She plucks a couple of stale butts from the sand and stuffs them into her army jacket. It happens once every couple of days, and every time it's as gripping as the times before because she is me, and she is my dark angel. She lives on the outskirts of Bel Air, and she comes to town to hang out all day with the addicts who live above my office. She babysits their grandchildren. It's ironic seeing her everyday...and awkward. Seeing my alternate fate in front of my eyes almost like a ghost floating past my office or by my car as I park it. I walk beside her in a parallel universe, but she's on the street and I'm in my office, living totally different lives.

On one high October afternoon, some twenty years ago, Jessie and I had a private wedding ceremony in the woods. Both of our minds reeling from heroin, sitting in the parking lot of Harford Community College waiting for a friend who was driving us, we decided to walk to the back of the parking lot and take a stroll through the woods. I don't remember our conversations that day, I vaguely remember the woods, but I do remember that in our fragile godless minds we were going to be together forever. My young heart was in love with hers. Jessie was six years older than I, and she was magical. She was everything I thought I ever wanted and I was under her spell, or the deceit of my own misguidance. All I knew that afternoon was that she was everything. Together we could shoot heroin, smoke cigarettes, and talk about life and magic, and God and drugs. We could steal and deal, and grow old, and pick cigarette butts out of ashcans together, and none of it would matter because I was with her. So, when she suggested we get married right there in the woods, I agreed. It wasn't a typical wedding. Ours was a magical ceremony in which we were going to be one forever. Our blood would unite.

"I will carry you, and you will carry me," she explained, "and we will never be apart."

We each withdrew our syringes from our pockets and for the first time stuck ourselves while they were empty, drawing up blood until we were each sure that it was enough to carry the very essence of ourselves. We pulled out the blood-filled syringes and swapped them. Maybe we even did something corny and intertwined our arms as we each injected the other's blood back into ourselves. I vaguely remember anything more about the ritual, but I do remember small details like not being able to measure an exact amount because the numbers on the syringe had been worn from overuse, as is often the case. Diabetic syringes are intended for one use, and then to be discarded. To a junkie though, a syringe is more than a needle, it is a passport. You don't throw your passport away, nor leave home without it.

I felt emptiness after the ceremony. Maybe I expected spirits to whirl about or for our souls to temporarily glow the same light, but what I was left with instead was silent disappointment and momentary disgust. Even in my lowest moments, there was always a flash of morality and a slight semblance of sanity. A voice in the back of my mind shouted from the void, *this is wrong!* But I carried on anyway. Life instantly went back to normal and felt no differently now that we were "married." She sat on a log and fell back into her nod, and I crouched at the bottom of a tree, both of us lighting up fresh cigarettes.

"We became blood forever. Our hearts and souls are one," she spoke in a raspy heroin-laced voice, then blew her smoke out.

I could die right now, I thought, *perfect lovers together forever.*

XI.

Jessie and I split for good and never got back together after she left me for someone else approximately twenty-four hours into my second incarceration. I wanted to take my life in that jail cell. The thoughts of her leaving me, of us never being together again, almost killed me. The thought of me getting out and seeing her again may have saved my life. She did what she had to do to stay high: follow the money. I was of no use to her in jail, even if it was only for twenty-some days. It was a hard hit—calling my soul mate, my life, my dream—when I was dopesick, cold, and in the darkest place of my life, and she didn't answer.

I called her parents and was cussed out and hung up on. I called mine and cried into the phone. My skin was hot, my body ached, and I couldn't sleep for days. My world was black, but none of that mattered. It was her I wanted to die for, and her I wanted to live for. It was misplaced hurt, a missing light at the end of the tunnel. Never mind the withdrawal, never mind the environment I was in, never mind my lack of a future, lack of a plan, or my family who had seemingly turned their backs. It was Jessie, and only Jessie. I had to get out for her—to smell her, to touch her, to shoot heroin with her, and to nod out into her arms.

Looking back, I never loved that girl. I was in love with the idea of her and all the possibilities she represented. At one of the weakest times in my life, she was my security blanket. I wrapped her around me and fell into her. I carried her with me. She was my comfort, but also my belief in magic. I met Jessie when I was seventeen and she was twenty-two. I had just started bussing tables at a new brewery/bar in town, and she was a waitress there. She had jet-black hair and wore sterling silver and amber. She looked like she practiced black magic, and so did her friends. They represented experience, and mystery, and everything I wanted a taste of. I would find my way into the break area whenever I saw them in there smoking, just for a chance to smoke and talk with them. I was drawn to older girls since I was a little boy. I always wanted to hang around them in the neighborhood, on the school bus, even my older cousins. I looked up to older women, and I wanted to be noticed by them. I wanted one—to learn from one, to be with one, and to be accepted by them all.

I would sit and listen to Jessie and her friends chat in the break room and would chime in whenever I had something worthy to add or had the confidence to speak and be noticed. The conversations often drifted into partying and drugs and alcohol. When it came up in conversation that I had never taken ecstasy, I quickly became her pet project. Suddenly, she became more interested in me than ever, and we had a definite reason to hang out. Then one day it happened, I was invited into their world. When I obsess over something and focus my intent on it long enough, it eventually manifests. Unfortunately, my intent was usually fixed on something poisonous. Jessie was definitely the one who would pluck the heroin apple from the tree and encourage me to take a bite, and I would willingly let the world collapse around me as I ate with her. The appetizer before the apple was ecstasy.

She told me in the break room one day that she and her girlfriends were going to Paradox on Wednesday night to Fever, an ongoing biweekly rave party in Baltimore, and I was invited to come. This was what I'd been waiting for! My heart raced at the thought. I couldn't tell my friends about it, or they'd try to barge in on my plans, beg me to come along, and ruin my vibe. But I couldn't wait to tell them afterward…just me and four older women going to my first rave party. I was beyond proud of myself. Up to this point I was an alcoholic, a thug, and a drug dealer. I never sold designer drugs because I was never accepted by that crowd. I wasn't accepted by much of anyone in my hometown or even my own color, which is why I stayed away from there as much as possible.

It wasn't their fault, I chose not to be like them. I was what they called a thug and a "wanna be black." I floated between two worlds, and they didn't understand it. I had sold crack, and powder cocaine and was a full-blown alcoholic by the time I was fifteen years old. I got into fistfights just about every night of the week, and ran with a crowd of the same type. I felt unaccepted everywhere I went in Bel Air by older generations, so when I got the chance to go experience something new with four older girls, I jumped on it.

The night came, and Jessie called me from out front of my parents' house around 9:00pm, and I went out. They were in a brown old-school work van, like the kind people got kidnapped in in the movies. I climbed in through the back doors, and Jessie and two of her friends welcomed me in. The welcome felt more like an initiation, like they were proud to be taking me into their world and as of tonight I would be one of them. The faint smell of recently smoked weed hung in the air.

"You ready?" one of them asked me.

"Can we stop at the store? I need some beer." This was the part I had worried about all night. How do you explain to someone that you need alcohol to function, but conceal the fact that you're an alcoholic? I didn't want to show weakness, but I couldn't socialize without it. These girls only drank on occasion, and tonight we were going to a rave party. People take drugs at rave parties. Only normal people drink. It's almost taboo where we were headed.

"Beer? What do you need beer for?" Jessie asked in a condescending way that almost made me shrink. "Here, smoke some bud," and she reached into her pocket.

"No, no, I don't smoke. It gives me anxiety attacks. Stop up here at the store, please." I knew I was slowing these girls down from their destination, and minutes matter when you're not fucked up yet, but I was crawling inside. *I'll freak out without it.*

She hollered up to the driver to pull in at the Beverage Barn, and as we pulled in, she said to me, "Go ahead."

"You know how old I am," I said. "I can't buy it here. I'm not twenty-one, and they won't take my ID."

"Oh, shit," she took the money and hopped out, looking back into the van. "What do you want?"

I told her to grab me two forty-ounce bottles of Mickey's.

"Holy shit babe, it's only a thirty-five-minute drive," she laughed, back turned, as she headed into the store.

Thirty-five minutes of me pounding that beer in between cigarettes, listening to some unfamiliar ska-style music. I felt like I was in a hippie van headed to Woodstock. Throughout the ride they built up my anticipation, saying things like, "You're going to love it!" and, "You're in for the night of your life!" and, "Are you ready?" through mischievous smiles. Part of me could have sworn that I was taking all of these girls to bed that night by the vibes they were giving me.

Once the van came to a full stop at our destination, I had already drunk enough that I had a solid, comfortable buzz. I was ready to take on the night and everything it had to offer.

We pushed the doors open and stepped out into the chilly darkness. We were in Baltimore City, parked underneath an overpass next to railroad tracks was all I knew. I heard cars whirring past us on the highway above. The parking lot itself was abuzz with traffic, and people moved about everywhere. Music pushed through the walls of what looked like an old warehouse, and a line had already formed outside full of some of the city's finest freaks and lost young souls. I couldn't wait to join them. The girls paraded off like they were on a mission, pulling me along with them as the van drove off behind us.

"What the fuck? You didn't tell me we were getting dropped off," I said.

"Don't worry about it. We got a ride home. Her boyfriend has to work in the morning."

That's a lot of trust, I thought to myself, walking quickly to keep up with them as we approached the line. I saw two bouncers checking IDs and women's purses on their way into the building. All of the girls went in, and I handed my fake ID to the bouncer.

"Naw bro, you can't come in," he said, handing back my ID like it was a bad joke.

I didn't even argue. I could walk somewhere and get some more to drink, then call a ride home. My anxiety started to ease at the thought. The girls were already in, so they'd have no idea what happened to me. This ID worked at half of the places I tried to use it. We didn't think there would be any question of me getting in here. According to the girls, they didn't even card here most of the time. They must be cracking down. This was before the days of holograms and fancy driver's licenses. I bought this fake for $15 at Lexington Market where they took my picture and laminated two cheap stock cards together with my basic information that said "Maryland Identification Card," and I was good to go. Even the police officer in the club raid some time ago had taken a good look at it and let me go.

I began walking into the dark night under the bridge and lit a cigarette, trying to figure out where I was and in which direction to head out. That's when Jessie came out.

"What happened? They didn't accept your ID?"

"Yeah," I said. "Go on though, have fun. I'll get a ride out of here."

"No, no, no, give me a second. I'll go talk to him."

I watched her magic unfold from a distance as I nervously puffed my Newport. She disappeared, then reappeared with the other girls. They all stood around the bouncer, talking to him, then I saw him shrug.

I'm in, I thought to myself.

She came back, "You got $20?"

I handed it to her. We walked in, and she slipped it to him.

The club was dark, and the entrance was a wide hallway that seemed to lead into a network of rooms. I could hear a variety of music coming from several directions. In front of me beyond the crowd, I saw a small makeshift bar, like the kind you'd see at sporting events. To the left was a dark cavernous room, and to the right, a set of restrooms. There appeared to be many more rooms beyond the hallway where the bar was. The place was bigger than I ever imagined, though I'm sure if I were there today, it would only appear to be half the size. I was excited, and yet overwhelmed at the same time. I needed a drink, or a drug, or something to numb my thoughts quickly. Jessie grabbed me by the hand and led me into the dark cavernous room to the left, which she called the "Jungle Room."

We walked into a room where people milled around in crowds in the dark, some stood chatting in circles, some danced alone. We reached a wooden stage off to the back. The rest of the girls were already sitting there on the edge of the stage with their things. I hopped onto the stage and sat with the girls, and Jessie handed me a pink pill. I quickly threw it in my mouth and swallowed it. I sat there in the dark with the girls, quietly listening to the thundering bass of the music—music like I'd never heard before—with extremely fast drumbeats and low bass intertwined into an almost futuristic voodoo sound. I sat and watched the rhythmic sway of a few of the solo dancers in the dark as my mind wandered off, awaiting the barrage of feelings that a new drug would bring. I waited, and smoked, and watched, and smoked, and waited.

Jessie had disappeared into the darkness of the club, and I was left alone with the other girls. The music was too loud to make unimportant conversation, and my unfamiliarity with them was beginning to make me feel uneasy. *Where had she gone? Why wasn't I feeling anything?* I started to get paranoid and suspicious. *Did they rip me off for $20 and plan on ditching me here and leaving me?* My mind raced. I hopped off the stage and went into the bathroom, where the music was at least a decibel or two lower, and pulled out my phone.

"Bro, I'm down here at Paradox. You ever been? I'm down here with four older girls. See if Mark will bring you down, and you guys come hang out." My fear caused me to betray myself. I needed backup, someone I trusted. I was scrambling, I can't believe I put myself here. *Hopefully they will show up, and I can hitch a ride home with them.*

I walked back out of the bathroom, wandered through the corridor, and grabbed a plastic cup of beer from the bar. I noticed that the majority of people in line were buying bottled water, definitely not what you'd expect from your average club. I wandered through the large hallways into other the rooms, scanning the crowds, looking for Jessie. I entered a huge auditorium with house music playing and crowds of weirdos sitting on bleachers that lined the wall smoking cigarettes and massaging each other. I sat down and lit up another cigarette so I could study the room to see if I saw her. There had to be nearly a thousand people in this building, or so it seemed. I might have been the most sober one, oddly enough. I looked at my phone, only a quarter after ten. I knew she hadn't left already. These girls wait every two weeks for this. I hear them talk about it at the restaurant all the time. I walked back slowly to the first room where the rest of the girls were, sipping my cheap beer and scanning the freak show around me for a familiar face. When I returned to the stage, she was there.

"How is it?" she asked.

"I don't feel anything. Either it's bunk, or it's super weak, but I seriously don't feel a thing."

"How long has it been? We all had the same thing," she stated matter-of-factly, like she felt it.

"It's been almost forty minutes," I said.

"Do you want to try something else?" she asked.

"Yeah. I mean, I do, but I can't waste any more money if it's not going to work." I was afraid she had ripped me off and was going to do it again, maybe so she could get her own for free and give me the fake stuff.

"Hold on, I got you. I'll go see my boy Jason. Be right back."

She came back in less than ten minutes and held my jaw in her hand. I stuck out my tongue, and she placed a gel cap onto it.

"This is pure MDMA," she said. "If this doesn't work, I don't know what to tell you."

I swallowed it, hoping she didn't just take me for another ride. The night was becoming miserable, and I felt like a fish out of water. She danced around in front of me, and I tried to make out whether she was high or mock-enjoying herself. I lit her a cigarette and passed it to her and tried to smile at her amidst my concern. I couldn't even catch a beer buzz through my anxiety, and the music was only annoying at this point. I couldn't hold a conversation because it was too loud. The bass was vibrating the wooden stage we were sitting on. All I could do was chain-smoke in the dark, watch the dancers come into my field of vision, and wonder when my pills would kick in.

Twenty minutes in, and my stomach started to turn. I didn't know if it was from my nerves or from the pill. I got up, mind reeling, and wondered if I had just been given something bad. My stomach wrenching, I headed toward the bathrooms in the hallway fast. *Did she give me something toxic? Am I going to die in this nasty ass place?* I swam through the blackness, fighting to get away from the music as beads of sweat formed on my forehead. I made it into the open hallway and busted through the bathroom door. The bathroom was packed with people hanging out and talking, but the first stall door was open. I practically fell into it, hit my knees, and started vomiting into the toilet. It wasn't horrible and never-ending like a food poisoning, but it was enough to bring tears to my eyes and knock the wind out of me for a second. I climbed up onto the toilet and sat there with my pants on, sweat running down my forehead. I took in my surroundings, every inch of the walls around me were covered in graffiti. There was moaning in the stall next to me. I looked down and saw two pair of men's shoes under the divider. *Fuck me*, I thought. The music, and the voices, and the moaning from the men next to me formed a toxic soup of sound. Reality spun in my mind like a vinyl record until I placed my head in my hands, and it was no more.

When I came to, I was still in the same stall, looking at the same graffiti, with the same music, but now I felt like I belonged. I knew what it was. I was rolling. I don't know if I had slept on that toilet for five minutes, or fifteen minutes, or thirty seconds, but everything seemed just the way it was, except the stall next to me was now empty. Sweat poured off of my forehead, and every time the bass dropped, it rolled out of the subwoofer and up through every fiber of my body until it resonated with my soul. I stood up and marched out of the bathroom like I was the king of this new jungle I'd found. I walked into the dark room and headed for the stage where I'd left everyone. Jessie was there.

"Are you ok—?" she asked, then cut herself off. "Yeah you are. You're rolling, aren't you? You like it?"

I was in their world with them now. I'm not sure whether it was a level above reality or a level below, but I knew I wasn't in reality anymore. I looked over, and the friends I had called were sitting on the stage, looking like guardian angels who appeared out of nowhere to come protect me.

My friend Jay looked at me, "You're rolling. How you like it?"

I sensed I had been initiated, like anyone who's previously been here knows and can come back here at any given second. *How did he know? Did he eat some too?* My mind, and everything that filtered through it, was both translucent and vivid at the same time. I was hot, and my skin was flushed. I felt a warmth I had never quite sensed before, a comfort that soothed unlike anything I'd ever felt, and an otherworldliness similar, but quite different from any acid trip I could remember. I fell in love with the deep, heavy, rolling bass that night. It started at the floor and massaged every cell in my body right through to the top of my head. I didn't want to think tonight, I wanted to let loose. I wanted to bond with Jessie. We were on another level, and I wanted to meet her there, talk to her, dance with her, seek her out on this wavelength. I wanted to learn this world, and I wanted her to be my teacher.

We didn't talk much that night but we touched a lot, never sexually, more like mystically. We took turns massaging each other sitting on the stage, she and I, and my friends and the other girls. I followed my more experienced friend Jay's cues and found the beat while I massaged her and moved with it. My fingers were the bass rolling through her neck and back tissue. I longed to impress her. We danced, and in that state of mind I fell into a sweet abyss. I moved without moving, my body finding its own rhythm, and I lost myself there in the darkness. A piece of my soul stayed there that night.

The lights came on, and the police flooded into the club. I was still sweating profusely. People scattered in the light like

Daniel McGhee

roaches, everyone headed for the front door. I wasn't sure what was going on. We all got up and joined the flow. The floor was littered with bags of pills, vials, weed, and pipes. They crunched underfoot as we shuffled along with the crowd. People ditched their goodies, afraid that they would be searched by the police at the door. It was tempting to scoop up the littered drugs off the floor, but city jail wasn't nearly as tempting. I kept moving forward in spite of my inclinations.

The cold night air has an extremely mystical, and yet sobering effect, when leaving a place like that. It's almost like stepping into another world, a sudden, cold, new reality. With the police everywhere, people yelling, and car horns blaring, there wasn't a moment to enjoy the effect. There was only a sad recognition that this evening was over, and I could never get it back. My initiation was complete, the ceremony had ended, and another piece of my innocence had been lost.

I hugged the girls and said my goodbyes. It was somehow understood that I was leaving with my friends. I don't know where Jessie and her friends headed off to that night. I assume to more parties. They were the professionals after all. What I do remember though, is how she turned and looked at my friends, even though I was standing right there, perfectly fine.

She said, "Guys, take care of him please," almost like I was her prize. It was like she cared about me. I smiled out the window the whole car ride home.

XII.

After that night, I didn't see Jessie for a few weeks. Even then, we would randomly hang one night here and there. We had our first annual employee Christmas party at the brewery, and I had looked forward to it for weeks. I wasn't sure whether or not they'd be letting those of us who were under twenty-one drink at the bar that night, but I did know that they were going all out with a DJ and twenty-five cent draft beers. Everyone was allowed to bring one non-employee friend. I couldn't go to a party of this magnitude without drinking. As a matter of fact, I couldn't go a single night without drinking, so I got an older friend to buy me and my friend some forty-ounce bottles of malt liquor. I guzzled a couple before I arrived to the party.

When I showed up, I was already buzzing, only to find out that they were letting everyone drink. I don't remember much of that night, but I do remember being so drunk that at one point I gave up waiting to pay for drinks and started reaching behind the bar to refill my own cup when the bartenders weren't looking. The action that night was centered around the pool table, and that was where the staff, mostly all older men and women, were hanging out. There were a few older waiters who were arrogant and had attitudes with me during work hours, so I decided this was the time to provoke one of them into a fight.

I couldn't stand Jack. He always had something smart to say, always something in reference to me being a "wiggery" or a "wannabe." I had always hoped to catch him outside of work. Like so many others, he stood at about 6'1" and 200 pounds, and I was at 5' 8" and 140 pounds, so he felt like he had free reign to say whatever he wanted. My vendettas came out when I drank, and things would tend to get ugly. I tried provoking a fight with random comments, but no one was feeding in. After all, it was a work Christmas party, but my mind was so far gone that none of that mattered.

There was a long line of teams waiting to use the pool table. I gave up even trying to get on that list, even though I was a beast with a pool stick. I had learned how to hustle pool in an arcade earlier in life. I'm not sure exactly how long it had been escalating, but I saw Jack and one of the cooks, Chris, arguing over who was shooting next on the pool table. Chris was one of those light-skinned, Bob Marley type of hippie black dudes, and he had the dreads to prove it. Nicest guy in the world, but he backed down from no one. As soon as I heard the argument, I moved in close. I was drawn to fights and chaos like a moth to a flame. I don't know what took it to that level, but I saw Chris pick up a stick and start moving to the table to start his game.

I heard Jack say, "Fuck you, nigger!"

This was my opening. "What'd you just say, pussy?" I charged at him.

"What the fuck are you gonna do?" He managed to say, just before the beer mug in my hand smashed into his forehead, and he fell backward into the high table and stools surrounding it.

He fell all the way to the floor, the stools and tables covered in glassware fell with him. As soon as he hit the floor, I pummeled him, landing blow after blow on his face. Just as quickly, there were multiple arms lifting me off of him and dragging me out the side doors to the bar. Between my drunkenness and adrenaline, I'm not sure exactly what was said, but I specifically remember standing out in the parking lot with two of the managers in front of me.

I danced around saying, "Come on, I'll fuck both of you up out here."

They probably threatened to call the police and I left. I don't know if I walked home that night or how I got there, I don't remember much of anything. I never did, except for the extreme highlights of my alcohol-fueled nights. I do know that I showed up the next morning for my busboy shift in full uniform, feeling like a train had hit me.

I walked in the front door only to be asked, "Ummmm, what are you doing here? You no longer work here."

I felt internally crushed because I loved that place, but also relieved that I could go get drunk. I also remember getting a bill in the mail for over $400 in glassware that I had supposedly broken. This was not the last employee Christmas party that I would ruin and get fired for, nor was this the last time that I'd beat someone unconscious in that very same bar.

Over the next year or so, I only saw Jessie occasionally, but I had taken up a new interest in going to rave parties. I still drank regularly every night and sold coke whenever I could get my hands on it, but on certain nights I would convince my friends to go to other cities to attend various rave parties there. I found a whole new line of drugs to experiment with and sell as well. So, it went, during the week I was still drinking, fighting, and selling drugs, but occasionally on the weekends now, I was getting blasted out of my mind at underground parties in warehouses. I would sometimes run into Jessie late into the night at those parties, and it was like running into a long-lost lover or family member. Often it was on the dance floor.

I was a B-boy. I liked jungle music, otherwise known as drum and bass. I would get blasted out of my mind and dance all night to it. A typical night like this would involve me drinking a few forty-ounce bottles of malt liquor before, and on the way to, the club. Then I'd tuck one or two more forties into the waistband of my oversized camouflaged army pants, hidden by my oversized sweatshirt or jacket. I'd have bundles of pre-filled vials of ketamine (Special K) and baggies of ecstasy pills in my pockets, along with my Newport's and a lighter. Once in the club, the drinking took a backseat. The beer bottles came out of my pants and got stashed somewhere in a dark corner or on a dark stage where my friends set up camp. I would either pop an ecstasy pill or start dumping little piles of ketamine powder on the back of my hand on the fatty tissue between my thumb and forefinger and sniff them up in one quick inhale. Depending on the club, I either worked out of a dark corner or spent a large portion of the night in a bathroom stall sniffing ketamine and hitting off buyers.

The ketamine was a wish come true at the time for someone who wanted to make money off drugs and get mind-blown at the same time. I could get a bottle of liquid ketamine for $60, cook it up, and vial up the white crystal flakes and make over $400 off of that one small investment. I could sell a few bottles worth in a night at the club so it paid for my drinking and drug habit, as well as food for the entire week with just one night at the club. If I did an ecstasy flip, I would buy twenty pills for $8 a piece and sell them for $20. Nothing major, but to a loser like me, it was all a goldmine.

As the alcohol was flowing through me, and the Special K pushed me into what was called a "K-hole," I would feel loose enough and brave enough to dance. The Special K distorted reality so intensely that I often lost track of time or even where I was. A few times I was so out of my mind that at the end of the night, my friends had to carry me out of the clubs because an owner asked them to remove me. The world spun either faster or slower when I was in a K-hole. Everything was twisting and melting, but somehow, I could find a bass-line and move to it. There would be circles around me on the dance floor as I tore into the pounding rhythm. I could breakdance, I could lose myself entirely, and I think that was the beauty of it all. I had out-of-body experiences on more than one occasion in those dark sweaty clubs. I vividly remember being so far gone one night that as I danced wildly in the center of a small crowd, I found myself standing in the crowd alongside everyone else watching the dancer in amazement—only to realize I was outside of my body watching myself. Then, as the realization hit me, I was suddenly thrust back into my own swinging body and slowed tempo, and I quickly walked off the dance floor amazed at what had just happened.

I tried to recreate that scene many times. Jessie would find me on the dance floor, always after I was wasted, and she would jump in with me. We would just sync together in dance. Not once did we rehearse or practice, but the drugs must have united us somehow because we fit together like two pieces of a puzzle. We never ceased to draw a crowd when we danced together. It was like we knew how to anticipate each other's next move. We would fight-dance when the hard jungle music would come on. She would punch, and I'd move to the side. I'd throw a haymaker, and she would duck. Then she'd roundhouse kick, and I would slide under her leg and pop up behind her. It was beyond magical, and these were the things that constantly brought me back and enticed me about the drugs...and about Jessie.

Jessie was all about the hippy vibe. She liked the same hard music that I liked, but she believed in free love, free drugs, and no drama. She wasn't a fan of my thug side, or me hustling drugs in the clubs because she saw that business bring out the ugly side of me. The alcohol did as well. She didn't like that I drank the way that I did, and it almost always ended up in a fight, either inside the club or out in the parking lot.

I had received my final warning from the owner of my favorite weekly party. He knew I dealt drugs in there, and he let it slide because I always brought a small crowd and we spent money, but he was tired of the fighting. On my last night in that party, we had to have security bring the owner to the door so we could plead with him to let me back in. After some consideration, he gave me one more chance and emphasized, "No fighting!"

I spent the majority of the night in and out of the bathroom selling Special K. Toward the end of the night, a dude named Scoob tried to strong arm me for some reason. My guy Marcus put his back to the door so nobody could get in. At the same time, I cracked a bottle over Scoob's head and drug his head over to the urinal.

I began flushing it on him saying, "You like that shit? Huh?"

The owner pushed through the door right at that very moment to witness the ridiculous scene. That was my last experience there and at any local rave parties.

I was seventeen. I had been working at a warehouse stocking and sorting dental products and had done very well there. Every single day, I would come in hung over, or still drunk from the night before, and the afternoons would drag. But the idea of getting off work and getting a drink kept me going. The staff was a mix of black and white, but almost everyone was over forty. They liked to party on the weekends, so I would hang with various friends or drink by myself on the weeknights.

I lived in a middle-class single-family neighborhood with my parents, and I quickly learned that their cordless home phone still worked on my favorite smoking corner a couple houses up the street. I would stand on the corner and make cocaine sales right in the middle of suburbia like I was standing in the inner-city projects. People would pull up, I'd hop in their car and ride around the block making the transaction, then they'd drop me back off at the corner. Between that and my day job, I never saved a penny. It was all spent as soon as I got it, usually on fresh clothes and shoes or a piece of gold jewelry. I was always chasing an image, always chasing the wrong things.

On the weekends I'd hop a cab twenty miles across county to Aberdeen to the apartment complex to where my coworkers lived, and I would drink and sell and snort cocaine with them. I fashioned myself a "pretty boy." I always liked to dress fresh, keep a clean haircut, and wear jewelry. I liked all the attention I got from the older women I worked with, even the sexual comments. Even though I didn't find any of them attractive enough to sleep with, the ego boost was enough. I was always seeking affirmation. That's what insecure people do. The women would make comments, or try to lure me into their bedrooms or talk me into staying the night. Even though I was uninterested, I secretly fed off of their attention. So, I liked going over there. I had something they wanted, I made money off of them, and they were able to buy me alcohol. The whole scene was fun, until one particular night.

The night before Thanksgiving things took a twist. I had about half an ounce of coke bagged up into sixteenths, twenties, and fifties when I arrived at "Uncle Mike's" apartment that night. Uncle Mike is how everyone at the job referred to him, I guess because he was the senior employee and the oldest one working there. He was a goofy-looking white guy with a big build, pushing fifty years old. He and his sister shared the apartment where we would come to party. Within a couple hours of drinking and occasional trips to the bedroom to do lines, Mike started geeking out. He came back for more, and then more, until finally he sniffed up my last sixteenth. He kept asking for more and waving money around. I was thinking to myself, *how does this man pay rent after he blows his entire check on coke the same day he gets it?* I dialed people, but it was after midnight, and I was in Aberdeen, so I couldn't make anything happen. He was adamant and pestering me for more, fiending out.

After I finally laid it out for him that I couldn't get any more that night, that it was flat out impossible, he said, "I'm gonna go to the Park then. You coming with me?"

Washington Park is a project apartment complex in Aberdeen that I had heard about many times, but never been to. My running always had me between Edgewood, Bel Air, and Baltimore, so this was uncharted territory. The women tried to talk him out of going down there at that time of night, and when they saw that it was futile, they pleaded for me to go with him. I agreed to, but I wanted to bring the .38 pistol that Uncle Mike had shown me on a previous occasion. I had never been to the Park, but I didn't expect to see any other white folks down there. I had heard about shootings happening up there on a regular basis. I tucked the pistol into my front waistband, and we threw on our jackets and left the apartment.

Mike walked into the Park knowing that he would likely only be able to score some crack, but it really didn't matter to him. I was embarrassed to be seen with him, but it was late at night, and this wasn't my hood. I felt the need to protect him even though I was half his size. I tried to tell him to let me handle negotiations, and we argued about it on the way, walking three quarters of a mile or so down the highway to get there. It was his money though, I was just along for the ride.

We reached the end of the highway and made a left on Post Road. The apartments were lit up like a beacon in the night. We crossed through the grass into the cluster of buildings and saw several figures moving around in the streets in the moonlight. There were a lot of people out for 2:00am on a cold evening. We walked past a couple. Finally, a dude approached us.

"What's up? What you need?" he asked Mike.

"What's out? Coke or readies?" Mike asked.

The guy said he could get either one. Mike said he was looking for $50 of ready. I rolled my eyes to myself. He'd smoke that up in twenty minutes and be up all night jonesing for more. The guy told Mike to give him the money, and he'd run into the building and bring it right out. Mike handed him the cash, and the guy walked off into the darkness never to be seen again.

I finally broke my silence.

"Why did you just do that? You know he's not coming back. Are you really that drunk?"

We bickered for a few minutes, and the more time that elapsed as we stood in the dark in that sketchy situation, the more reality began to sink in for him. Figures moved through the streets in the dark, but no sign of our guy. Mike fidgeted repeatedly, then asked how much money I was holding. He knew I was holding all of the money that he had just spent with me, and more.

"I'm not giving you any more cash to give away out here. Let's just roll," I said.

He asked for a loan until payday. We argued some more, then out of the darkness I heard shouts, "Whoop! Whoop!"

Somebody was alerting the complex that the police were nearby. We had to get out of dodge. The streets cleared out almost immediately, and we were two of the only people left somewhere we clearly didn't belong.

"Let's go!" I insisted.

The walk home was a quiet one. I know Mike was miserable. His night had ended abruptly. The party was over. The serotonin in his brain was quickly decreasing, and the chilly air was sobering. As we reached an intersection about halfway home, two black men approached us. They walked straight up to Mike.

"Hey homeboy, you got a cigarette?"

I sensed this was a robbery. I reached into my waistband in the dark. They were focused on him. We kept walking. We never stopped moving to acknowledge them. It was after 2:00 in the morning. It was no time for casual conversation with strangers.

"I ain't got none," Mike said, never breaking stride or looking at them.

They must have taken offense to this because one of them snapped, "Fuck you, white boy!" at our backs as we were crossing the street.

Mike spun around in the street, and all of his rage from what had just happened reached a boiling point. His anger from getting burned for his last $50 was directed at them, and he snapped.

"Fuck you nigger!" he roared with a voice full of anger.

I had never heard him speak like that, but I knew he was out of his mind. Two feelings hit me immediately: embarrassment and fear. I didn't want to be in this situation, but I was. Now I was guilty by association, and I couldn't abandon the man I was walking with. I didn't want to be associated with racism, let alone fighting for it, but I was in a jam. We were on the other side of the street looking across at them, two shadowy figures in the dark. They immediately turned and started crossing the street in our direction.

"Oh shit," Mike said, immediately realizing his mistake, but stopping and getting ready to fight.

I wasn't fighting for this I told myself, as I pulled the gun from my waistband aimed above their heads, letting off two shots. I simultaneously screamed out, "Fall back, motherfucker!"

I heard an "Oh shit!" and watched the shadows disappear into the dark in the other direction. And just like that, the night was quiet again.

Mike turned to me, "What the hell got into you?"

I told him I was cleaning up his mess and that we should just hurry back. We broke stride all the way home and managed to make it to the parking lot of his apartment complex just in time to hear police sirens. I reached into my waist once more, retrieved the pistol, and slid it across the asphalt under a minivan literally seconds before two squad cars pulled in behind us. We were fifty feet from the steps to his building. We almost made it.

The police pulled in quickly and immediately hopped out, guns trained on us. Within minutes we were up against the parked cars being patted down and pockets searched. I was still drunk, so my nerves were calm.

I played coy with them, "What happened officer? What's going on?"

When they told us there were reports of a shooting in the area and two white males running from the area where the shooting supposedly occurred, I played dumb.

"Oh wow, were they hurt bad? We didn't hear any shots at all. We just walked out here."

Eventually they let us go and drove off as we walked into the building. I thought I should wait a few minutes, then go back out to get the gun so I wouldn't get caught. But there was a new face in the apartment that night, and he took an immediate interest in me. Cujo was a black dude with crazy, random braids like Coolio. He looked cold in his eyes, like something was missing.

"Yo, who is you? I like how you handled that shit, my nigga."

I was wary, but intrigued, and glad to be back in the apartment where there was more alcohol. We all drank and talked. We told them all, including Cujo, about the whole night, not leaving out the "nigger" detail.

Cujo laughed, "Y'all motherfuckers, crazy."

Eventually Cujo went out and got the gun from under the minivan for us, and he told Mike he owed him for the favor. Cujo asked me to get more coke, and hounded me the same way Mike did. I could tell by his eyes that something wasn't right with the dude. He was definitely drugged out, but I could tell he was thorough too. He called me a "thorough ass white boy" that night, and it stroked my ego. At that time in my life, those were words I lived for. Little did I know, those words were intended to stroke my ego.

Cujo was a con himself. Everybody in the hood has a game. Cujo wasn't just a fiend, he made his living and supplied his habit off robbing drug dealers in the county projects. I didn't know these things at the time, but I felt enough of a vibe not to let him know that I had a wad of cash in my pocket.

"You ever rob somebody?" he asked me.

I told him, "Yeah," and I wasn't lying.

"You wanna go make some money?" he asked again.

I went all in. While everyone else went to sleep in the apartment, my new friend and I headed back out into the cool night. We ran through the apartment buildings and crouched behind cars smoking cigarettes looking for victims on their way home or on their way out to work. At one point around 4:30am, we beat on the door of an apartment of someone Cujo had said owed him money, but nobody answered. No one in the building even came out to see what the racket was all about. In hindsight, that was actually amazing in itself, because they would have most likely become innocent victims and gotten beaten or robbed too. I was in over my head, committing felonies in an unfamiliar neighborhood with someone I barely knew, but could sense was dangerous, and yet I loved every bit of the excitement.

Nobody got robbed that night, but I had made a new "friend," and we parted ways just as the sun was coming up. I called a cab to take me home. The ride home in the early morning sunlight was miserable, as I prepared to walk into my parents' house just in time to catch the Macy's Day Parade on TV and Mom's pumpkin pie, a Thanksgiving morning tradition. The next time I saw Cujo was under different and less friendly circumstances.

XIII.

About three weeks later, the warehouse where I worked was celebrating their annual Christmas party at a popular bar and restaurant in Aberdeen. I decided I was going to get dressed up and pre-game at Uncle Mike's apartment. I arrived an hour early and started drinking to get my buzz in preparation of the night's festivities. As I drank, I started changing into my dress clothes and getting fancy for the night. I had brought a change of clothes and intended on coming back to the apartment after the party, getting back into my casual clothes, and spending the night. Once dressed, I sat on the couch pounding drinks and smoking cigarettes waiting for everyone else to get ready. The door opened, and a woman entered, crying. She shut the door behind her and locked it.

The ladies came out of the bedroom exclaiming, "Oh my God! Amy, what's wrong?"

She looked up, her face red, and one of her eyes severely bruised. It turned out that she was Cujo's girlfriend at the time, and he had just beat her up.

Uncle Mike said, "Don't worry, you can stay here as long as you need while we're at the party."

She introduced herself to me and asked if I knew her man.

I said, "Yeah, not well. But we sort of became friends the other night."

"Well, please don't tell him I'm here. Please!"

"No, of course not," I said. "I don't even know how to get in contact with him." The whole situation was uncomfortable to me, and I didn't want any part of it. I didn't support anyone beating their girl. But I didn't know the situation, and I didn't want to get caught hiding her out either. I finished my beer and just wanted to get to the party, but the women were taking forever. I told everyone I was going out front, hoping that would encourage them to hurry the hell up.

I walked out of the apartment door and down two levels to the building entrance. As I stepped out into the daylight, I saw Cujo and four other brothers sitting there on the steps. The whole scene felt bad. It was like I just walked into a trap, and I knew he was not going to be friendly with me in front of his homeboys.

"Hey yo, you seen my girl Amy?" he asked.

I hesitated for a minute, but decided to do what I thought was right, "Naw, I don't know who that is bro. I've never seen her." I lit up a Newport and looked up, and my heart skipped a beat.

Amy came walking out of the same apartment where I just exited. He followed my gaze until he saw her through the front glass of the building.

"M-o-t-h-e-r-f-u-c-k-e-r, you lied to me! I thought we were cool, but you just lied to me about my girl!" And just like that, I was surrounded by his homeboys, with him facing me. "You lied to me, bitch!"

He leapt at me and swung. I was able to duck his punch, break through his circle of goons, and run up the street. When I was a safe distance away and confident no one was following me, I got brave and shouted, "You gotta wait til you got all your boys with you, pussy! I got you. I'll fuck you up alone though!"

I knew at this point I'd probably be followed by the whole

crew, so I cut through a yard or two and up a side street until I was face-to-face with a ten-foot chain link fence. It belonged to the Amtrak railroad. I climbed the fence in my dress clothes, adrenaline pumping through my body, alcohol fueling it. I hit the ground and crossed the tracks just in time to feel a train blow past me with the horn sounding wildly. *What the hell was I doing?* I knew that on the other side of these tracks was Route 40, and somewhere along that stretch was the Eagles Nest Bar and Restaurant where our party was being held. I franticly scrambled over that fence too, adrenaline surging even more after my near-brush with the train. Once my feet hit the pavement on the other side, I felt safe. I slowed my stride and began brushing off my dress clothes as I crossed a parking lot to the shoulder of Route 40.

I'm in a suit walking up the shoulder almost at the parking lot of the venue, preparing myself to enter into a whole different world, when I hear from behind me, "Ayooo, what was you saying? You gonna see who?"

It was Cujo pedaling up behind me with a smirk on his face. The bike he was riding was clearly stolen because it was way too small for his body.

"What was you gonna do? Huh?"

I kept walking, rounded the corner into the parking lot, and entered the bar where I felt safe, like I was on home turf. I knew I had fucked up, and now I had to straighten it out. I looked out the double doors behind me into the parking lot and saw Uncle Mike's car, he and the others climbing out of it. I also saw Cujo pedal over to them. I waited around the corner, thinking he wouldn't dare come in here, at least I hoped.

When they came into the building I popped out from around the corner, "What's he talking about? He's not coming in here, is he?"

They told me not to worry about it and to enjoy the party, that he wouldn't come inside.

We walked into a huge room with white tablecloths and flowers and glassware on the tables. The executives and higher-ups of the company were all there. I vaguely remember drinking champagne, a few toasts, and listening to various lackluster speeches before finally excusing myself to the restroom. I ducked into the bar, ordered a mixed drink, and smoked a cigarette. My dress clothes and association with the party must have been my free pass to order a drink without being carded. One drink turned into two, then three…

I don't know how many I had, but I spent at least an hour on the payphone dialing everyone I knew off the little list I kept in my pocket. One by one, I called all my guy friends telling them to come up and bring me a gun because I was going to kill this dude who was after me before he killed me. I dialed all the women on that list trying to get them to come hang with me at the bar. I never went back into the party. I had the payphone ringing as I bounced back and forth between there and the bar ordering drinks. At some point, someone overheard me in my drunkenness talking about getting a gun up there and shooting someone. They returned back to the work party and told someone, who then notified my manager. She came out to the payphone where I was, and seeing how drunk I was, she asked me to leave, and she yelled at the bartender for serving me. Eventually, I was escorted out of the building and told not to reenter. Cujo was gone, and the parking lot was empty. I'm not sure how my father was contacted, but he arrived to pick me up. I remember climbing into his car, but not much about the ride home.

The rest of that night was a blackout, but the following is what I've been told. I was brought back home, and once there, I decided I didn't feel like staying. I told my parents I was leaving and going back to Aberdeen, that I had unfinished business out there. When they tried to stop me, I tore my room apart, cursed them out, flipped my bed over at my mother and swung at her.

I never even cursed in front of my parents when I was sober, but drunk, I had no bounds. The police were called. When they arrived at my house, they entered into my basement bedroom where I was sitting in the wreckage and gave me a stern warning about how they could take me to jail that night. They said they would let me slide this time if I just stayed home and slept it off.

About ten minutes after they left, I snuck out the backdoor and started walking the twenty-mile journey back to Aberdeen. When the police found me again, I was out of my mind hitch-hiking up a backroad. As they approached me, I am told I threw rocks at them and shouted for them to "leave me the fuck alone."

I don't remember any of that, but I don't remember many nights from back then. I do know that somehow, some way, I didn't end up in jail that night. I ended up back home in my own bed, in my own trashed room. I was charged for drunk and disorderly conduct and malicious destruction. I also initiated the process of getting thrown out of my parents' house that night. I had gone too far. The idea to quit drinking wasn't even an inkling of a thought in my mind; it wasn't even a possibility. Alcohol made me who I thought I needed to be. I thought alcohol made me into superman, but really it turned me into an asshole centered on self-destruction. That night was a tiny drop in the bucket of the madness that alcohol caused in my life. There would be many more just like it.

As for Cujo, we never saw each other face-to-face again. A couple of years later, he was on trial for attempted murder. One of the witnesses was a white female who worked at a convenience store in Aberdeen. He walked into the store one night and shot both of the female store clerks in the head and killed them, and walked back out like it was business as usual. He's now serving two consecutive life sentences in the Maryland prison system. The news articles I read said that he expressed no emotion regarding his crimes, nor when he was sentenced to life in prison.

XIV.

Nothing changed for me except my surroundings. I left my parents' house—the feelings were mutual. I was wasting my life away, I was a terrible influence on my younger siblings, and my parents were making it extremely difficult for me to continue my current lifestyle of doing whatever I wanted, while slowly killing myself. A couple of my friends were staying at a party-house a few neighborhoods away from where my parents lived, and we managed to talk the girl who lived there into giving me my own bedroom there for free. Kim and I met that day, and by that evening I had my own room in her house. It turned out that her parents were loaded and didn't want her living at home anymore. They were old enough to retire and wanted a simple, quiet life of their own at their house out in the countryside. Their daughter, as they were well aware, came with drama and tons of poor decisions that they did not want to deal with. So, they bought her a townhome about an hour away and let her have her way with it.

Kim was a fiend for popularity. Her house was modern and spacious and could have been beautiful if she had had the backbone to keep the riff-raff out. Instead, the inside of the house was covered with graffiti and holes in the wall, and it was littered with ashtrays and beer bottles of all shapes and sizes. In one part of the basement, there was a human-sized hole in the wall where a human body had literally been thrown into it in the middle of a fist-fight.

I was right at home. The upstairs living quarters were much cleaner and more organized. Kim had the master bedroom suite, and my friend Tina had the bedroom next to mine, which she often shared with her boyfriend, Steve. We instantly became a happy family. We cleaned together, we went out to eat together, we clubbed together, and we got drunk out of our minds together. I kept a lot of the riff-raff away who wanted to come over just to use the place, and I cleaned every morning after we partied. Kim loved me. It seemed like I was the only one who actually cared. I had morals, but mostly I cared about making sure I had a place to stay and that a good thing wasn't ruined. I introduced Special K and ecstasy to the household, and sometimes even cocaine.

On an average night I was cooking up bottles of Ketamine, cutting it up, and putting it into vials at the kitchen table while drinking forties and occasionally snorting some. Ketamine was cat tranquilizer, and mine was coming from a guy in Philly. I don't know how he was getting so much, and I didn't ask questions. I just knew that it was cheap, and he seemed to have a never-ending supply. I would empty the bottle onto a plate and set the plate over top of a pot of boiling water. Eventually the liquid would crystallize, then I would scrape the crystals into a powder with a razor blade and package it up for sale. Sometimes if a stove wasn't available, or if multiple bottles were being cooked up, I could set the plate of liquid on top of a lamp to crystallize, but it took much longer.

Much of the traffic in and out of the house was to buy the drugs I was selling. Otherwise, mostly only close friends came there to party. I introduced the crew to the rave scene, and we began frequenting clubs together. I was back in my element, and it wasn't long before I ran into Jessie again and told her about my new place. I had to get her there to check it out. I knew she would love it. Jessie was dating a guy who owned a rave club up in York, Pennsylvania and was hanging up there with the DJs and drug dealers, spending her time bouncing back and forth between the two states. When she was in Maryland, she would come hang with me. I was crushed that she had a boyfriend, and I wanted to steal her away. She would sit in my room, and we would watch movies together and cuddle. We shared the same bed, but she would never take it past friendship. Things started changing though.

Jessie started hanging with the other couple in the house, Tina and Steve. They didn't want to go out much anymore. I wanted to get out to the clubs and do things, but they weren't interested. There seemed to be a secret vibe going on that I wasn't let in on. They started to give me a hard time about wanting to drink and party all of the time. I didn't know what was going on. I don't remember exactly when it was, but at some point, I found out they were sniffing raw heroin, something I never had any interest in. I often heard one of them vomiting in the bathroom. I wanted to help, but they told me they liked it.

I didn't understand this sickness. It was taking over our home and ruining the vibe there. They were often pale-faced and broken out with red pimples, always scratching themselves, and falling asleep sitting up. I had no interest in trying any of it, so I started keeping my distance from them. I got very bitter over it. I would call other friends to come pick me up and would go out drinking while they would sit around the kitchen table playing cards in slow motion. They talked in slow, hoarse voices and always had some kind of cocky sarcastic attitude. We'd fight often about my drinking and partying and their heroin use. It was three against one. When I was in the house I'd sit up in my room and drink alone, watch movies or write poetry, and wait until Jessie was ready to come to bed so I could have some alone time with the girl I was in love with. My other friends had stolen her from me. Occasionally I would bitch about her sniffing dope, only to have her throw my drinking back in my face. I will never forget my disgust back then at that drug, I couldn't understand for the life of me why someone would want to look that way and tolerate feeling itchy and nauseous. When I tried it once a few years prior, it made me miserable. I hated it.

Jessie disappeared for almost two weeks at one point, then randomly showed back up at our door. I was angry and relieved at the same time. She told me that she went up to stay with her boyfriend in Pennsylvania, and he did some sort of intervention with her. They all did cocaine and sold cocaine, but heroin was off limits. When he found out that she was sniffing heroin, he gave her an ultimatum. He told her it was either him or the drugs. I imagined she could stop instantly if she cared about him, but I knew nothing about the drug. She said that he locked her in his home and kept her there, and that either he or his friends kept an eye on her. She was there for almost a week. She said she lied in bed almost the whole time. When she was feeling a little better, they went out to a fancy dinner and had wine. I was thinking how I couldn't compete with this guy. He was definitely older and more put together than I was. I scraped by every day and had nothing to offer her except my love.

Something bad had happened though toward the end of her visit there. Apparently, while she was laid up sick, one of his friends had tried to take advantage of her and sleep with her. When she told her boyfriend about it, her boyfriend confronted his friend, who called her a liar and a junkie whore. Her boyfriend took his friend's side, and according to Jessie, he showed his true colors. She never planned on going back to him after that. I couldn't imagine how awkward that hour-drive home from York must have been as he drove her back home for the last time.

Nobody had seen nor heard from Kim, whose house we were

all living in, for weeks. She showed up one day and told us that we all had two weeks to get out of the house because she had a date set to go into rehab. Her parents had given her an ultimatum to go into treatment or they would take the house from her. Jessie had been staying away from heroin and had been spending a lot more time with me. We spent almost every night together in bed stroking each other's skin. I would kiss her all over her exposed skin and play with her black hair. We grew very close. I was like a little boy in love. She was here, but just out of reach. I had nothing to offer her. I was six years younger than her at an age where six years made a huge difference.

The other couple disappeared daily all day long and would come back at night. We could hear them fucking for hours through the bedroom walls. It was awkward, but especially awkward as I lay there sometimes wishing it were us making those noises. Sometimes they would ask Jessie if she needed any heroin, but she would say she was good. I was proud of her.

Kim went to rehab, and nobody left the house. Her mother showed up a couple of days later, livid, and said everybody needed to be out within two days or she was charging us with trespassing. Steve and Tina left. They were only staying there for fun. I was staying out of necessity. I did what I knew best when faced with no real option; I drank. I drank away my anxiety, fear, and hopelessness. I invited people over. People showed up, and more people after that, until the house was packed with people drinking and partying in the middle of a weekday afternoon. When the doorbell rang two days later, I wasn't prepared for how to handle it. Instead of thinking that morning, I had started drinking. I was sure it was Kim's mom showing up with more threats, but it was the police.

Before anyone even opened the front door, we heard the police radio go off, and people panicked. Everyone in the house scattered and fled out the backdoor, except Jessie and me. She didn't want to run, so she offered to answer the door. I was totally unsure of what to do, so I sat back and listened. The police were very reasonable, and to my surprise they didn't ask to come inside. They gave us one hour to leave the house, or they would be back to arrest us. We were gone in twenty minutes, walking up the sidewalk in the middle of suburbia with no plan and no home. Jessie had a room at her parent's house. I had an empty stomach and a heart full of fear.

I felt absolutely lost walking up that sidewalk through rows of townhouses and single-family homes with nothing but the clothes on my back. At that moment I was helpless. Helpless, except for this woman by my side who always seemed to have the answers. I needed her. I latched onto her like a little brother to his big sister. Maybe that's why it was so hard for me to break through to her on a romantic level. I was weak and lost, I had nothing to offer, but at the time my ego told me I was special that I was a prize. I thought I was attractive and had style, and that I was tough. To me, those were the only attributes that mattered in the world. Forget my alcoholism, my inability to hold a job or a place to live, my emotional insecurity. I felt I deserved everything just because I was me. It's funny how many people around me had the same distorted beliefs about themselves, and how later in my bail bonds profession I saw those characteristics in all of my clients.

Jessie called a ride to come pick us up and take us to her parents' house. We spent the afternoon at their kitchen table smoking cigarettes and making phone calls. It wasn't long before a plan had come into effect. She had made some friends up in York, PA apart from her ex-boyfriend and his crew. One of them was a female DJ named "L Boogie." Her name was Lana, and I had never met her before, but I would be meeting her that night. She was going to come down and take us to New Energy, the club in York where she spun, and afterward we could stay with her for a while.

When she picked us up early that evening, we had her pull over onto the shoulder of the highway near the house we had just vacated. We ran up over the hills that served as a sound barrier for the highway and darted through some pine trees until we were in the back of the townhouse row. It was a corner house, which made it a little less suspicious that we were lurking around. We tried the back doors and the front doors, but they were all locked. I had to get in to get the rest of my possessions, as well as a stash that was hidden under the kitchen sink. Looking out for any watchful neighbors, I crouched low and kicked out the basement window and slithered inside while Jessie waited on the outside for me. Once inside, I loaded up a bag with clothes, hygiene products, and other belongings I had left behind. I scurried through the house as quickly as possible keeping an ear out for police sirens. I finished loading up in less than five minutes and paused in the kitchen on the way out. The most important bag was under the sink. I reached in the cupboard and pulled out an Army-green duffel, checked the contents, and then hurried out the backdoor. Jessie was anxious. We smiled at each other, then darted back through the trees toward our waiting ride.

"Did you get it? How much is in there?" Jessie asked.

On the last day in the house, we had invited a bunch of people over. One of them was my drug connect from Philly. Jessie had invited him because he had an obvious thing for her and was always trying to take her out on dates. When the police banged on the front door earlier, she had seen him toss the duffel under the sink before he ran out the backdoor with the rest of the crew. Had the police come in and raided the house, we would have caught that charge because we stayed behind to talk to them. I would have been arrested without even knowing there was a duffel bag of drugs underneath that sink. Luckily, they didn't search the house. The bag belonged to us now.

"Twelve bottles of Special K," I replied, counting them out.

This could last us a little while until I came up with a new game plan. I could make about four grand off of these if I cooked them and broke them all down myself. I knew in the back of my mind that we'd end up sniffing half of it though. I had to get my life together. This was a scary new beginning in a new town, and I didn't dare think about my future beyond that.

XV.

Lana was a good girl in a bad world. She intrigued me because she had her life together more than anyone else in my circle. She DJ'd at the parties we went to, she went to college, she had her own place in York, as well as a college dorm room in Lancaster. She even had a gig on the college radio. She also instantly had a thing for me. If I had any sense back then, she could have been my ticket to a new world, maturity, and an escape from a fate of drugs and homelessness.

Lana cared about Jessie. She liked to party in a normal way, she occasionally dabbled in designer drugs and drank, but it didn't affect her life the way it did ours. She didn't rely on it. I soon realized that she had an extreme interest in keeping Jessie away from heroin, which is why Jessie was coming to stay with us. Jessie had made it sound like she was doing all of this for me, that she had a place to stay, but she was coming to York with me to make sure I was okay because she didn't want to ship me off to this new world of strangers alone. That was partially true. The part she didn't vocalize to me was that she was back in York to kick heroin again. At the time, I didn't realize the exceeding power of heroin addiction, nor did I understand how it worked.

We were in York as a wakeup call. It was a roof over our heads, being surrounded by good people, and a chance to somewhat dry up and get a foothold back in our lives. It turned out to be everything but that, because we were, after all, our own worst enemies. On the way up to York that first night, Jessie spent the ride doing her make up in the rearview as the girls talked about various people from the scene up there. I sat in the backseat in silence smoking cigarettes. We were going straight to a rave party because Lana had to DJ that night. I just wanted peace. After the turmoil of the day, I needed to relax and sleep, but that wasn't about to happen. I had no choice but to go to the club. I hadn't had time to cook up any bottles, so I had to sell a bottle in the club in order to have money. Jessie told the bartenders in the club not to serve me. Because I was under twenty-one, I was only allowed to stay on the second floor and not come down to the first. Jessie's ex and his buddies owned the club, so I wasn't going to catch a break. I was trapped here. I got strangers to buy me drinks. I spent all of my money on ecstasy that night. I tried to fit in with strangers, dancing, and eventually sleeping in the stairwell and dark corners of the club.

My entire time in York was a blur. I don't know whether it was two weeks or three…it may have even been a month or two. I met a lot of people I don't remember. I went to many different clubs, fancy restaurants, and ghetto alleys, but there are only a few random memories of my days in York that stick out. I shot ketamine for the first time, intramuscularly, sitting in various houses all day smoking cigarettes and drinking, while strangers watched TV and passed around joints. I vaguely recall several row homes on Chestnut Street and sitting in a laundromat full of Latinos doing laundry on more than one occasion. My life back then is nothing but a smear on the fabric of my memory. I recall bits and pieces, and they're usually accompanied by vague feelings of despair and heavy depression. I was in a helpless state, and I believed I was worthless. The only thing I held onto was my love for this woman who led me around like I was her pet project, and maybe I was.

One night I got kicked out of the club where Lana worked because I was selling drugs in the stairwell, all of the Special K that I had cooked up and brought with me. Since the owner was Jessie's ex-boyfriend, their vendetta against me was strong. They cornered me in the stairwell with security, took the last I had, and threatened to call the police. I was out of the club, empty-handed. They had strong-armed about $450 of Special K from me, and I had no clue where Jessie was. When I finally found her, she and Lana did some snooping around and found out that the owners turned around and sold what they had taken from me. They didn't care that drugs were being sold in the club—they cared that I was stepping on their toes and taking sales away from them. I was weak, and I wasn't used to this kind of stuff happening to me. I was used to being the one with the upper hand.

Weak wasn't the word, maybe pathetic was. I was broken, my spirit was gone, just chasing a dream. I had no future, no identity, no plan, and I was out of hope. I laid on Lana's floor quite a few nights while the girls went out, unable to sleep, lying in wait, smoking cigarettes and listening to club tracks until early into the morning hours, like a dog waiting for his owners to come home. I couldn't go to the club anymore, and I wasn't old enough to get into other establishments. The only thing I had left were several bottles of Ketamine, and then the entire well would run dry.

I wasn't interested in Lana, and probably even bored her with conversations of the details of my feelings for Jessie. She was growing disgusted with the people and the scene in which she worked. She had higher plans and aspirations for her life, and one day she announced that she was moving out of her apartment in York to go back to school in Lancaster. This naturally meant that we had to go, too. Somehow, we managed to come along for the ride. She took us into her dorm room in Lancaster and let us stay there.

Jessie and I would stay up all night in that room, drinking

and sniffing ketamine. Then, she would smoke weed and talk. I loved the conversations Jessie and I had regarding spirituality, witchcraft, world peace, and anything else intriguing and remotely esoteric. She was amazed at my knowledge on all religions, astrology, masonry, alchemy, Wicca, and how I could tie them all together. Through my wild youth, I always found time to read and study, and spirituality drew my interest above all.

One night we got so blasted listening to sublime and blowing lines of Special K that I vividly remember having a full conversation without ever speaking a word. There were times when we connected outside of the physical plane, just like when we danced. It was real, but somehow the drugs loosened up our minds to find the same channels. I strongly remember the details of that night, the looks and smiles, the ability to communicate without ever saying a word. Drugs could do a lot of amazing things, but using them was like putting a tool in the hands of someone who didn't quite know how to use it. I thought I was using the tool wisely, but in truth I was turning it in on myself and destroying myself with it.

Lana was gone most of the time to her college classes or one of her DJ gigs. All three of us were in a tiny, one-bed college dorm room in a shared house, with shared bathrooms and showers. It was awkward, and we almost never left that room except to shower or go to the bathroom. We were a secret. There was no stove, so at any given time, there were plates of Special K drying on the top of every lamp. I would fill the vials, and Lana would take them out to her gigs and sell them for me. We began to run low though.

One night Lana took me to her studio at the college to watch her work on air. She allowed me to announce songs and spin records on air. She was a sweet girl and did more than enough for me. She tried to reel me in and change me, but I only had eyes for one thing and that was my obsession for Jessie. One day,

Lana finally gave up and told us we had to leave. Someone had reported that we were staying there, and she had been threatened to be kicked out if we didn't go. I knew this was a lie, but I felt horrible for her. She'd done more than enough for us. It was time to head back to Maryland and face the nothingness that lie ahead.

Lana had a gig in Philly. Following, we went to an after-party somewhere else, then another after-party in Annapolis, and then somewhere else after that. I don't recall all of it, but I spent a few days living and sleeping in rave clubs. It was a never-ending party if you followed the trail correctly. When a party in one city finished, another was just beginning somewhere else in another city. The final party I ended up at was called Ultraworld, and it was in DC. It was massive and held inside an arena with inter-national headliners performing. It was one giant freak-show, and I was burnt out beyond relief. All I wanted to do was sleep off days of drug and alcohol abuse that seemed to never end. I walked through Ultraworld like a zombie, feeling lost and tired of it all, wanting something better, but in the back of my mind knowing that I was entirely homeless and broke once this party came to an end.

Jessie and I were inseparable at this point. She had made it her mission to take care of me, maybe because she felt somewhat responsible for my situation, or maybe because she truly cared about me. I clung to the hope that it was the latter. She snuck me into her parents' house to sleep that night and snuck me out the next morning. She called around to all her friends who owned their own places to see if anyone would take me in. Her best friend Kali had an apartment with her boyfriend in the middle of Bel Air, but her boyfriend said no, and I didn't blame him. We'd never even met.

Still, Kali agreed to meet Jessie and me and help us lay out a plan. Kali and her boyfriend had a work van parked out front of their apartment on a side street in Bel Air that they weren't currently using. She was going to put blankets and a pillow in the back with the tools and junk. She said I could sleep there, and that in the mornings after she and her boyfriend were off to work, I could come into the apartment and shower. It was the only plan I had. I couldn't believe my life had come to this. I was too proud to even try to move back home or to let my parents know how bad things had gotten. I couldn't stand the thought of receiving a lecture from them instead of open arms.

At this point my belongings were scattered everywhere. I had one book bag with some of my things and no more Special K, which meant no more money. I stole whatever hygiene products I needed, and I switched outfits in department store dressing rooms and walked out with a new one almost every other day. My future was inconceivable. I couldn't even begin to think about how to get my life together at this point, so I drank. I had to drink to be able to sleep in the back of that van, and even drunkenness made it hard. To top it off, I wasn't with Jessie on those nights, so I'd lay there uncomfortably, thinking of what she might be doing. I drank and tried to think of ways to get money for a security deposit and first month's rent. The second or third night in, I decided I had to make a move. I couldn't stay in this van forever. I was out drinking and had my ride drop me off a couple streets over from the van. I was too embarrassed to let anyone know where I was staying. That night I came up with a plan.

I got back to the van and undressed down to my boxers and socks. I had only one change of clothes, so I couldn't afford to be identified by my outfit or clothing. Drunk, but coherent enough to know exactly what I was doing, I dug around in the back of the van and found a tennis racket. I imagine I looked like someone who had just escaped from a mental asylum, as I slid back out of the van and ran through the back neighborhoods of Bel Air wearing only my underwear and carrying the tennis racket.

It was about 2:00am, and a twenty-four-hour gas station was

open about five blocks away. I stayed low and out of the street-lights, occasionally ducking behind a car, tree, or bush when I saw oncoming headlights, but for the most part the streets were eerily silent that night. When I hit the small street where the gas station connected the neighborhood of homes to downtown Bel Air, I waited until there was no traffic in sight and darted for the fence that ran along the gas station property. It was a tall wooden fence lined with bushes, and it gave me the perfect cover while I collected myself.

Out of my mind, desperate and drunk, I ran my fingers through my thick brown hair, pulling it out in every direction, giving me the appearance of craziness and desperation. The gas station had several pumps and a small glass-enclosed walk-in kiosk in the center where the cashier sat, surrounded by chips and candy and a cooler stocked with drinks. There was a door on either side. I just hoped that they were open. There were no cars at the pumps, and what appeared to be a twenty-something young girl reading a book behind the counter. Timing would be everything here. I turned the fence and marched as fast as I could toward the door, yanked it open and screamed wildly. I had to catch her by surprise and scare her. I felt bad for her, but I needed money. It wasn't her money, I justified. The company could recoup.

"Give me all the fucking money in here!" I yelled. "Now! Or, I'll split your fucking head open!"

I used the racket to sweep all the candy and chips off the counter inches from her face. It flew into the walls and onto the floor, as I continued swinging wildly for extra drama. If I had a gun, I could have been calm. But a tennis racket was ridiculous, so I needed extra effect. She was terrified as she popped open the drawer, rapidly shuffling out bills.

I smacked the racket into the counter, "Hurry the fuck up!"

She was hurrying, but this is how they do it in the movies,

minus the tennis equipment. I snatched the bills from her hand and crashed through the door sideways. I hauled ass all the way up the street and down the wrong way, in case she was watching me. I doubled back thirty seconds later, cut a couple of corners, and before I knew it, I was diving into the back of the van and pulling the door shut behind me. I lay there for a long time listening for police sirens that never came and waiting for a knock at the van's backdoor that never happened. I finally slept and woke up to a normal day, only I was $172 richer.

The money would only last me a few days between food and bars. I saw Jessie occasionally, but I think she felt relieved to sort of get rid of me. I was an extra responsibility in her whirlwind of a life. She was in her mid-twenties and already pushing the envelope by living at her parents' house when all she did was party. She would let me come hang for a few hours here and there, and even though her parents liked me, there were strict rules. We were constantly watched and never allowed upstairs alone. She had gone back to work as a waitress at the Red Lobster, and I had started hanging around Social Services looking for jobs and housing. I applied for food stamps and assistance. I got a food stamps card, but no other assistance.

One day Kali came out and told me they were getting rid of the van and that I couldn't sleep in it anymore. So, I went to the local police station and gave them my homeless sob story, minus anything that was my fault, like drinking and drugs. I had heard that they would put a person up in a hotel for a night, and they did. I went to Red Lobster the next day on Jessie's referral, met with a manager, and landed a job as a dishwasher. This, I knew from prior experience, was completely miserable work, but I had to do anything I could to get by. Besides, I'd be close to Jessie. I worked there a week or two, sleeping where I could on people's couches—anywhere. Jessie had started sniffing heroin again. A handful of coworkers also did heroin, including an older married couple who had supposedly been getting high on the stuff for over twenty-five years. I was in my own horrific little world in the dish room, just me and an older, gay man named Eddie. Outside of him, very few people spoke to me, even Jessie. I wasn't cool enough or old enough to be in their inner circle. That, or maybe if you weren't sniffing dope or coke with them, you weren't let in on their secret fun. I was annoyed by it all, and my life was pointless and empty, but somehow, I kept pushing. Then it happened.

One of the older guys, who I wasn't all that familiar with, said he was making a run to pick up some goodies downtown, and he asked if I wanted anything. He said he was picking up some ecstasy, heroin, and coke. My curiosity and my emptiness got the best of me, and I handed him $30 to bring me two pills of dope and keep the other ten.

"Are you sure? Have you ever done it before?" he asked.

"Yes," I said, being partially truthful. "Just don't tell anyone, especially Jessie," I pleaded.

That night I connected with my old friend Rico. He had some girls out in Aberdeen, who he wanted to go over and chill with, one black and one Latina. He wanted me to come along and meet the black girl. He had a friend scoop us both up. On our way, we hit the liquor store and grabbed a bunch of forties for us and wine coolers for the girls. I wasn't going to tell him about the dope I had on me. This was a whole different crowd of friends. We got to the apartment, and the girls were both gorgeous, so we immediately cracked open the drinks to calm our nerves. Rico had obviously seen the Latina girl on a few previous occasions, but he saw a lot of women. The guy was known for the number of women he messed around with. They introduced me to the black girl, and we all hit it off, chatting, joking, and drinking. At some point I dipped off into the bathroom and sniffed half of my pill of heroin. I came out as if nothing had happened and returned to our small party.

I didn't want anyone to know about my experimenting. It was just my curiosity to see what had Jessie so caught up. I sat back on the couch and felt my body flush over warm, and a familiar feeling came flooding back into me that I hadn't felt in a long time. It was very reminiscent of the first night I had tried ecstasy. I had only felt this warmth one other time before, many years ago when I tried heroin for the first time and hated it. This time I liked it.

I welcomed it, and my soul smiled. I knew it was bad. My whole body was on a cloud, and I didn't care about the drink anymore. I drank to be social, but I didn't need it. I sat there embracing this new, old feeling. I found my inner sanctum. I floated on warm internal sunshine, and my fears and worries evaporated into the present. There was nothing except for the simple "now." I slowly dragged cigarettes, and talked and smiled. I finally told my friend Rico about it and offered him some, but he wasn't interested.

He responded, "Yo, you better be careful with that shit!"

I told him, "It's cool. I'm just trying it this one time to see what all the hype is about."

He eventually took his girl into the bedroom, and I was left with my new friend. Our awkward silence became comfortable, and then our lips met, and I melted into her. We made out for a while, but something was wrong. I was sweating a bit too much. Just as we were going to move from one of the couches into one of the bedrooms, I had to call it off. My stomach was knotting up, and sweat was pouring off of me. I felt like I had food poisoning. I sat there hot, stomach turning and uncomfortable, alone with this new stranger I was trying to impress. I apologized maybe five times, then started dialing numbers in my phone for a ride out of there. Eventually, I went into the bathroom and vomited, and shortly after that everything in my body started to return to normal. It was too late though. I was already too embarrassed, and my ride was on its way. Rico came out of the bedroom just before I left.

"It's that shit doing it to you. I told you," he said.

"Naw bro, I got sick off something I ate, or I got the flu. It's something more than that," I said in denial, already protecting my future love.

I got a hotel room in Edgewood that night and walked eight miles to work the next day. I felt great, not hungover. I started my shift with the idea of flushing the other pill and a half that remained. The problem is that good intentions can quickly turn bad the longer that you think about them. I stood in that miserable kitchen bogged down in dishes, feeling cold and alone with my own thoughts and despair. As the dishes piled up and the work never ended, my loneliness caved in on me. That pill began to burn a hole in my pocket. *Maybe if I dip off into the bathroom and snort the rest of this heroin, my night will go by quicker and my motivation will change.* Maybe then I could get through this miserable shift and face the great emptiness I felt every night when my shift was over and I was unsure of where I was going to stay. The more my thoughts brought me back to the pill in my pocket, the more I couldn't resist it.

I broke for the bathroom, sat down in a stall and took the half-filled clear gel cap from my pocket. I carefully twisted it open and emptied its beige powdery contents onto the back of the square, metal toilet paper dispenser, rolled up a dollar bill, and inhaled it all into my nostrils. The warmth returned. My worries were gone, and I could finish this shift alone and confident, without the great depression that usually pulled at me from within. I went back into the dish room and started working hard. I broke a sweat and hustled. I suddenly cared about my performance and the effort I put into it. I moved fast and caught up quickly, but as my performance increased, my inhibitions lessened. I bounced back and forth to the bathroom several times, taking small bumps from the second pill that I was still holding onto. I sat in a stall smoking cigarettes in the main bathroom meant for customers because I no longer cared. I felt good, and I wasn't going to continually ask a manager if I could smoke outside only to get denied, plus I didn't want them to possibly notice that I wasn't myself. I made repeated trips back and forth because this new feeling made me want to smoke more often.

A couple hours into my shift, I saw Jessie arrive for work. I finally realized why she had been pushing me away. She didn't want to expose me to this. This drug had come between us. It had pushed us into two entirely separate worlds, and now I was in. I had crossed the line without her knowing. I couldn't hold back, I had to tell her. As soon as I got the chance, I told her I had something for her and to meet me back at the dish room. When she came back, I proudly handed her the rest of the second gel cap full of heroin. She lit up for a second, then she looked at me closely. She could tell I was high. Her face changed to disappointment, or was it mock disappointment because that's how she was morally supposed to respond, even though she was happy inside.

"What the fuck, Danny?" she said pretending to be a woman of responsibility. "When did you start doing this?"

"I do it every once in a while," I lied, trying to be cool and a man of mystery. "I love it. I can work so much better, plus I'm not hungover."

"Not cool. Not cool!" she said, and she stormed off in feign anger. I knew it was all an act. We'd be closer now than ever before. And damn, was I right.

XVI.

I got fired from my job that night at the end of my shift. Somebody told the manager that I was going in and out of the
bathroom snorting cocaine. I wasn't even mad. I focused on
the fact that I was fired for something I didn't do, snort cocaine,
rather than the fact that it was close to the truth. I used that
minor detail to garner pity from anyone I spoke to, telling them
that I was falsely accused of snorting cocaine in the bathroom
and that's why I was fired, never mentioning the fact that it was
actually heroin that I was sniffing.

Now I was back to square one, jobless and homeless without
a plan. This time was even worse, I couldn't spend almost every
waking second with Jessie because she was working and running
back and forth to the city to get high in between. We fell out of
touch for a week or so. I finally made some headway at Social
Services and got a voucher for a one-week hotel stay at a motel in
Edgewood. *I'll stay in this hotel, dry out, and start over,* I thought
to myself. Again, I had good intentions, but the isolation got
the best of me.

Chase Manor Motel was a crack motel on the side of Route
40 in Edgewood, surrounded by swamp land. There were only
a number of reasons why anyone would stay there, and none of
them were good. I hit the lotto when Social Services granted me

a one-week stay there, paid for by the county. I hitched a ride to Edgewood and checked in with the Indian lady behind the counter. I could barely understand a word she said, but I knew I had a week, and it was like heaven to me. I checked into the tiny room and threw my book bag on a chair and hopped into the shower. I remember feeling clean and refreshed and at ease with the idea of a second chance, as I settled into the freshly made bed and lit a cigarette. I didn't even want to turn on the TV. This was my first night without a drink in as long as I could remember, and it felt good to be free. I laid there for a long time with mixed feelings, drifting in and out of comfort, depression, and anxiety. The walls started closing in on me and then expanding. The room swallowed me up.

Eventually, I awoke bright and early. I needed a plan, but more importantly, I needed a drink.

The sun was out, and I was feeling good as I drank that afternoon. I had a hotel room, I had a guaranteed place to lay my head, which meant no stress—which meant I could get drunk early and know exactly where I would be sleeping that night. As I continued drinking, I started calling friends to celebrate with me. Jessie was first, and I told her to invite others. At some point, I was back in the hotel room with a few people I barely knew drinking and waiting for Jessie and some others to arrive. In my intoxication, I had the brilliant idea to turn the party up a notch by going on a liquor run, but while we were there, I would use my food stamp card to buy a ton of whipped cream canisters to do "whip-its." This was a spur of the moment, ridiculous plan, but it worked. I laughed hysterically as we exited the store with an entire case of twenty-four whipped cream canisters and a sack full of alcohol. "Whip-its" is the act of holding a whipped cream canister right side up and pressing the valve into your mouth to release all of the nitrous oxide gas and inhaling it as quickly and deeply as possible. The reaction is an extremely euphoric head rush that only lasts about thirty seconds. It was a ridiculous waste of time and money, but alcohol and boredom are usually the recipe for disaster, at least in my young experience.

We returned to the room and more people were there waiting. There were probably ten of us in the tiny hotel room now drinking and doing whip-its, and I was having fun playing host. Jessie showed up, as well as some other people I invited, but I was already beyond drunk. A friend of a friend was cutting up raw heroin on the counter and selling pieces of it to people in the room. I had never even heard of "raw" before. It looked nothing like the gel caps of powder that I had seen on previous occasions. They were little dark beige rocks that had to be crushed into a powder and sniffed.

"Let me try some," I said.

"Naw bro, you got $25?" the guy replied.

Feeling like a big shot, drunk and belligerent, I replied, "Who's fucking room are you in selling this shit right now? You can get the fuck out then. I don't even know you!"

"Okay, okay. Just hold up one second," he said.

I sat down and waited my turn while he cut off little pieces for the other paying customers. Then he called me over. He cut me off a tiny piece about half the size of a match head and slid it my direction with his driver's license.

I looked at him with an expression that said, "Are you kidding me?"

He told me, "Be careful, it's a lot stronger than you think it is."

I shook my head thinking, *whatever, this guy's just being stingy.*

I determined that if I didn't feel anything, I would throw him out or possibly whip his ass. I already didn't like his vibe. I laid a dollar bill over top of the tiny, tan rock and rolled my lighter over the top of it to flatten it out onto the wooden countertop. Then, I used my ID card to dice up the flattened rock into a powder and scrape it into a line. I rolled up the dollar bill and snorted the tiny line up my nose.

I don't know how long it took, but the last thing I remember is being in the bathroom projectile vomiting into the sink, then hovering over the toilet throwing up almost all night, shaking and sweating. Jessie had stayed to take care of me, and that was the only thing that made me feel safe. I thought that dude with the raw had poisoned me. I thought he intentionally gave me something bad for threatening him. I was extremely sick and embarrassed, I felt like I was dying. I was acting like a big shot, just hours before, threatening people, yelling at people, playing host. And now I had embarrassed myself and looked weak in front of everyone. Jessie left while I was unconscious. I fell asleep over the toilet and eventually climbed onto the bed.

I awoke the next morning to a knock at the door. It was the hotel owner's wife. I winced at the sunlight as I looked out at her. She asked if she could come in.

I told her, "no," as she craned her head to look behind me through the crack of the open door.

I quickly shut the door and went back inside. The room looked like a frat house. There was someone asleep in the bathtub and someone asleep on the floor by the door. Whipped cream was splattered all over the walls and ceiling, and the number of beer and liquor bottles that populated every countertop, nightstand, and square inch of the floor was unbelievable. There was vomit on the floor and in the sink. The whole place would take an entire day to clean. I felt half dead. It was already 11:00am, and I had no clue what I was going to do at this point.

Five minutes later…another heavy knock at the door. It was the Indian owner along with his wife, both dressed in traditional, full-color garb with red bindis on their foreheads. I didn't want to answer. Maybe if I didn't, they would just go away. They knocked and knocked. The guy on the floor began to stir and curse to himself.

"You have to leave our hotel. We are calling the cops," they said from outside.

Oh shit! This was serious. They must have known about the party and waited until the morning to confront it. They knocked repeatedly and threatened to open the door.

Finally, in a fit of hungover rage, the guy sleeping on the floor got up, opened the door, and said, "Fuck you! Why don't you go back to your own country!"

My heart immediately dropped. That was too much. I didn't want to be a part of this ignorance. I'd already done enough damage. These people had done nothing wrong, and I had nothing against them. They repeatedly shouted that they were calling the cops. My stay was over. I packed up my book bag and walked off leaving the other two behind. I walked to a payphone and started calling around until I could find a ride.

I had my ride drop me off at the 7-Eleven in downtown Bel Air. I had no plan. Once again, I had screwed myself. No place to go, no money, no job, and not even a smidgen of hope. I sat on the curb out front of that 7-Eleven for hours smoking cigarettes and bumming change to make phone calls from the payphone in hopes of finding somewhere to lay my head that night. I was so tired and weak, I couldn't begin to explain it. My world was closing in on me. Waves of despair crashed against me, as I sunk deeper into myself. I didn't even have the energy to ask for change anymore. I curled up under the payphone and started to doze off. It wasn't long before I startled myself awake—I couldn't breathe.

I didn't know what was happening. I'd had anxiety attacks before, but this was different. My lungs were literally closing up. I had noticed tightness in my chest throughout the day and thought that the night of partying and chain-smoking cigarettes had taken its toll on me. This was different though, unlike anything I'd ever felt before. My lungs were closing in on themselves, and it took everything I had to pull deep breaths of air into them. I became frantic and thought for sure I must be dying. My head spinning, I hit my feet quickly and started walking to the nearest drug store, gasping for breath.

About a half mile later, I approached a Rite Aid and frantically rushed in. It was just me versus the world. I didn't notice anyone around me, nor did I know what was wrong with me. I had one prayer to rely on, just one chance that medicine would help, or I was done and I didn't even know why. I worked my way through the drug aisles until I found what I was looking for. I slipped a small box of bronchial dilators and an inhaler into my hoodie pockets and left as fast as I had come in. I didn't care if I looked suspicious. It didn't matter if I was stopped. Whatever was going on with me was clearly serious, and this was my only chance to remedy it. I popped two of the pills and hit the inhaler as soon as I turned the corner, out of sight of the store. I made my way back to the 7-Eleven, where I aimlessly dwindled away the rest of the night. My time on that curb for the next few hours shifted between filling my lungs as full as I could and praying that a familiar face would stop to shop, see me and take pity on me. My lungs returned to normal, but no helpful, familiar faces ever came. Eventually, I wandered back into the neighborhood and into the park and spent the night under a tree, sober and somewhat happy to be alive.

I'll never forget that night and how my lungs felt. I will always remember the panic and hopelessness of not knowing what was going on inside of me. It would be a long time before I found out what had caused it and how close I really came to death. Years later, and several dead friends along the way, all of whose lungs had collapsed from sniffing raw heroin, I finally realized why I stopped breathing out front of that 7-Eleven. That would be the first of many times heroin tried to pull me to my grave.

XVII.

I contacted Jessie the next morning. She had to work that evening, and I wasn't exactly welcome at Red Lobster. She promised to find someone on the job who would let me crash at their place. One person stepped up, Eddie, my coworker in the dish room. We didn't see each other often because we generally worked different shifts. But, I knew Eddie had a thing for me. (He was about fifteen years older than me and gay.) I was reluctant, but I knew I could hold my own if anything sketchy happened. Jessie swore he was cool, and that it would be okay and only temporary. He got off at 10:00pm, and I was to meet him out back in the smoke area around that time. When I arrived, Jessie was there waiting on me. We smoked a cigarette together, and she consoled me again. She said she had plans that night, but might go downtown to an after-party at Club 1722. I got into the car with Eddie when he came out, and we made a stop at the liquor store. He was already showing off, but as long as he kept his hands to himself, I was set to take full advantage.

"What do you want?" he asked.

I was going to drink, and drink hard. I needed to drink my way out of the awkwardness of this situation. He came out with a thirty-pack of Red Dog beer cans. He lived about twenty minutes away in a townhome in Belcamp. I pounded beer the whole way there. Once we arrived at his place, he changed, I showered, and we drank more. For every one can he drank, I had three. He commented on how much I drank and was puzzled by why I drank so fast. Occasionally, he would steer the conversation toward sexual innuendos, and I would blow it off.

"You're cool, but I'm not into that shit," I would tell him.

I couldn't sit there all night just he and I, drinking myself into oblivion. Nor could I stay there with him for more than one night. I didn't know what I was going to do. We talked about my future plans, and I told him how lost I was. He told me that I couldn't stay there forever, but that I was welcome to stay a week or two. Then it happened, the moment I was afraid of. He told me that he was willing to pay me a substantial amount of money if I were to let him give me a blowjob.

"Just one," he said, "I'll give you $250, and you'll love every minute of it!"

He pressed the offer all the way up to $400 before I cut him off and said, "Can you just cut the dumb shit before I leave? I don't even care if I have nowhere to go."

He suddenly changed his tone and claimed he was just messing with me. He asked if I wanted to go to the club. It was already midnight, but he told me they were open until 5:00am. I jumped at the chance to get out of this weird situation and be around other people, especially Jessie or other females. I wanted to cuss her out for putting me in this predicament. She had to have known his intentions. We drove all the way downtown to the club. I finished the remaining beers while riding shotgun and blowing cigarette smoke out of the window. Eddie remarked that he'd never seen someone drink so much.

It was a quiet ride downtown, with the exception of pulling off once to take a leak and hearing Eddie shout out behind me, "Do you want me to come hold it for you?"

I bit my tongue, I had to lose this clown when we got to

the club. Things would work themselves out after that. Things didn't. I got to the club and looked for Jessie, who was nowhere to be found. The place was a freak show, all kinds of strange characters, and more gay men than I had ever seen in any one place. Eddie was following me around, and I was trying to lose him. I started a fight with him, but I'm not sure what about. I cursed at him and threatened him enough to make him leave me there. The next thing I remember was being in a car with four other guys—clean-cut white guys, frat boy looking types. We were driving around the city, sniffing coke in the backseat. I have no idea how I ended up there, but I was in the back telling them the story about Eddie and his offer to give me a blowjob.

The big one next to me said, "Shit, I'll give you more than that if you let me."

I waited on him to laugh. I was drunk and not sure what to believe. At that instant I realized that I was in a car full of gay men and that his proposition was real. I freaked out internally, and then externally.

In a drunken rage I said, "Pull the car over before I fuck your faggot ass up!" I climbed out yelling and punching at him as he tried to grab ahold of me...and then I don't remember anything.

When I came to, I was covered head-to-toe in blood. I was in a building lobby, and I was so disoriented that I didn't realize what kind of building it was. There was a young black lady at the front asking me to come in. I told her I didn't need to go anywhere, that I needed a phone. She pointed me to a payphone across the lobby by the front doors, and I dialed. I don't know what I was doing. I was blacked out like so many other nights, and I don't remember a thing. Of all the people I could have called, I called my parents' house, after not speaking to them for weeks. My mother picked up the phone at whatever ungodly hour it was and tried to talk to me, but I was in hysterics and had no clue where I was. She asked me to wave down anyone who was nearby and put them on the phone. The lady at the front got on the phone and told my mother that an older, black man had found me on a corner downtown completely covered in blood and incoherent. He put me into his car and dropped me off there, at the lobby of the University of Maryland Medical Center. Ironically, out of all of the hospitals in Baltimore City, this was the one where my mother worked as a registered nurse.

I don't recall any of my actions in the hospital, but from what I was told by my mother and other staff members, I became so unruly that they had to lock me in a room on one of the wards. I pushed one nurse into a wall and tried to punch another one. I refused treatment and screamed out repeatedly that I just wanted to die. My mother had gotten out of bed and rushed down there, completely embarrassed because this was her place of employment and these were her coworkers who I was cussing and assaulting. She tried to talk sense into me and calm me down. In a drunken rage I did the unthinkable. I lashed out at my own mother, called her names, dropped my pants and told her to suck my...

The nurses got me sedated and on IV fluids. I was treated for alcohol poisoning and multiple surface wounds. My face was beaten, and my arms and legs were torn up from the sidewalk. Worst of all, I had been sliced open. I had knife wounds running down my back from just below my neck to just above my tailbone. I had been jumped, cut up, and left on the curb like a piece of trash. What a big gangster and tough guy I had become. All the work I had put in on the streets, and all the things I'd done to prove myself and my strength, and here I was getting jumped by a carload of gay men. Not only jumped, but cut open. I could have been raped, and I thank God I wasn't. It would have only fueled my fire to drink more. This was the lowest of my lows. What I did to my mother was heartbreaking. I had never even cussed in front of my parents. I was a criminal and a deviant, but I always showed them respect in person. As terrible as it was, it was certainly nothing another drink wouldn't eventually make disappear.

I woke up the next day late in the afternoon on the hospital bed with an IV still bringing fluids to my weak body. I looked at the time and decided I had to go. I pulled out all of the IVs myself and got dressed. The nurses urged me to stay another night, but I wouldn't listen. I needed my freedom. I was in a rush to go nowhere—except to escape all the damage I'd just done. I called a cab company and begged them to take me as far away as they could for $25. I had to flee from the scene I had made. I had to get away from myself, but I just couldn't run far enough.

XVIII.

I met up with Jessie and discovered that a friend I had grown up with had moved out to Fallston with his parents into a huge half-million-dollar home. It was Steve, the guy who was dating Tina, who shared the room next to mine at Kim's townhouse. His parents were gone for two weeks, and he said I could stay there the whole time—a beautiful home with a fully stocked kitchen, clean showers, a comfortable place to sleep, everything. It was another chance for me to regain my footing and formulate a solid plan. When Jessie and I arrived at his house, he was there with a bunch of guys from the neighborhood I grew up in, all of them old friends. It was a warm welcome, and I felt refreshed to be there.

I have no idea how, but somehow, they too had gotten involved in sniffing raw heroin. Steve and Tina would make daily runs in his pickup truck from his huge home in Fallston to the West Baltimore neighborhood near Druid Hill Park to pick up small $20 baggies of raw heroin for everybody. I had no idea this drug had become so popular with all of my old friends. It shocked them when I said I wanted some. I was in now, no longer an outcast among them like I had been when we lived at Kim's. I used to fight it and call them names, and talk down to them because they got high, and they talked down to me about my drinking.

They won. My drinking life had gotten so out of hand that I finally threw in the towel. I needed a new remedy to get outside of myself and make this world slip away. My time spent in that house that was supposed to serve as a reprieve. Instead, it started me down a path through hell that would change my life forever, and ultimately save my soul.

We drank occasionally, but with heroin I no longer relied on alcohol to help me sleep or function. It was a slow, easy transition. I would sniff a small bit of heroin and drift off into a soft numb state where I was free from all inner and outer turmoil. There were no outside troubles, no worldly stressors. I lived in the moment. I felt no pain and no anxiety. The only stressors in my life were those immediate ones of the moment, when I needed a cigarette, when I nodded out and burnt a hole in a piece of furniture or clothing, or when I had to take a piss.

The bathroom became my home base. Raw heroin did something to my body that highly affected my ability to urinate. I felt like I had to go all of the time, but then I couldn't. I would get tired of standing in front of the toilet, nodding out, and would actually sit down and do the same. My bladder would be on fire, but nothing would come out. The toilet was my cloud. I would sit there for hours nodding out, burning my legs with cigarette ash, waiting for the tiniest bit of urine to come out of my body. People would bang on the door, only to stir me from my daze, and twenty minutes later I'd head back in.

It was blissful. From an outsider's point of view, it probably sounds horrid and insane, but to an addict, there's no better feeling. Heroin erases all anxiety and worry. It takes away all cares of the future and the past. It numbs emotional pain and physical pain. It is worth the trade off to experience urinary discomfort or an occasional spell of nausea in exchange for feelings that nothing really matters in the end anyway. Heroin let me just "be." That's what I did, and I became good at just being nothing. Slipping into the abyss and accomplishing nothing, doing nothing, and feeling nothing—I loved it.

Eventually I had to leave that house to go home and visit my family for Easter Sunday. I had been getting high on raw heroin for four consecutive days and hadn't urinated in three. Not a single drop. I was getting terrified. I figured I'd speak to my mother before I admitted myself to the hospital. I hung with the family and faked enjoyment and participation in the Easter Sunday events as much as I could. I hadn't gotten high that day, and I couldn't wait to return to the Eden I'd found out in Fallston. I took many trips back and forth to the bathroom at my parents' house, frustrated beyond tears that I wasn't high, and still I couldn't pee.

Finally, I pulled my mother aside and told her the whole story, minus the heroin use. As a nurse, I hoped she would know what I could take or if I should go to the hospital. She took me upstairs and had me lay on the bed to examine me. My bladder was extremely distended, and she said I was going to need a catheter. She said she could give me one, or I could wait until the Easter gathering was over and she could take me to a hospital. I didn't know what a catheter was, so as she described it to me, I became alarmed. Not only was it terrifying, but it would be extremely awkward. Why did my mother even have this device in her home? I had to do it though. There was no way that I could wait hours more.

She had me pull my pants down to my ankles and lay there as she pushed the tube into my urethra. The pain was so excruciating, I don't know how I survived or could ever survive that again. And the fact that it was my own mother having to do it to me makes my heart sink. Somehow, I think she was enacting her revenge on me for giving her such a painful birth. *Should I even trust her?* I thought to myself in mock comedy. I had put her through hell, and I was in the most vulnerable position I may have ever been in. The remnants of the heroin in my system from days previous may have done their part to numb the pain because I didn't pass out. Eventually, warm yellow liquid began filling the tube and running into the bag, and before long the whole debacle was over. I had to get back to my new home. I needed to get high, and I didn't care if it stole my ability to urinate. I had to make these feelings dissipate. As soon as the Easter festivities were over, I got a ride back to the house in Fallston, and that's exactly what I did.

Little brown rocks. I was living off of those little brown rocks. For two weeks I stayed in Fallston, and the majority of those days were spent high from those rocks. I could take one about the size of a match head, crush it with a credit card, chop it to separate it, and then scrape it into a line. One line from a little brown rock that size would bring me all the comfort of a thousand pillows—pillows for my emotions, my stress, my fears, and any physical pain I had. During those two weeks in that big fancy house, I got high more days than not. There was a rumor among the group that as long as you didn't do it three days in a row, you wouldn't get addicted. I played with it, doing two days then stopping for a day, then one day, then my willpower left me, and I did it every day.

All good things must come to an end though, and Steve's parents were coming home from vacation, which meant I had to go. My brief vacation from the streets and not having to wonder where I was going to lay my head at night was over. I was headed back to fear and confusion, except this time I had a new habit that even I didn't quite realize I had yet.

I came around Jessie's house and met her mother and father. She was trying to warm me up to them, hoping that they would give me a place to stay there with her and off of the streets. Her parents were much older, and their home was an old farmhouse. Her mother would sit in the kitchen and smoke cigarettes all day looking out the window. Her disposition wasn't all that pleasant, but she broke down a few barriers for me. Jessie was quick to let me know that her mother liked me, and that that was unusual.

Her father, however, wanted nothing to do with any of the men Jessie hung around with. She was in her mid-twenties, but she was still his little girl.

I was trouble for sure, in the worst kind of way. I talked to Jessie's mom for a while one afternoon giving her my sob story about how my horrible parents had thrown me out for no reason, and now I had nowhere to go.

It worked. She gave in and made up a creepy room in their old house for me. Jessie's room was down the hall, but in no way was I ever allowed in Jessie's room. One of Jessie's own stipulations was that I was to stop drinking if I was going to live there. Heroin was okay, but alcohol was off limits. I vaguely recall the first couple of sleepless nights in that cold, tiny attic of a room. I felt haunted inside and out, as the alcohol left my bloodstream for the first time in nearly a decade. I had visions in the dark, hallucinations in and out of my mind. I wished for death, as I shook and sweated up the bed. When the lights went out, I drifted into a hellish world all alone where I teetered very closely to the edge of sanity. I couldn't wake Jessie up, I couldn't cause a commotion, so I'd lay there in the dark wrestling with demons. I didn't know at the time that I was going through alcohol withdrawal. I didn't even know such a thing existed. I thought I was losing my mind and possibly the spirits of this old house were tormenting me. But I hung on. I hung on for Jessie. I knew she would be there in the morning. I would think of her all night. She kept me afloat. Although sometimes, I wondered if she had done this to me, if I were under her spell, if she was a witch, and I was her prey to toy with. A million thoughts pushed me in and out of the web of fear that I lay in for those few days, but with the sun and the warmth of her near me the next day, I would quickly forget about the night terrors.

By the third day we scored some heroin. Those couple days of torment quickly disappeared, and I slept like an angel. Under my new courage formed from the heroin, I would gather up the nerve to sneak across the squeaky floorboards and into Jessie's room at night. Together we would lay there in the dark and drift in and out of a heroin trance, holding each other and tracing circles on each other's skin. Then, I would tiptoe back out before the light of dawn when her father would awake for work.

This went on for a few days, and we managed to duck the responsibilities that her mother had laid out for us, as far as saving money and finding an apartment. I mowed their huge farmland on the riding tractor or did a few chores around the house for a few days, while Jessie went downtown with friends to score us both heroin. Then at night, we would enjoy each other's company in the dark of her room. Eventually, I stayed back to help Jessie's mom sand and paint some antique furniture, while Jessie went to the city with some friends and promised to be back in a couple hours with dope. I yawned as I attempted to sand the bench, and my arms quickly became weak. I forced myself to work. I sanded and sanded, checking my watch every five minutes, stopping often to smoke. I couldn't finish the job. I had no energy. I knew something wasn't right. Intuitively, I knew that something terrible was happening to me, and that I wasn't going to be able to stop it. I felt panic rise from deep down in the pit of my stomach as I gave up on the sanding job and called Jessie. No answer. I waited fifteen minutes and called again. Over and over, I did this, smoking nervously and hiding from her mother. Finally, when her mother came looking for me, I told her that I didn't feel well and that I needed to lie down.

I'll never forget that first dose of discomfort. I'll never forget lying on that old antique couch in that old house kicking my legs up, feeling exhausted, but unable to sleep. I'll never forget the panic in my heart when I began to realize that something was happening to me, something not good at all. I lie there for hours wide awake, skin crawling, and miserable until early that evening when Jessie came through the door, her eyes pinned up, lower lip hanging loosely, and scratching at her face.

"Please tell me you've got some shit," I pressed.

I don't remember what excuse she gave me, but it crushed me from the inside out when she told me, "No."

I told her what I was feeling.

"Oh shit, you're illing. Just hold out tonight. We'll try to get you something tomorrow."

Illing? What is that? I had broken the mysterious three-day rule of heroin. *I am addicted. Or am I?* I was never told the consequences of using heroin for more than three days, I was just told not to. It had never come up in a discussion what the effects of heroin addiction actually were. Whenever I was told not to do something, it came across to me as a challenge. *It couldn't have control of me that fast or that easily. I just won't do it again,* I lied to myself. Sickness was too easy to fix, rather than go through it another day.

I was angry, resentful, and crawling out of my own skin. I should have been angry at myself for not asking what I was getting into by joining them in their heroin club, instead I was angry at her for leading me here. I was angry at her for leaving me here to crawl in my own skin while she was getting high all day, and then coming home and treating me with such nonchalance. I knew one thing for sure, I wasn't sending Jessie down without me anymore. I was going to learn where to cop my own raw heroin from now on…that is of course, if I ever did it again.

Shortly afterward, my mother and Jessie's mother spoke. My mother told Jessie's mother the true story of why I was living on the streets and expressed that I was welcome back home. Little did my mother know, how far gone I was at this point and the monster she was letting back into their lives. I moved back home, worse than when I had left. I was in the full throes of early addiction now and had to figure out where to get raw dope on my own. It wasn't long before I found a spot just outside of the boundary of the Baltimore Zoo, in a neighborhood known as Woodbrook. It was about a forty-minute drive every day. Once we got to the dilapidated neighborhood of Whitelock, I usually began to get butterflies in my stomach because I knew inner peace was just blocks away. There were numerous ways in and out of the Woodbrook neighborhood, but we all became familiar with entering through a side street called Parkwood, so much so, that we began referring to the whole area as "going to cop down Parkwood." We would turn onto the lane of row homes that towered on each side of the narrow one-way street. Once in, we were somewhere we weren't supposed to be. On any of the main streets, a car containing white people could be en route to any number of locations in the city. But once we turned into this neighborhood, the police knew we were there for one thing. If stopped, the common excuse was that we were lost and trying to find the zoo. Although that usually didn't prevent a thorough car search and warrant check. Parkwood was a straightaway that ended at an intersection with a small corner store called Chang's Store. It was interesting to watch how rapidly the market for raw heroin grew in the area in the course of time that we were going there.

When I first started going down there, we would pull up and get $15 bags of raw heroin from one or two dealers who would hand it out in front of Chang's. Within weeks, there were several different brands of dope being touted on that strip, and fifteen to twenty people hanging out in front of the store at all times. They had brand names for the dope like Green & Whites, Tutti Frutti, Good & Plenty, and New Jack City. Some of the raw heroin was a light tan, and some got almost as dark as chocolate, but it was all legit. There were several dealers we knew by name such as Twon, Fats, Peanut, and Bright Eyes. Bright Eyes was our favorite. She was an older addict who hustled Good & Plenty. She looked like a dark-skinned Michael Jackson and always wore a black leather biking glove on her left hand. When we first started going down there to cop, it would take eye-contact and a nod to get them over to the car. Then we'd conduct the transaction through the car window. Before long, as soon as we'd come pulling up the street and they saw our white faces, a dozen of them would bum-rush the vehicle, shouting out the brand names of their dope and holding it in through the open window. On one occasion, I actually had a guy throw the baggies into the window onto my lap and demand I pay for them before I even said what I wanted. Whoever we were buying from would back off the other dealers, or we'd have probably gotten beaten and robbed when I handed the bags back and said I didn't want his.

It was rare to be in the neighborhood buying dope when police were around because the neighborhood boys had look-outs on the rooftops who would alert everyone when a police car entered. If we made the trip to Parkwood, and no one was out on the street or in front of the corner store, we automatically knew there were cops in the area. We'd go over to Mondawmin Mall and wait fifteen minutes and drive back. Usually the whole strip would be alive again. On the rare occasion that we did have dope in the car and a police officer was in the neighborhood, we'd duck through the maze of back streets and alleyways playing a tense game of cat and mouse, usually evading them. If we got pulled over before we had time to crush the dope up and sniff it, then we had to swallow it or pray we didn't get searched.

The ride to the city became a ritual. It was almost as much of a high as sniffing the heroin. I loved every second of it! It was tense, dramatic, and exciting. I never knew what I was going to get when we turned the block into the neighborhood. I never knew what dealers were going to be out, police officers, guys at the bottom of the street trying to sell fake heroin. You had to know who was who, or have a real keen sense for the streets, or you would get burned. There were addicts working for the dope shop selling dope, but there were also addicts hiding in the shadows waiting to hop out and sell you fake garbage. There was no worse feeling than driving forty minutes to chase your sickness away, then spending the last of your money only to get a bag of drywall or dirt. The transactions were always rushed so there was no time to sit in your car and taste test the product. Even then, the dealers would sprinkle a touch of real heroin in with the fake stuff in order to beat the taste test.

I got to know the lay of the land and the players very quickly. I studied the streets intently. I noticed the guys on the rooftops, the stash spots in a car wheel well, or a flowerpot or even under a random piece of trash on the curb where they hid bags full of dope. I knew all the names and faces and could barter with them for deals, or push them off when they tried to scam or sell fake product. I became an asset to any junkie heading downtown to cop and landed myself many free rides to the city that way. If there wasn't already someone going down to cop, rides to the city were not cheap. A cab would run about $100 round-trip. A non-addict friend, if they were even willing to do it might want $50 to $60, and an addict friend would want at least their own bag and gas money. I prided myself on getting a lot of free rides because I could cop dope for people without them running the risk of getting burned.

Once the dope was in hand, we'd get out of the neighborhood as fast as possible and to a more commercial or mixed-use area where we didn't stand out. Then, we'd dump the contents of heroin into a dollar bill and crush it with a lighter. Once crushed into a powder, we'd use a cut straw or another dollar bill to sniff it. The bitter taste of the heroin would drip from my nasal cavities into the back of my throat, but with that nasty taste came the warmth. A blanket of peace would cover my soul and my skin. It would cradle me for another twenty-four hours without worry. I would be okay until the next day when the process would begin all over again.

SEASON THREE

FALL INTO WINTER

*"I do not understand what I do.
For what I want to do, I do not do.
But what I hate, I keep on doing."*

-Romans 7:15

*"I'm gonna try for the kingdom if I can
Cause it makes me feel like I'm a man
When I put a spike into my vein
And I tell ya things ain't quite the same
When I'm rushing on my run
And I feel like Jesus son
When It shoots out the dropper's neck
And I'm closing in on death...*

*Heroin.   It's my wife and it's my life.
It's gonna be the death of me."*

-Velvet Underground, "Heroin"

XIX.

Heroin made life extremely simple. That is one of the most powerful lures it has on an addict. The United States in particular has major problems with anxiety, stress, and depression. There are an overwhelming number of modern stressors like college, careers, reputations, popularity, family, sex life, retirement, mortgages, insurance, health, taxes, failure, success, children, dying parents, disease, vehicles, brand name clothes, the Joneses, judgment, sleep deprivation, holidays, being fake, being real—the list goes on and on. As a world power we are in a mental health crisis. We make up only five percent of the world's population, and yet we consume over eighty percent of the world's psychiatric medications. The human mind was not designed for these levels of prolonged stress.

The pressures and stressors are coming at us from too many angles. It's too much to balance or to even keep track of. People find their own coping mechanisms. Heroin for one, numbs all physical and mental anguish and stress. For a young, fragile mind, heroin is an all too easy way out, despite all of the adverse consequences we may have been warned about. Sometimes, to a weak mind, it could come down to a choice between heroin or suicide, although they are close to being synonymous. In a world full of overwhelming stress, and responsibility, in a place where fear is the catalyst behind almost every decision, and the slightest mistakes can feel like permanent failures, heroin is an easy escape. It's like the Zen Buddhism of the streets, like a warped vacation from the insanity that we call a normal functioning society. The masks we wear become uncomfortable, and the worldly pressures that tell us we're not good enough or that our future is bleak and hopeless drive us away from normal society. Working to live and living to work, living to make others happy, and living how "they say" we should is exhausting—and nearly impossible. Many respond by pushing away. They drink or drug all the negative feelings down that arise from others' expectations, and the escape brings temporary relief—like a vacation within your own body. It's a way out of the mountains of pressure that close in day after day. The problem is, when the high or the drunkenness wears off, the societal pressure remains. Then, the voices of authority, the judgment, and the damage of whatever you did while high or drunk constricts even tighter. With no apparent means of escape, the cycle begins again.

Heroin makes it all so simple. Heroin is a Zen teacher, a cult leader, or a Shaman who teaches without words. It teaches from within, by breaking the user, by simplifying him and by making him into nothing. Heroin is a killer. Not everyone comes back from the teaching, and no one should willingly take it. It is a last resort for lost souls who stumble into its clutches, sometimes accidentally and sometimes by being led there with no viable alternative. In a culture where stress, anxiety, and depression permeate, where media saturates our minds with mental terrorism, and where peers condemn with finger-pointing and judgment, heroin boils down an addict's life into the mere basics.

You might envision an addict's life as stressful. In a way it is, but it's a simplified stress. On heroin, life becomes a game of survival, almost a caveman-esque way of living. The pressures, the thousands of variables and factors that confront us every day are gone, and life reverts back to the way it was many millennia ago: basic survival. Now each day is boiled down to waking up and finding a way to get high—that's it. Life becomes a selfish fixation on getting money to get the drug, finding the drug, enjoying the drug, and that pursuit is subconsciously more appealing than the effects of the drug itself. Everything else in the world stops for the addict. Nothing matters anymore. Life is now direct, one way, and completely self-focused. Even though the cycle of addiction is painful, it feels refreshing to an inner part of us. There's sickness, there's physical and mental pain, there's crime, and the damage done to ourselves and others physically, mentally and emotionally. But in the end, none of that matters because once we get our heroin for the day, we can make it all go away. Until then we can channel our thoughts on getting the heroin, or getting money to get the heroin, and the stress of the outside world temporarily disappears. Just like that, life is broken down to the very simplest form. Just as the caveman wakes up and leaves his den to go search for food for the day to satisfy his and his family's hunger, the addict does the same. Life is physically miserable this way, but for the soul, it is very easy and simple.

In the beginning of human life, it was man versus nature and man versus the elements. Now through modern technology, we manage those things, and we are left with a new battle. This new battle is more that of man versus himself and his own thoughts. It's no longer as simple as a physical battle anymore. We face a spiritual, mental and emotional battle every day. We are at war with ourselves. In a strange way we are bringing ourselves back to the Garden of Eden, where everything we want is at our disposal, and we experience very little physical threat from the world around us. Only now there are billions of other humans in the Garden with us, and we are destroying the Garden and each other. In the Garden of Eden, man had no threat from the physical world around him, and everything he wanted or needed was at his fingertips. There was no battle against the elements of the world around him. The only battle he faced was the inward battle against himself that he ultimately lost in that garden.

The snake within his head, the snake within my own mind, within every would-be-addict's mind, urges us to pluck the apple. The street corners, the doctor's offices, the house parties are the trees of good and evil that bear the fruit, and the apples are laced with heroin and fentanyl. In a world like a garden where we can pluck any fruit we want, our inner mind can't escape from itself, and so we pick the fruit that we believe has the answers for us. We eat that forbidden fruit usually knowing that we shouldn't be eating it, but hoping it's a better way out. We are looking for a reprieve of warmth from the cold world around us, and it works. It works so well at first, that we don't even realize we've been duped. We don't realize that we walked right into a trap, and that the snake in the tree who convinced us to eat the apple was in fact ourselves. Once we've taken a bite, the world will never be the same, and the garden will never be an appealing place to live again. Instead, it becomes an obstacle course in the way of the one thing we desire: more apples. Until eventually it kills us, or turns us inside out trying.

My life fell into this deep, mindless pursuit. My daily rhythm was sleeping until 10:00 or 11:00am, then hopping out of bed with one thing on my mind and one thing only. I didn't hunger for breakfast, I didn't care about work, or making anyone happy. I didn't care about any responsibility in the world. I could worry about those things once I got high. My mission every single day was to get out of the house, get at least $15 together, and catch a ride to the city. Depending on the quality of the heroin, I might need to make a second trip in the early evening. Like alcohol, and pretty much any other drug, regular usage meant a rise in tolerance. As weeks went by, eventually the same amount that almost killed me in the beginning would barely get me high.

In the beginning, a $20 bag could keep me high for three days, now it only lasted several hours. The daily rat race increased in intensity as the days went on. I never missed a day without getting high, so I never felt any true pangs of sickness, and I couldn't fathom the thought of facing it, so I did what I had to do every day to secure a fix.

I met a wide assortment of people who I didn't even realize got high, and unwittingly went back and forth to the city with them to cop. I was beginning to understand that there was a whole underbelly of society that I never knew existed. Even in my days of nonstop partying and drug use, in my alcoholism, and cocaine selling, I never knew this world existed. *These* people didn't party; they kept to themselves. They had no time, or even desire, to party. Life was basic. It was about securing the next high and enjoying it, and only attempting to do normal human things and face responsibilities once the high kicked in.

My eyes were opened wide to an entire undercurrent, both in the county and in the city. The city had it bad though. Through the eyes of an addict, everyone in the city got high. I saw it everywhere I turned: on street corners, in courthouses, businesses, and offices. The telltale slurred speech or hoarse voice, slack jaw, droopy face muscles, itching, acne, and nodding out were common traits on people everywhere. I began to realize how common my condition was. I knew it was wrong, and I didn't want to be in this vicious cycle in which I had found myself, but it was easier for me to get high than to face the unknown sickness that I was told lie in wait if I quit.

Jessie somehow held onto her job at Red Lobster all this time. I found various ways to get money. I would sell other drugs to get dope money, or steal whatever I had to. It wasn't beyond me in a fit of desperation to take things from the people in my own household that I didn't think they would notice. I would take $20 at a time from my sister's secret stash, or my father's wallet. Or in even more desperate situations, I'd pull twenty or thirty dollars of change out of their change containers. I hit those change containers time after time until the silver ran out and there was nothing but copper left.

Jessie was excited to tell me that she'd been hanging out with an older married couple at work who had been shooting heroin for almost twenty years. They showed her how to do it for the first time. She bragged to me about it with stars in her eyes like she had just passed a new threshold in life, her voice lilting as if she had struck gold. Anything self-destructive was exciting to her. She once told me that she liked teetering on the edge between life and death, and I silently agreed. We were both lost souls who enjoyed playing with fire. Fire just never seemed to burn her the way it did me. I listened intently, I knew this day would come, and it intrigued me but also scared me. Shooting up…I wasn't sure I wanted to cross that threshold. I mean, I was already trying to find a way out of my sniffing habit. The possibility of feeling a new kind of high, one that surpassed all the others was too intriguing for me.

So, when Jessie called me late one morning and simply said, "Meet me out front of your house in thirty minutes. I'm coming to pick you up. I've got a surprise," I jumped to it and stood on the curb eager for what the day had in store.

An old Buick pulled up to the curb with two guys in the front and Jessie in the back. I hesitantly hopped in. She introduced me to Jay and Leon. Leon, the driver, had stolen his mother's credit card and taken out $1,200. He was taking us on an all-day binge in the city. I didn't want to bombard these strangers with too many questions, but I assumed that Leon wanted to get with Jessie, and I was just a nuisance in the way. Nevertheless, they welcomed me with open arms, and included me in on the excitement of how high we were going to get.

He made it apparent that he "didn't give a fuck" if he got

caught, and when it came to his mom, "fuck her!" I didn't know the woman, but I felt sorry for her. I couldn't imagine being so cold that I stole from the woman who birthed me, knowing that I was going to get caught and didn't care. Either way, some of that money was going to me, and I was excited to blow it. Leon was a huge guy, over six feet tall and well over 280 pounds. He was loud and obnoxious, but he had a teddy-bear-softness about him. He talked about shooting cocaine to the point that we had to pull over so that he could throw up from the excitement once we got closer to the city, and he laughed about how he had shit himself before from the same eagerness. This wasn't uncommon among cocaine addicts, the butterflies in the stomach knowing that you were just moments away from experiencing nirvana would cause their stomachs and bowels to go awry. I never had that experience, but the butterflies and anxiety would have me trembling and nauseous at times. Jessie looked at me in the back seat with her soft brown eyes brimming over with the devil's handiwork.

She clenched my hand and said, "This is it. Are you ready?"

I replied nervously, "Yeah."

I knew what she meant. I was graduating to the next level. She was lonely there by herself. Today I was going to inject heroin. We pulled up to a row home somewhere in East Baltimore and knocked on the door. Four white faces crowding the front step, I looked up and down the street nervously not knowing what to expect.

A window slid open, and Leon hollered up, "It's me, open up."

An old black woman with a scarf on her head squinted down at us and said, "Aww-ight, be down in a minute."

We waited a few seconds before the door opened, and she motioned us in and up an old rickety stairwell to the second floor. It was more like a loft with nothing but a couple of stacked mattresses on the floor that served as a bed and some milk crates being used as tables. An old black man in sweatpants with gauze wrapped around his forearm sat on the bed pulling on a cigarette. Leon introduced us to Penny and Chick. Penny was the lady at the window, and Chick was going to be our runner. It wasn't safe for a white boy to be seen out in these neighborhoods copping, neither by the police nor the stick-up boys. Some of the best dope shops on the Eastside refused to even serve white people, not because their money wasn't green, but for fear that they might be undercover police. It was right around that era in the late nineties that the sitting mayor, Martin O'Malley, of Baltimore dressed himself in disguise and bought heroin from several Baltimore dope strips in an effort to show the public just how prevalent and easy to buy heroin was in the community.

We weren't taking any chances. Chick would run and get whatever we needed, and in return Leon would get him and Penny high. Leon was obviously in a rush and was putting pressure on Chick while giving him his shopping list. Jessie and I crouched down against a wall across from the bed and lit up cigarettes.

She leaned over and whispered in my ear, "Don't tell them you've never shot dope before."

I kept it cool. Leon was tallying up what to get and asked me if I was going to do coke with them.

I told him, "Sure."

Then off Chick went out of the house. We struggled to sit still for fifteen minutes. This was my first time using a runner to get drugs for me. I was used to a different world of heroin. I had been copping in West Baltimore where they sold raw heroin and stood on the street corners. Raw heroin was more for sniffers, though it could be injected. Over in East Baltimore they sold the more common form of heroin called *scramble*. Scramble comes in clear gel caps. It is raw heroin cut with various types of agents from vitamin B, to laxatives, to quinine. It was the far more common form of heroin and preferred among those who injected.

In East Baltimore, they typically didn't stand on corners selling the drug, rather there was a whole shop set up that included a money man, touts, lookouts, and hitters. The lookouts and touts were sometimes one and the same. These guys stood on the surrounding corners of the dope shop and shouted out the brand names of the heroin all day long, while keeping an eye out for stick-up boys and police. Stick-up boys were just that, they were coming to rob the drug dealers. The police were generally referred to as Five-O, although on certain occasions the police and the stick-up boys were one and the same. The cash man was the one who took the order and the money. He would shout how many you were buying down to the hitter, who would hit you off with the pills. These transactions often took place in an alley, which would be referred to as a "hole." It wasn't uncommon to hear many different brand names being yelled out as you drove through West Baltimore.

I can only imagine the confusion on the faces of those unfamiliar with the drug game as they passed corners and heard things shouted at them such as, "Tiger Woods hitting in the hole."

Or, "State Property hitting in the hole!"

Or, "Homicide hitting in the hole!"

At one point in time there were two shops right across the street from each other off of Washington Street with unique dope names.

It was quite amusing to drive by and hear men and women shouting from their prospective corners, "Good pussy hitting in the hole!" and, "Big dick hitting in the hole!" at 6:00 in the morning while the rest of the world passed by on their way to Hopkins or other jobs downtown.

We heard the front door open, and Chick came stumbling up the stairs. I could almost hear everyone's hearts begin to race. He sat down on the bed, dug into his coat pocket, and pulled out an old raggedy napkin. As he unfolded it, we saw about a dozen gel caps full of heroin in the middle. Then, he pulled out a handful of new syringes, still wrapped in their packaging, followed by another handful of tall skinny vials of cocaine. I was the outsider, so I waited my turn with bated breath while everyone else scrambled to get theirs in. Leon tossed the syringes to us, and Jessie immediately went to work performing her ritual. I watched, patient on the outside, but crawling with impatience on the inside. Penny and Chick argued over which of them was going to go first.

I heard him say something like, "Fuck it! I'll do it myself then."

And I watched as Penny slowly unwrapped the gauze from around Chick's wrist. After the last of the gauze came off, Penny took the needle of dope that Chick had cooked from between his teeth, and he picked up what looked to be a shard of a broken Popsicle stick. What I saw next will forever remain burned in my memory. Chick turned his arm over, and I saw an open, bloody hole where his wrist was. From across the room I couldn't see too clearly, but I could see enough to make out what was happening. He used that Popsicle stick to either move something out of the way inside that hole or to pry his vein up because Penny then inserted the needle and pushed the contents in. *Is this what my future has in store for me? No, never me*, I thought. *I'd die before that ever happened.* Turns out, through later conversations I learned that the hole in Chick's arm was an abscess caused from shooting excessive amounts of cocaine and heroin.

It was my turn. I let Jessie do it all. I was a little traumatized by what I had just seen. Hesitant, a little scared, and past the point of no return, I committed. There was nowhere to go now. When she pushed the needle in, I melted. I dozed in and out of consciousness. I blew lines of cocaine off of CD cases on their milk crate night stands, maybe even smoked some at one point. I passed out for a while in a separate room, and then came to and rejoined the party that seemed to last for hours. Chick went out and came back again, and again, and again, until the money was gone. The rest of the day, the ride home, walking into my house— it's all foggy to me. I was high for two solid days after that, and then the cycle picked up momentum.

I got a job as a busboy at an Uno's Pizzeria in Bel Air. I worked nights, and I got cash in hand at the end of every shift, so it was perfect for me. I had enough time to get to the city to get high before work, so I would come in ready to go. I was everyone's favorite busboy. Heroin put me in the zone. I would run around like a crazy man all shift long, bussing and cleaning. Typically, heroin is a downer that will leave you numb and tired if you let it. But if you exercise any kind of physical activity, it will hone your focus and energy in on that activity so that you give it your all. I know people who would get high and clean their house top-to-bottom, behind refrigerators, under stoves, and everywhere else you wouldn't normally think of. Then, when the work was done, they'd nod out in a chair and drop their cigarette in their lap.

I busted my ass making big tips in that restaurant for the week or two that I was there. The problem came when I got a couple of days off. I spent all of my tip money before my next shift. So, the day I came back into work, I was miserable and weary and couldn't fathom having to work an entire shift without my fix. As I came into the building, I walked into the locker room and got an idea. I quickly tried the handles on all of the lockers until I found one that was open, and at the bottom of that locker was a black leather wallet.

As quickly as I could, I grabbed the three twenties that were tucked inside and a credit card from within. I snuck over to the payphone and called a junkie friend. We had been trying all day to figure out how to get money.

"Come pick me up. I've got money."

He pulled up out back of Uno's in twenty minutes, and I hopped in. We went directly to Parkwood, and I scored us three bags of raw heroin. After we got high, I suggested we go shopping at White Marsh Mall out in the county. We went into Hecht Co., and I started browsing. High and with no fear whatsoever, I asked my friend if he wanted anything. He was nervous and said no, so I grabbed up some essentials for myself. I walked to the counter with two pair of white Reebok Classics and two Nautica sweat suits, worth about $350 and charged it all on the stolen card. That was just for fun. Now we had to grab something that would ensure tomorrow's "get high" money. We went into the parking lot and stuffed the bags of clothes into his trunk and then drove around to Sears on the other side of the mall. Once inside, he and I began picking out what we thought would bring us the most cash from a pawn shop. I grabbed an expensive home stereo system and a TV. I handed the card to the cashier and eagerly awaited my bags full of goods—only something different happened. The cashier picked up the phone. I sensed something wasn't right.

I turned to my friend and said, "Go!"

We split into two different directions. Security intercepted me before I made it to the doors. My friend got away, and I was going to jail.

XX.

My booking process at Baltimore County Detention Center is hazy because of the high I was on. I remember walking on the tier called 2B, which was a "low bail" tier. I was being held on a $2,500 bail, which meant it would cost $250 to get me out. I walked up the stairs to the second floor and found my cell. My cellmate was an older black man who was friendly.

"You're gonna be sick, aren't you?" he asked me.

"I don't know."

"Yeah, you are," he said confidently. "I don't know what's wrong with you young kids. Y'all gotta stay away from that shit, man."

I heard him, but I didn't. I crawled up into the top bunk and slept for maybe twenty-four hours. When I awoke, I couldn't believe I was still there. I made my way to the payphone on the wall the first time I saw it open up, and I called my parents. I was scared to death to call them, to disappoint them, but what the hell, how many times had I already done so? I cupped the receiver so nobody could hear me, and I ducked my face into my elbow.

I heard my mother's voice, "Hello."

I bawled. I bawled like the little baby that I had become. I spilled my guts about the heroin addiction, and why I had done what I'd done. I begged for forgiveness, I beat myself up and asked for their help and mercy. I hung up the phone and looked up to see my cellmate and several other older black men looking down at me from the second tier. I was humiliated. I knew where I was, and nobody was supposed to see me like this here, but I was broken. I didn't know why I had put myself in this position. I used to look down on fiends, make fun of them. They were once my clientele, and now I was one of them.

I sulked up the stairs, and my cellmate said, "Here, sit down with us, bro."

I felt safe and special for a brief moment to be able to just sit with these older men who probably knew the ropes of this system inside and out by now. They said a few words lecturing me about getting high, and how I needed to let it go, but mostly we sat in silence.

Before I made my way back to the cell to return to sleep, my cellmate reassured me, "Don't worry. Your pops will get you out."

"I hope so, but I doubt it," I replied, holding back tears.

I walked into the cell and climbed back up into my bunk to return to hibernation. I never got a chance to feel the fangs of withdrawal sink into me. My cellmate tapped my bed and woke me up. He said they were calling me to be released. I hopped up and packed up and waited for the big metal door to slide open. I stepped into the sally port and waited for one steel door to slide shut before the next would open. For a minute I was alone with my thoughts and scared. I was going to be sick soon, and I didn't want to get high, but simultaneously I did. I was convinced I didn't want to get high when I talked to my parents on the phone, but now that I was getting out, I felt differently. My mind raced, torn between two forces pulling at me from different directions. *Maybe I should have just stayed inside.* It was easy to think those kinds of thoughts now that I was being released. There was no way I wanted to go back into that hell hole. I played the game with myself. I pretended to be righteous and do the right thing, but subconsciously, I knew I was getting high as soon as I possibly could.

My father was receptive. The ride home wasn't as awkward as I imagined it would be. I was craving McDonald's, so he stopped and got me some. I had come clean about my heroin habit, so there would definitely be discussions when we got home, but for now he left me to ride home in comfort and silence away from the steel doors, hard bunks, and orange jumpsuits. My parents gave me space when I got home. I didn't even stop to think about how they might feel raising a son like me, having a child in jail and addicted to heroin. Given the opportunity, my mind went straight into addict mode. My basic survival instincts took me right to the phone when no one else was around. I started dialing. I went out front to smoke a cigarette on the corner where I always did. (I wasn't allowed to smoke on their property.) Jessie pulled up and met me with a tiny blast of dope to ease my nerves. I slept well in my bed that night and was back at it by morning.

As far as my folks knew I was out job hunting. Really, I was copping heroin for county kids who were scared to go into the Westside dope holes. I had found another dope shop about three blocks from Parkwood called "Black and Whites." At the time, these were the best quality bags of raw heroin available. The shop was run by a dark-skinned bald guy named "Ice." He had it set up like an Eastside scramble strip. I'd have the driver park up on Woodbrook Avenue, then I'd walk down the alley and turn right into another alley, which then turned into an intersection of alleys. The first backyard in the alley is where they would have me wait after I had paid, while the runner would run up a board, through an abandoned house, then back down another fence. Half the homes were boarded up and dilapidated. Watching the guys run through them was like watching hamsters run through a network of tunnels. There was no way any number of police could catch them or find their stash. I began to realize why police finally got frustrated and planted drugs on these kids.

My heart would beat out of my chest back in this network of alleys—anything could happen. The police could see a white boy sitting here and automatically know what I was doing. The stick-up boys could take what little money I had. A body could easily be disposed of in one of these vacant houses and not be found for days. Still, I always managed to come walking out of the alley proudly, humoring myself at the car full of county kids biting their fingernails off waiting on me.

My grandmother, who had co-raised me and had me at the campground every summer, was getting older and senile. She had both Alzheimer's and Parkinson's disease. It broke my heart watching her decline. She had always wanted to go to Vegas, so my mother booked a trip to take her before the diseases advanced even further. My mother purchased a ticket for my sister and I as well. My responsibility was to help to take care of and support my grandmother on the trip. I was eighteen years old, and it was my first real trip anywhere off of the East Coast. I had no idea how I was going to handle the whole week without dope, sick on the other side of the country, but I had no choice. If I had even one ounce of goodness left within me, then this was something I had to do.

I don't remember the flight to Vegas because I shot heroin in the airport bathroom moments before we walked through security, so I slept through the whole flight. I was too afraid to bring my needle and any heroin with me, so from that moment on I had no clue how I was going to operate. The first night in Vegas was a blur. I was high out of my mind, roaming through the casino and exploring. We stayed at the Luxor, which was the newest hotel on the strip back then. I spent a lot of time in the gift shop stealing souvenirs and trinkets and other goodies. I was a kleptomaniac in my addiction. I shoplifted everything, even things I had no use for. I filled up the nightstand drawer in our hotel room with stolen merchandise. Eventually, a hotel manager contacted my mother and advised her that they caught me on camera stealing. She burst into the room with tears in her eyes, angry and disgusted at me.

"I was just trying to get gifts for you and Nana, and I didn't have any money," I said.

It was only partially true, and I knew it was my only hope of diminishing the backlash. Embarrassed, she took all the stolen merchandise back down to the management, and they let things slide with the understanding that I was to never go back into the gift shop. On top of that, my grandmother was out of her mind. She would wake up at 3:00am and wander through the halls of the hotel while we were asleep and have to be brought back by security. My poor mother was in over her head. I had to do my best for the family in spite of the oncoming dopesickness.

The four of us shared a double-bed hotel room, my mother and grandmother in one bed, and my sister and I in the other. Lying in bed all night wide-eyed, legs kicking and skin crawling, while sharing a bed in a room with three others wasn't exactly comfortable.

In the daytime once my family awoke, we walked and walked through the strip, casinos, and resorts. Dragged from one place to another, I was hyper-aware, anxious, and completely sore. Each place was filled with loud noises and bright lights that permeated every one of my senses. It was torture. Once I got clean, it would be decades before I ever went back to Vegas. The whole experience left me scarred and jaded.

I was my grandmother's favorite, and I was invited on this trip to be her partial caretaker and to help lighten the load on my mother. I was expected to walk with her when my mother and sister walked ahead, to take her to bathrooms, to help her sit down, anything she needed. It would have been an honor had

I been in a sane and normal frame of my mind, but I drudged through it knowing that it was what I had to do.

We went to the old Vegas strip one night, and I saw an opportunity to finally break free. I told my mother I wanted to go explore, so she let my sister and I wander. She gave us an hour to do our own thing and then meet up at a rendezvous point. I ditched my sister and headed quickly toward the bottom of the strip, where I had heard the casinos got seedier. I walked briskly, block after block, asking people who looked like they may be addicts where to find heroin. I quickly discovered that people in Vegas in 1997 had no clue what heroin was. I asked every-body—white, black, bikers, homeless people. Finally, I spoke to a young, black man who gave me directions to a corner where they were selling it. I got down there quickly. When I walked up to the corner, I saw it was actually a bus stop with a bunch of black men and women, obviously Crip gang members because they were all adorned in blue bandanas and blue hats.

I asked a large woman, who was selling heroin, "How much?" She said, "$20."

I handed her the money. She reached into her mouth and pulled something out that had been tucked behind her gums. Then, she held out her closed hand and dropped it into mine. I closed my fist and walked quickly back toward the loud, bright strip.

Once I was a safe distance away, I opened up my hand and looked at it. It was a big crack rock. *Shit!* They thought I was looking for crack, or they didn't care. I wanted to throw it, but I couldn't even do that. Cocaine is the last thing in the world you want to do when you're dopesick, it will only exacerbate the symptoms. In true addict fashion, I kept it anyway. It would at least take me out of myself for a few minutes.

Once reunited with my family, we headed back to the Luxor, and I snuck out of the room under the guise that I was going out to smoke a cigarette. I went to the casino and found a coke can. I used a pen to puncture holes in the side of the can, went into a bathroom stall, layered the holes in the can with cigarette ash and placed the crack rock on top. I smoked that piece of crack in that bathroom stall for no reason, knowing it would bring me absolutely nothing but misery and pain. I did it knowing that the only thing it would do for me would be to take me out of reality for just a moment. That's not what cocaine really does though. It just made reality more vivid. It made me crave more, and it made me go back to the room wide-eyed and lay there all night, unable to sleep. I laid there in a hotel room next to my sister and six feet away from the woman who gave birth to me and the woman who gave birth to her. I laid there crying, asking God why I do what I do. I wished for death, or at least that God would somehow stop me from being the person I was. I hated myself.

My parents wanted me in rehab, and I agreed. If not, I was back out on the streets, homeless. I had nothing. Rehab wasn't such a bad idea anyway. Maybe I could finally get my life in order. I was still on my folks' insurance at the time, so they found me a bed at a rehab called Oak Crest. It would be two weeks before it was available. Like any good addict, the fact that rehab was around the corner gave me an excuse to use freely until I went in. I had exhausted all of my funds, so I snuck a check out of my parents' checkbook and wrote it out to myself for about a hundred dollars. I cashed it at a local bank with no problem. *They'll never notice*, I thought to myself. *I will just intercept the mail whenever it comes and throw away their statement before they get to it.* The problem with that was that when I got away with it once, I did it again and again and again. I ended up writing just over $700 worth of checks within four different occasions. I knew at that point that I was bound to get caught.

I managed to keep myself high for two weeks straight leading up to rehab. Three months into my addiction, and I was already going to rehab. I fought it inside and out. I would argue how ridiculous I thought it was to my parents. No one else I knew had ever been to rehab. Jessie and I had been getting closer than ever now too. We had begun telling one another that we loved each other. We had kissed and made out. My persistence had finally landed me the girl I was in love with. I couldn't stand the idea of being away from her for thirty days. I was dying inside at the thought of having to go away. Everything in me fought it. To a rational person, the concept of going to rehab at this point was clear, but to me it was the end of the world.

The night before I was scheduled to leave for rehab, I talked to Jessie on the phone. We shared our love for one another and how much we were going to miss each other. She offered to walk to meet me halfway to say our goodbyes. We lived about twelve miles apart. It just wasn't possible. It would take us four hours round-trip to meet, not to mention our time together. So, I did something I had never done before, I stole the keys to my sixteen-year-old sister's car and snuck out. I got in the car, drifted down the street, started it up a few houses away and was off into the night.

I met Jessie in a parking lot down the street from her parents' house, and my heart was full. I could do this for thirty days as long as I knew she loved me and was waiting for me. She got into the car, and for a little while we were no longer junkies. For one night, we were teenagers in puppy love caught in the middle of some skewed fairytale existence where the prince was being whisked away from his bride for thirty days of torture, and this was our final embrace. We kissed and held and stroked each other. We cried and promised to write, and then we broke free from one another. I drove home ready to face my fate in the morning.

I arrived at Oak Crest as high as I could get. It was the only way I thought I could face the unknown. My father dropped me off early in the afternoon with my belongings, and I slept the majority of my first twenty-four hours away. I was in detox mode for the first three to four days. During that period, classes were optional, and I opted out of all of them. When I wasn't asleep, I would sit in the common area, or mostly the outside courtyard to smoke and talk to the other clients telling stories about where we copped and how we got high. I got on the payphone whenever I could sneak a call, even though I wasn't supposed to use them while in detox.

I tried to get ahold of friends to see if I could convince someone to bring me some heroin or stash it out front in the garden. I hadn't even started feeling withdrawal sickness yet, and it was calling to me hard. I knew I wouldn't be able to get anyone to bring me dope without any money, not to mention I was on the other side of the city, so I gave up. I called my parents' house to check in, and I broke down in tears at the sound of their voices. I was emotional and fragile as the heroin was leaving my system. I sobbed into the phone, telling them how sorry I was and begging them to forgive me. I came clean about the checks that I had written, and they hung up the phone on me. I called back, no answer. I felt weak and abandoned. I got paranoid, I got scared, and I got angry.

I couldn't take personal responsibility for where I was and what I had done, no addict ever can. It's part of the nature of addiction. Personal responsibility means accepting consequences for my actions without accepting outside help. Fear is an addict's most effective motivator, and it surely was mine. My fear told me that I couldn't do this alone, at least not without a chemical crutch.

I started to get extremely fidgety as the sickness began to arrive in my body. I had never really gone through full withdrawal before, and I determined I wasn't going to here. There was a med window where we could get a Dixie cup full of medication several times a day. One of the medications they gave was Klonopin, which I learned was a distant relative of Xanax. It was a tranquilizer in the Benzodiazepine drug family. I was relieved to be getting some kind of drug, even though it would only be for my first three days, and then they cut us off.

My second night in the program, they were taking the entire group out bowling, and asked if I wanted to come along for the ride, even though I was still in detox. I was going to stay back until I heard them talking about stopping at a 7-Eleven along the way for cigarettes and snacks. I immediately devised a plan. I had no money, but I was an excellent thief, and I knew they sold alcohol at most 7-Eleven's. I would find a way to beat the system one way or another. We stopped at the store, and everyone unloaded out of the van and into the store. To my dismay, there was no alcohol there. I wandered through the aisles looking for anything that caught my eye. Stuffing a few bags of Reese Pieces into my pockets, I rounded the corner and saw bottles of Robitussin lining a shelf. I quickly shoved two bottles into my waistband and hurried out of the store and back to the van.

A young girl I had been flirting with and swapping drug stories with sat in the back with me, so I showed her the bottle and offered her some. She wasn't interested, and neither was the guy on the other side of me. Apparently, no one was on the same suicidal crash course to hell that I was. I tilted the bottle back in the darkness of the back of that van and downed the whole thing. I saved the other for later. The driver dropped off all of the residents and two counselors at the bowling alley, then we returned to the center. I wasn't as high or drunk off the bottle of Robitussin as I expected, but it definitely had an effect on me. By the time the residents returned from bowling, I was wound up and cocky. I was dancing around in the hallway, showing off for the girl I was interested in, and inviting people back to my room after our last med call for a "Robitussin party" with the other bottle I had. The girl asked me if she could have my Klonopin at med call because she was off detox and feeling a little sick still, and that I didn't need it because I had the Robitussin. I agreed to give her one of the two pills.

When we lined up for our meds, I dumped the Dixie cup in my mouth but didn't swallow the pills. She asked me if I saved her anything.

I said, "Come here, I've got something for you," and in my cockiness, I grabbed her head, leaned forward and kissed her, pushing one of the pills into her mouth.

She looked taken aback, and I couldn't tell whether I was overstepping my bounds or that it was okay with her, but at that point I didn't know what was going on. I spread the word that we could party in my room until lights out, but really, I only wanted her to show up. Then I went back into my room and patiently waited. People were there to get clean, not party, so nobody showed up. I couldn't do this. My brain and my emotions were scattered, going a million miles a minute, trying to do everything I could to dodge reality and the horror it would bring. I cracked the second bottle of cough syrup open and drank, then I lit up a cigarette and began to smoke. Rules didn't matter anymore, nothing did. As the Robitussin mixed with the Klonopin, the room started to spin, and I was out.

The only way I knew how to survive was with drugs and alcohol to numb myself down to a point where reality was tolerable. I didn't want to think about the past, present, or future because it filled me with fear. I needed to soften my reality into a foggy blur—a brainless, thoughtless existence was what I hoped for. Anything else, and I was riveted with fear... fear for what I had done, and fear of where I was headed. Fear of failure, and fear of success. Fear of losing what I had, and fear of gaining things only to lose them. Fear dominates an addict's life and is the catalyst behind all of their self-destructive behavior. I numbed my fear so diligently that when it would return, it would come back with a vengeance.

Daniel McGhee

At some point in the middle of the night, when the security guard came around to take a head count to make sure no one had escaped the facility, he found me passed out in my bed with a bottle of Robitussin and a sheet smoldering from being caught on fire by my lit cigarette. I don't remember him waking me up or having the small fire extinguished, but I know when I arose the next morning around 11:00am and walked out into the common area, I was greeted by a counselor who informed me that I was being discharged from the facility immediately and that there was no hope for me.

Fear came at me in waves. *What had I done? And why?* I didn't even know what motivated me anymore. This was embarrassing and stupid. I was ashamed. I went back into my room and grabbed my belongings. They told me that a driver was going to take me back to my parents' house. That was the last thing I wanted. *How the hell am I going to explain this?*

I climbed into the van with the older, black man who would be taking me back to face the inevitable disappointment and anger of my parents. I tried to convince him to take me somewhere else, anywhere but there. *I can lay low and pretend like I am still in the program*, I thought irrationally to myself. He wouldn't budge. He told me that he was legally obligated to take me there. I could tell that he looked at me with disdain, and I didn't blame him. It was an uncomfortable ride home, being driven for an hour by someone who clearly thought I was a piece of trash.

"How did you even manage to get Robitussin?" he sneered.

I told him I stole it.

"What are you going to do with your life? You think you can live like this forever?" he followed.

Good question, I thought to myself, *I don't know.* I rode the rest of the way in silence wondering how in the hell I was going to explain this once I got home. The van pulled up in front of my parents' house, and I hopped out. He had done his job. What happened from here was up to me. I was just going to walk up the street with my bags and not go in. I'd figure it out somehow. It was too late though. I saw my mother on the cordless phone standing in the frame of the screen door. She must have heard the van pull up. I had no choice but to approach. She hung up the phone and opened the door.

"What the hell are you doing here?" she scowled.

I told her they had released me without further explanation.

"Bullshit!" she said. "You're not welcome here. Get the fuck away from my house!"

It crushed my soul, but I deserved it. *Fuck them*, I thought, *I'll go get so high I don't wake up. That will fix all of my problems.* I walked up to the shopping center, bummed change for a phone call, and dialed Jessie.

I greeted her with "Hey, I'm out!"

XXI.

Jessie was upset. She sincerely wanted me to do better for myself. I told her the story, and I could hear the disappointment in her response, but the damage was already done. She told me to catch a cab up to Red Lobster. She'd be off soon, and she had money in her pocket and a ride lined up to go downtown. I hitchhiked to Red Lobster, and just like that I had a goal again. Nothing in the world mattered to me except attaining it.

I waited around Red Lobster until Jessie got off work, then a carload of us headed down to Parkwood. We got several bags of dope, but the driver was a sniffer, and from his position of so-called moral ground, he didn't want anyone shooting up in his car. We headed into Druid Hill Park and found a secluded gazebo. I emptied my bag into a spoon and fired away. Blackness swiftly came over me.

I don't know how much time elapsed between firing up in that gazebo and when I began to awake, but when I came to, I was on a strange couch in a row home full of people I didn't recognize. There was an older, black man reaching into the front of my pants, but I couldn't feel what he was doing, nor could I stop him. Jessie was on the couch next to me, though I'm not sure if I actually sensed her or just assumed her presence, but I couldn't turn to look at her.

"He's awake!" I heard her shout. "Are you okay?" she said looking into my eyes.

I couldn't move my lips to form a word. Fear reverberated through my entire body. I tried desperately to move a hand, a finger, to even blink an eye, but nothing moved. I was imprisoned in my own body. I wanted to cry, but I couldn't. Sheer terror gripped every fiber of my being. My worse fear had come true. I was buried alive in my own skin. I kept trying to communicate to my hands and fingers to move, but nothing. A thousand voices came at me from all different directions.

"Give him more ice," someone said.

"What about salt water?" I heard another voice say.

Other people were asking me questions, but I couldn't reply. *Is this going to be my forever? Is this what I brought upon myself?* I was paralyzed from head to toe, and if this lasted for eternity, then it would be the worst thing I could imagine happening to anyone. I wanted to piss myself, but I couldn't even do that. The terror rocketed through me as my mind scrambled. I called out to God in my silence. I pleaded to anyone who would listen, but even my inner voice was gone. I just was.

I remained that way for maybe five minutes, but it felt like forever. It was the scariest thing that had ever happened to me. Then suddenly, my fingertips twitched. I focused on moving them until I was slightly bending my fingers. Then, I focused on balling my fists, and then moving my wrists. My eyes could look around now. I could see Jessie next to me, looking intently concerned. I felt wetness all over my lap. I had pissed myself. *How embarrassing.* I stretched my arms, and then my neck. Life began to return to every single part of my body, and relief flushed over me. *I am alive. I am normal.* I never thought I'd be so happy to acknowledge that. I turned to Jessie and hugged her. I wanted to cry, but I couldn't because the heroin wouldn't let me. I had so many questions...

It turns out that I was carried back to the car from the gazebo in Druid Hill Park, then frantically driven to the house of an older, black couple who lived near the city jail. The black couple reluctantly brought me in to try to revive me. They were junkies too, and apparently were sometimes runners for one of the guys in the car with us. They were pissed that I could have died in their house and brought trouble there, but were also happy to help bring me back to life. That wasn't piss in my lap—it was melted ice. Apparently, it is an old junkie trick to pack a man's balls with ice and inject him with saltwater in order to bring him back from an overdose. It worked.

No one in the room that night had ever experienced the paralysis that I just had. They all swore that I must have done something other than the same heroin they all had done, but I hadn't. Maybe it was the prior night's affairs mixed with the heroin. Nobody knew.

"We cool. But don't ever bring that shit to my house again. You take him to a hospital next time," I heard the man say, whose couch I had been laid out on. "You good? You got to be careful bro," he turned and said to me.

I thanked him. Everyone agreed that I needed some cocaine to wake myself up, so I blew a couple lines with them. The homeowners went out on a run and came back with some more dope and coke, and I remember shooting more heroin before we even left their house in order to bring me down from the coke high. My life was lived with reckless abandon, with no care of the consequences until they were actually happening.

That night, I slept in Jessie's parents' van in their driveway. It was a big family-style van that her mother sometimes, but rarely ever, drove. In the early morning hours, I could hear her father come out and get into his truck, and I lay there peeking out the window, praying that he never had a reason to get in the van or look inside. When Jessie woke up, she came out and tapped the side of the van a few times to let me know the coast was clear. I walked down to McDonald's and waited an hour or so, then came back up to her house like I hadn't been there all along. I did this for two or three days. The weather was getting cold though, and it took forever for me to fall asleep in the back of that van, even though I was high on dope.

Jessie was heading into town with some mutual friends to a party at a warehouse loft. The guy who lived there was very eclectic and made abstract sculptures and various other forms of art. He was setting up the warehouse like an art gallery and hosting a formal party for his artist friends and potential buyers. I didn't know the guy personally, only through association. Jessie told me I could come along and stay down there for the night as long as I didn't drink at the party.

"No problem," I assured her that I had no need for alcohol anymore.

Before we headed to the party, we stopped on Westside to score some heroin, and that's the last thing I remember. When I awoke, I was on a fire escape outside of a window on the top floor of a huge warehouse building downtown. Apparently, I had overdosed again, and when we got to the artist's apartment, I was foaming at the mouth. Jessie and the rest of the guys with us carried me from the car to the elevator, and we went to the top floor. Luckily, they got me there before the guests started arriving, but the host of the party was freaking out on Jessie for bringing me there. When the guests began coming in, he had them take me out onto the fire escape until they were able to bring me back to some form of normalcy. I woke up several floors up above the city on a fire escape, high and confused, and extremely embarrassed. I was embarrassed for Jessie and for myself. I had become a huge nuisance to have around and was quite possibly destroying her friendships. I wondered how long it would be before I wasn't included on anything anymore.

Once I finally became coherent enough to act somewhat normal, we snuck back in through the window, and they took me to a couch in a side room. I remember walking past strange sculptures and people dressed in blazers and gowns drinking mixed drinks and wine, and I thought how stressful it must be to have a situation like this here. Jessie and the crew left me on the couch so they could mingle and party. I cracked open a beer, lit a cigarette, and eventually drifted off to sleep. I woke up late the next morning with her beside me on the couch and other people sleeping all over the floor in the same room, including the owner of the loft. I casually made conversation with him, and congratulated him on his party and artwork.

I never once mentioned my episode the night before except to say, "Hey, sorry. I appreciate you letting me stay."

XXII.

I f there was one thing I excelled at, it was "boosting." Boosting was just another term for shoplifting. I was the best-dressed, cleanest, most well-groomed homeless person around. I stole all of my food, my snacks, my hygiene products (all top of the line), as well as my name-brand clothes. I could steal anything, and in the 90s, baggy clothing was in style, which made it incredibly easy for a booster. My jeans were already five sizes too big, and my shirts came down to my knees. I could hide a whole grocery list around my waistband and sometimes did.

For a good shoplifter, there were plenty of ways to make money. At that time there were numerous stores that would give a person cash for returned merchandise without a receipt. Word quickly spread through the junkie community as to which stores had these kinds of return policies. Sears would only give cash back up to $15, but they had various counters throughout the store. The Harford Mall was within walking distance from Jessie's house, so it was a common destination for me in the beginning. I would put a plastic grocery bag in my pocket and find something in the store as close to $15 as possible. When no one was watching, I would pull out the plastic bag, drop the item in, and walk directly to the return counter. Once I did this three times at three different counters, I'd have enough money for myself, plus a ride to the city for the day.

When we had enough money, Jessie and I would go together. Other days it was every man for himself. Home Depot also became a hot spot for junkies all across the state of Maryland for about a year or so in the late 90s. When I first went in, they would give cash for returned merchandise without a receipt up to $150. That worked the first time or two. It was like striking gold for a junkie. One quick transaction, and I was set for a couple of days. It wasn't long before the amount of cash they would give without a receipt dropped to $60. They would check my ID each time I returned an item, and only allow me to make three returns per location. Every junkie I knew was onto the Home Depot scam. No matter where I went, or who I talked to, they all knew about it. It got to the point that we were hitting every Home Depot in the tri-state area, from Maryland to Delaware to Virginia.

I started getting cocky and lazy with it. I started bringing my own plastic bags in there as well and dropping a telephone or a thermostat into the bag and walking straight to the return counter. Not long after, they set up merchandise sensors between the inner store and the return desk so you'd have to pass through them to get to the cashiers. A couple of times, I got brave and swung the bag up over the sensors as I casually walked through them whistling a tune out loud. I prided myself on this horrible talent. I had no shame, nor did I give thought to the ramifications all of this theft had on society. We were just small timers looking to get high.

There were ways around everything. If a store didn't give cash, we'd take the store credit and sell it at half-price for cash. Or we'd buy something with the store credit, then visit another location with the item and receipt and get cash for it. I was a mastermind when it came to inventive ways to get money to get well. Every day was a never-ending hustle to get more money to get more drugs so I could fall asleep with some semblance of peace and wake up the next morning just to do it all over again. Every day as a junkie was about pushing back the sickness that was inevitably coming for me to another day. Each day the sickness is prolonged, it is also intensified. A night without heroin meant a night without sleep, and there was nothing scarier than a night without sleep anticipating the oncoming sickness and anxiety that would follow.

I finally slept with Jessie—not once, but a few times. We went at it all night long. Heroin was known for giving men what's known as "dope dick," meaning a guy can hold an erection for hours even after an ejaculation. Not only that, but because heroin desensitizes your physical body, it takes forever to reach an orgasm. It's because of this effect that a lot of dealers also occasionally sniff heroin in order to impress the women they sleep with. I would venture to say that more dope habits begin from inner-city males using heroin for the purposes of "dope-dicking" a female down, than from any other use. I felt like Jessie and I were closer than ever. After almost two years of pursuit, I felt a certain level of manhood regained now that I had finally slept with her. Jessie did drugs and a lot of other crazy shit, but she did not sleep around. I had a new reason to live now, a small glimmer of hope. That light was quickly extinguished.

After a full day of boosting and getting high one day, our ride said he had to run home and needed to drop us off somewhere for about thirty minutes until he could come back to get us. It was night time when we got out at a shopping center and wandered into a TJ Maxx. The store was packed with Christmas shoppers, and carols played overhead as we wandered around. Jessie was looking at the women's clothing, and I made my way over to the jewelry. Feeling no pain from the heroin in my system, I began doing a little Christmas shopping of my own, stuffing my pockets with jewelry that I liked for Jessie, and some for myself, plus toiletries, leather gloves, and gifts for friends. When I had reached capacity, I headed out front to smoke a cigarette and wait for Jessie. Only I didn't make it out front.

Just as I was about to cross the threshold of the front doors, I felt a heavy hand on my shoulder. Security grabbed my arm and marched me directly into a backroom. There was no way out of this, so when confronted, I began emptying my pockets, hoping for leniency. I dumped handfuls of merchandise onto the table while giving some feeble excuse about not having money for Christmas gifts for my family. None of it worked. The police were called, and I was loaded into a squad car and taken off to jail.

All I could think about was Jessie and the ride coming back to pick her up. How they would continue feeling the warmth of heroin in their bodies, and sleep in the warmth of their beds, and I was being taken to a cold holding cell left to wonder when I'd see their faces again. *Why am I the only one who is constantly suffering?* Tears rolled down my cheeks in the back of that squad car. Bits and pieces of my life flashed before me as I was being shocked back to reality and away from the world of heroin. Thoughts of my family and the warmth of the holidays with them, my grandparents, my siblings, happy times, my days selling drugs and fighting and feeling powerful, all leading to this: a shoplifting junkie being carted off to jail alone while his friends go free again.

I sat for hours in the cold holding cell clinging to the last remnants of my high and the hope that the commissioner might let me go so I could find my way back to Jessie that night. The commissioner, however, saw fit to give me a $10,000 bail. Neither my parents, nor anyone else I knew, was going to post that. It was over. I was stuck.

My first time in the Harford County Detention Center was by far the worst. I was sick, weak, and fragile—and only eighteen. Since it was my first time in, the correctional officers put me in a laidback dorm. Dorms in the detention center consisted of ten steel bunk beds squeezed together in one room with a steel toilet in the corner, the whole thing surrounded by bars. During the day, a barred door would slide open extending the living quarters to a tiny day room with three steel tables, a toilet, and a television. It is far worse than any situation you've seen on TV where someone gets the privacy of their own cell, or maybe one cellmate. This was twenty to twenty-four males of all different walks of life piled on top of each other for twenty-four hours a day in one loud, smelly room. Some men slept all day, and some slept all night, so it was never quiet. It was winter time, so it was freezing cold. Each man was issued a recycled scrap blanket to try to keep warm on his plastic bed roll that had almost no stuffing in it. There was never an ounce of privacy. All eyes were on everyone at all times, but somehow people get used to it. The human mind and body adapt very quickly to the most extenuating circumstances. I learned to sleep with people talking over top of me, or even fist fighting ten feet away, because I simply had no choice.

The correctional officers were in tune with which dorms had rougher populations in them and which dorms were calm and civil. So, in order to prevent newcomers to jail from being harmed or taken advantage of, especially tiny ones like myself, they sent us to the more civilized dorms. Two years prior I would have preferred a rougher, wilder dorm, but now I was a different person, broken by heroin.

I went into the dorm, claimed my top bunk, and laid there awake for the first couple of days tossing and turning, trying my best to hide my tears. The sickness and cravings weren't nearly as bad as I had expected, although they were definitely there. I wasn't throwing up or having diarrhea like I was told I would, but I was weak, my skin crawled, and I couldn't sleep for days. I never noticed a craving to smoke. This was my first understanding of how powerful the mental addiction to heroin was, in addition to the physical addiction. When I went only several hours without heroin on the streets, I went crazy inside and out. My skin crawled and felt on fire. My physical symptoms were magnified when I felt certain there was a possibility to get more.

I called my parents from jail and bawled into the phone just at the sound of their voices. I was never coming back here. This was my first and only time. I told my parents as much on the phone, and I meant it. I meant it with every fiber of my being. My father informed me that he had found a bed for me in a 28-day treatment center on the Eastern shore of Maryland upon my release. I agreed to go, and I knew better than to ask them to bail me out, so I just rode it out.

The guys in the dorm were surprisingly helpful and supportive. I felt like God had specifically led me to this place. The older men schooled me and tried to talk me straight. No one wanted to see me go back out and get high, most of all myself. But truly, deep down inside I always felt a hesitation. My lips said I didn't want to get high, my heart sang it out, but there was something deep down in my gut that told me I was lying to myself and everyone around me. It was a tiny, evil place way down deep that I tried to step on and hold down. I needed it to keep quiet so I could keep up this facade for myself. The voice intensified one morning.

I awoke early on my top bunk and looked over several bunks away. A young black guy who had been brought in late the night before lay in his bunk sniffing something up his nose while the rest of the dorm slept. Just like that, a battle welled up inside of me. I wasn't ready for it. I had no control. I felt as though I was looking at my one opportunity to feel the best feeling in the world. If I didn't grab it, he would finish it, and I would spend the rest of my day in miserable guilt.

I got his attention, nodded to him, and quietly walked over.

I whispered a lie to him. I told him I was sick and asked if he had any more. He cut me a small line on a piece of paper. I excitedly crept back over to my bunk, pulled the sheet over my head, and inhaled. Then, I waited. Nothing. I waited longer. Nothing. It wasn't even enough to get me high. The joke was on me. God put the spotlight on me right then and there, and I saw how powerless and worthless I really was. ~~I traded everything for nothing. I laid there in guilt and shame for the rest of the day. I knew at this point that I would never get clean. I wanted to give up and die.~~

XXIII

I spent about thirty days in jail and was released in time for Christmas. My family figured with thirty days under my belt, they could take me back in. I convinced them that after thirty days clean, it would be redundant for me to go to rehab. But within a couple of days, I was already getting high. Christmas Day with my family, I was nodding out and looking like death warmed over. Part of my release conditions required that I go to outpatient meetings and submit to drug testing. I did, and as usual I cheated the system. I went to the meetings high, and I beat the urine tests with other people's urine. Once more, my parents had enough, and they issued an ultimatum. I was not welcome to stay there anymore. They told me I needed to get into a halfway house, or they would throw me back out onto the streets.

We found a halfway house which was owned by the same gentleman who owned the outpatient center I had been attending. As far as he knew I was clean and had just slipped up once or twice. The halfway house was a rickety old row home in the town of Havre De Grace, about forty minutes away from where my parents lived, which meant even forty minutes further from the city. Once there, I unpacked my things, was led through the rules of the house and gradually introduced to the other guys who lived there. I had no intention of making friends.

I felt like an intruder in this house among all the other older residents. So, after I tossed and turned all night in my bed, dreaming of getting high, I left early the next morning to explore the town of Havre De Grace. My first duty was to find a job. I planned to start working and do things the right way. I got lonely fast and started calling all my friends, the only friends I had—which were of course, junkies. Nobody wanted to ride to Havre De Grace to pick me up when they were already in a rush to get to the city. It was almost an hour and a half roundtrip out of their way. I sat in the library killing time, my stomach flipping and legs aching. I wandered the streets of Havre De Grace with flush, crawling skin, putting in job applications, and sitting on curbs and under payphones smoking cigarettes all day, while secretly I just wanted to just shrivel up and die. Another night in that old house with strangers, lying in bed tossing and turning without sleep sounded like a nightmare. But if I just pushed myself through it, I could catch the first bus to Bel Air at 6:00 the next morning.

When I arrived back at the house that night, there was a message to call the Tidewater Grille in Havre De Grace. It was a fancy restaurant where I had submitted an application earlier in the day and spoken to a manager. I called in, and they said they desperately needed someone to wash dishes. I had put in an application for busboy or waitstaff, but they said if I came in and washed dishes for a week or two, they would move me to a busboy position. I had washed dishes before, and for me, it was one of the single most depressing, isolated jobs I could have. Just me, alone with a sprayer, steel wool and all of my negative, depressing thoughts.

I would start in two days. It was time to celebrate. The next morning, I caught the 6:00am bus, walked two miles to Jessie's from the Bel Air courthouse, and together we found a ride to go boosting and get high. That night I came back to the halfway house ten minutes after the 10:00pm curfew, walked directly up the stairs, avoiding everyone as much as possible, and went straight to bed. I slept like a baby. The following day I started work at Tidewater Grille. I dragged myself out of bed and put on the outfit they required, although my shoes were not the right color. I did not have money to buy the proper dress shoes for the job. The manager warned me, but let me continue with my shift. Moments later into my first shift, I was pulled aside by another manager who had a massive problem with my tennis shoes.

"What does it matter? Nobody sees me. I'm in the kitchen," I debated.

This led to an argument, which then led to me saying, "Fuck this place!"

Just twenty minutes into my first shift, I walked out. I went down to the library payphone and called a friend who surprisingly had no options for money and was willing to come all the way to Havre De Grace to pick me up to try to get some. I went back to the house to prepare and wait for him. I had a stupid idea that just might get us out the gate ("getting out the gate" is an addict term for getting well) and high enough to come up with a better idea. I loaded up a large black trash bag with laundry and sat on the curb waiting for him to arrive.

When he pulled up, I said, "Take me to my parents' house. I'll get us some money."

I figured my mother would be there. My plan was to stop by and say "Hi" and pretend I needed to do laundry. While I was there, I could attempt to borrow money, or check her purse or my sister's secret stash for $30 or so. We pulled up, and I told him wait about a block up the street, and that I'd be out in ten to fifteen minutes. I walked inside, and my mother was on me right away.

"What are you doing here?" she snapped.

Sarcastically, I retorted, "I love you, too," and said that I was just stopping by to do some laundry.

I walked down to the basement to do laundry and knew my plan was thwarted. She paced around on the level above me talking on the phone. There was no way I was sneaking around up there. I began loading my laundry into the machine and scanning the basement for anything that could go missing without being noticed. There was a small TV and VCR in the back of the room that wouldn't be missed. It was just collecting dust as far as I could tell. I stuffed it into the black laundry bag, and fluffed some clothes around it. I immediately headed upstairs carrying the bag next to me, and my mother stopped me on the way out the door.

"You're done already?"

I told her that I had a ride waiting and that I'd be back.

"Don't come back. We'll bring them to you," she replied.

She knew I was up to something, but she couldn't tell what. I hopped into the car, and we took off up the road. I showed the goods to the driver. We went to a city pawnshop, then to the dope hole and got high. Afterward, we came back to the county and picked up Jessie, went on a boosting spree, and got even higher.

I had the driver drop Jessie and me off at my halfway house in Havre De Grace. All of the other residents were at work during the day, so I knew we would be safe. We sat inside and got high and started making out. We made our way to the first-floor shower and were having sex when the front door of the house opened up and one of the other residents walked in. Women were not allowed in the house. We came out of the shower, and the resident was in the kitchen grabbing lunch.

"You know you can't have women in here..."

The heroin did the talking for me, "So the fuck what? Are you gonna snitch?" I already knew he was. I just hoped he didn't realize I was high.

"He's probably just mad that he doesn't get any pussy," Jessie said to me, loud enough for him to overhear.

If he wasn't going to tell, I knew he would now. He was too embarrassed to speak, but I knew he was going straight to the house owner. The next morning, I was called in for a urine test. I was also told that I was no longer allowed in the house because the other resident was sure that we were getting high and that I had a woman in the shower—blatant disrespect for the rules and for the other clients' recovery. Of course, I denied everything about the drugs, but I knew was caught red-handed with Jessie. I never once looked at the other residents of that house as people motivated to get their lives together and stay clean. I didn't see them as fragile addicts walking a tightrope, nor did I consider how my actions could jeopardize their recovery. As an actively using addict, I had tunnel vision. The only thing I saw was how circumstances affected me. I was a perpetual victim, always perceiving everyone else to be against me.

I told him the urine test would come back clean and would prove my story. I asked that if it did, would he consider putting me back into the house. I knew the test would come back clean, and it did, because I had rigged it. However, by the time he got the results back, I was living back on the streets again and getting high daily. So, when he called me back in to talk about returning, he sprung another test on me. This time I was unprepared and told him that I would fail it. Naturally, I blamed it all on him, stating I only relapsed because I had nowhere to live since he had thrown me out of the halfway house. Like any other addict, I lied so much that even I began to believe my own lies. I actually believed that I was a constant victim of circumstances and not of my own volition.

The bed in the rehab that I had lined up while I was in jail was still available, and I still had pending court dates. I had to do something fast. I had numerous court dates for theft. My TJ Maxx incident was a felony because I had $600 worth of merchandise on me. I had a credit card case at White Marsh Mall, which was also a felony because it was over $1,000 in merchandise. And the checks I stole from my parents created another felony because they were over $700, not to mention numerous smaller petty theft charges also pending against me. As luck would have it, the courts assigned me a pro bono attorney instead of a public defender. It was like a random lottery, and I was the lucky winner. Every attorney was required to do a couple of cases per year pro bono to keep their law license active. My new attorney understood that while all of these cases were separate incidences, they stemmed from the same cause—heroin addiction. The charges individually added up to over eighty years in prison if I was given the maximum sentence. She felt that the only way to avoid an extremely harsh sentence would be to combine them all into one case, which she was able to do. The court date was set for almost six months out, which meant I had plenty of time to either continue to destroy my life or work on putting back it together.

I agreed to go to the rehab this time. Now it was more than necessary. I checked into the Whittsitt Center way out in the Eastern Shore of Maryland for a 28-day stay. I was more than a model student this time. This experience was very different than the one at the last rehab because I began to realize that my way didn't work—I had lost all control of myself. Here though, I actually followed the rules. I participated in all the classes, did my homework, and had a great relationship with my counselors. I made friends with everyone in the program, but gravitated to the older, black folks. During the day we would participate in classes and meetings with smoke breaks in between. At night we would either have an NA or AA meeting in the facility, or we would pile into a van to attend meetings outside of the facility. I enjoyed all of it and was very passionate and active in taking my recovery seriously. At night, we would often play spades and listen to Baltimore club music. I would dance around show off. They loved me there, and I loved them.

As always, I found a female there who piqued my interest and quickly became infatuated with her. Every chance I got, I would hang out with her, smoke with her, and talk with her. We formed a very unclear bond there. I wasn't quite sure what we had, but it felt important. We talked many times about sneaking out of our bedroom windows at night and going to the liquor store across the field from the center, but neither of us ever had the courage to pull it off. In spite of everything they taught us in rehab, we were addicts. In our estimation, alcohol did not fall under that category, because after all, it was heroin that landed us both there. This was a hard lesson I'd have to learn repeatedly throughout the course of my substance abuse: alcohol is a drug.

Nevertheless, I graduated the program with flying colors. My counselor ranked me "Very Likely to Stay Clean" on my final report. I was eager to return home and get involved in meetings and practice this new way of life. My parents came to pick me up and bring their new son home. They had set a bedroom back up for me in the basement of our house. I unpacked and sat on my bed, overwhelmed. I decided to check in with the old friends and let them know where I'd been and find out what I'd missed. I called a friend up the street. I could tell by his voice that he was high.

"You wanna meet for a cigarette?" he asked.

"Yeah, meet me on the corner," I said. As an afterthought I added, "You got anymore dope on you?" just testing the water. I knew he wouldn't actually volunteer to give me some. So, his reply rattled me.

"Yeah, I'll bring you down a half bag."

XXIV.

And just like that—within two hours of being home—my entire twenty-eight days of passion and progress were flushed away. My soul was torn in two walking up that street to meet my friend, but something inside me had already committed. Like so many times before, I did exactly what everything inside of me screamed not to do. I made the worst possible decision at that moment. I can't expect an outsider to understand it, I can't even understand it myself. It defies all reason and logic. I knew it was wrong. I knew it meant more pain and suffering for me and more hurt for everyone around me. But it was a thousand times easier to take the dope than to walk away from it. I was a loser and a bottom-dwelling junkie, and apparently, I just hadn't had enough pain.

Things were only getting harder in the heroin world. People were starting to overdose and die. In one year, 1998, I lost eighteen friends and acquaintances to heroin overdoses. Almost every one of them were under the age of twenty-five, and the majority of them were only sniffers. Raw heroin was killing novice users. The junkies who had been shooting heroin for years and were using the scramble heroin were staying alive, but the raw heroin was somehow closing up the user's lungs. Many young people were dying in their sleep or bathtubs as the heroin relaxed their lungs to the extent they couldn't breathe anymore, so they literally suffocated.

On top of that, the local stores were getting wise to our theft scams and tightening up on their return protocols. We were now hitting various Walmarts because they would give up to $10 cash back without a receipt. This meant a lot of work to just build up $40 or $50 to take a trip downtown. Portable CD players had just come out, and I seemed to be the only one brave enough to go into electronics departments and boost them. I would grab two or three at a time and shove them in my armpits under my big down coat and walk out. Then we would have to find a pawn shop to buy them. If it was nighttime, we were screwed. One night my ride and I had gotten $17 together, but we were too impatient to make any more stops. So, we pulled down at Parkwood at night, and I asked for three bags from a guy I had never seen before, who looked kind of like Suge Knight. He handed the bags to us, and we simultaneously handed him the money and pulled off as quickly as possible, knowing we just shorted him. In the rearview, I could see him standing in the street pointing at the back of the car with an "I got your ass" look in his eyes. I would definitely have to find a new spot.

Two weeks later, I was with Jessie and the older married couple from her work in his huge window-cleaning van. They were trying raw dope for the first time. They were old school scramble shooters, both on the methadone program for about fourteen years, and had been shooting heroin for over twenty years. Somehow, they managed to have jobs, raise three children, never once get locked up, and yet never miss a single day of shooting heroin. These rare cases are what gave kids like Jessie and me hope for the future. We rolled down Parkwood to a busy corner, and I pointed out a guy and placed an order. I sat in the passenger seat with my window down and hoodie up in hopes not to be recognized, when I heard a knock on the side of the van. I turned to look out the window and caught a fist to my eye. The same big boy I had ripped off a couple weeks ago in the dark somehow recognized me and caught me so good with a right hook through the car window that I fell off the seat.

I hit the floor and yelled, "Go! Go! Pull off!"

He looked in and said, "Don't leave without your shit," and the other hitter came back and dropped off the baggies to me.

'Suge' looked at me and said, "You got me good. You're brave coming back here. But you good now. Just don't do that shit again."

I nodded fearfully but respectfully. I felt a bond with him after that, and he was my go-to guy whenever I saw him out. However, it wasn't long before the entire Parkwood strip started becoming unreliable, and the Black and Whites shop over on Woodbrook became the only place to go. This was good news for me because I was one of the only county kids brave enough to get out of the car and walk down those alleys to cop, which meant I would be invited on a lot of dope runs without having to pay for a ride.

After a tax check came in, I was in the position to buy quantity and bring them back to the county to sell for almost twice the price. I could charge $25 a bag for what I was paying $15 for downtown. This would allow me to keep my habit going for a while...until I went to meet a friend of a friend in my parents' neighborhood one afternoon for a deal. He pulled a gun on me and took the rest of my dope. I had become a weakling. I wasn't the guy I once was. I couldn't feel sorry for myself. I just got high to forget about it all instead.

I was up at the shopping center the next day and ran into some old friends. I had no clue they had started getting high. They hadn't gotten habits yet, but had done it several times before.

The oldest one, Dave, said, "I wanted to get in touch with you. I heard you've got a good dope spot downtown and can get it for anyone. I'm scared to even park my car down there. I don't fuck around."

I told him sure. He said he was getting a brand new car the next day and his paycheck, so he could take us all downtown to get high, as long as I would run into the hole and cop for him. I happily agreed. This was like Christmas in July for me—a free ride and free dope. The next morning, he and the other two guys pulled up at my house, excited and ready to go. I hopped in and started giving directions. Dave was wound up. He clearly had some kind of hyperactive disorder, but his excitement got me excited too. As we got off at the exit and turned into the ghetto, the three of them became terrified. They wouldn't even park within three blocks of the dope hole. I prayed that they wouldn't leave me down there as I ran into the alley and grabbed the dope, but then I remembered how much they needed me.

I disappeared into the network of alleyways for about ten minutes, and I came back to find them frozen in the car with the windows up, panic-stricken. They unlocked the doors, and I hopped in. They started telling me how nervous they were and how they thought I got killed. I just wanted to get high, but they wanted to get out of the city first. I bit my tongue and waited patiently to get somewhere they deemed safe so we could finally get high. We made it out of the city and were flying around the beltway in his brand new car, all four of us anxious to get high, though I was the only one with a full-blown habit. I noticed Dave glancing up in the rearview.

"Who are these clowns in back of us?" he said.

I turned around to look. I saw a young white guy and black guy in the car behind us. "What are you talking about?" I asked.

I'm usually up for a good fight, but I didn't have time for this. I needed to get high, then I'd fight. He kept glancing in the rearview at them, braking, then hitting the gas. *I need out of this car*, I thought. Everybody in the car was turned around looking at them now.

"Pull over then!" I said, "See if they pull over too, and we'll fuck 'em up."

He ignored me and kept looking in the rearview. I didn't understand what was going on. They didn't seem to be doing anything behind us.

"Holy shit!" the passenger in our car yelled, immediately followed by a loud crunch.

Our car went spinning into about six other vehicles. Cars smashed into each other everywhere. The sound of tires screeching and metal crunching was so loud that it was terrifying. Dave had been so busy watching the rearview that he plowed straight into standstill traffic on 695. Not a single person in our car was hurt, but his brand new car was completely totaled. The front engine was pushed in almost to the windshield.

I climbed out and surveyed the wreckage. It looked like a war zone on the highway, cars crumpled up and spun out everywhere. A BMW was crushed into the median and looked like a tinfoil ball laying there. The guys behind us swerved to miss us and plowed into someone else. There were a total of eight cars smashed up and destroyed, and miraculously no one seriously injured. A few people left in ambulances. It was over ninety degrees outside. We stood on the side of the highway for almost an hour with our shirts off, watching helicopters circle around above. All I wanted to do was run up into the woods on the side of the road and shoot my dope.

It wasn't long before a tow truck driver arrived. We all squeezed in, and the driver dropped us off in Towson. We went to the mall to get high and figure out a plan. Towson Mall was four stories high and full of high-end shops. It was a playground for an addict like me. We went into the bathrooms. I shot my dope, and they sniffed theirs. Then we went our separate ways. I went on a shopping spree with no money. I'm not sure what they did, but when I ran into them again a couple of hours later, they said Dave's mom was coming to pick them up if I wanted a ride home. I graciously accepted. I couldn't imagine what his mother thought about him totaling his new car within four hours of getting it. That was the last time I ever went downtown with Dave, but there were hundreds more county addicts where he came from.

Not long after, Jessie's parents went out of town, and she decided to have some people over. Everyone coming to the party gave me money early in the day for a dope run. I was nervous about going into the hole to cop twenty-three bags of dope. I had never gotten more than six or seven at a time. I had my ride park a block away from the top of the alley. I went in and worked my way through the back alleys looking for the hitters and found them sitting on a back stairwell. I told them what I needed. They had me sit down and wait about ten minutes, then it was delivered to me. I quickly made my way out of the network of alleys, looking over my shoulder as if I had the Hope Diamond on me—because in that world, I practically did. We hopped in the car and made it back to the party with everybody's goods.

An hour or so later, a guy pulls up who is one of my most reliable rides downtown. He needs to go down and get well. Nobody at the party had any dope to spare, and he didn't want to go downtown alone. I had just gotten back, and I really did not feel like taking that ride all the way back down, but reluctantly, I went. I had to maintain favor with anyone in the circle who had a car. I knew I would need favors from them in the future. We drove all the way back down to Woodbrook, and I had him park in the same place as the last car. I walked into the alley to get his one measly bag of dope. As I come down the bottom of the alley, I see the hitters on the same steps, and I hold up one finger.

They say, "Black and whites out. Black and whites out, y'all," to let the other guy passing by me in the alley know they're open for business.

I grab my bag and start walking out the side alley onto Fulton

Avenue when I hear the guy that just passed me in the alley ask, "What is it? Weed?"

They replied, "Naw, it's dope."

I didn't think anything about it as I was turning the alley onto the busy street and was suddenly lifted in the air from behind. I felt a big strong arm around my neck as I was literally lifted off my feet and shaken side to side.

"Give it to me!" he said.

"I don't have no money," I cried out.

"You know what the fuck I want!"

Then I felt a heavy piece of metal press against my temple as he continued holding me in the air. The cars were lined up at the red light, all black faces watching me out of their car windows as I dangled in the air. Some looked horrified, while others looked as if it was nothing they didn't regularly see. Cars jumped forward as the light turned green. Just another day in the hood… nobody cared about me.

I wasn't about to die over someone else's dope. I reached in my pocket and dropped the single $15 bag onto the ground. He released his grip and scooped it up. My legs lurched forward up the street in the direction of the car. I turned back to see his bald head and jet-black sunglasses, and I watched him stick that big, shiny gun back down the front of his pants right in plain view of traffic, then turn and walk away like nothing happened. It was the Wild West out there. At least thirty people watched the whole thing go down, and no one cared. Once I saw him round the corner, I came back down the street and into the alley to tell the dope boys what had happened. Unfortunately, they must have seen it, because they were already gone. They had packed up instantly and left because they couldn't risk getting robbed of their entire stash. I headed back to the car. My friend was never going to believe what just happened. It was normal for junkies to pretend like they just got robbed so they could keep the dope. I pulled some stunts sometimes, but that wasn't one of them.

I got back in the car, feeling horrible for him. That was the last of his money, and I had none either. As we drove away, I told him what happened. I don't think he ever trusted me again. That was our last ride together.

XXV.

My sickness was arriving earlier and earlier each day. I used to be able to do a shot in the afternoon and be good for over twenty-four hours, but now I was waking up sick. There's nothing more miserable than waking up every morning broke without a car, while being sick from needing and craving a substance that is forty minutes away—and knowing I still needed to find money to purchase it. Every morning meant waking up to the same nightmare all over again. I didn't want to get out of bed, but I had to before the sickness got worse. My sickness did get worse, which meant my desperation got worse, which in turn meant the actions I took to get money also got worse.

I found a new regular ride to the city from a guy in my parents' neighborhood. Pope was a hippie who wore Grateful Dead shirts, smoked weed, and listened to Clapton the whole way to the city. In spite of the whole hippie-love vibe, Pope was a dope fiend first and foremost, which meant doing whatever it took to get money to get well.

One sunny day, we were flying down I-83, excited to be nearing the exit into Druid Hill Park, when a police officer got behind us with his flashers on.

Pope handed me a bag of weed from under his seat, and said, "Help me eat this!"

It was about a quarter of an ounce of weed, and we were stuffing it into our mouths, chewing up the dry buds and leaves, and trying to swallow them down with a quarter of a bottle of Snapple that was left in the car. I finally gave up and tossed the rest of the bag back under the seat as the officer approached. It was just a speeding ticket, so no search. The party was back on. We got into Woodbrook, and the neighborhood was quiet. Nobody was out on Parkwood or Black & Whites, so we circled the block a couple of times. A guy I'd never seen before flagged us down.

"What's out?" I shouted.

"How many you need?" he asked as he approached the passenger window.

I explained to him that we want five bags, but that I need to taste it first. He leaned in to listen to me, and before I knew it, he swiped the money from under my leg, then turned to haul ass up the alley. I didn't even realize the money was visible. I always kept it tucked under my leg so no one could grab it. We were screwed. Two sick junkies, who just spent the day getting money, drove all the way to the city to cop and got beat. There was no more hopeless feeling than that, it seemed.

We had to get money somehow, and fast. His plan was to go to a nearby shopping center and do driveway purse snatchings. He said he had done it before with another guy. We went to a nearby shopping center to pull it off. He told me that he'd just ride up close to a lady, and I'd hang out the window and yank her purse off her arm. I envisioned old ladies falling in the street, or being dragged behind the car while all of their identity and money was whisked away in front of their eyes. Even I, in my desperation, couldn't follow through with this one. I told him to go back to the county, and I'd find us some money somehow. What we ended up doing wasn't much better.

I had him take me to a Rite Aid, and I stole one of the most authentic looking black water pistols I could find. Then, we went to his house and got gloves and hoodies. He wore some kind of half-mask for his face. We parked a couple of blocks away from a sno-ball stand in Bel Air, put on our attire, then crept between trees and parked cars until we were right next to the sno-ball stand. We waited until there were no customers, then I turned to him.

"Are you ready?" I asked.

He nodded, and we were off. I kicked the side door of the little wooden stand wide-open and ran inside while Pope stood in the doorway clutching what looked to be a gun in his waistband for extra effect. Two teenage girls froze, looking shocked.

"Get the fuck up against the wall!" I yelled slinging one of them into the wall. My adrenaline was surging, and I was in full character like I was robbing a federal bank.

"I'm taking all the fucking money. Turn around and face the wall!" I shouted.

As they cowered with their backs turned to us, I went to empty the cash box, then thought twice and grabbed the whole thing.

"Now count to thirty before you turn around!" I yelled as I made my way out the door.

We darted through the trees, and into the open parking lots of shopping centers in full attire, carrying the cash box. I saw two mechanics at a car shop look over at us.

One of them yelled, "Hey!"

But I kept trucking and didn't look back. We both made it to the car, dove in, and were off. Within five minutes we were on the highway headed back to the city. No one would find us down there. I counted the money. There was $76 in the box. All of that effort, and it might last two days if we were lucky. I just risked ten to fifteen years in prison for $76, and it wouldn't be the last time, by far.

One is too many, and a thousand is never enough. This is a common saying in the rooms of NA and AA. It applies to the drug or drink itself, but honestly to an addict it applies to almost everything in their life. We are obsessive, and we don't change until we self-destruct. Such was the case with the sno-ball stands. It had worked once, so why not do it again, and again, and again? That's exactly what I did. I did it so frequently that a friend (who had no idea what I was up to) notified me one day that there were now rough sketches of a guy who looked just like me hanging in all the sno-ball stands around the county.

I had the fever. I had to lay low from doing anything in Harford County for a while, so I started hitting gas stations off of the highway near the city lines. Every time, I put on a full production like I was doing a major hit somewhere important, but never actually scoring over $200 anywhere. It was always just enough to last me, and whomever was driving, a couple more days.

It wasn't long before my parents realized that I was getting high and showed no signs of stopping. I'm sure they had an idea that I was getting high sooner than that, but they likely held on to a thread of hope that maybe, just maybe, something from rehab would sink in, and I would stop. Once again, I was tossed out of the house, and I went back to hanging with Jessie on the streets.

We went to stay with some friends who lived on a little side street called Tyrone in West Baltimore. It was a raggedy old row home across from Westside shopping center. The good news for us was that we were a couple of blocks away from the nearest dope hole. But the bad news was that it was hard to get money there to get high. The majority of white people in these areas were junkies, so they were automatically watched when they entered a store. Most stores had their own security guards due to the high rate of theft. We still managed to spend our fair share of nights getting high, but I spent a few nights laying on that wooden floor dopesick—both of us sick, skin on fire, legs aching, feeling like we were in actual hell.

I couldn't take it anymore. Life down there was miserable, dark, and depressing. The couple who lived in the house were addicts, but they both had jobs. We were just intruders who sat around dopesick half the time, and we were starting to feel unwelcome. Jessie had a bed at her parents' house. The only reason she was putting herself in this messed up situation was for me. We packed up and headed back to the county, I was going to do the noble thing and fend for myself. I wanted her to go back to her parents' house as the weather was starting to get cold.

Times were changing in the city. Old dope shops closed and new ones opened. Druid Hill dried up. There was no more dope to be found over there, but we found somewhere even better. The whole Edmondson Ave was jumping. Almost every side street had a dope shop on it. I found a new favorite strip on Edmondson & Warwick and another on a small street named Lauretta. The strip was just like Parkwood back in earlier times. There were tons of various vials of raw dope being sold here for $20 each. It was even better and came in greater quantities than what we were used to getting in Druid Hill. It was the same drive-through concept though. We would pull up and get bum-rushed by many different dealers trying to push their product on us. The best part about this particular dope strip is that there was a McDonald's and a KFC just a block away, so we could run in and shoot our dope in private in the bathrooms before leaving the area.

This quickly became the new dope strip. Many times I would be down there copping and run into old friends of mine from the neighborhood I grew up in. I never even knew they got high. These were best friends of mine growing up, who I hadn't spoken to in years since we went our separate ways. Now, I had access to another group of people I could conspire with to get high and get rides to the city with.

On one occasion I saw a carload of junkies down there. I recognized the driver. It was Kim, whose house we had once stayed at until she went to rehab and the police chased us off. She was excited to see us and invited us back to her house. We accepted and met up at the same old house in the county where we had once stayed, a place where my adventure with Jessie had begun. The house was different on the interior. The graffiti had been removed, and the walls had been patched up, but otherwise the vibe was still the same.

She told us about the bloody handprint we saw smeared down the neighbor's door, which had apparently been there for two weeks now. One night, my friend Steve, who also used to live there, and another friend, Charles from Edgewood, busted in there on a rampage. Steve's ex-girlfriend, another girl, and two guys were all in the basement tripping on acid, and Steve didn't like it. They went into the basement armed with a hammer and a pool ball in a sock and beat the guys unconscious. After they left, one of the guys managed to crawl out of the basement and over to the neighbor's door. The police were called, and both men were hospitalized with severe injuries. One of them never woke up from his coma, the other hasn't been mentally normal since. Steve's parents had money, and his father was a local attorney. Somehow, he never did a single day in jail for the crime, but Charles got two years.

I'll never forget that night at Kim's house. It was my first night there in a while, and my last night to ever set foot in it. I began realizing that night just how far backward we had gone. Being in that house reminded me of when the magic began, before I became a puppet for heroin, back when I had a puppy-love crush on Jessie and thought she was the most magical creature in the world. We would sit on my bed and watch movies like *True Romance* and *Crazy Love* and cuddle with one another. Even though my life was headed nowhere then, I still had hope and childish dreams.

Now I stood across from her in Kim's upstairs bathroom, as

she waved a needle around like a mad woman wielding a knife. I was just high enough already to not be afraid of the situation in front of me. She had blown her dope earlier in the car on the way here trying to hit a vein and missed. Both of us were running short on veins. Tracks lined up and down our arms from wrist to elbow. The veins eventually stopped surfacing and would roll off the needle tip, especially since the needles we were using were so dull from repeated use. I watched as she stood there sick and plunged the needle repeatedly into her bruised arms. With each strike the needle was getting even duller, but due to her thirst for the drug, the pain just didn't matter anymore. The scabbed tracks on her arms, the bruises, the damaged veins, the bloody mixture in the needle, but most of all her anger, all combined like something out of a horror movie, as she cursed and screamed in frustration. Imagine the pain of finally getting what you need after hustling for it all day, finally getting to that blissful moment you've been waiting for to inject the magic potion to take all of your sickness and troubles away, but your own body won't cooperate with you. Her veins were worn, and the needle was old, and she couldn't seem to land on one no matter how hard she tried.

Sick and frustrated and on the verge of going mad, she reacted without thinking and plunged the needle in midair, shooting the bloody solution all across the bathroom wall. She stood there immediately regretful, insane, and hopelessly crying. All I could think about is how she just wasted all of that perfectly good heroin. I paused there, thinking about licking the bloody mixture up off of the wall hoping to absorb some. She collapsed to the floor in disbelief over what she had done. My dream girl, dance partner, and biggest crush ever lie on the floor in a heap with trails of blood trickling down her arms. She knew she wouldn't get any sleep that night without a fix.

As horrific as this all sounds, this wasn't even close to her rock bottom. There is no bottom to addiction. People talk about rock bottom, but that's just a myth. No one has seen their rock bottom. If you think it can't get any worse, go back out and shoot heroin again, it will get worse. I broke through many bottoms and did things I never thought I would do. Life can always get worse as an addict, no matter what. There are a lot of things I didn't do when presented the opportunity. I know if I go back out and shoot heroin or have a drink today, that any of those things are possible, and more.

I was living homeless in the streets of Bel Air again, hustling rides to the city, and running theft schemes at any store where I could still pull them off. I called my mother and spoke to her one day on the phone, and she said there was a lady at her church who wanted to speak to me. I got excited because I knew that sometimes churches found places for people to stay, and even gave them money. Either one was good for me at the time. The day I wandered into the church to meet this lady, I was already borderline sick. I hadn't gotten my dope for the day, and I was completely out of options.

I walked into my old church, a completely different person than the last time I had been there many years prior. I found my way to the front desk, and they rang the lady for me. Sharon came out and introduced herself as a new pastor at the church. She was a middle-aged, black lady with a warm demeanor and a soft smile. I was instantly drawn to her. We walked back to her office and talked a while. I was honest for the most part. When she asked what I needed most, I told her I needed a place to stay, knowing that money was off the table given my drug problem. She said she would look into a few things, but for now she wanted to pray for me. I gladly accepted her prayers—I needed them. I prayed every night while I was high for a way out of this addiction. On the nights when I was sober, I was too sick to think about quitting.

We prayed. She said she would look into some resources and asked that I get back in touch with her. For now, she said she had gift certificates and coupons from various local restaurants, if I would wait while she went to retrieve them. Of course, I would. She got up and left me in her office by myself. I immediately jumped up and started going through her things, looking in her desk drawers, hoping to find some cash or jewelry. The only thing of value I found was her personal checkbook. I quickly tore out a check and stuffed it in my pocket before she reentered the office. She handed me some $10 gift cards for a couple of fast food restaurants, we hugged, and I walked out of the church.

I left feeling more hopeless than when I walked in. Hopeless, not because she didn't give me a place to stay, but hopeless because no one was off limits to me anymore. *What have I become? Stealing from a Pastor? She was trying to help me and pray over me, and I stole from her.* I felt sick, but I had to get well. I had to push it out of my mind and keep moving.

XXVI.

As soon as I left the church, I got in touch with Jessie. She had a ride lined up to go to the city with Steve. She was meeting him at 6:00pm at a shopping center and had only enough money for herself and him. I took it upon myself to just show up and intercept them before they headed downtown. I couldn't get stuck out here sick, no way. I got to the shopping center an hour early and waited on the curb for them to arrive. When Steve pulled up, he looked frustrated to see me. I wondered if he was trying to have Jessie all to himself.

"Look, just let me ride along," I said. "Just get me out the gate. I'll find a way to get some money."

He wasn't budging. If I didn't have my own money, I couldn't go along.

Then I remembered the check in my pocket, "I've got money for us all to get high, plus gas," I said. "Just take me to cash this ch…"

I stopped myself. Something inside of me couldn't go through with it. I couldn't do that to the lady, not a pastor. I clutched the check in my pocket tight and balled it up in my palm, my eyes welling up. *Tonight will be a long night alone.* I turned and walked away, as they drove off toward freedom.

I sat around the shopping center hopeless. I had absolutely

nowhere to turn and not a dollar to my name. I don't recall what led me there, but I sought refuge about a half mile up the street from Jessie's house at an apartment building to keep dry. I walked in and went down to the bottom level in search of a laundry room to sleep in. I had done it before in other complexes. Laundry rooms and post offices were two places I knew that were generally warm and open twenty-four hours. One night, I had slept in a post office all night drunk. I was huddled up on the floor in the early morning hours as people stepped over me to get to their PO boxes.

There was no laundry room here, but I found a door on the bottom floor with no apartment letter on it, and it was unlocked. It was an electrical and storage room. Lucky for me, nothing was currently stored there. There was even a light switch and outlets in the walls. I couldn't wait to tell Jessie about this. I curled up into a ball with my coat on in the dark corner and tried my best to sleep. Hours ticked by, as I tossed and turned, legs kicking, skin crawling. I slept for maybe fifteen minutes at a time here and there in between fits of flailing myself around in misery all night long. When the morning finally came, I snuck out of the electrical room and walked a mile down to McDonald's to brush my teeth, apply deodorant and hair gel, and wash my face in the bathroom sink. Then I killed time until it was safe to go to Jessie's. I walked into her house and sat on her couch to watch TV, feeling miserable. She was still feeling fine from the night before, but I was starting to feel symptoms of heavy withdrawal. I sat next to her writhing inside while she relaxed, watching TV and waiting on the phone to ring with a plan.

Jessie was fun, and she was female, so people called her to go downtown just to hang out. I, on the other hand, was a common nuisance because I was Jessie's man, and therefore stood in the way of them getting anything in return from her for their kindness. God only knows what she told them to lead them on to give her free rides and dope. I didn't want to think about it. She tried to comfort me on the couch and reached into my pants. Almost as soon as she touched me, I ejaculated abruptly. I had never experienced anything like it before, but she knew I was ill, so I wasn't even embarrassed.

Heroin numbs your body and your feelings, both physical and emotional for so long, that when you experience withdrawal, they all come back to you tenfold. Physical sensations are magnified immensely. Anything sexual causes almost immediate release. The only times I ever had wet dreams in my life were during periods of heroin withdrawal, and sometimes twice in one night. It's not even pleasurable. It's more of an uncomfortable, messy feeling than anything else. Emotions come flooding back as well. Fear and anxiety are intensified, as is sadness. I could be cold and callous in the face of anything that would normally stir up my emotions, but when I would go through withdrawal, I became a sobbing ball of tears. It was scary to be normal and have feelings again.

We managed to go downtown and get high that day. There was a spot on Edmondson and Pulaski Street that was my new favorite. They had $40 miniature amber glass jugs of some of the strongest raw dope that I had ever come across. This dope was called "Diamond in the Raw." It was by far the best product to get if you had the money for it. I got familiar with the dealers' names and looks, and I started taking other county kids down there. Jessie and I turned my electrical room into a dope-fiend apartment. She snuck me down blankets and a pillow from her house, and I stole a miniature alarm clock radio. We stayed there, smoking cigarettes, listening to the radio, making love and cuddling for two days straight off of a good batch of Diamond in the Raw.

The next day I had to get up early to go to court, but I was nervous that I was going to jail. I wanted to press for a postponement. I set the alarm and woke up early, kissed Jessie goodbye and walked two miles into town to the courthouse. When I showed up, I saw my father there in the courtroom.

"What are you doing here?" I asked.

"I just wanted to make sure you showed up. You're still out on our bail, you know," he replied.

I sat down and waited for my turn in front of the judge. When my name was called, I explained to the judge that this case was being combined with my other cases, and that I needed a postponement for the same date as my other trials. This is what my attorney had instructed me to tell the judge. The judge agreed to do so, and I was free to go.

As I turned to walk away, I heard my father's voice say loudly, "Wait, your honor!"

I froze in my tracks. The judge asked him what was wrong, and he said that he would like to revoke my bail. He proceeded to tell the judge that I no longer lived at home, and he didn't know where I was staying, and that I was using drugs.

The judge shocked me, but made perfect sense, when he replied to my father, "Sir, the reason for a bail is to guarantee that a person shows up to court. Now I understand that you don't know where your son lives, and that he may be on drugs, but it looks as if he's still responsible enough to show up to court. I'm going to have to deny your motion to revoke his bail."

With that, I spun around and continued out of the door.

My father scowled at me, "I hope your happy you won."

It wasn't about winning at that point, it was about survival. I actually felt horrible and broken-hearted for my father, watching the Judge deny his motion. I could feel his frustration and hopelessness, but I wasn't ready to face jail and dopesickness at the same time, though I knew it would come eventually.

Jessie got her job back waiting tables at Red Lobster. She was working a lot of day shifts, so she stopped spending the night with me in the electrical room. She would still come hang out, but kiss me goodnight and head home. I rarely saw her over the next several days. And the next week was hell on Earth. There were downpours every single day for a solid week, and Jessie wasn't around. I would wake up and leave the apartment building every morning and walk a mile in the pouring, cold rain to McDonald's for my morning hygiene routine, then I would walk another two miles in the rain to the Harford Mall—shoes, coat, and clothes completely drenched. I was a sorry sight sulking through the streets of Bel Air.

The rain was so horrible that strangers stopped and gave me rides on several occasions. Once I explained that I was homeless, they generally gave me anywhere from five to twenty dollars. I would hang around the mall all day working on ways to get more money and eventually a ride. I would scour the sidewalks and parking lots for dropped cash receipts. I'd dry them out, locate the store and item on the receipt, steal the item, and return it with the receipt for cash. Finding a ride to the city was the hardest part. Nobody wanted to drive to the city in that kind of weather, even for fifty bucks. I remember calling my little brother one time and convincing him that I needed to go down to get some weed. I had him park down the street while I hopped out of the car and copped heroin around the corner.

On about the fifth rainy day in a row, I was weary. I was sick of the rain and sick of scraping all day long just to get well. I wanted to die. There had to be a way out. My life was a never-ending series of disappointments and failures laced with pain and anxiety. Every day was the same miserable quest to get a drug that wouldn't even get me high anymore. I had to rob and steal just to feel normal for a few hours, and then the sickness would start creeping back in. I couldn't think of a more miserable existence. I had to end it. I didn't want to be sick on the streets anymore, and I certainly didn't want to be sick in jail.

I was too much of a coward to take my life in any painful way. So, I cried out to God daily on my walks, my tears blending with the rain. The whole world cried with me. I was caught in a rainstorm inside and outside of myself, and I needed it to stop. I determined to make it end once and for all the only way I knew out, the easy way...death by dope.

I stopped to rest about a half mile from the apartment, to smoke under the overhang of a store called C-Mart. I had to find a plan and an easier way. There had to be something I could do. I stood there smoking, when an employee came out front and lit up a cigarette. I recognized him from high school. It was Cody, always a good kid in school, but he was cool. I reintroduced myself, and we started chatting. Turned out, he was the manager of the store. I wanted to try to work out some kind of hustle with him at the store without letting him know I was a junkie. Then I decided just to drop it on him.

"Do you get high?" I asked.

"Yeah sometimes," he said.

I told him I meant high on dope, not weed. He said that he knew what I was asking, and that he'd done it several times before with some friends. They loved it, but didn't know where to get it. This was perfect, I told him that, not only could I get him the best stuff in the city, but I could get enough money to treat us all, the only thing I needed was a ride. He told me he was off work in an hour, and if I met him at his house, he would get us the ride that I needed. He gave me all I needed from there, and it was set.

I killed time at McDonald's for about an hour, then walked a couple miles into the back of the suburban single-family home neighborhoods of Forest Hill until I found Cody's house. I rang the bell, and he let me in. He already had his friends there, two other guys and a girl. The driver was a light-skinned black kid named Chris. Chris' girlfriend was Roseanne, and the other kid named Zeke looked the youngest of all. I told them to trust me, if they would just take me to White Marsh Mall, I would get enough money to get all of us high and put gas in the car. They agreed, and off we went on an adventure.

When we got to the mall, I asked them to sit in the parking lot of JCPenney be patient—and to please not leave me there. I told Cody to go in and get a JCPenney bag even if he had to pay for it and meet me back at the car. I went in and headed straight for the men's dress clothes section. I found a suit that was priced at just over $100, took it off the hanger, rolled the pants tightly, then the blazer, and stuffed them in my waist and exited the store. Once I got back to the car, I climbed in and took the suit from my waist. I put it into the bag Cody had gotten. Then I convinced Roseanne to go in to any cashier and return the suit.

I emphasized, "Do not settle for store credit!"

She came back out smiling twenty minutes later with $115 cash in hand, climbed in, and handed me the money. I hadn't been this happy in a few weeks. I was brimming with excitement and nobody knew why, but me.

I was going to get the highest I had ever gotten in my life, and if I didn't wake up, I didn't care. This was the end of the road, a lifeless waste finally gone and out of everybody's way. I would finally be free, free from sickness, free from hurting other people, and free from being a burden on this world and everyone who loved me. I guided them into the city and took them straight to Edmondson and Pulaski to cop some Diamond in the Raw.

When the hitter came up to the window, I held up two fingers. He took the money, and a young boy on a bicycle came up and handed me the two jugs of raw heroin. I guided Chris to take the car over to the KFC parking lot and park in a dark corner. I pulled out one of the $40 jugs and handed it back to Cody.

"There, that's for you guys if you want to get high."

They decided to wait to sniff it when they got back to the

county. I told them that I couldn't possibly wait. I laid down low in my seat, knowing that they had never seen anything like this, and I was putting on a show for them. I felt a little evil having them watch the last stages of my life play out like this, as I dumped the entire jug of raw heroin into the spoon and cooked it up. I drew it up in the needle, planted it in my arm, and pushed it halfway in. I waited a second and pushed it the rest of the way, and I was gone.

Forty-five minutes later, my eyes cracked open. I was still in the passenger seat. We were parked in front of Cody's house all the way out in the county.

"Holy shit! Are you alright?" Chris asked.

"We thought you were gone!" Cody said from the back.

I looked down. The front of my shirt was all wet. I was covered in sweat. They told me I had gone unconscious and started seizing and flopping around like a fish in the seat, and that I was foaming out of my mouth. They said they were scared that I had died on them. I thought that was too good to be true. In the back of my mind, I wondered what they would have done if I had died. Granted, they did absolutely nothing when they thought I had died. We went into Cody's house, and they split the other $40 vial four ways between them, sniffing their little portions. We shot a couple of games of pool and played some music. Cody, Roseanne, and Zeke went out to smoke on the front porch while Chris and I finished up a game of pool. Roseanne came down a few minutes later in a huff. She said both of them had fallen asleep out front in the rocking chairs. We all went out front to smoke and to laugh at them. As we got out onto the front porch, I saw Cody's head laying slack into his chest and heard an odd snoring sound coming from him.

"Wake him up!" I shouted.

I had heard that sound before, the "death rattle," and it is not a good sign. Chris shook him, then slapped him a few times in the face. Cody woke up and fell forward out of the chair. He was okay though, and we got a good laugh out of it. I suggested that we wake Zeke up too, just in case, although he didn't look half as bad. The problem was that Zeke wouldn't wake up.

We crowded around him on the porch in the middle of suburbia, yelling for him to wake up, slapping him, and shaking him…but nothing. He was still breathing, but it sounded extremely labored. I had no idea what I was doing or even what to do at that point.

"Lie him down on flat ground," I said quickly, running up the steps to help them carry him out of the chair.

We laid him in the grass in Cody's front yard, and I told Roseanne to go inside and grab a glass of ice water. Everybody else was in a frenzy, going crazy with fear. I had no idea what I was doing, but I felt like the self-appointed leader of this group. I kneeled down and listened for a breath, and heard nothing. I performed CPR, exactly the way I had always seen it done on TV, breathed through his mouth a few times and then pumped his chest a few times, then repeat. Roseanne came back out, and I instructed her to pour the cold water over his face. I repeated the sequence again, and he came back to life, delirious, but alive. Everyone breathed a huge sigh of relief. That was a close call.

The party was over at that point. Things had gotten serious, and nobody was having fun anymore. They agreed that they should do something with Zeke. They got him to his feet and walked him to the car, but he could barely stand on his own.

"Thank you so much," they said, followed by, "What do you think we should do?"

I advised them to get him to a hospital, not to worry about getting in trouble, that they wouldn't be arrested.

"No way. Our parents will kill us!" they said.

I shrugged my shoulders and walked off into the night. Funny how life happens sometimes. I set out to kill myself and instead

I ended up saving someone else's life. I walked home three or four miles by myself, peaceful and content in the night, looking up at the stars in a clear sky. I was a loner, always would be. I preferred it that way. I could have gotten a ride back with them, but I wanted this walk and this time alone, as long as I was high enough to appreciate it, this world wasn't so bad after all.

The next morning, I woke up feeling okay. For once, I wasn't waking up ill. I wanted to embrace the feeling and get a jumpstart on the day so I didn't have to do my dirt when the illness started kicking in. I walked straight down to the payphone to call my new friends. Cody picked up after a couple rings.

"Hey, what's up bro?" I said.

"What's up?" he echoed back.

"You guys wanna go down again, or is it too soon?" I asked, crossing my fingers.

The reply was short and unexpected, "Dude, Zeke died last night."

I paused, then smiled, "Stop fucking with me. You wanna go down or not?"

His reply wasn't a joke, "Dude, I'm serious, he's dead. He's fucking dead. His mom found him in the middle of the night in his bed, dead."

"Oh my God. I'm sorry to hear that…" I trailed off, and my stomach dropped to the ground.

Whatever his reply was, I didn't hear it. The world stopped spinning for a second. *How could God let this happen? Why would this happen?* I was a homeless junkie, piece of shit, who deserved to die and wanted nothing more than to die, and I couldn't even do it when I tried. Yet, here was this good kid, good student, good grades, only eighteen years old, who had his whole life ahead of him. He had only tried heroin a couple times. I shot the entire jug of raw dope, and they divided theirs into four parts and sniffed it. *Why is he the one who died?* I silently screamed at God. *Why does he get the easy way out?* My family wouldn't miss me. All my friends were junkies, so they definitely wouldn't miss me or even care. I had no future, literally nothing, and yet I helped kill that poor kid instead of myself. This was literally hell on Earth..

Nothing got better. Naturally, my life only spiraled further into misery. I got so desperate that I began to despise myself, I couldn't even kill myself correctly. It was as if I was being tortured by being kept alive while everyone else around me died. I was a leech, and my addiction knew no bounds. When we first started, we had rules, such as only steal from corporations and retail chains, never from Mom and Pop stores. Or, never steal from or hurt the people you know personally. None of these boundaries even mattered anymore. I was like a vampire who needed blood from the community around me in order to fulfill my thirst, and even then, I was only okay for just one more day until the thirst for more blood returned.

At that moment I found myself standing at the counter of a 7-Eleven with a handful of change to buy a pack of cigarettes, when I noticed a donation jar for a foundation for children with muscular dystrophy. I didn't pay attention to what it was. I'm not sure in my closed-off little world that I even knew what muscular dystrophy was. I just knew that what I was about to do was extremely wrong and defied any bit of moral fiber I had left within me, but I didn't care. There was money in there that I needed to get well. I stuffed the jar under my armpit inside of my coat when the clerk turned his back to get my cigarettes, and then I quickly exited the store after he handed them to me. There was almost $60 in there. I was happy. I had secured my ride downtown, so I couldn't think about the low I had just reached. Heroin would make all those feelings go away soon enough.

I got back that night and the door to the electrical room was locked. I was expecting this to happen eventually. One thing I knew for certain about life was that everything changes. And in my experience, good things never lasted. The life of an addict is constantly changing, and surely wasn't meant to be easy. I struggled with the lock trying to break in until eventually I had to give up and walk away. I walked off into the night wondering where I would go now. I wandered for about a half mile until I found another apartment community. I went inside one of the buildings. I found a door that led to a small concrete platform underneath the stairwell. I climbed inside and curled up to sleep with my coat still on. I was hardly able to sleep because the concrete was so cold and hard, and I couldn't even extend my legs, but I did my best. My daily hell awaited me in the morning.

There were a couple 7-Elevens in the area, and I assumed they all had similar donation canisters, so I visited one a day. On the third day, I had walked all the way into the town of Bel Air and had some friends meet me at the 7-Eleven there. I walked out with a donation jar under my coat and went around back to check how much money was in it and dispose of the container in the dumpster. When I got to the back and twisted off the cap, there was eight measly dollars of change in there. I sighed and tossed the jar into the dumpster. That wasn't going to get me a ride downtown. My friends would go without me. I had them meet me there before they left to head down because I was sure I'd get at least $20 out of the container. I sighed and trudged back around the corner of the building. Then I did, I walked right into the police who were there waiting for me while they interrogated my friends.

The officers were disgusted with me, and rightfully so. I was disgusted with myself. They asked me where the jar and the money were. I tried to deny it, but they had camera footage of me. Not only camera footage of what I had just done, but they collected camera footage from the previous two days at the other 7-Elevens. At that point, I relinquished control.

There was no fight left in me. I couldn't die If I tried to, so maybe jail was the only place I belonged. They handcuffed me, walked me to the back of the police car, and I watched as my friends climbed into their car and took off for the city. It was painful to watch, and even more painful to think about. I was headed for a long road of sickness and despair, and they were headed into the warm awaiting arms of heroin.

XXVII.

It's a gut-wrenching feeling to reenter the jail I swore I would never come back to—time and time again—the sound of the steel doors sliding behind me, the smell of the cheap state supplied soap and cleaning supplies, the feelings of permanence and complete helplessness, especially after several hours in holding cells when finally, the commissioner sets a bail that no one will pay.

Today, I can confidently say that jail saved my life on more than one occasion, though you couldn't tell me anything good about it back then. I had been locked up several times, but at the age of nineteen, this was my first time being locked up sober. Usually, I spent my first day or two sleeping off a massive high. There's something both awakening and chilling to the core about being taken in when the onset of withdrawal is already upon you.

Heightened sensitivity and awareness plagued me as I was paraded through the bright white lights of booking to get my picture taken. I stood there covered in goose bumps, shaking and yawning, as they snapped pictures of my lifeless caricature of a face. I was escorted back to the showers, my skin burning and sweating one minute, then flushing over ice cold the next, and told to undress while a guard in full uniform watched. I barely had the energy to inhale and exhale, or the motivation to do so, but I followed orders, as I stood there naked and ashamed.

"Lift your right foot. Now spread your toes. Next, lift your left foot and do the same. Bend over. Now cough. Lift up your ball sack. Hold your arms up. Run your fingers through your hair. Now open your mouth, and lift your tongue. Okay, now move it side-to-side. Okay, finished. Hold out your hands."

They'd squirt lice shampoo into my hands and tell me I had five minutes to shower. I'd stand there in the shower, too tired to cry. I lavished every second of that hot shower water as it rinsed off every last remnant of the outside world because I knew it would be the last time I'd have a moment to myself in a long time. Once I exited the shower, I was freezing. It was a chill that stuck with me for a long time. I smelled like the facility that I was now a resident of. I blended in. I was now the property of the county.

In black and white stripes and orange rubber shower slippers, yet again, I walked through a series of steel doors, one shutting before the other opened. Guards walked me down a series of long hallways. I stepped into a sally port, and as one door slid shut, I waited for the final one to open, to release me into the unknown. On the other side of the door were twenty men, waiting to see who would walk in. I stepped into the dorm and everything stopped: it was all eyes on me. It was dirty, crowded, and loud. I heard shouts of "new guy" or "fresh meat" joking around, and as an addict, I hoped it was just jokes. The last thing anyone wants to do is defend himself while dopesick. The toughest guys on the street become prey when they're going through withdrawal. Likewise, sometimes the toughest guys in jail are nobodies on the street. It's a whole different world. The first thing I did was scan the room in hopes of seeing some familiar faces. Not this time.

I found an open top bunk and made my bed up. I climbed in, sat back, and surveyed my surroundings. This promised to be an extremely long couple of days of pain and misery. I tried hard not to cry, which meant I had to keep myself away from the phone. I had to call Jessie though, I couldn't fathom being away from her for any period of time. Maybe she could even put together bail money with her cash from waiting tables. I hopped down when the phones cleared up. I would wait to call my parents. I was too ashamed to tell them where I was again. I dialed Jessie…no answer. I called Jessie several more times, still no answer. Over the next few days, I tried again and again. Finally, once I talked to her, she told me I had to quit calling there because her parents were getting angry and taking it out on her.

Later, I found out through a letter from a friend that Jessie had moved on to another man a few days after I got locked up. It's a dog-eat-dog world out there. I knew this was bound to happen, but still I couldn't accept it. My insides turned, and I fell into one of the darkest places my soul has ever been. I went through withdrawals from Jessie in that jail worse than heroin withdrawal, and my dopesickness was bad. My bones ached, my legs kicked all night, my skin was ablaze and my bedroll was drenched in sweat. I couldn't sleep, I couldn't read, and sometimes I felt as if I couldn't breathe. I only thought about Jessie, our life together, and our adventures. I daydreamed about getting high, and I dreamt at night about getting high. I dreamt with my eyes closed, but my mind awake, kicking sheets, hugging my blanket and begging God for mercy, and for sleep. Neither ever came.

My second day in, I was called to the front by some correctional officers.

"Mr. McGhee, some homicide detectives are here to see you."

Was this a joke? My heart was beating out of my chest. *What have I done that I don't remember?* I was already in the throes of dopesickness and anxiety. This was a cruel joke. I entered a room where two detectives sat across from me with grave expressions on their faces. I sat down across from them.

"So, you know, Mr. McGhee, we're here about Zeke. We're

told that you sold him the heroin that killed him, but the stories we've gotten are mixed and not that clear. So, we would like to hear your side of the story."

I could not go down for murder. That could not be how my story ended. I was terrified, so I told them the truth. Quite matter-of-fact, I explained to them how we all went downtown together to get high, that I was only an addict and not a dealer, and that I had handed the money through the window to the dealer and bought the heroin for us.

Their reply was, "That's kind of what we figured. Thank you for your time. We'll be in touch if we need you."

That was it? I felt like they were being truthful with me, but this was just one more worry that would loom in my everyday thoughts. It was bad enough that I felt a thousand pounds of guilt on me for what had happened to that young boy. I simply couldn't imagine doing a sentence for murder.

The jail didn't even give me a Tylenol for withdrawal, not that it would have helped, but they literally gave me nothing. They called me out to Medical three times a day for a vital check because they knew the severity of the symptoms I was going through, but they offered me nothing to ease them. I wouldn't die on their watch, that's all they cared about. Heroin withdrawal, as horrible as it is, will not kill you. It is a major physical withdrawal, more than any other drug, however it cannot kill you. Alcohol, and possibly complications from Benzos, are the only drug withdrawals a person can die from.

I laid in that top bunk for a few days straight and only came down for meals, but one night I rolled over and looked right into the eyes of a familiar face. It was Leon, the guy who stole his parents' checkbook and took us downtown when I shot heroin for the first time. We hit it off right away. We reminisced over drug stories and people we knew in common. As bad as I felt, it was slightly comforting just to have a friend and a familiar face next to me. He was leaving in two days though, so our reunion would be short-lived. He kept talking about how he was going to get high when he got out, and I told him how insane that was. I was done. I wasn't getting high when I got out. There's no way I could go through this again for the rest of my life. He was adamant. Maybe he had some secret clue to life that I had missed out on. How could you look forward to getting out just to get high again?

The more I thought about it though, the more I understood. It was simple. Just the thought of taking the responsibility to stay clean and not come back to jail was overwhelming. How could we trust ourselves to do it? To a non-addict it may sound easy, but to an addict it is a trillion tons of pressure. Even if I managed to get out and stay clean for any extended period of time, it wouldn't matter how many steps or precautions I took, how much success I attained or work I put in to it, one single moment of weakness, one split-second poor decision could ruin it all. That's a massive amount of stress to walk around with.

It makes being released from jail or prison absolutely terrifying. Submitting to the drug was the easy way out, but it made getting released much less scary. Maybe Leon had it figured out, either way I couldn't give up so easily. Leon was released, and we hugged goodbye as he left. Several days later, word made it back to the jail that he had overdosed and died on his second day out. God rest his broken soul. Leon was finally free.

Time went by, and I got my weight up in jail. I was eating as much as possible and working out every day. I was still a small guy though, maybe around 135 pounds. My attitude came back, and I became the fighter I was before the heroin. A couple of brothers I knew from Edgewood came to the dorm. I established myself. We fought a few times, and I won. I became comfortable, and jail started to feel like a home to me, a nasty, smelly, boring home, but I made the best of it.

I'll never forget the day Steve came in. It was the day before my big court date. Steve and I grew up together down the street from each other and our lives intersected repeatedly over the years. When he came in, I was guiding a couple of brothers through a workout routine. He was excited to see me. I found out that he had just left the padded room for suicide watch, and he told them that the only way he would go back into population is if he was placed in a dorm with me. I couldn't believe they granted his request.

He was doing dope a couple of years before I started, so I imagined his withdrawal must've been hell. He wasn't cut out for jail. He always acted tough and did some crazy things like beating that guy with the pool ball in the sock. But outside of that incident, it was usually just to show off for the rest of us. He watched how I interacted with the other inmates. This was my dorm. I did what I wanted, I talked shit, I used the word "nigga" freely with the black folks in there and practically was one of them. I could tell he envied it, but he was brand new in the dorm, and it just wasn't in his persona.

The morning after he arrived, I went to my big court date for all of my combined cases. When I came back, Steve was gone. I was told that he started mouthing off while I was gone, and used the word "nigga." He got beaten up badly and taken out. I felt bad, but how could he think it was okay to come in on a brand new dorm and act like that while I'm not there to defend him? That was the last time I ever saw Steve.

His folks were wealthy, so they got him out of jail and admitted into a fancy rehab program down in Boca Raton, Florida. He did well in there for a little while, and then something happened. He was found nodding out in a pickup truck in a parking lot back up in Bel Air. When police searched the vehicle, they locked him up for a quarter ounce of weed. After almost two days in jail, they ran the tags to the truck and found out that it belonged to his roommate in the program down in Florida. They had officers down there go to the house, and they found his roommate stabbed to death forty-five times. For whatever reason, Steve had killed his roommate, stolen his truck, and driven sixteen hours straight into Baltimore to buy heroin. He's now doing life in Florida without possibility of parole. His father couldn't save him from that one.

XXVIII.

At my court date, I received one year in the Harford County Detention Center. I leaned over and asked my attorney to ask the judge for work release, and he granted it. Once I was sentenced, they moved me to a nice unit with two-man cells, and I worked desperately to find a job through the work release classifieds within the jail. I had been in for a few months at this point and had gotten my health back. I recommitted my focus on changing my life. I participated in Bible studies with other inmates and attended meetings on addiction and recovery in the jail. I quickly became passionate about life and living right, as was customary when I was in a position that I was practically forced to. There were other groups of inmates who constantly talked about getting high and illegal things they planned to do, but I kept my distance from them. I didn't want any more pain. I couldn't understand why anyone else did.

I got word back from the McDonald's up the street from the jail that they would be pulling me in two weeks for work release. It wasn't the ideal job, but I'd be thrilled to work anywhere and get out of that jail and have fresh air. I could save up money for a place to stay, and gain some real-world experience to prepare for my eventual release. As the days passed while I waited for work release, something changed within me. All it took was one evil thought to enter my subconscious, and it would begin to plague me and eat me alive, day after day. Freedom meant that I could go downtown. Going downtown meant that I could taste heroin one more time. I laid on my bunk day and night, daydreaming about what it would be like to feel the freedom, satisfaction, and excitement of going down to the city with a wad of cash on me, and how hard that dope would hit me after all of this time without it. It was an inane thought, pointless and self-destructive.

I lay on my bunk in tears praying that it would go away and leave me alone. But there it was, day and night, eating away at the pit of my stomach. I didn't want work release anymore. The bile in my stomach was causing me to throw up, and my nerves grew raw the closer I got to being called downstairs for work release. I tried talking with the other inmates, and they reasoned with me the only way they knew how, by telling me that those thoughts were stupid, and that I was an idiot if I messed up work release.

I already knew that. I was reaching out for help everywhere, but nobody could help me except myself. The problem was that I was my own worst enemy. I hated myself because I was spineless in the face of heroin. I had three months clean now. I was supposed to be strong. After all, I did everything I was supposed to do, and now I was getting a second chance at life. I knew I was going to screw it up. I almost cancelled my work release, then I reasoned that cancelling it was almost just as cowardly as going downtown and screwing it up by getting high. I couldn't avoid the outside world forever, although I wanted to. As much as I hated jail, I feared the outside world much more, because I hated who I had become in it. At least in jail, I was a better version of myself. I was terrified of freedom, well not exactly freedom, but my response to it.

I was moved downstairs to a work release dorm. These dorms were just like the first ones I had been in upstairs, except that people left at all hours of the morning and came back at night in their normal street clothes. They had just thirty minutes after returning to change into their black and white stripes. It would be a few days down here until I would leave for my first day of work at McDonald's. I had to lay around in my own anxiety and watch as people left for work all day and then came back at night excited about their experiences from the day. I noticed immediately a couple of young guys who came back high. All the telltale signs…eyes pinned out, scratching and nodding out. I wondered how they weren't caught, or even noticed by the guards, and I lay there envious, daydreaming sick thoughts. I wondered to myself, if I bit into their neck like a vampire, would their blood get me high? I'd lie in my bunk and write poetry about my sickness and my sick thoughts relating to it. I was on the verge of tasting freedom for the first time in months, but it was truly one of the darkest places I'd ever been.

I went out for work release at 5:00am and started my first day at McDonald's. I stopped at a gas station on the way and bought a pack of Newports. It was my first cigarette in three months, and it was a completely unnecessary evil. It made me nauseous, but I kept smoking. I went to work and learned the ropes, and I hated it. It was better than sitting in jail though. The world is an extremely small place. When I arrived for my first day, there was another familiar face there: Nick, the first guy I ever went to the city with, the first one to ever give me heroin. He was not only working there, but was also on work release in another dorm, and was dating one of the managers there. It was as if everything always lined up perfectly to point me in the wrong direction.

My third day out was the day after Thanksgiving. My mother met me at the Park-n-Ride on my way back to jail from the McDonald's in her minivan with a plate of leftovers. I sat in the van with her and ate. I tried my best to enjoy the moment, but I was dying inside because I was going to let them down yet again, and they didn't even know it yet. I was already committed. When my paycheck came, I had plans to head downtown. It made me sick to think about the sadness and pain I'd cause, but no amount of willpower could deter me from my personal commitment to self-destruction.]

The McDonald's was a half a mile from the detention center, about a ten-minute walk, but they gave us thirty minutes to travel back and forth. I would climb up an embankment underneath an overpass and smoke cigarettes before I had to go back in. This was also where I stashed my cigarettes. The lead manager there would often break the rules and let the work release guys out a couple of hours early on payday or special occasions in order to handle whatever business we needed to attend to. The day before payday, I told Nick my plan, and he gave me some money to score him some dope as well. I charged him $40 for $20 of dope because I would definitely need ride money.

The next day, when I got out for work release, it was snowing. The snow was coming down pretty hard. I chomped at the bit all day, stomach turning in knots waiting for the end of my shift to go on my adventure. I called around to local cab companies during my shift, and got ahold of Big Ben. I'd used Big Ben before. He was an older, heavy-set, black man who took his job very seriously. His cab was lined with CB radios, radar detectors, and police scanners. It looked like a space shuttle control panel from the driver's seat. Ben was also cool with the hustle. I had used him before to go back and forth to the city to cop dope. He said because of the snowy weather, he wouldn't make a round-trip to the city for less than $120. My paycheck was $190, but whatever. I didn't care, I was already committed. The manager cut me loose three hours early, and I walked out in my uniform into the snow. Big Ben was there in his van waiting.

"Take me to Westside," I said.

The whole ride downtown, I loathed myself. The excitement was gone. I had crossed the threshold, and there was nothing left but panic attacks and nausea. I had gone too far to turn back. I was a complete failure. I tried hard to dissuade the anxiety and be in the moment, but it ate at me the whole ride down. I could hardly breathe in the back seat of the cab until we pulled up on a snowy Warwick and Lauretta. It was a ghetto winter wonderland, a snowy ghost town. Nobody was on the corner…I was afraid of that. The weather was keeping them in. *There has to be somebody out somewhere though.* We pulled down the street to the corner of Wheeler, and there were a couple teenagers hanging out.

"Anything out?" I yelled out of the window.

"Yeah, how many you need?" was the response.

I told him three, and he pulled three vials of brown rock out of his mouth that were tucked between his cheek and gum. I gave him $60, then looked down. *Wait a minute.* Something didn't look right. I tapped a vial onto my palm and licked the substance. It was fake. It confused me because the teens didn't even disappear. They went right back to the corner. I tried it again.

"Fuck!" I said to Ben, "I just got burned!"

His response shocked me, "Not in my car, you didn't. Give me that!"

I handed him the vials, unsure what he would do. I knew he was strapped. He kept a gun on display in a shoulder holster.

He hopped his three-hundred-pound body out of the driver's seat and yelled, "Hey!" as he approached the boys.

I lost sight of him in the rearview at that point, but sat there with my fingers crossed. He came back to the van moments later and handed me back my $60, "Be careful from now on."

I guided him up to Edmondson and Pulaski, and there was a young child, maybe nine years old on a bicycle on the corner.

"What you want?" he asked when we pulled up.

I was tempted to ignore him, but I took a shot in the dark, "Is anybody out around here?"

I couldn't believe when he replied, "Yeah me. Diamond in the Raw. What you need?" He was a child, practically a baby. I couldn't believe it. "Let me see," I said.

He pulled out a couple big vials of chunky brown rocks.

"I'll take both of those," I replied, and the exchange was made. There was no doubt it was real, and not only real, but some of the best. I had never bought off of a child that young before. Why was he even out there alone? There had to be eyes on him at all times, I hoped. I had already gotten a pack of needles the day before at Rite Aid, and kept them stashed, so I was ready to go when I scored. I leaned back in Ben's taxi, just out of the sight of his rearview. I put the dope in me, and it all came rushing back in. The warmth was there. The anxiety and fear were gone, and the terror disappeared. Nothing mattered anymore. I had Ben drop me off up the street from the jail, so I could stash everything under the overpass. Then, I walked back to the jail.

I was blasted, but somehow the guards didn't notice. They strip searched me and then sent me back to the dorm. There I sat in oblivion, in full view of everyone else in the dorm. At one point, somebody woke me up to tell me that I was going to get myself busted and the whole dorm raided. I had nodded out upside down on my bottom bunk with my body on the bunk and the top of my head touching the floor. I didn't even care. I was empty inside, the way I longed to be.

The next morning, when I left for work release, I went straight to the underpass. I was still high from the night before, but I couldn't wait. I had to do another small shot before work. I dumped some of Nick's vial into mine and brought his half of a vial into work with me to give to him. I warned him about the potency before I handed it to him. Nick went into the McDonald's bathroom, and I went in the kitchen to work. I didn't think anything of it until almost forty-five minutes had passed with no sight of him. Right as the realization hit me, there was a commotion by the bathroom. A customer had gone into the restroom and seen Nick's legs sprawled out on the floor under the stall door. An ambulance was called, but Nick was okay. He was borderline overdosed, but he was coherent. The dope had knocked him out hard, and he had nodded out and hit the floor.

Despite his dating relationship with the manager, there was nothing that could be done at this point. They had the courtesy to dispose of the dope, so he wouldn't catch a new charge. But nevertheless, the jail was notified, and he was taken back and removed from work release. I knew they had to know who supplied it to him. I waited for the repercussions. That night when I returned to the jail, the entire work release unit was hit with random urinalyses. Of course, I failed. I was taken back upstairs to medium-security immediately. All the guys there shook their heads to see me come back so soon. After only two days of using, I looked like a different person. My skin was pale and extremely broken out from stress and the impurities in the drug. It had turned me back into a zombie in just forty-eight hours. At least I was back in a safe place now.

I finished out the remaining six months of my sentence. Once again, I was fully ingrained into the Bible and other spiritual texts. I attended in-house meetings and recovery classes. When I was strong, I really desired to live clean. However, all it took was one moment of weakness to bury all of my positive growth. I knew I had to be strong. I was certain that if I had any hope of sobriety, I had to go to a meeting within the first twenty-four hours of being released. The first twenty-four hours were the most important. The majority of relapses happen in that tiny window of time.

In jail, my senses were deprived. There was a lack of color, smell, and members of the opposite sex. When I had been locked up, even the slightest scent of perfume or cigarette smoke would be overwhelming, that when on the outside, I normally wouldn't even notice. The female guards, whom I might never find attractive, became beautiful to me. Everything is different when a person is caged in from the outside world. I knew that once I touched down on the street, it would be overwhelming: colors, sounds, smells—everything—flooding me all at once. I knew my anxiety and energy would be high, and my awareness heightened. It would take everything I had not to overreact and want to numb it all back down. I made sure my parents understood this. I had nowhere to go when I got out, not a single opportunity, except for them. I was doomed for failure if they didn't help me, in my opinion. So once again, I put the burden on them.

XXIX.

I came home and went immediately to a meeting that night. I started going every night. I made some friends and hung out with them occasionally. The lure to drink was there though, and I couldn't convince myself that it was wrong. It was normal. Everyone, everywhere seemed to drink. My entire family drank at every get together. They made comments about how one drink wouldn't hurt me, and they couldn't understand why I couldn't have any. Nobody seemed to understand that it was poison to me, except the people in the meetings who told me it was a drug.

I couldn't accept that I wasn't able to drink. I thirsted for it. I wanted it so badly, and it was so easily accessible. So, I started drinking. I drank with my family. I drank with my friends. I managed to drink daily, but eventually my Dr. Jekyll and Mr. Hyde personalities resurfaced, and I was back to hurting people again. The violence and blackouts quickly returned. I began hanging with old friends, going to house parties and bars, and doing normal things people my age were doing, except that I couldn't do them normally. I couldn't go to a bar or house party without punching somebody in the mouth or hitting them with a bottle. I had managed to get myself banned from every bar in the area before I turned twenty-one and was even legally old enough to be in there.

Alcohol is the original gateway drug. People claim marijuana is a gateway. It wasn't for me, nor many people I knew. I didn't even like marijuana. It gave me anxiety attacks. If marijuana had been the only drug I ever tried, then I would have likely been turned off from all drugs after that. Alcohol is the first drug that almost everyone tries. For me, it was the drug that caused me to beat someone half to death and not remember it the next morning. Alcohol is responsible for more deaths each year than all of the other drugs combined, and is the catalyst behind nearly 100% of domestic violence cases. Alcohol is poison to me and anyone else who lacks the ability to take it in moderation. It was essentially poison to anyone who chose to be around me when I drank it.

I could fill an entire book with stories of fights, beatings, property crimes and strong-armed robberies that took place while I was under the influence of alcohol, but it would be pointless. With the tremendous guilt or embarrassment that followed one night's actions, came the next day to drink it away. I was a thug. I hung out with other thugs, which made my behavior acceptable, and most of the time even championed. It was an honor in my circles to brag about the damage one had inflicted on other human beings, and that made it even more twisted. Alcohol completely removed my inhibitions and fears, which would be fine if it didn't take with it my morals and boundaries, too.

I hadn't been home long before it took me downtown to buy heroin one drunken night. Within days, I had a full-fledged habit all over again. Heroin picks up right where you left off. It alters the chemical structure of your brain permanently so that every time you stop, no matter how long, the addiction begins again as if you had never stopped using at all. That's exactly what happened to me. I dove right back into the depths of addiction at full-speed. Naturally, my parents caught on and threatened to throw me back out on the streets if I didn't find treatment.

I procrastinated as long as I possibly could, until one day they took things into their own hands.

I came home high one night to find my father loading my things into his trunk. It was dark out, and I caught him on the way inside. I asked him what was going on, and he told me he had found a halfway house for me. My heart leapt. I wasn't ready. Deep inside, I knew I never would be. I started asking him a million questions, searching for an excuse or a loophole. It turned out, it was located in East Baltimore.

"I'm not going down there to get clean in a row home in East Baltimore. That's where I go to get high. How am I supposed to get clean there?" I snapped.

We started arguing. He was well beyond the point of frustration. I can only imagine the talks and disagreements he and my mother had about what to do with me. I was destroying their lives, as well as my own, and they had other children to think about. I was high and knew I would be sick the next day. I fought with him the best I knew how.

"Give me my stuff! I'll just go live on the streets then!"

He lost his mind in rage and yelled, "Walk away from this, and you're not my son anymore!"

My father is a docile, peaceful, good man, and I was blessed to have him. I had brought a world down upon him that he never even knew existed and wasn't prepared for. I'm sure he understood nothing about why his son would be living like this or doing the things I did. Honestly, I didn't even understand it myself. To watch him stand there, angry to the point of tears, and make that declaration to me put a hairline crack in the facade that heroin had built around my heart. I turned around.

"I'll go down and check it out with you. That's it," I said, knowing that once I had committed that much, I had basically committed to the whole thing.

It was a long, quiet ride to the city. I was nervous about

what was in store for me. We pulled onto a little side street in East Baltimore called Leverton and parked several doors down from the corner of Highland Avenue. The street was little more than an alleyway boxed in by row homes that loomed above it on both sides. It felt claustrophobic. I followed him up to the door of one of these row homes and waited as he knocked. We were greeted by an old man, maybe in his late sixties, named Lenny. He welcomed us into his cluttered front room which served as his office. He took a seat at his busy desk sitting right next to the front door and introduced himself. He said he'd been talking to my father and was expecting me. There were religious paintings and crosses all along his walls. Angels looked down upon me from the walls, seemingly frowning at the evil inside me, as I sat nervously in his wicker chair. He spoke about God, and recovery, and what it would take to stay clean. He spoke a lot about how great his halfway house was and how I would be well taken care of there. I noticed that almost all of his talk was directed at my father, the financier, and not at me. He had little interest in speaking with me. I was just a number to him. He spent his time assuring my father that this was a "place of God" and that it was the best place for me.

The plan was for my father to cover the first couple of weeks' rent and for me to find a job and finance my own way after that. There were very few rules at the house, except for a weekly Sunday dinner, and that everyone had to be out of the house by 7:30am and was not allowed back in until 7:00pm. He walked us several houses down to the corner house right next to the alleyway, and showed us inside. He gave me a tour of the old row home, covered in dust, with its shoddy furniture looking like a memoir from a half century ago, and continued rolling through the rules as he showed us around. Rules about groceries, and telephone use, and showers and such. It all went in one ear and out the other. The only thing I could think about was how I had to be out of the house at 7:30 the next morning with no plan. I hadn't even been detoxed. I was still dopesick. I had no clue what I was going to do.

"What am I supposed to do out on the streets all day from 7:30am?"

The reply was to find a job, sit at the library, go to interviews, or attend meetings. It sounded easy, but not to an addict out of his element with no guidance. They walked me upstairs and showed me the bed in the corner of a cold room sandwiched between two antique bookshelves that served as makeshift privacy walls for my portion of the room.

"This is it," he said, "and over here is your bathroom and shower."

He walked me over to show me, but it was currently in use by one of the other residents. He explained to me the rules about buying toilet paper and soap, and our responsibilities for cleaning the bathroom and the rest of the house, but it was all far beyond the realm of my thinking at the moment. I heard nothing. I just needed to escape. I started acting tired. I was overwhelmed and needed to be left alone. When he wrapped up his tour, we went down and retrieved my bags out of the trunk. There was really no turning back at this point. I either take the bed in the house being offered to me and figure things out in the morning, or I get dropped off somewhere on the county streets with all of my belongings in trash bags. I didn't want to deal with either option.

They left me alone, and I put away my belongings and lay down on the hard bed. The house was old and creaky, and the air was cold and stale. I had yet to see another resident. They were all off in their own rooms doing God knows what. I felt like an intruder. I laid there in the dark anticipating the onset of dopesickness, and it came. I tossed on that bed for hours and spiraled into a dark depression. The house felt haunted around me, and the city screamed my name outside. I knew that just beyond those walls lay endless possibilities. It was all I could do to wait for the morning. I felt trapped in a dark corner of a row home, among hundreds of thousands of row homes in a city of sickness, forgotten, and about to enter the hell of heroin withdrawal.

The feeling of oncoming withdrawal is like walking through spider webs. Your skin crawls, and transitions between hot and cold, goose bumps, and sweat. Cold sweat is the most uncomfortable feeling, especially when you are laying in it wide awake at night in the cold dark. Your anxiety and depression heighten, and your nerves become raw. A cigarette is usually a brief break from what ails you, but when you're dopesick they actually taste bad and leave an uncomfortable dryness in your mouth. I laid in these feelings all night with maybe a fifteen-minute reprieve of sleep here and there.

The sun came up, and I learned a lot. At 7:30 I stepped out onto Leverton, where I saw several black dudes at the entrance of the street working the corner. I watched as they walked a white lady into the alley and handed off something to her. Then I saw a young Latino guy get the same treatment. I had a feeling this wasn't heroin. I started walking quickly past them and out onto the Highland Avenue. As I rounded the corner, I caught up to the lady who had just gotten served.

"What are they hitting? Coke?" I asked her.

She looked me up and down and said, "Yeah, readies."

"Okay, that's what I thought."

Her response was the typical required inquisition, "What are you, a cop?"

I shook my head, "Do I look like a motherfucking cop to you? I'm looking to see if it's dope."

"Oh, not down here," she retorted, as if I had just asked her about rat poison. "You've got to go up to the Monument area for that."

Monument Street was a major thoroughfare in East Baltimore that had a large shopping district. It ran right alongside Johns

Hopkins in one direction, and parallel to Madison Street in the other direction. I shook my head to myself at her disdain toward me that she was only a crackhead and not a junkie. It's funny in the drug world that people will feel better about themselves by justifying their own addiction against someone else's. I've witnessed full-blown junkies on many occasions talk down about what a junkie another person is. Junkies will look down on crack addicts, and vice versa, and alcoholics will look down on them all. As long as people can identify someone they believe to be worse off than them, they can focus their negative energy on others and justify anything about themselves. An addict might look at people with healthy relationships, careers, or physical fitness as "losers" or "nerds," and wholeheartedly believe it because it helps them justify the life of misery they live in.

I surveyed the area…crack dealers in front of the halfway house, a liquor store a few doors down, and on the end of the block were a couple Spanish bars. I started walking south into the Highlandtown district to explore with the full intent of finding a job. I had a little over $10 in cash, and the lady's words were ringing in my head incessantly, *Monument Street is where the dope is.* It took me about fifteen minutes of walking through the streets before I surrendered to the cravings and sickness and made up my mind to go get high. At that very moment, all the sickness subsided and something new took over.

It was a passion, or strong desire, that fueled me. My once cold body turned warm, and my walk became faster. I headed toward Monument Street on a mission—nothing could stop me. There is a certain kind of walk that a dope fiend gets when they either have money in their pocket and are on their way to score some dope, or they have the dope in their pocket and are on their way to get high. It's triple the speed of a normal walk and recognizable to the anyone who knows. Nothing short of a tackle could slow their momentum or stop them. I perfected this walk. I moved through the streets like a swift train of desperation.

It was about twenty blocks from where I started to where I was headed. The neighborhood started changing from mixed black, white, and Latino throughout the first half into all black neighborhoods for the second leg of the journey. The Latino-owned grocery stores and bars gave way to Asian-owned stores and bars. The houses progressively became more run down and dilapidated, a lot of them outright abandoned. The neglect of the neighborhoods was much more apparent, and a lot more people were on their front steps or out milling around in the streets. The fast walk meant to show, that not only were you were on a mission, but that you had no time to stop for harassment or trouble. I got to Monument Street, and it was packed. There were people everywhere, and very few of them were white. The closer I got to the hospital the more mixed the crowd became, but down at the bottom away from the hospital, I stood out like a sore thumb. They knew I was there for only one thing.

There were corner boys on almost every corner. I heard several different brand names being shouted out.

"Muddy Waters!"

"Tiger Woods!"

"Harrison Ford!"

I saw a white guy coming up the street walking fast like he had just scored, and I asked him, "What's the best out?"

He replied, "Go see Rivers on Monument and Bradford."

And that's exactly where I headed. I got to the corner and there was a crowd there in front of a small carryout.

I asked a big dude, "Are you Rivers? I'm looking for Rivers."

"Go inside," he said and nodded at the door.

I walked into the small lobby of the carryout, which was filled with young black men in winter coats. The carryout itself looked like all the other ones in the city, with bulletproof glass partitions separating the customers from the workers and product.

The second I walked in, I was asked, "How many you want?" I pulled out the ten from my pocket and answered, "One."

I was handed a gel cap of scramble from one of the black hands in the crowd, my ten dollar bill was taken by someone else, and I was back out in the winter cold and up the street.

A couple streets up someone was shouting out, "New ones!"

I handed them a dollar, they handed me a clean, packaged syringe, and I was off to find a bathroom. Burger King was up the street by the hospital, so I ducked in there. I had grabbed an aluminum bottle cap off the street during my walk to cook the dope in, so all I needed was a source of water. When you're sick, being sanitary is the least of your issues. You are in a feverish race to get well. So, I stuck the syringe into the porcelain bowl in front of me, drew up a few cc's of toilet water into it and began the ritual. My bloodstream welcomed the warmth that cold autumn day, I sunk down on the toilet and embraced my accomplishment and my failure. I had failed to make it a single day clean in that halfway house, but I had found a new stomping ground. A whole world of possibilities had opened up right in front of me.

XXX.

I was feeling normal, and I was in the middle of the city alone with a full day ahead of me to explore. I was excited about all of the possibilities and needed to figure out how to get some money to not only stave off this sickness every day, but also to live and survive. Now that I wasn't sick anymore, I could start looking for jobs.

Without enough money to even catch a bus, I walked across half the city until I reached the Inner Harbor of Baltimore. This was the fun touristy area of Baltimore, and if there was money to be made somewhere, this would be the place. When I finally got to the Inner Harbor, I took my time exploring all the small malls and stores, looking for money-making opportunities. Not only were there a lot of tourists in the area, there were also a myriad of junkies and homeless people. These were the people I knew that I could learn from most.

I sat on benches observing people and smoking cigarettes, striking up conversations with young people who looked like they also got high. I met a guy about my age, only a bit dustier than me because he had lived on the streets for a while. After a brief chat, he invited me to come with him to show me his current hustle. Box sets. CD box sets was where the quick money was at. There was a well-known record store in Fells Point that bought new and used CDs, and box sets were apparently top sellers. They would pay anywhere from $15 to $40 a set, and I could easily steal three at a time from a store.

There was a fairly new, three-story Barnes & Noble bookstore in the Harbor, and on the second floor they had a music section. They also had a Starbucks on the second floor with a balcony where people could smoke and sip their coffee while overlooking the Harbor. The good thing about the Harbor, even though it was crowded most of the time, was that nobody actually lived there, so people generally minded their own business. This meant that when I walked out onto the balcony with a couple of CD box sets and casually dropped them from the balcony into my partner's waiting arms below, nobody was invested enough to report what they thought they just saw. We made off with our stolen goods and walked another twelve blocks or so to the record store in Fells Point, where we each earned $45. It was approaching dark, and I was comfortable enough to go back to the house. There was no need for any more running today; I could score some more dope in the morning. That's what I did, and when morning came, my new way of life came with it.

I went to Monument Street first thing, then back to the Harbor by 10:00am to our rendezvous point to wait for my new partner. He never showed up. After waiting on the bench smoking cigarettes, I finally acknowledged that he wasn't coming and decided to wander into Barnes & Noble myself. I waited until they opened at 10:00am, then wandered in and started browsing the store. I picked up a few box sets and quickly hid them in the bathroom trashcan underneath the liner before anyone else came into the restroom. I went back out into the store and started browsing. Since I had already gotten high that morning, I wasn't in a rush. I felt like I was better safe than sorry, so I walked around the store, went out onto the balcony to smoke, and tried to formulate some kind of plan. I didn't have one.

There didn't appear to be an alarm by the door, but that didn't mean there wasn't one. Finally, I decided *better now than never*, and returned to the bathroom when the coast was clear, tucked two of the box sets into my waist and headed downstairs with the third in hand. I ducked between shelves making sure no one was watching me and made my way into the line. I saw that a young black teenage girl was working the register, so I went to her and told her that I really wanted to return this box set. I explained that it was given to me as a gift, so I didn't have a receipt. She told me she could only give me store credit or return the money to the card from which it was purchased, which is what I had expected and hoped that she would say. Now I had a reason to walk through the sensors with the product in hand, to find out if there were in fact alarm sensors. I gritted my teeth and made my way through the front doors expecting the shrill sound of an alarm, but nothing happened. I knew this would be a free-for-all every day until they caught on.

I still had a pill and a half in my pocket from copping earlier in the morning, and with the whole day to kill, the city was my oyster. I got a bag to carry the merchandise around the harbor and started exploring. In between nodding out while smoking cigarettes on park benches and buying coffee and food, I decided it was time to find a job. I would have to pay rent eventually. The Hard Rock Café was located next door between the Baltimore Aquarium and Barnes & Noble, so I wandered in once they had opened for the afternoon.

I picked up an application and was seated at the empty bar filling it out when a voice said, "Heeeyyy!"

I turned around to find this blonde Barbie doll looking back at me with smiling eyes. It was Lindsey, probably the prettiest girl I had ever done heroin with.

"I had no clue you worked here!" I replied, knowing she would be my "in" for a job here.

She explained to me that she had been there for about a year waiting tables, that her boyfriend lived over in West Baltimore, and that they both got high daily. She worked, while he roamed the streets looking for hustles. She told me to give her the application, and she would probably be able to get me a job waiting tables. I stayed and ate a sandwich and left feeling accomplished. Things were working out for me. Now I just had to get off the dope, and I could move forward in life.

Quitting heroin is almost a daily thought, even an obsession, for a using addict, especially when they are high. It is easy to face possibilities that arouse fear and anxiety, like quitting, when you're comforted by the pillow of heroin. Once the high fades, all of those noble thoughts of self-improvement fade and survival instinct kicks back in. The obsession to get clean is quickly exchanged for the obsession to get high. The drug makes us bipolar. There is always a war within that no one from the outside can see. I lost that war so many times that, for me it was no longer disheartening to lose. Failing became a normal routine, and once failure is expected, it is no longer feared. Life is eerily comfortable at the bottom with nothing to lose. It's simple and carnal once you've accepted that you're worthless to the society around you.

I became familiar with the Baltimore bus lines, hopping the 23 back toward Highlandtown at the end of my day, then hopping the 8 to Towson Mall to boost from there. Sometimes, I'd get blasted high and ride out to Mondawmin Mall and hangout or ride various bus lines around the city just to learn the area and nod out. I worked Barnes & Noble and other stores around the city for everything I could, and I met different junkies on the streets every day to run and hustle with. Half the time, I didn't even know their names, just that we were lost souls on a mission. I met a lot of prostitutes and older women, white and black, that I'd get high with, but never had any interest in sexually. Heroin took the desire for sex away from me. I was only interested in one thing only, getting high and finding money to continue to get high.

I met women on the streets copping. They'd invite me to come back to their row homes to shoot dope. Sometimes their husbands would be upstairs, and we'd walk right past them to go into their bedroom or basement to get high. It was nothing for a woman that I met fifteen minutes earlier to drop her pants and underwear in front of me, hike her leg up onto a stool or dresser, and shoot dope in a vein way up on her inner thigh or next to her vagina. I saw a lot of nasty things, a lot of bloody, bruised scar tissue on a lot of vacant souls—abscesses, scabs, swollen feet, hands and legs, and track marks on their crotches, necks, feet and hands. My own arms were lined with bruises, dots and scabs from using the same needle hundreds of times. There is nothing glamorous about heroin. Still, we'd kid ourselves, acting like we were the rock stars and wild ones.

I literally took every worthwhile box set out of Barnes & Noble and moved on to single CDs. I would walk around the Harbor selling them to tourists and locals for $5 apiece. The harbor was full of hustlers. I was sitting on a bench when three older, black men came over to see what I had. One asked to see the CDs, and as I handed them to him, he tossed them one at a time about twenty feet behind him to a friend, and they kept moving. The precision and quickness with how they did it proved they were professional hustlers. They kept moving down the crowded Harbor, as if they hadn't done anything and didn't expect me to give chase. They knew I was selling stolen merchandise and figured they could steal it from me.

But I chased after them yelling, "You aren't going to steal my shit that easy!"

A group of sailors overheard me and came running to my assistance.

One ran up to me, "What did they steal?"

Now I felt like an idiot. I didn't want to get people involved. I told him, "They stole CDs that I got for my birthday!"

I stood there in horror. *What have I done?*

The sailors caught up with them and surrounded them. A couple of police officers arrived on the scene as well. Suddenly the whole mob of them came walking back to me. I thanked the sailors and the police as they handed me my stolen CDs. The police asked me where I got them and why I was selling them. Hoping that they had no knowledge of the thefts at Barnes & Noble, I told them that they were gifts for my birthday, and that I didn't listen to that kind of music. They presented paperwork for me to fill out, but I refused to press charges. They let the guys go, and we all went our separate ways.

A day or two later, I was walking out of Barnes & Noble for maybe the tenth time, and the alarm randomly went off. I was stunned. I turned around, made eye contact with the girl at the front desk, and showed her that I was removing the merchandise from my waistband. I sat it on the floor inside of the sensor alarms and took off out the door. I was sure that since I didn't actually make off with anything, that the police wouldn't be called.

I found another mall near the Harbor that had a record store on the second floor. I took the long escalator upstairs with Lindsey's boyfriend to check it out. There was a young girl working the counter and an alarm sensor at the door. As I moved through the store, my new partner sat outside in the mall hallway. When the clerk went to the back of the store to continue stocking, I grabbed box sets and tossed them up and over the sensors and into his waiting hands out in the hallway. He caught them and quickly stuffed them into his waistband. I asked the girl if she would be back the next day under the guise that I would have money then and was just browsing today. She said she was off the next day, which was good because it bought me another day of stealing from them.

The next day we went in to pull off the same routine. Every time the clerk would look down, I would toss a box set out to Lindsey's boyfriend. The second one I tossed was too low, and it passed right through the alarm sensor. As soon as she heard it go off, she snapped up in time to see it bounce across the floor of the mall hallway and land at his waiting feet.

"Oh my God!" I blurted out. "I'm so sorry, I was just playing with him. I didn't mean that." It was the only thing I could think to say. I went out, picked it up, and brought it back to her.

"Get out!" she barked at me glaringly.

I turned and walked away back through the alarm sensor with my arms up to show her I was empty handed. We ducked out and jumped on the first bus out of there in case the police were coming.

The Harbor became off limits to me now. So, I started getting up in the morning and walking straight to Monument Street because I knew that certain dope shops gave out "testers" in the morning. Testers were a small, sample pill of heroin that they would give out for free to advertise their product. Particularly, the dope shops would give out testers to announce a new product or a new batch of product. They would make the tester batch of heroin more potent than the rest of their batch because they knew that word would spread throughout the junkie community about its extreme potency, and people would flock to buy it. Testers were given out early in the morning because a large number of addicts had to get high before they went to work. Dope shops generally opened early, sometimes as early as 4:00am, and were closed by noon. Only a few stray shops would stay open into the evening hours. Junkies would come from all over to wait for testers to come out, or to wait for dope shops to open. It wasn't uncommon to ride through East Baltimore and see large crowds milling about on street corners at daybreak…and they weren't waiting for the bus.

Handing out testers, just like selling dope, had to be done quickly and carefully because police were always around the corner, and addicts swarmed like piranhas in a feeding frenzy. Instead of handing testers out, a dealer would generally come out on the street, make his presence known, then toss handfuls of pills into the air toward the waiting crowd. A small mosh pit would break out as addicts of all colors, sexes, and sizes would scramble and dive after the fallen pills, then rush off to their individual holes to shoot and sample the drug. This was the easiest way to "get out the gate" in the morning, especially if you were broke. A full-blown heroin addict goes through a grueling process of robbing and stealing and hurting those they love just to find the money they need to search for a drug that no longer gets them high. At a certain point they need the drug just to stave off the sickness, just to feel as normal as anyone else feels on any given day. An addict has to pay daily to feel comfortable in his own skin. They become a monster, a zombie, who has to feed his inner need in order to function. "Getting out the gate" meant getting out of the starting gate and into the human race with all of the other humans.

I wandered up to Monument Street to catch the free testers. I missed them most mornings because I woke up too late. By the time I made the walk up there, they had already been distributed. One day, I arrived in time and still missed them. A new dope called "Stars" was coming back out, and everyone was excited to sample it because it was rumored to be top-notch quality the last time it was around. When I arrived, there was already a large crowd of maybe thirty people on the corner. After waiting almost half an hour, people were getting antsy. There was a lot of sickness in that group of early morning addicts. A runner for the dope came out and announced that they were going to be handing out testers soon, and for everyone to line up in the adjacent alley. Asking a bunch of sick junkies to form a single-file line in an alley is a recipe for disaster. There might not be enough, and only the people in the front may get pills. Everyone was in a panic, running, and jockeying for position. Amidst the screaming and pushing, the hitter came out and announced that "Rico" wasn't going to hit anybody with pills until everybody was quiet and lined up. *This is like elementary school*, I thought, *a bunch of rowdy children fighting over toys, except these are adults fighting for survival.*

A large black man in line shouted, "Tell him to hurry the fuck up!"

The hitter hollered back, "Why don't you tell him?"

They exchanged a few words, but everybody shouted disapproval at the large junkie for holding things up and he quieted down. After another five minutes, we started wondering if this was a hoax and if the dope was even coming out. Big Guy started mouthing off again and got into a shoving match with the lady in front of him. The hitter popped back up, this time waving a gun around in front of him.

"Y'all niggas gonna shut the fuck up and line up now, or you can bounce your bitch asses out this alley."

Silence. It may have been quiet for a whole two minutes more before Big Guy started complaining again about having to wait and began fighting, trying to cut in front of the people in front of him. This time I knew it was over. Nobody was getting dope from this shop today.

The hitter came out with the devil in his eyes, and commanded him, "Get the fuck out of the line!"

Before Big Guy could finish the "Fuck You!" that was coming out of his mouth, the pistol came up and flared off a foot from his face. A torrent of blood flew out the back of his head and onto the trash that lined the sides of the alley floor. His body fell sideways like a tree. People scattered for their lives, afraid more shots would follow. Some of us stepped and jumped over the body on the way out of the alley, careful not to get blood on our sneakers, while others tripped over it in their frenzy. Over thirty of us addicts witnessed the scene in that alley, but I would bet not one called the police or an ambulance. We were bottom feeders, more concerned that there would be no testers that morning, and that the man who lie dead in the alley had ruined that opportunity for all of us. Like many other tragedies I witnessed as an addict, I wouldn't think much more about this incident until after I got clean and returned to some semblance of a normal way of thinking. But in that moment, I was focused on getting high, and I didn't care who might be a victim in my way.

XXXI.

Monument Street became my new playground. For one thing, unlike the Harbor, a junkie blended in with the crowd here because there were so many of us. Also, there were dope shops everywhere around here, so once you got money, getting high wasn't an issue. There were all walks of life on this street from the hospital workers and patients, to the people who came here to shop, down to the dealers and addicts. I quickly blended in and adopted ways to make money. There were many stores up and down this strip to steal from and quite a few pawn shops to sell the stolen merchandise to. If that didn't work, I could sell it out on the street. And if that was a dead end, I could hit the Spanish bars and sell the goods there. I was stealing everything from disposable cameras, pocket knives, and Zippo lighters to Sony Walkmans and boomboxes that I shoved under my coat and slid out of the store with. These were long days of sickness, until I finally got enough goods sold to maintain a stable high that would stave it off.

Lenny, the halfway house owner, wasn't nearly as stupid as I thought. I truly believed I had him convinced that I was out looking for a job every day with no luck, but he knew I was getting high. He just never said anything to me. One day, he asked me if I wanted to make some money cleaning out one of his rental properties on Lombard Street, which was just a couple streets over from the house. We negotiated $50 for the work and headed over to the row home. He said he was selling the home and had to get it completely cleaned out before he did so. He handed me a trash bag and asked me to clean out the attic for him. What I saw up there gave me an eerie, gut-wrenching feeling.

Scattered across the dusty wooden attic floor were dozens upon dozens of half-full urine sample bottles. My stomach dropped. I lived a life of crime and destitution outside of the normal world. I expected things in my life to be chaotic and disturbing, but the outside world was supposed to be normal and upright. When things in the outside world mirrored things in my world, it scared me. This wasn't how it was supposed to be. These hundreds of urine samples meant that Lenny wasn't testing his house tenants. They had been hidden up here collecting dust, carelessly tossed across the floor, as if someone had opened the latch to the attic and just tossed a handful in from time to time. Lenny obviously didn't care what went on in his houses, which explained why I had never been tested. But the fact that he let me see this also made me question how much he thought he knew about me. *I can't do this. I have to get out of here. It's too strange for me.* I had to find an excuse to get away and go get high. I came down the ladder quickly and asked Lenny for gloves.

"You don't have gloves? I'm not picking all that up without gloves! I'll come back another day and do it with gloves," I told him and made my way out of there.

I felt like maybe now that I knew his little secret, I was safe in his house. He couldn't throw me out as easily. I made my way up to Monument. There was a crew of black folks whom I'd been hanging out with, mostly addicts and drunks, who lived on the block of Montford between Monument and Madison. It was a safe zone for me because they all lived on that block and hung out on the stoops and let me hang there with them. They loved me, black women always did. They were often my protectors.

I would go into the alley and remove the plywood from the side window of the abandoned row home on the corner and climb in to get high, then come out and hang on the block with them until the sun started its way down. The police wouldn't mess with me here. They would assume I was one of the few white folks who lived on the Eastside.

I got up to the strip, and it was quiet. The whole Monument was quiet, which meant police must have been through conducting raids. It was a Tuesday, and Tuesdays and Thursdays in Baltimore were known in the streets as "jump out days." The police were also known as "jump out boys," usually plainclothes officers who had the ability to pull up on anyone on the street, jump out, and search them for no reason, other than looking suspicious. This basically described anyone in those neighborhoods who was alive and breathing. Dope shops were a lot harder to find on these particular days, or just like the weather, the dope climate in different neighborhoods changed from day-to-day depending on things like police presence, stick-up boys, and murders in the area. But, today it was quiet. I didn't see any familiar faces as I made my way over to Madison.

Two young attractive black girls were walking up the street. "You cute as shit!" the better looking one said, "You looking?"

"Yeah," I replied, and she told me to follow them. My curiosity was piqued, as I caught up with them. She introduced herself to me as "Princess," and she looked like one too. She had straight black hair past her shoulders, brown skin, makeup and clothes that did not make her look like she got high. She asked me what I wanted, and I told her I just wanted two pills of dope. She stuck out her hand, and I put a twenty in it.

"Get some coke, and get high with me," she said.

I had never shot coke before, but I was willing to explore with this beautiful female.

"We can go back to my place after we cop," she turned and said to me.

We rounded the corner and stepped into an alley off of Ashland Avenue. There were dope boys in the alley, and they tensed up when I walked in.

"He cool. He's with me," she said.

They exchanged their drugs for our money. We got out of the alley, and she handed me two skinny vials of cocaine and a pill of dope. I was eager for the adventure. The other girl split from us, and Princess and I walked several blocks toward the hospital. She had her own row home over there, where she said she lived by herself. This was perfect! Now I had a beautiful girl with her own place, where I could go whenever I wanted. She unlocked the door, and we walked in. The house was like many city houses I'd been in. The furniture was very scarce on the main floor and dusty, almost as if no one lived there. The house definitely didn't match her appearance, but as she led me up the stairs and into her bedroom, it started to look more like a home.

She had a huge, comfortable-looking, unmade bed stacked high with clothes, which she sat on. She began cooking her dope and cocaine up at the same time. I watched her and mimicked her. I had never "speedballed" before. This was the last stop at the end of the road, or so I had heard. You couldn't get much more extreme than this. I dumped my usual half of a pill of dope into the spoon and then tapped out maybe $2 worth of coke, just a couple of little rocks, and started cooking.

When the high hit me, it lifted my head tall. I was instantly elated. My pulse began soaring, and I felt like I needed to shit almost immediately. I got off her bed instantly, made my way into the bathroom, and sat on the toilet. I was zooming. It was terrifying, but amazing, at the same time. I felt instant elation and clarity, as if I were floating on a cloud of ecstasy. Words fail me in describing the pure bliss I felt. As I type this now, my rising pulse and racing heart have caused my body to shake. My stomach is in knots remembering this indescribable feeling—this indescribable, amazing, horrible feeling. Horrible, because in spite of the sheer ecstasy that came with the massive amount of dopamine released into my body, I found myself in a state of paranoia that I would have a sudden heart attack due to my elevated pulse, the shaking, and my hyper-awareness. It was hellish until the cocaine high subsided after several minutes and the soft pillow of heroin comforted me. A speedball went through brief levels of happiness and ecstasy, followed by fear and paranoia, and finally warmth and comfort. These two drugs were the exact opposite of each other and yet worked together with uncanny chemistry that was both beautiful and inherently evil.

I finally wandered back into Princess' bedroom. She was stretched out on her bed in a bra and panties, smoking a cigarette. I wanted to sleep with her. I had to, I felt like I needed to complete this bond between us, which would secure this house and her as a refuge site for me in the future. Not to mention, she was beautiful and mysterious to me. She invited me back over to the bed, and I sat next to her and lit up a cigarette. I was still trying to ground myself from the experience with the coke. But now I was in a frenzy. My mind was off-kilter from the drugs, and I had this beautiful woman next to me wanting me to put it on her. I couldn't though, because I was uncomfortable. The whole scene had unfolded so fast, and the cocaine had my mind going in two different directions. It had me anxious and paranoid, and it was calling to me from my pocket to do more. I pulled out a vial and turned to her.

"You wanna split this?"

She sat upright, stroking my back, as I dumped the remaining contents of the vial into a spoon and heated it up. I drew up half of the liquid and passed her the other half. When the cocaine entered my bloodstream, it hit me like a train head on. My head spun in pure euphoria, as I floated back into bliss. Then, my heart pounded loudly in my chest, and my pulse quickened until my paranoia sent me reeling into the bathroom again. This time I didn't land on the toilet. I set myself down on the floor, sweat pouring from my forehead. I sat there massaging my temples as the high took me on a rollercoaster that came crashing down into my stomach. I began to vomit profusely into her toilet. I couldn't be sure whether or not I was dying, but I knew my pulse was dangerously high. Sweat was pouring, and my stomach was flipping in circles, and still somehow it was all mildly enjoyable. I laid there reeling with energy, and yet not wanting to move at the same time. The house was suddenly cold and scary, but the bathroom felt like it was a hundred and fifty degrees. I knew I couldn't face the idea of sleeping with her anymore, much less talking with her. I was lost in the prison of my own mind and stumbling for a way out.

She hollered out from the bedroom, "Are you okay?"

I realized that I had better make a move. I got up and walked out of the bathroom, soaking wet from sweat, and grabbed my shirt off of the bed.

"I'm sick. I need some fresh air," I said.

She giggled, but looked frustrated, in reply.

"I'll come find you tomorrow," I said, but had the feeling that she was annoyed.

She didn't bother getting up from her bed as I left the room, went downstairs, and let myself out into the bright afternoon sun.

There was a message for me back at the house from the Hard Rock Café, so I caught a bus there. Lindsey was working. She greeted me at the door and took me to a table to wait for the manager to arrive. He sat down and briefly went over my application, but he had already decided to hire me if I was willing to start out bussing tables and work my way up to a waitstaff position. Of course, I said yes, but deep down inside I was nervous. I didn't know how I could possibly hold down a job after all this time. The thought of being responsible and accountable for something terrified me. All I knew was failure, and I was sure that's all I'd ever know. I was to start the next day, and I assured Lindsey that if she'd let me hold a few dollars, that I'd give it right back when I got my money at the end of my first shift.

She hesitantly agreed, followed by the words, "You'd better show up!"

The following day, I was only set to work a few hours in the afternoon, and I needed to get well first. So, I took the walk up to Monument Street as soon as I awoke. I was relieved to run into Princess and a different girl out on the street that early. She acted extremely happy to see me. *Maybe I could make this relationship work after all.* I was on my way to a different dope hole, but figured she knew what she was doing, so I tagged along with them. She said she knew where some good $6 pills were, and I just so happened to have only $12 to my name. Occasionally, though rarely, there were certain dope shops that sold $6 pills, which were slightly smaller than the usual $10 ones. As we came up to a corner house, Princess told me to wait on the steps while they ran into the alley around the corner.

"They might not serve us, if we are with a white boy," she said.

I sat on the steps, and that was the last time I ever saw Princess again. I waited for almost half an hour for her to return with the heroin, but she never came. I walked the streets looking for her, and went to her house and banged on her door. She seemed genuinely interested in me, so I refused to acknowledge that I had been taken. After giving up and hopping a bus to the Harbor, I sauntered into work fifteen minutes late, sick, and miserable. After a quick four hours of bussing tables, I walked back out of the restaurant with almost $40 in ones after being tipped out. I caught a bus down to Patterson Park Avenue and started up the hill toward Monument Street. I was starting to feel sick, but the idea that I had $40 in my pocket was helping to keep the illness away. A couple of blocks past the park, one of the prostitutes I was familiar with came down my side of the street.

"You holding?" she asked.

"No" I told her, "I'm trying to get well now."

She asked to come along. I told her absolutely not, but that I'd give her a couple of dollars, and it was up to her to find the rest. I wanted to make sure she was okay because I never knew when I might need her help in the future. We looked out for each other on the streets, only when we had thoroughly looked out for ourselves first. A person I'd help one day when I was well may be the same person I'd rob the next day when I was sick. I was walking quickly as I pulled out my wad of ones in order to recount them before handing her a couple.

"Be careful out here. The jump-outs have been heavy today pulling everybody up," she leaned over to tell me while we were walking.

It couldn't have been two minutes later that an SUV came screeching up to the curb, and two plainclothes officers hopped out and had us up against a wall patting us down and running through our pockets. It happened so quickly after she had mentioned them that it almost felt unreal. I felt like an idiot being patted down in my work uniform. I wanted to ask what I did wrong. He pulled out my ID and cash from my apron pocket that I had dropped next to me on the ground.

Looking closely at my ID, and then at me, he said, "Mr. McGhee, do you always pick up prostitutes when you get off work?" I explained that I had just gotten off work, but that we were just talking, that I never spent money on prostitutes.

"You're either getting your dick sucked or selling her drugs, which one is it?" he scowled.

I ignored him.

After the pat down for weapons, he said, "I'm going to search your pockets now. You got anything in there that will cut me or stick me?"

I told him I had a needle in my front right pocket and a closed pocket knife, both of which he carefully retrieved. He then removed the rest of the contents of my pockets. Luckily, I hadn't gotten any dope yet. They sat us both on the curb while they ran our names for warrants. After a few moments they returned, and he snapped the needle in half in front of me and tossed it into the street against the curb, which was customary even though they weren't illegal. He then handed me back my ID card, and they hopped back into the SUV and took off. I dug in my pockets. The money was gone. They had just robbed me of my little bit of tips for the day. What could I do? Who would believe me? Nothing was going to help me get it back in time to get well before the night was over.

XXXII.

I trudged up to Monument Street, desperate and exhausted. I had been burnt twice in one day, once by Princess and then by the police. There was no mercy out here, and no way I could get any more money from anyone. The stores on Monument were surely all closed or closing soon. The pawn shops definitely weren't open anymore; they closed at 6:00pm. I walked to Monument anyway. It was a different world at night, a complete ghost town. The majority of the people were in cars leaving their day jobs and just passing through. Trash blew across the streets everywhere. There was no action and no dope shops yelling out brand names. I walked the street aimlessly heading east in the direction of the halfway house, when I got down to the bottom of the strip, where I rarely passed through.

There was a big black guy on the corner of Belnord Street who looked my direction and hollered, "We open! Hitting in the hole."

I looked at him with desperation in my eyes and said, "I wish, bro. I just got beat for the last of my money, and I'm sick as shit."

At that moment, something happened—something I'd never heard of, something that would go down in the history of all Baltimore dope tales.

He looked at me and said, "Here, I got you bro," and dug in

his pocket and handed me a fat gel cap of dope. "You'll love it," he said. "Just make sure you come back and see us."

I promised that I would and headed up the street quickly with renewed energy. I had never experienced such kindness out here on the streets. A stranger, a dealer no less, just gave me something for free, and it genuinely felt like he didn't want to see me sick. I was excited and eager to get well, but had forgotten that I didn't have a needle anymore. I scoured the streets and alleyways for one as I headed east, until I found one on the sidewalk near some steps in front of an abandoned house. I scooped it up quickly and continued toward the Burger King where I needed to get high. At this point, I didn't care about what was in that needle. I only cared about getting high. Everything else could be dealt with in the future, if I lived long enough to have one.

The thing about needles is this, if you don't have one, you're screwed. All of the dope in the world won't help if you don't have a needle. Once you've crossed the line between shooting and sniffing, and felt the raw power that comes from shooting heroin, you can't bear to go back. Once you've become a veteran addict, sniffing your dope is akin to wasting it. Needles are fragile, they get dull, they break, the cops break them, and there are very few places to buy them in the hood. There's a needle exchange bus that travels around the city and exchanges new needles for dirty ones, but it may as well have been a mythological creature to me because I never caught up with it. Needles weren't illegal, but they weren't legal either. I could walk into any county pharmacy and buy a ten pack of needles for $2.50, and it was up to the discretion of the person working the pharmacy counter on whether to sell them to me or not. It was easier to pretend to be a diabetic or to be purchasing them for someone diabetic in the family. Some pharmacists still wouldn't sell them without a diabetic ID. That puzzled me because as pharmacists, I felt like they should prefer addicts to be buying clean needles rather than sharing dirty ones. Whether I said diabetic or not, it wasn't hard to tell what I really wanted them for, especially if my arms were visible. Some inner-city entrepreneurs, mostly diabetic, took full advantage of their ability to purchase needles and in turn sold them. There were places known as needle corners where several people could be heard shouting out "new ones," which were always sold for a dollar apiece. Every inner-city junkie was also familiar with where the needle shops were. There were certain houses in every neighborhood that sold needles, and once you became familiar with the neighborhood, you learned where they were. You could show up at these houses at any reasonable hour and knock on the door. A voice would usually ask through a cracked door or a slot how many needles you wanted, and the exchange would be made.

A needle was cheap at a dollar, but sometimes that dollar was critical. Or sometimes the time it took to go find a needle was too much to bear when you were dopesick and had dope in hand. I shared many needles, sometimes with people whom I presumed had AIDS or other diseases. We all started out saying we would never shoot, then once we started shooting, we swore we'd never share needles. All your "nevers" come back on you once you're caught in the grips of addiction. This evening wasn't the first time I had picked up a dirty needle off the ground and used it, and it surely wouldn't be my last. I'd inject the dried blood in that needle into me if it meant getting dope into my system faster. I didn't expect to ever live long enough to face the negative consequences that could possibly arise from those bad decisions.

I got into the Burger King, fired that whole pill in the bathroom stall, and wandered back to the halfway house, high out of my mind. I couldn't wait to get some money and get back to see my new friend on Belnord and show him that I appreciated the favor. Even in my lowly condition, I was concerned about repaying a good deed. When I arrived back to the house, Lenny was there. He wanted to make room for a newcomer in the house, so he was moving me to his other house across the alley. He waited until 6:30 at night to spring it on me. I tried to keep my eyes low and avoid eye contact. I had never been around Lenny in the evening when I was obviously high, and the last thing I needed was confrontation. I begrudgingly packed up my few belongings and followed him out of the front door. We made a right into the alley next to the halfway house and walked halfway down the alley and into a back gate. He opened the back gate for me, and we ascended a long wooden staircase to a back door. This new place was a two-bedroom apartment above the liquor store on Highland Avenue, and the only way in and out was through this back door. We got inside, and he pointed to a couch where he said I would be staying until a bedroom opened up. I wouldn't even have my own room. *This was ridiculous.* But I dared not to argue about it in the condition I was in. I was lucky I still had a place to stay. I wondered what the other two working men who stayed there would think about this newcomer sleeping on their couch. It didn't much matter though because I was high out of my mind, and would try to stay that way during the duration of my time there. I knew no other way to cope.

The next morning, I hit the streets early. I had been in the same stores too many times on Monument and was running out of hustles there, so I decided to go back to the Harbor. I had to be to work at 2:00pm, so I killed time until 10:00am when I knew Lindsey would be coming in to open. At 10:01am, I popped into the Hard Rock asking her to let me hold $10 until my shift. She claimed to have no cash on her, and then proceeded to point out that I was on expediter training this afternoon, which meant I wouldn't be making tips. Rather, I would be garnishing dishes, making salads, and helping to serve food. I had to act fast. I had to figure out how to make money and get to Monument and back all within the next couple of hours.

I wandered around for an hour or two until I ended up back at the mall where the record store was. I made my way up to the second floor to the Brookstone electronics store. I browsed around for a moment. I found a speaker system that I was able to stuff up my jacket, and then I exited the store. There were two ways into this store. One was from the inside of the mall, the other was from a walkway that stretched above the busy Pratt Street below and into another Harborplace Mall located at the Inner Harbor. I used that walkway on the way out, cut through the other mall, and out into the busy Harbor.

I had to find a pawnshop to sell the speaker system. I made my way up the streets of downtown Baltimore until I reached the red-light district of Baltimore Street. This section of Baltimore Street in downtown Baltimore, otherwise known as "The Block" is interesting because it is a couple blocks of nothing but strip clubs, sex stores, prostitution and drugs. Directly at the end of the strip is a pawn shop, followed by the huge Baltimore Police Headquarters building which looms at the end of the strip like a bully just daring the rest of the street to act out of order. "The Block" is the sex capital of Baltimore. Even I, a full-blown criminal and junkie, felt dirty being there.

I walked into the pawn shop and got the expected attitude from the man behind the counter. He knew I was an addict and needed money, which automatically gave him the upper hand. I had a Bluetooth speaker set, which was almost unheard of technology at the time.

When I pulled it out, he said, "What the hell is this?"

I tried my best to explain it, but in spite of the $120 price tag in the store, I walked away with a measly $25 and knew I was lucky to get that.

"Come back when you get more," he called out to my back as I rushed out the door. I got to the bus stop just in time to miss the bus. I asked someone for the time. It was already 1:30pm.

There was no way I would make it to the Eastside and back in time for work, so I went in early. I'd just have to make it through the shift borderline sick, and go cop as soon as I got off.

I went in to my second day of work and lasted about three hours. I stood in that hot, loud kitchen as everyone ran circles around me, stressed, impatient, yelling and rushing. I had no idea what I was doing. I was trying to learn and do my best, but my mind was foggy and my bones were weak. I couldn't operate at that speed, not then. Their mouths were nasty and full of venom and anger. Waiters and waitresses act like they are saving lives. The level of stress in any given kitchen I've ever worked is akin to the level of stress you'd imagine firemen having going into a burning building. For the most part, they take their jobs very seriously. When a new employee like me stood between them and getting their food out to their table, they tore me apart verbally. I walked out, or rather, I snuck out. I casually walked away from the kitchen like I had to use the bathroom, but I never came back. I was sick, I was empty, and I needed to feel normal, which meant I needed to get high. Most of all I needed to get to the strip before it was too late and there was no dope out at all.

When I got off the bus at Johns Hopkins, the whole Monument Street had an eerie feeling to it. It was dark, and I hated being up there after dark. It was reminiscent of an "end of the world" movie, where everything in a once busy shopping district is abandoned, and there's nothing but trash blowing down the empty sidewalks. A few homeless drunks were scattered here and there, bundled up against brick walls. A few young boys stood in clusters on corners, but I paid them no mind. I was on a mission to travel the fifteen blocks or so to Belnord and see my savior from yesterday.

As usual, I moved swiftly, one hand in my front hoodie pocket holding the money for the drug, my other hand in the other pocket holding my pocket knife, just in case. He had told me yesterday that he'd be out, and I expected him to be posted up on the corner just like he was before. I got down to the corner and there was an older, thinner black dude standing there. "What's up? They out?" I shouted.

"Yeah yo, in the alley. What you need?" he replied.

"Hold up, this the same shit that dude had yesterday when I came through?" I asked hesitantly. I felt uneasy about this dude, but my craving didn't care.

"Yeah, in the alley...fuck I just said?" he replied impatiently. His frustration made me think he was legit. A scam artist would've tried to explain himself, I reasoned. I walked into the dark alley alone, my hands still in my pockets clutching my blade, and the other clutching my money even tighter. It was dark back there, and as I walked in, it got quiet. There was nobody back there. The further I walked in, the more paranoid I became.

I hollered out into the darkness, "Yoooooo!"

I wanted so badly to show my support to this man, who had shown me mercy the previous evening, that I stupidly walked into this trap. I realized suddenly what was going on and headed back out of the alley. The man who had led me in there stood at the entrance.

"What the fuck? There's nobody in there," I said.

"You didn't go in far enough," he said. "Go back in there!" He snapped.

For a second, I actually questioned myself and thought about going back in, but then decided for the better and went to walk past him out of the alley. His arm shot up and pressed just below my throat, pinning me against the brick wall at the entry of the alley way. His hand went to the front of his waistband like he was reaching for a gun.

"Kick that fucking money out, boy!" he snarled.

I had enough. I wasn't going to constantly get taken advantage of out here. My hand was already in my pocket clutching the knife in the ready position. My heart was racing, and cornered, I withdrew my hand and rammed the knife into his side just below the rib cage. His hand released from my neck almost instantly as he buckled quietly in front of me. I yanked the knife back in the same direction as I had plunged it in, and I felt warm fluid on my fingers. His blood was on me. I shoved my hands back into my pockets, slid past him, and headed for the corner. My mind immediately went to the gun. *Did he have one, or was he bluffing?* I rounded the corner walking as fast as I could, wincing inside, waiting for the gunshots to come that never came.

I got about a block away when I heard him yell, "Come back here! Wait!"

I turned back to see him stagger around the corner with his arm outstretched toward me like something from a zombie flick, and his knees half-buckled under the weight of his own body. I moved quickly, block after block, and dropped the bloody knife onto the street and kicked it into a storm drain. I had to get out of there fast. For once, I felt something was more important than finding heroin. The fear of going to jail for life was stronger than the fear of being dopesick, because going to jail for life meant never touching heroin again. I walked and walked until I got back to the halfway house. I climbed the long wooden staircase to that dusty old apartment like it was the stairway to the warmest refuge I'd ever known.

I got into the house feeling safe and secure inside, took a hot shower, skin crawling, and wishing I had gotten high. That night I laid on the couch tossing and turning, feeling like I was wrapped in cobwebs of misery, legs kicking, sleeping in cold sweat, and occasionally drifting off into a brief moment of sleep in which I dreamed. I dreamed of blood and butchery, and jail, and all of the things I was terrified of. Those were just figments of fear though. Jail was a reprieve. My real fear was having to face life without heroin and having to look at myself with sober eyes as well as all the wreckage I'd caused.

I got out of bed the next morning sick, but felt a renewed sense of pride in myself. I may have killed that man. I couldn't go back to that area for a while just in case I did, but I still had money in my pocket. I also still had my pride. For once I felt like the old me, like the bully instead of the bullied. I left the house and caught the 23 bus over to Westside. They would still be serving raw dope on Lauretta, this I was sure of.

I started catching the 23 regularly over to Lauretta to the raw dope strip. The dope there was $20 a vial, so I had to hustle a little harder, but I found new ways to do that as well. Portable CD players were new on the market, and I could get $30 for just one at any pawn shop. I would catch the number 8 bus out to Towson Town Center, which was a huge mall in Baltimore County and boost the CD Walkmans from the record stores there. They had alarm sensors on them, so I'd take them to a back corner of the store where the noise wouldn't be too loud and snap the sensor off, which usually left my hand bleeding. Most of the time I could sell them on the bus on the way back to the city without even going to a pawn shop.

I would cop dope on Lauretta, then walk across Franklin Street to the McDonald's to get high in the bathroom. It was a daily ritual. One day Lauretta was quiet, and there was no dope out. So, I was milling around McDonald's wondering what to do, when I started talking to a middle-aged black dude outside. He told me he was getting ready to cop some morphine-based dope up the street and that I should follow him. We walked a block up Franklin and to the median strip. There was a huge old metal staircase leading up to the train tracks above that crossed over Franklin. At the train stop on the top of the bridge was the hitter. He gave us our bags of dope, which had little Red Devils on the front. Unsure how much of this dope I could handle, I did half, and it rocked me. I came back looking for this dope many times and was never able to find it again. However, that night I caught a bus to the Harbor to play.

I roamed around the Harbor and decided to get a jump on the next day's "get well money." I wandered into the mall with the Brookstone, made my way up to the second floor, and into Brookstone. Just like the time before, I walked around expressing fake interest in a few items before stuffing another Bluetooth speaker set under my coat and making my exit. I left out onto the bridge walkway that spanned Pratt Street below, which was packed with shoppers and back-to-back traffic. Making my way across the bridge, suddenly the door in front of me opened and a security guard appeared. I tried to act casual, but realized he was coming right at me, so I turned and doubled back. Another guard burst forth from the other set of doors, and I was flanked by them. Surrounded, I climbed onto the railing, trying to estimate how to get over it and drop onto Pratt Street below without breaking something. There was no way I could pull it off, so I slowly stepped down and let them apprehend me.

They took me up to a room somewhere, in what I believe was the top of the mall, although it very well may have been the basement. I was way too high to remember. The room had three security guards in it and was covered with monitors and TV screens, like the ones in the movies. I cooperated as best as I could and followed their every instruction. This, I knew, was my only saving grace at this point. They asked me to empty the contents of my pockets, so I handed my possessions over to them. I fed them a lie about how I was Christmas shopping for my family and didn't have any money. I had a new knife in my pocket that they questioned me about, and kept. I didn't argue. They rifled through the rest of my possessions, threw my needle in the trash, and asked if I had drugs on me.

"No sir," I replied, immediately realizing I had put the rest of the bag of heroin in the cellophane of my pack of Newports.

He picked up the Newports off the desk, opened them, and looked inside among the loose cigarettes for drugs. As he held them, my heart raced, staring directly at the small bag of heroin that was staring back at me. Somehow, he never looked at the other side of the pack. He tossed them to me, and I quickly stuffed them into my pocket.

I got a lecture from them about heroin, and doing the right thing. I was also told that since I didn't have any actual drugs on me, and since I was so cooperative, that they were going to let me go—but if they ever saw me on the property again, I would be arrested immediately. I promised that I would never return and quickly exited into the cold night air, walking as far and as fast as I possibly could.

XXXIII.

Two nights before Thanksgiving, I was in the McDonald's bathroom on Franklin Street shooting dope. I heard a lighter and then a flick in the stall next to me. So, I lit my lighter and flicked my needle loud enough that they'd recognize the irony of me doing the same thing in the stall next to them.

I heard a voice say, "Hey, are you white?"

I chuckled to myself, "Yeah," I replied. "I'll be outside smoking. Come holla at me."

I went out front and lit up a cigarette. A white person in this area only meant one thing, and the telltale sounds of the lighter and the flick of the needle told it all. A young guy about my age came out and introduced himself as Chris. We started talking, and I found out that he was from Edgewood out in the county too, and that we knew a lot of the same people. He invited me to come out "hacking" with him in his Mustang, so I did. Hacking was picking up hacks or the act of being a hack. A hack was someone who stood on any given street corner waving their hand up and down pointing at the street, which was a signal that they were willing to pay for a ride somewhere. Since Chris had a car, we had the option of driving around all night making money by picking up hacks. Chris didn't know me, and owed me nothing, but he was willing to let me in on the money he made that night, I guess because the junkie life gets lonely and boring at times.

We rode around the whole city that night picking up hacks and copping dope and coke until it was time for me to get back to the halfway house before curfew. He dropped me off, and I even had a pill for the next morning. Life was good. I didn't ever expect to run into Chris again, but as fate would have it, his father would end up being my urinalysis supervisor while on probation in Harford County half a decade later. Then a decade after that his father would come into my bail bonds office to bail Chris out. But that was the one and only time I ever got high with Chris, the "white boy" in the next stall.

That Thanksgiving was a day I will never ever forget. As far as Lenny and my father knew, I was still working at The Hard Rock. My father was coming to pick me up to go to my grandmother's for our annual Thanksgiving tradition at her house in the county. I was already feeling the pangs of sickness because the last time I had gotten high was the previous morning, and he was coming to get me at 10:00am. I lied and told my father that I had to work at 4:00pm in order to buy myself time to get well before night fell. He picked me up for an awkward, uncomfortable ride to the county. We got there early, so dinner wasn't ready yet. I tried my best to be normal, but I couldn't. My skin was on fire, and I had goose bumps all over me. My muscles and tendons were crawling with sickness, and my anxiety and depression were screaming out from within. I went into my grandmother's bathroom at one point and rummaged through her cabinets.

There were various medications in there that I was unfamiliar with, but one caught my eye. It was quinine. I had no idea what quinine did, but I knew it was used to cut heroin. I thought at minimum it might make my withdrawals subside a little bit. I sat in there cooking the quinine in my spoon, while my family fellowshipped outside. While they enjoyed each other's company,

I hovered in the bathroom like a fiend cooking white mush on a spoon. It wouldn't even draw up in a needle or fully liquify. I was out of my mind with fear and pain, so I sucked up the chalky, white, powdery liquid into the needle and fired it into my arm anyway. My arm swelled up. I tried cooking muscle relaxers and shooting them. My arms were swollen and throbbing. I was waiting for one of these medications to clog a vein and to be rushed to a hospital, but that didn't happen.

I sat through Thanksgiving dinner trying to be normal, forcing myself to eat, forcing myself to keep up appearances because I didn't want to ruin anyone's holiday. I sweat, I froze, I pushed down fear while I sat at that table watching everyone around me talk and laugh. I resented their happy little lives and the simplicity of it all. As soon as I got a break, I snuck into the bedrooms. I found a container full of change and scooped out a handful of quarters. Then I thought about it and went back again to scoop out another handful...then another. I put the change in the pockets of my coat, and I started getting antsy. I had to get downtown. I had to "work."

I finally coerced my father to take me back down to the Harbor so I could go to The Hard Rock. I had him drop me off nearby, under the impression that I wanted to walk and smoke a cigarette before my shift. Of course, the real reason I didn't want him dropping me at the door was because I didn't want him to see that the place was closed. As soon as he dropped me off, I doubled back into downtown Baltimore and started walking to the Westside. Through rows of tall buildings in the business district I walked, stopping occasionally at bus stops, but getting impatient and walking onward. Nobody was out, and the city was quiet, especially the otherwise busy downtown area. I made it over near Lexington Market and stopped to ask an older, black woman at a bus stop what was going on. She explained that due to the holiday, the buses were only running once an hour. I couldn't sit still, I was too sick and fidgety, and walking made it temporarily easier.

I walked all the way to Lauretta until I reached the dope strip. It was quiet. Nobody was out. I saw a young black girl come walking out of the alley who I had seen on the corner hustling before.

"Hey pssst…" I got her attention. "Is anything out? Why's it so dead?"

"No, honey. They closed up earlier, but I can get you something."

I was disheartened. I didn't trust anyone out here unless they were selling the product on hand. I asked her if they would take $20 in quarters.

She said, "Hell, no. You better come back with some bills."

I told her I'd be back in a few minutes and ran across the street. I was too sick for all of this running around. I couldn't believe I was so close. I crossed back over Franklin and was crushed to see that the McDonald's was closed. Not only was it Thanksgiving, but it was also dark out by now. Everything was stacking up against me. I jogged over to the gas station next door. There was an Arab behind the glass who turned me down when I asked about cashing in my change.

"Look, what if I buy something?" I pleaded. "What if I give you $20 in quarters and you give me back $18."

He finally gave in and counted out $18 in cash for my $20 in quarters. I was going back to the dope strip with short money. The hood feeds on desperation. They can smell it a mile away, and they'll use it to their advantage every time. Unfortunately, after running all day and being dopesick, I was past that point. I reeked of desperation. I got back to the alley on Lauretta, and the girl came walking down to greet me. I told her how much I had.

She said, "Fine, but you gotta split it with me."

I didn't care at this point. I was sick. I had no choice and no one else to turn to. I had to get well. I couldn't go home feeling like this. She disappeared into the alley, and I prayed she would come back. I had no choice, but to stand there like a helpless fool, waiting. After a few minutes in the cold, I saw her shadowy figure coming down the alley, and my stomach started turning. I would finally get well. I had new hope. She handed me a small bag of heroin, which had nothing but minuscule crumbs in the bottom of it.

"What is this? You took way more than half." I said.

"Nope, that's all it was," she claimed and headed back into the alley.

There was maybe $5 worth of heroin in that bag, if I was lucky. It would hopefully be enough to make me feel temporarily normal, but definitely not enough to get me high or carry me through the night.

I scurried across Franklin. It was fully dark now, and I had to find a place to get high. McDonald's was closed, and that was my only resource within walking distance. I had to find isolation and light because I couldn't risk spilling my last little bit of dope. I walked across the McDonald's parking lot, and spotted a light out back by the drive-through with a little concrete stairway leading to a door. I looked around, then went down the concrete stairway and sat on the bottom step under the flickering light. Bugs and moths danced around the light as it buzzed and flickered above me. My hands shook as I pulled out my needle, my metal bottle cap to cook the heroin, and of course the dope. I was missing water though.

I hadn't even thought about that. I was so used to water being readily available everywhere on any given day. Water, the essential element of life, is also an essential element of a dope fiend's habit. The four elements of the universe: earth, air, water, and fire are all needed to make the black magic of a heroin high. The heroin from the earth, the water as the dilutant, the fire in the lighter's flame, and the air inside of my lungs which was essentially the puppeteer that pulled my very strings. Water was usually easy to find. It's everywhere, and I would use it in whatever shape it was found. Just like the dirty needles I found in the street, I would use water in whatever form it was readily available to soothe my ills. I had used toilet water, stream water, puddle water, or even dew in dire circumstances.

Unfortunately, tonight was the direst of circumstances and no water could be found. I had sunken to horrible lows as an addict. My shame was one of the factors that kept the gears of addiction in motion, but tonight I would cross another low. I considered spitting in the metal "cooker," but my mouth was so dry from sickness that my saliva was bubbly. I had no other choice. I had to get high immediately, or feel like I was going to curl up and die in that stairwell. I unzipped my pants and started urinating at the bottom of the stairwell. Toward the end of the stream, I dipped the metal cap in and caught a few drops of urine, then zipped up my pants and got to work. I dumped the heroin into the cap, cooked it, and shot my own urine that night. I laid my head back and waited for a rush that never came. I felt nothing.

I sat alone in my despair, horror, guilt, and a million feelings I never wanted to feel. I didn't want to get onto a bus to go home. I wanted to walk in front of the bus, but I couldn't even do that. Heroin had broken me. It made me filthy and disgusting. It made me pray for death, but also made me too weak to pursue it. It was a slow torture, a horror movie that never ended, but I just couldn't stop myself from going back.

When I reflect back on my addiction, this is where I measure my rock bottom. Of all the events from start to finish, this very day is where I found my rock bottom. I know if I get high again, my bottom could go lower. I did a lot of terrible, immoral things in the name of getting high, but I know they could always get worse. I never killed anyone that I loved. I never had sexual relations with another man. I never willingly let anyone hurt me. Somehow, I managed to hold onto the tiniest sliver of pride. I was lucky to be intelligent and resourceful, but I never kid myself. If I were to go back out and start using heroin at any time, anything is possible. The possibilities of a so-called "rock bottom" are infinite.

I eventually trudged my way to the bus stop and rode home for another wide-eyed night of tossing and turning, nightmares, and pain on the old halfway house couch. Tomorrow morning would be a new day. I'd be even worse in the morning, but with sunlight there came promise. In the heroin world, just like everything else in life, where there's a will, there's a way. I would get high, no matter how much it was killing me.

The next morning, Lenny called me over to his house and said he wanted to do a late Thanksgiving meal for all the guys in the halfway house. He asked me if I could go pick up some things from the grocery store since I was the only one who was off that day. I was sick as hell and quickly agreed, telling myself that I could figure out how to handle things after I got high. He gave me $30 and a grocery list. I showed up two hours later with the items on the list that I was able to steal, and fed him some ridiculous lie about getting robbed in the parking lot of the store for the rest of the money. I knew even in my high state that there was only a small chance he would possibly believe me, but also that he had no way of proving that I was lying.

I don't remember that meal. I got myself nice and high with the grocery money in order to have to sit down with these strangers I lived with. I assume they all had to know that I was high, but no one ever confronted me. They all must have had their own thing going on with Lenny, or maybe they had their own dirt. I didn't question it. I just ate, did the dishes, and got out of there as fast as I could. The next day I boosted a CD player, showed up at the back door of Hard Rock where the employees smoked, and begged Lindsey to buy it. She did and told me when she got off, she'd drive to go cop. The next night I met her and her boyfriend outside of the restaurant when she got off. I had promised them that I could get us all money to cop if they took me somewhere to boost some CD players.

It was around 8:00pm when we went to Eastpoint Mall on the east side of Baltimore. I went into the music store and grabbed two CD players, snapped off the alarm sensors, and stuck them under my coat. Once out in the mall, I found a big plant to hide them in, then I went back into the music store for more. This time, I figured I'd grab a couple box sets, but as I went through the alarm sensors, it started blaring. I panicked and started sprinting through the mall, and two security guards gave chase.

I dashed across the food court and through the glass doors into the parking lot. The security guards were close behind me, as I ran around the outside of the mall. I came up to an enclosed dumpster area and cut to the left around it. When I did, I grabbed the box sets from under my coat and tossed them up over the wooden fence into the dumpster enclosure. Still moving as fast as I could, I jetted around the wall of the dumpster and collided into a security officer and went skidding across the asphalt on my side. The other officer was on me immediately. They both got ahold of me. I was trapped.

They took me into their security room and told me that I was not only being charged with theft, but that I was also being charged with assaulting a police officer. These were apparently sworn officers assigned to this mall. I argued with them, saying that they knew I didn't intentionally run into them, that they knew it was only an accident. It was clear I was going to city jail. I was screwed. This was going to be a horrible night. I cried, I surrendered, I knew I was out of options. They did the usual search to make sure I didn't have any drugs or weapons or additional stolen merchandise on me.

After about ten minutes, they returned and said, "Tonight's your lucky night. We decided not to charge you with assault on an officer."

They handed me a citation to appear in city court for misdemeanor theft charges, then released me. Once again, I was told that if I was caught setting foot on mall property ever again, I would be arrested. I walked into the cold night air, refreshed and feeling like I got another chance at life. I walked quickly across the parking lot, knowing that I still needed to get high and unsure where to even begin. Suddenly a car pulled up next to me. It was Lindsey and her boyfriend. I hopped in. I couldn't believe they hadn't abandoned me. They were about to leave the mall and take me home, when I reminded Lindsey of the CD players inside the mall that I had stashed in the plant. I gave her directions to where the plant was, just outside of the entrance of one of the department stores, and then convinced her to go in and retrieve them while we sat in the car. After ten minutes anxiously laying in that car, I poked my head up to see her walking across the parking lot smiling ear to ear. God bless America, I wasn't going back to the house sick again.

One day, I caught the 23 bus over to Lauretta and walked up to cop dope. The strip was crowded, and they were competing for my business. A black girl I knew on the corner nodded in the direction of a young dude, so I walked toward him. Instead of doing the transaction right there though, he told me to walk with him. We walked down to the corner and turned onto a busy street. I was a little leery.

He said, "We good yo, right here," and pointed to a house a couple doors down from the corner.

I realized he didn't have the dope on him in case any cops were around, and he didn't want to lose my business. He opened the small gate, and we walked the large flight of stairs onto the covered porch of the row home. Between the door and the screen door, he kept a bag full of vials of raw dope. It looked to be fifty or sixty of them in there. He pulled one out and gave it to me. I was taken aback by the fact that he would show me where his stash was, but it was good to know. That much dope could keep me high for weeks and bring me a good chunk of money to pay rent and to play with.

The next day I caught the bus over to Lauretta. I sat on a stairwell at the bus stop, which was across the busy four-lane Franklin Street, near the house with dope between the door and the screen. I eventually saw the boy run up and down the steps a couple times hitting his stash. I waited until I knew the bus was coming again and got ready. Once I saw the bus crest over the hill where it makes its descent from the intersection of Edmondson and Poplar Grove, I casually started walking across the street. I turned and looked as the bus pulled up to the last bus stop before mine. As soon as it scooted off, I broke through the front gate of that house. I scrambled up the steps, grabbed the bag from between the doors, and hurried down the steps so fast that I ripped my leg open on a post. I made it back through the gate and onto the bus without being noticed. I slouched down in the back of the bus and watched out the window, but there was no action as we lurched forward and down the street.

Easing down into my seat, I slipped out the worn, rolled up brown paper bag, unfolded it, and looked inside. Where once fifty to sixty vials were stashed, now only three measly vials remained, bouncing around in the bottom of that bag. I had just ruined my chance of ever going back to Lauretta over $45 of dope. *Oh well,* I thought, *at least I am getting well today.* I felt bad for the young boy I had just ripped off. There may have been serious repercussions for him, but there were lessons to be learned in these streets. Never show a junkie where you keep your stash. I got off at the next stop and found the nearest bathroom to get high. I knew I'd have to start figuring out my next "get rich quick" scheme, and I'd be heading back to Monument Street again.

A couple of days after the grocery store incident with Lenny, he called over to the house early one morning before I left and said he wanted to have a serious talk with me. My heart raced. *He must finally be throwing me out. Or maybe he is going to actually give me a real urine test.* On top of the stunts I'd recently pulled, my parents had stopped paying my rent, and I hadn't given him a dime in almost three weeks. This had to be my eviction speech. I walked timidly down to his house. He opened the door with a serious look on his face.

"Sit down," he said, his old brow furrowing as he crossed one leg over the other in his chair as if he was going to talk philosophy with me. "How would you like to make some serious money doing some things for me?" he asked.

His question caught me off guard. This was the opposite of what I had expected. At this point, anything further that came out of his mouth could only be good news.

"Absolutely," I agreed, eager to hear what he had to say. I got the feeling that this wasn't about cleaning out houses, but something easier, something not-so-legal.

"Can I trust you? I need to know that I can trust you," he said. I assured him that whatever it was, it couldn't be any worse than anything I'd already done. He continued by telling me that he could have regular work for me as long as he knew that he could trust me not to tell anyone what we were up to. I assured him that he had no worries with me.

That's when things went way off the course I had expected them to go. Lenny casually told me that he was willing to pay me $1,200 if I was willing to follow his exact instructions. I eagerly accepted. He said there was a particular woman he knew who was a prostitute. He said to never mind the backstory or why he was doing this, but that he wanted to rent a van and pick her up. He wanted me to be in the back of the van with her while he drove, and that he planned to videotape the whole thing. He wanted me to befriend her, smoke cigarettes, and talk with her, and to ask her very specific questions. He then wanted me to pay her for a blowjob and make sure I got the whole thing in front of the camera, while I smack her around and call her a "whore" and a "slut," and ask her if she likes to "fuck niggers." I cringed inside. I knew immediately that I wasn't doing this, so I asked no further questions.

I simply said, "Sure, no problem. Just let me know when you're ready." I was willing to do almost anything for money, but I wasn't doing that. None of it made any sense, and Lenny was one of the creepiest old men I'd ever come across. I walked out of his house cool and collected that day, but inside my world was spinning. It felt surreal.

I ventured out into the city confused, but not so confused that I didn't get money to get high. What just happened was so unbelievable that right before I went to score some dope, I called my father. I told him exactly what had transpired, expecting him not to believe a word I had just said. The story was so insane, I doubted that I'd believe it if I were him. Not to mention, I was a junkie, all I did was lie. This time though, I had to make sure he knew that I was telling the truth.

"I'm leaving tonight after everyone goes to sleep," I told him. "I'm not worried about myself, but I have nowhere to put all my stuff. I can't leave it there," I told him.

The words that came through the other end of the phone blew my mind. I couldn't explain why or how they happened other than pure love.

Instead of anger and disappointment, I heard my father say, "I won't say anything to Lenny. Be ready. I'll pick you up at 11:00 tonight. And Danny, be careful."

I wanted to cry, and maybe I did, but I also got high. Then, I did exactly as I was told. When 11:00pm hit, my dad came, and we drove off into the night.

SEASON FOUR:

WINTER THAWS INTO SPRING

"Well, I've been afraid of changing
because I've built my life round you,
But time makes you bolder,
And children get older
And I'm getting older, too."

~Fleetwood Mac, "Landslide"

"I'm not the one who's so far away
When I feel the snake bite enter my veins,
Never did I wanna be here again
And I don't remember why I came."

~Godsmack, "Voodoo"

XXXIV.

The night my father picked me up from the halfway house was the first night in a very long time that I'd spent in the home I'd grown up in. However, it was only for the night. I was told that I could leave my stuff there, but I could not stay there until I got clean. I gravitated back to the city with all the possessions I could fit inside of a book bag. I bounced back and forth between different black women's households in East Baltimore. There was Rhonda on Ashland, and Kia on Castle Street. I would sleep on their couches or in their beds. They took care of me while I was there, and most of them didn't even get high. I would shove a machete in my waistband and walk the hill up to Biddle Street because that was the new hotspot. Sometimes I'd hit the intersection of Eager and Rutland Streets, but that was more of an early morning shop. Rico had opened up "Stars" again in a small alley off of Biddle, and all the junkies were raving about it. I ventured up there one night when I was half dopesick and found a crowd milling around at the mouth of the alley.

"They on hold. They'll be back any minute," one of the old black men told me.

There were never any white folks in these parts. If Monument was dangerous, this was an all-out war zone. I brought the machete to feel safe but couldn't imagine it ever saving my life, maybe fending off a couple of junkies at best. The hitters came up the block in a hurry, loudly barking orders.

"Okay everybody, line up with your back against the wall at the third stoop in the alley. Put both fucking hands in front of you with your money in your right! We ain't taking no shorts and no change!"

I recognized the face and the voice instantly. They were the same guys from the other Stars shop who shot the guy in the face in front of the crowd. Everyone followed orders immediately, and I placed both hands out with a twenty in my right, both palms up. He came through rapidly with the bag of gel caps, taking money, and dropping pills in hands. He paused when he got to me, the only white guy out of the fifteen or so in the alley.

He looked me in the eye and asked, "Why you shaking, ghost?" as if he thought my behavior was suspicious.

"It's cold as hell out here," I stuttered.

A big light-skinned dude next to me said, "It's cool. He with me," in reference to me.

The hitter dropped the pills in my hand, and I took off out of the alley following the other junkies who had just gotten theirs. I waited for the dude who spoke up for me and thanked him briefly.

He replied, "It's cool. Be careful out here, bro."

I never saw him again, but I always felt like I encountered random angels in the darkest of places, people who didn't belong in the situations in which I found them. They were almost out of place, as if they were only there to protect or save me.

Almost from the time I had begun getting high, I wanted to stop using. It was a worthless painful existence, but I couldn't seem to figure out how to fight the cravings. Willpower and inner strength seemed powerless. Many nights, I prayed with tears that God would take away the cravings and rid me of the desire. I prayed while I was high to be able to quit and never look back. Countless nights I prayed and cried, sometimes immediately after the high settled into my system, and I realized what I had done to myself again.

However, by morning the vicious cycle began all over again. My heartfelt prayers became a distant memory with the dawning sun. The desire to stay clean seemed almost ridiculous, and the carnal urge to get high was back in full force. I was possessed. My addiction was sorcery, and I was under its spell. I spent years in the same dismal, decaying lifestyle. I wanted to die an addict, not as an old man—I wanted it to end soon. That never seemed to happen. Even when faced with the possibility of death, my survival instincts kicked in, and I would somehow manage to escape its dark grasp. Something deep inside told me that I couldn't die like this, that my story was far from over, that I was here for a greater purpose. *But, what?* Not only was something inside of me keeping me in this prison called Earth, but something outside of me seemed to be as well. I had narrowly escaped death way too many times for it to be coincidental. I had also averted significant prison sentences in much the same fashion.

There was a new methadone clinic out in the county by my parents' house that I had been hearing about. I didn't know much about methadone, but I had heard that you could quit heroin by taking methadone and not experience any withdrawal symptoms. That is exactly what I thought I needed. So, one day when I was in the county, I convinced my father to take me to the clinic for an intake appointment. The clinical counselor I was assigned to asked if I wanted to invite my father into the room, so I did. He managed to convince my father and me that this would be the cure for my addiction. At $85 a week, I would have to come in every morning between the hours of 6:00-11:00 to drink my dose of methadone. I would get random urinalysis tests and have a biweekly visit with my therapist.

"If you're interested, you can pay the $85 and start tomorrow," he told us.

My father agreed to pay two weeks ahead, and I was on my own after that. I spent the night in my parents' guest bedroom and sweated it out that night, knowing that reprieve would come in the morning. We arrived at the clinic, and they started me on a dose of 60mg of methadone. I had to stand in line at a small window in the back of the clinic where they were dispensing the doses. When I got to the window, a nurse asked for my ID and checked my name off on a sheet of paper. She then came back and handed me a cup of a syrupy Kool-Aid like liquid. I drank it in front of her and handed her the empty cup. It tasted bitter and medicinal, but I was eager to feel its effects. Within an hour my chills and sickness subsided, and I rested into a state of normalcy. Within a couple hours, I sank further into a comfortable state, not quite high, more like the feeling of dozing off in front of the TV. But as the day went on, I started feeling nauseous.

My stomach started churning, and I broke out into a heavy sweat. I laid down sick in bed, wondering if it was from the methadone or from something else in my system. Around 6:00 in the evening I awoke with the uncontrollable urge to vomit, so I hopped out of bed. I didn't make it two steps before I pro- jectile vomited across the guest room vanity and the wall behind it, then collapsed on the floor. I cried out for my parents, afraid that something horrible was happening, but as I continued to vomit, the sickness subsided.

First thing the next morning, we were back at the clinic explaining the previous night's events to my therapist. He explained that it was likely that my body was adjusting to the medication and to give it a couple of days. If things didn't change, then we could lower my dose. I was an addict, so the idea of lowering my dosage didn't sit well with me. Fortunately, the methadone seemed to work. I began to regain my footing in life, despite the daily trips back and forth to the clinic. I got a job at the local 7-Eleven within walking distance of my house and was quickly able to afford the clinic costs. After a 30-day trial run of staying in my parents' guest room, my parents decided I could live there temporarily while I got on my feet. I agreed to enroll back into college and keep full-time employment while I lived there. I also agreed to pay them rent that I never paid.

I was no longer stealing to support my addiction, however my morals had far from changed. I was off of heroin, but I wasn't recovering. I was still stealing anything that wasn't nailed down in order to play "catch up" with my peers. I was stealing the best hygiene products, and clothes, and everything else I thought I needed to blend in as a normal, successful member of society. Even at the 7-Elven where I worked, I had perfected a way to steal cigarettes and scratch off tickets out of sight of the surveillance cameras. I would go home at the end of every shift with rolls of them, scratch them off and cash them in at other locations. It got so bad, they eventually removed them from that location.

After a couple of months, I put my name on a waiting list for a state-run methadone program in Bel Air and was accepted. My fees went from $85 a week to only $8 a month to get my daily doses. Most people who went to the clinic were long-term users who had been on methadone for decades and never intended to get off of it. That was a scary thought. Methadone was an easy way out, but it was still a drug that had control over me. I couldn't live without it. It dictated my life. If I missed a day, I was sick, just like with heroin. It numbed my experience and gave me a very mild high, but it didn't allow me to fully be myself.

There were a few drawbacks. I couldn't keep my eyes open through a book or movie. I fell asleep many mornings while driving the back roads to the methadone clinic. I would wake up miles down the road and not be able to describe how I was still alive and on the road. I would often tell people later that angels must have carried me. I was constipated for days, or even weeks at a time. I would take massive amounts of stool softeners, suppositories, and even enemas, still nothing could make me go. Methadone was a bandage. It didn't fix anything that was wrong with me; it just masked it for a little while. Another big problem was that in true addict form, I could never get enough. I would complain and push the limits at the clinic regularly in order to get my dosage raised. I got my dosage up to about 100mg daily, nearly double the dose I started with.

My life appeared to level out with Methadone. I re-enrolled in the local community college. I was promoted to night manager at the 7-Eleven. After a few months being incident free, I went to a car auction and got a cheap vehicle. I stopped stealing and became passionate about things I had been passionate about before. I started reading and studying a lot on religion, philosophy, and the occult. I studied everything from the Masons and Rosicrucian order, to crystals and astrology, to Jewish mysticism and the lost books of the Gospel. I read myself to sleep every night. I prayed heavily to the God I believed in and began meditating and exploring every avenue toward enlightenment. My new beliefs sank in. I became a new person free from crime and violence. I was okay for a brief period of time.

Through all the soul-searching and God-seeking, I never addressed any of my own internal issues. Eventually the demons came crawling back out. I began having anxiety attacks that sent me to the emergency room swearing that I was having a heart attack. My depression and anxiety started overwhelming me to the point that I was on my knees praying and crying regularly like I had done back in my heroin addiction. I worked the graveyard shift at 7-Eleven, and was the only person there. I barely saw sunlight. I talked to a counselor at the methadone clinic in Bel Air, and he put me on Ativan, which is another addictive drug similar to Xanax.

Around that time, I took a ride downtown and got high. Then, I did it again, and again…and again. Methadone was supposed to block the high of heroin. It did a little bit, but it didn't block the rush when the dope first hit, and it didn't block the excitement that came with the journey downtown to cop heroin. Methadone also complemented a cocaine high because it softened the crash from cocaine.

I heard that a lot of people started shooting cocaine while they were on methadone, but I never understood why, until I tried it. I began speedballing every day, mixing cocaine and heroin in the same needle. I was listening to old heroin-related rock-and-roll songs and bands, and I took on the persona of a heroin rock and roll star. I would drive ninety miles an hour down I-95 to cop heroin with a bandana tied around my head and tracks in my arm, while blaring songs by the Rolling Stones, like "Gimme Shelter." I felt like what I was doing was cool. But it escalated very quickly, and in just months, I was right back where I had been, only worse. The difference being that as long as I had methadone in the morning, I would never get truly sick. So, I could embrace the "good side" of getting high. I mostly shot dope with other methadone addicts, and since we had jobs, we had money. My arms started tracking up badly again, and my veins were knotted or not coming to the surface because of all the cocaine shots. With heroin you only have to inject a couple times a day, but with cocaine you have to go every fifteen minutes to keep the high going.

I had to start hitting my hands, feet, and neck with shots, because my arms wouldn't cooperate. Once I drove up I-95 hitting myself in my neck with a speedball in the rearview mirror while glancing over at the cars next to me to see the expressions of horror on their faces. I really thought I was cool, so to me the expressions on their faces were hilarious. I believed that being a loser with nothing left to lose was the only way left to be. I started hanging out with the older couple who had gotten Jessie started shooting back at Red Lobster. The husband, John, had been shooting dope for almost forty years, and I envied his ability to survive and live a somewhat normal life and raise children while doing so. We would sit downtown in the car and get high, and he would tell me how his brother from Seattle was the lead singer in a rock band that was going to blow up and make it big one day. I would shoot my dope and entertain his stories, but not really put any stock into them because everyone thinks their family member's or friend's band will be famous someday. I let him talk about it all the time and gave him mock fascination. His brother even flew into town one time, and he introduced me to him over dinner at the pizza parlor where he worked. A couple of years later, from my prison cell in a medium-security facility in Jessup, I saw a rock band introduced on Good Morning America. When they began playing their hit song, I recognized the band's name and the lead singer's face, and my heart lit up with joy and excitement. John's make-believe fantasies weren't make-believe after all. Something in this world really did have a happy ending.

I eventually gave up on college because I couldn't keep my eyes open during the classes, and it was interfering with my trips downtown. I had left my job at 7-Eleven because they were keeping me on graveyard shift, and the months without sunlight were affecting me. The depression was way too much to bear. I had found a job stocking and working in a huge arts and crafts store in Bel Air that had much better hours. The problem was that my dope habit escalated quickly too. Even though I was on methadone, I had a daily heroin habit, or at least in my mind I did. The coke was occasional fun for me, when there was money for it, but the heroin was a daily routine.

The spiritual books I was reading, the lectures, the meditations, and church all fell to the wayside, and I started back to my old way of living. I started stealing again, I sold anything I owned of value, and I bought a gun from another junkie looking for "get-well" money. I only used that gun a couple of times, mostly to rob other people in the city streets at night, and one time I got brave and robbed a dope man.

I drove down Madison Street early one evening and made a left onto a little side street called Rose Street. I pulled up on the strip and told the hitter I needed six pills. When he came up to the window for the hand off, I grabbed his arm, pulled him toward the window, and pointed the gun in his face until he released his grip on the pills. As soon as I released my grip on him, I heard a loud crack and my car shook. I ducked low and peeled out of the side street and back onto Monument. Somebody had swung a bat or pole at my head just as I started moving forward, and instead of connecting with me, it dented the strip of metal between my front and back windows. That split-second movement, and those several inches forward, saved my life. I could have easily been beaten to death or shot that evening.

On another occasion I was sitting around in my house on a Sunday going stir crazy. I had fought back the urge to get high all day until I couldn't take it anymore. I figured my only option was to pawn the TV and VCR I had just gotten. They weren't worth much, but they were practically new. I'd just get them back out of pawn when I got paid, I reasoned. I got a phone book and started calling every pawn shop in the area, but it was after 6:00pm, and they were all closed. I finally got ahold of the only shop that was open until 8:00pm. It was in Essex, about thirty minutes away, and it was already 7:20pm. I unplugged everything, loaded it into my car, and headed off. I flew down the highway as fast as I could and was barely going to make it just before the shop closed.

As soon as I got off the highway, I realized I had taken the wrong exit. So, I frantically made a U-turn and ended up going up over a curb I didn't see in the dark. My back tire was blown out. I pulled over to find that the tire was completely flat already, and the rim was bent. I was only a mile from the store though, so

I hopped back into my car and tore down Eastern Avenue. As I drove, I could hear rubber smacking the side of my vehicle loudly as the car wobbled down the road. I pulled up into the parking lot and ran to the front door, but I was minutes too late. I went back to look at the flat tire I had just sped down the street on, and it was literally shredded. The strips of rubber whipped against my car so hard, they cracked pieces off of my wheel-well and fender.

I sighed and began the process of removing the tire and putting on a donut when a young black couple showed up, also disappointed to see the pawn shop was closed. They offered to help with the tire, but instead of accepting their help, I talked them into buying the TV and VCR for the measly price of $30. Once I had the spare on, I discarded the remains of the shredded tire and headed downtown. I drove for months on that donut, never once being responsible enough to actually purchase a new tire for the vehicle.

I ended up failing a urine test at the methadone clinic. I blamed it on the dose not being high enough, so they moved it up to 120mg. The higher the dose, the more heroin I had to shoot to get a rush. I was spending a couple of hundred dollars a day on coke and heroin, and that kind of money wasn't easy to come by. I didn't have to be at the craft store until 10:30 most mornings, so I would be able to hit the clinic, run down to the city, get high, and be back before work by the skin of my teeth. I could work well while I was high. The place was big, and I had no real direct supervision. I often clocked in and hung out back smoking cigarettes all shift long.

I started stealing sterling silver from the jewelry display counters of local department stores. I was too lazy to remove the individual store tags from the necklaces, rings, and bracelets before I sold them to the pawn shop because I was usually in a rush to get high. Luckily though, I found a pawn shop owner who took them from me just like that. My last hit was The Hecht

Company in the Harford Mall, which happened to be right across the parking lot from where I was employed. I would go in there when I was sober and snatch handfuls of jewelry, stuff them in my pockets, and head straight for the door. At the pawn shop I could net around $200 per trip. I did this about half a dozen days in a row until the day I walked into the store high.

I had gotten high that morning and went into my job. After about two hours of boredom, I went out front to smoke a cigarette and decided to walk across the street to the Hecht Company. I confidently walked into the store thinking nobody would ever suspect me in my work uniform. As I approached the jewelry department, instead of snatching and walking out in one quick motion like I usually did, I bounced around in a blissful daze holding and eyeing various pieces. Prince was on the intercom singing "Raspberry Beret," and in my high, I danced around trying on various rings and bracelets, stuffing different pieces into my work apron. I moved about that jewelry section without a care in the world, whistling and singing and dancing my way toward the exit of the store into the mall.

Just as I stepped over the threshold that separated the store from the hallway of the mall, I heard "Freeze!"

I turned to see a large man leap out from behind a rack of women dresses. I pivoted and ran about two steps, and in those two steps something happened. It felt like a complete surrender of everything inside of me, maybe a wake-up call, or an utter realization of where this lifestyle had led. I thought about the fact that I was in my work uniform, and that I wouldn't make it very far. I stopped. I turned around, and I held out my arms. I offered myself up to him and the other security guard who had just joined him and all that came with it. They led me back to the security room and began to process me. That's when the demons arose. The slow realization began to settle in that they were not letting me go.

They called the police to come get me. I began to writhe. The more I thought about the methadone withdrawal, my job, and my car across the street in that parking lot, and of course, how long it would be until I got high again, the more I ripped apart inside. I freaked out. I screamed and cried and begged, to the point they had to handcuff me to a pipe that was protruding from the wall until the police got there.

The amount I had been caught with was well within the felony range. I was also on probation and had various pending charges. This would be the end of the road for a long time. I seized and shook, and bawled, and sobbed. I know I must have appeared absolutely out of my mind to those security officers, and in those moments, I was. I knew what lie ahead of me was going to be weeks of the worst sickness I had ever endured, as well as a long time behind bars. When the officer arrived, I knew it was too late. There was no hope of walking away from this. I surrendered my tired, broken body and soul to the punishment that was to follow.

XXXV.

They processed me into the Harford County detention center and sent me back to the dorms. There were already a couple of guys in the dorm dopesick when I got there, and I witnessed them as an omen of things to come. A young black dude, who had been using, lay up in his top bunk shitting himself until the inmates raised enough hell to get him out of the dorm. I knew what was coming for me was way worse. I had to find a way to get out of this dorm before the sickness kicked in. Heroin was bad enough, but at this point I was drinking 120mg of methadone every day, shooting almost ten pills of heroin a day, and taking an Ativan prescription daily.

The first two days of withdrawals were eerie. It was almost like the calm before the storm. I was used to dopesickness from heroin kicking in almost immediately, but I felt fine. I couldn't believe it. Maybe somehow, some way, God had spared me the sickness! But I soon discovered that was not the case. My third day in, flu-like symptoms began seeping their way into my system. I went to the medical department for check-ups three times daily so they could monitor my withdrawal symptoms. I became frantic as I felt the onset of the sickness coming, so I tried repeatedly to have them contact my methadone program to get my doses delivered to the prison. I had heard of this being done there before for inmates who could afford it. However, since my methadone clinic was through the state, they decided to kick me out of it the second they discovered that I had been arrested, especially since I had just failed repeated drug tests.

My sickness got so intense that they eventually moved me into a medical isolation cell. Normally, they would have left me to sweat it out in the general population dorm, but my saving grace was that I had been on Ativan. Ativan, because it's a Benzodiazepine, can cause seizures and possibly fatality during withdrawal. Though my dosage was not high enough for that to be a factor, the fact that it was combined with extremely high dosages of other drugs, and the intensity of my withdrawal symptoms, warranted me having my own medical isolation cell.

The cell was tiny. It contained of a small metal cot with a two-inch thick plastic mattress, a pillow so flimsy that I may as well have been resting my head on an empty pillowcase, a dusty sheet and a scratchy blanket. There was a small steel sink adjacent to an ice-cold stainless-steel toilet where I would be spending most of my time. Everything was cold, the cement walls, the floor, the ceiling, and the steel bars that lined the front of the cell with paint chipping off of them.

Seventeen days I spent in that cell, the longest days of my life. I slept maybe two hours total that first week, if I was lucky. My eyes were yellowed with jaundice from liver damage. The nurse weighed me in at 118 pounds as a full-grown adult male. The terror and torture that went on inside my mind and body are inexplicable. I tossed and turned in the fires of hell inside that cage as the devil stoked the flames. I eagerly awaited the delivery of my meals. I had no desire to eat, but I craved the two minutes of human interaction at the end of that dark hallway. I shed enough tears to fill the cell and drown in them. I kicked, and screamed, and vomited. I tossed and turned for days and nights on end. Every waking moment felt like an eternity, and the few minutes that I would finally doze off were full of nightmares that produced cold sweats.

Dopesickness is like the flu combined with high anxiety, cravings, and restless leg syndrome. The one reprieve of just having normal sickness is the ability to sleep for hours. This was not the case when I was going through withdrawal. Sleep is almost impossible to attain, no matter how broken and beaten down and tired you are, your body simply will not sleep. The muscle aches and restless legs felt like stingrays swimming through my tendons and the fibers of every muscle. I could not get comfortable in that cell. For days, I would switch positions every two minutes, sleeping on the floor, under the bed, or inverted with my legs up the wall. I would lay in bed and beat my limbs against the concrete wall all night long, or even my head at times, just to distract myself from the pain or discomfort within me.

I completely lost my mind in there at times. I prayed for a quick death in place of the slow one I was experiencing. I scraped my wrists on the metal edges of the bunk trying to slice them open and considered the idea of diving head first onto the concrete floor in an effort to either kill myself or knock myself out. I had gotten a pen somehow and drew graffiti and song lyrics all over the walls and ceilings. It looked like the home of a madman or serial killer in there. In my insanity, I used the pen to draw words and symbols over my entire body. I looked like I was tattooed from head to foot. I had gone mad.

After about a week, one of my favorite guards, who had tried to talk to me about real things like changing my life and getting off of drugs, came wheeling back a TV on a cart to put in my cell. Apparently, there were two TVs on the medical wing, and I was second in seniority. At that point in time, I firmly believe that television saved my life and my sanity. It was my seventh day in that cell, and my tenth since I'd been locked up, and I was still not sleeping a wink, but the background noise of late-night infomercials did much more for my sanity than the quietude of that dark hallway.

My emotions were extremely magnified from the withdrawal.

My memories and feelings were rushing back in after years of suppressing them with drugs. I would find myself crying at the simplest television shows. I vividly remember watching the movie *Speed* with Keanu Reeves, and crying hysterically. Sometimes even episodes of Baywatch would make me tear up. Everything triggers emotions for a person who has numbed every nerve and feeling for so long. On the seventeenth day they moved me into general population because they needed my cell, but to a "safer" tier where they had two-man cells. I wasn't better by any means, but I was definitely starting to head in that direction. On my twentieth day in jail, I was still unable to get more than two hours of sleep a night, but any sleep was better than none at all.

As I started to get well and find a rhythm there, I started to write a lot. I wrote volumes of poetry, and I went back to reading and studying all of the spiritual topics I enjoyed. I found a few positive men on the tier and participated in Bible studies with them regularly. After a couple of months, I reached the top of the waiting list for an in-house job. I was granted a job as a "hall trustee" where I was released from my tier during the day to clean the hallways and other main areas of the jail. I was friendly with all of the guards, and this gave me free reign throughout its inner confines. Regularly, I got to see all the comings and goings throughout the jail as well as all of the other inmates, most importantly the females.

I made eye contact several times with a young black female I had seen several times in the hallways named Kita. I finally got the nerve to pass her a note with my ID number on it for her to write me. This opened the floodgates. Soon I was writing five or six different women and helping other guys on my tier hook up with women on the women's tier. My time was breezing by, and I felt some semblance of importance, and all of the attention from the women made me feel special.

My cell buddy left, and they moved a big Marine guy into

my cell, who had severely beaten his girlfriend. For whatever reason, he decided he was going to "buck the system," and his way of doing so was to refuse to shower. I had the best cell on the tier at that time, and I had bottom bunk. I knew that anything I did could jeopardize my job within the jail. I tried to reason with him, but he wouldn't talk to anyone. He only left his bed to eat, and soon it began to stink horribly in our cell. I rubbed soap and deodorant all over the walls trying to mask his odor. I yelled and complained to him, but he ignored me. He walked around between meals, angry at the world, and wouldn't speak to anyone. One day I came back to the cell after being out all day and decided I'd had enough. I heard that the female guard working our tier had tried to get him up for a medical visit, and he refused and called her a "fucking whore." So, I figured there was no better timing than now.

I barged into the cell and started shaking him out of his sleep, shouting, "Come on! Today's the day! Wake up! You're getting in the shower!"

When he finally snapped awake, he swung his leg out at me with force trying to kick me in the head. I caught his leg and walked backward with it until he came out of the top bunk and cracked his head on the concrete floor. I was all-in at that point. I knew my job in the jail was gone, and I would be sent to lock up. I grabbed his stuff and threw it out the door of the cell and all over the tier. Then, I marched out huffing, looking at the guard, as she stood there in amazement.

I yelled, "I'm done. This bitch has got to go! He's not staying in here no more. I'll kill him!"

I swear I saw her fight to hold back a smile at the sight of this little guy throwing this big guy's stuff all over as she radioed for help. I don't know exactly what she said over that radio, but when the guards flooded into the tier, they walked right past me and into our cell. He had apparently climbed back into the bunk and laid there. When they came into the cell, he tried to fight all of them and ended up being escorted out in handcuffs and taken to lock up. My job in the jail was magically safe, but not for long.

As always in my life, once I got comfortable doing something wrong, I pushed the limit further. And when I got comfortable with that, I pushed it even more. Kita and I had a full-blown "jail house relationship" that was known throughout the jail. She was in on gun and robbery charges and wouldn't be going anywhere for a long time. We had ordered T-shirts from the commissary and customized them with our ink pens, writing our names on them in graffiti and phrases like, "I've got jungle fever." There was a cleaning station with a mop closet just outside the female's dorm. I would hang out there as much as possible. The guards always kept the door there cracked, so Kita and I would yell back and forth through it when they were around the corner. I got so comfortable with that, that when they went around the corner for a disturbance on another tier, I would have Kita use a broom through the bars to push the door wide open. Then, I would run up on the tier and make out with her, and we'd feel each other through the bars. I really thought I was in love, and I know for a brief moment she thought she was too, but we were just two crazy kids trying to pass the time.

There were various classes offered in the jail about substance abuse and about religion, and I was enrolled in all of them. Once again, I was taking my recovery seriously. Kita was enrolled in these classes too, but they kept the men and women separate for all of them except church. When they would call the women out for the classes, Kita would go to the back of the line, and I would hide in my usual mop closet. As the line rounded the corner, she would dip into the closet with me, where for a quick minute we would make out and explore inside each other's pants. It was the best life I could possibly imagine for myself inside of a county jail, but like anything else, it was subject to change. A jealous female inmate told on us, and I was removed from the "hall trustee" position and from my tier and sent back to the dorms.

I've done a lot of things in my life that I wasn't proud of, but one of those was in the dorm I was sent to. I volunteered to do it in order to establish myself in a position of trust and authority in the dorm. It's now something I feel guilty about often, that many people probably wouldn't. There were air vents between the dorms through which one whole dorm of inmates could shout messages to another. Early one morning after breakfast, the dorm next to ours began shouting through the vent about a new inmate who was just admitted to our dorm. They said he was a pedophile and that they had seen papers indicating that he was in there for raping a minor. By the common ideal of what a pedophile is "supposed to look like," he didn't quite fit the bill. He was a clean-cut Puerto Rican dude, probably in his early thirties, with a rough look about him. The young black dude in our dorm, who was yelling through the air vent to his cousin, seemed convinced that his cousin and the other guys in the dorm next to us knew what they were talking about. After breakfast, he asked who was down to get involved in beating this man, and I, being one of the only few people up, volunteered.

He walked over to the bunk and asked the guy to see his paperwork. "Paperwork" meant his statement of charges, which would reveal exactly why he was in there. In jail you had better be ready to show your paperwork when asked, or fight, because refusal to show paperwork was considered proof that you were either a snitch or a pedophile. The guy refused to show his paperwork, and the young black dude braced himself like he was getting ready to hit him. He asked to see the paperwork one more time. I dropped off of my top bunk, wanting to be the first in on the action. I dove into the lower bunk connecting my fist below his eye, which sent him rolling feet-over-head off of the bunk and onto the floor behind him. Another young black dude blocked his exit between the bunks and swung at his head, as he dove over the bunk next to him. Scrambling to his feet, the new inmate ran into the small dayroom where the television and steel tables were. There was a tiny window embedded in the concrete wall where we would knock if we needed the guards' attention, and this is what he was going for. Three of us gave chase. Two cornered him in the dayroom and started hitting him as he tried to ball up. I grabbed the mop from the mop bucket and cracked him on his back and on the back of his head with the handle. What haunts me to this day was the way he screamed. He screamed out loudly, more from fear than from pain. It was something inhuman, like I'd never heard before. His yells were more like howls that sounded like a wild animal caught in a trap.

I dropped the mop and stood back, feeling bad for him as the other two worked on him, attacking him as he moaned loudly. It was a horrifying sound. It made me think of Jesus on the cross moaning out, asking why God had forsaken Him. At that moment I felt sick to my stomach.

I yelled out, "Chill! Chill! The guards are coming," not knowing if they really were, but secretly hoping.

They began to relent, and almost as soon as they did, we heard the click of keys in the door, which meant officers were coming onto the tier. Everybody ran back to their bunks, as the guards walked in to see his bloody, beaten body clutching the bars, begging for their help. He was removed from the dorm instantly, and the situation was never mentioned again. Later in my stay I learned that he was, in fact, being held on charges for rape of a minor. But the story involved him and his fifteen-year-old girlfriend, whose parents had found out about their relationship and pressed charges. It was not exactly the usual type of sick pedophilia we imagined it to be. Another human being had suffered at my hands because I wanted to fit in.

XXXVI

I never got high or used any kind of pills during those nine months in the detention center, although drugs were very hard to come by in the county. We tried making wine a few times with sugar, bread, and fruit, but it never quite turned out right. The correctional officers usually smelled it and raided the tier before it had time to fully ferment. Other inmates got into the medication game heavily, which meant trading their meals and snacks for other inmates' medications. There were always a few "crazies" on the tier who were on very high doses of psychotic meds. Those medications could induce sleep or turn an otherwise normal person into a lifeless zombie, which in turn made life in jail much more pleasant. I wasn't interested and kept away from it all.

One evening the sally port door to the tier opened up, and John came walking in, the same almost fifty-year-old John that I had been getting high with on the street. He set up his stuff on the bunk over mine, laid out his bedroll, and we started talking. He told me that he was serving weekends and had been doing so for a while. "Weekends" meant that he had a sentence of any number of days, and instead of serving them consecutively, he was able to serve them only on weekends. This meant coming to jail at 6:00pm on Friday and being released at 6:00pm on Sunday. The purpose of these sentences was typically so people could serve their time without losing their jobs. As long as they showed up every Friday at 6:00pm, they were fine. If they didn't show up on time, they were charged with second degree escape and kept in jail until a judge was ready to see them. John had been sent to a different dorm every weekend and just happened to end up in mine this weekend. This was a dangerous game, sending these inmates into population with other inmates facing lengthy jail sentences. Naturally, John was very relieved to see me.

He asked me how much control I had in the dorm, and if I was plugged into everything happening in there, and I assured him that I was. I knew he was still drinking methadone and shooting dope every day and had probably not gone a day without either in many years. I asked him how he was getting through the weekends, and he said he was going to show me. He told me he had brought pills and cigarettes into the dorm. He wanted to know if I could get the cigarettes into the hands of the right people so they would leave him alone about everything else. I told him it was no problem, to just give me the cigarettes and that I would handle it.

That night after the majority of the dorm had fallen asleep, I watched him intently as he sat on the top bunk, his hands fiddling around inside of his open mouth as if he was picking food from one of his back teeth. Then, it dawned on me what he was actually doing. I was both amazed and disgusted at the same time. He had somehow managed to tie one end of a small string around his back molar, and the other end around a tiny balloon, which he swallowed before coming to jail. I was witnessing him as he slowly pulled the string until the balloon attached came up and out of his throat. I wondered if he was even human. My eyes were watering at the mere thought of doing that. I reminded myself that he was high now, and also high when he put the balloon into his throat, and more than likely high when he concocted the whole scheme.

As he pulled out the small balloon and sat it onto a folded piece of paper, I was relieved that it was over without complication. He broke open the balloon using the tip of a pen and his fingernails, and the contents spilled out onto the piece of paper: a few Percocets, a few Xanax, a bunch of finely ground tobacco which he had ground down himself, and a few folded up rolling papers. *This is insane, and more than likely not worth it,* I thought to myself. He was only in for two days, and would probably have his wife waiting for him in the parking lot with heroin when he was released. Once again, I saw how the obsession of addiction can take over the mind and use it to do irrational things.

I smoked the cigarettes, and they made me miserable. At least they earned me some favor among my fellow inmates with whom I shared them. I never asked John for any of his pills. For one, I thought I knew the answer. And two, I didn't want to open that can of worms. I had been several months without a single drug. As tempting as it was to numb myself for one night in there, I knew that the guilt would eat me alive for the next week. It was a guaranteed set up for failure.

Nine months I sat in that jail awaiting all of my court dates to be consolidated into one final date. It finally came, and I got fifteen years in prison, all suspended except for three years in the Harford County Detention Center. I asked my attorney to please request my time be served at the Maryland Division of Corrections instead of the county jail. Judges sometimes looked at small, young guys like myself and figured that maybe the prison system was a bit too harsh for us. They would try to keep us "safe" by keeping us in the county jail. The judge had no idea what I'd been through or was capable of. Looks were quite deceiving. Furthermore, the county proved to be much more hostile than any prison I had ever been to. He also put me on five years of supervised probation. In a stern voice he told me that he wasn't playing with me, and that if I came back in front of him for any reason, including violating that probation, he would love to send me to prison to finish out my fifteen-year sentence.

This was the trap, the revolving door that the system is for addicts and all the people caught within it. I understand the scare tactics, and I was grateful to only have three years in jail, but the chances of anyone fresh off the streets completing five years of supervised probation without a blemish are very slim. There are court costs, probation fees, restitution to be paid, weekly appointments that interfere with work, urine screenings, and a host of other hurdles to stay on top of. The whole process of setting out on your own as a young adult with no real resources, while trying to find and hold work, and balancing all of the conditions of the court is nerve wracking. It's enough to throw a person into a whirlwind of anxiety, and then seek drugs to make it all go away. For now, I was focused on one thing, and one thing only, getting the rest of this three-year sentence behind me.

I had mixed feelings that day. I was apprehensive about heading into the unknown territory of the Maryland prison system and sad to be spending another two years and change behind bars. However, I was extremely relieved to finally have an end goal. All of my cases had been consolidated and taken care of, and I was no longer in limbo awaiting the unknown. Early the next Monday before daylight, they called my name and told me to pack up my things. The crisp morning air was exhilarating as I was lined up and loaded onto a bus with other inmates headed to the Division of Corrections to finish our sentences. We were hauled into Baltimore City to an underground garage to face the unknown. We were then unloaded, caged and transferred all day from bullpen to bullpen with other inmates from all over the state who were being processed to begin their journeys through the system.

Finally, I was taken up to the sixth floor of the Maryland Reception, Diagnostic, and Classification Center to be housed until they determined which prison they were sending me to. They put me in a cell for twenty-four hours a day, where I'd lay looking out over Greenmount Avenue and Latrobe Projects. I lay there caged like a rat on the top bunk, day and night, staring out of a huge window overlooking the city and neighborhoods I had once frequented to get heroin. It was torture, taking in the city and the projects below me, watching addicts nod out at the bus stops, seeing hustlers from the projects move about on the streets, and observing the same lifestyle that had brought me here continue on without me. All of those people breathing in the fresh cool air, tasting real food, and putting heroin in their veins, while I lay here watching their comings and goings on the streets below. I daydreamed about the adventures to be had outside of that window, until they called me to see Classification.

Since this was my first time in the Maryland prison system, and because I wasn't being housed on a violent charge, I was eligible for a boot camp program they offered. This was a rigorous program involving military style training, day labor, and rules. However, it would allow me to be released in just three months if I completed it successfully, rather than having to serve my full three years. I was eager to sign up for it. There were no beds available immediately, but I was put onto a waiting list. I was advised that it would take anywhere from two to four weeks before a bed became available there. In the meantime, I was being sent to a pre-release facility in Jessup called JPRU.

I spent another few days in the downtown diagnostic building watching the city below. They had me pack up and move to another tier for one evening before being transferred to Jessup. My new roommate in this tier was going to the same place as me. He was a larger black guy from DC who had some kind of reflux disorder, which literally made him burp every five seconds all day and all night long. It was horrible and loud. I laid in my bunk all night stewing in anger, but knowing there was nothing he could do about it. On top of his medical condition, he was obnoxious. He would pace back and forth in the cell all night long, beating his chest, rapping out loud at some points, or screaming out into the tier at the officers. I was just trying to chill and get through my sentence. I imagined my previous cell buddy on the sixth floor being stuck in a cell with this guy, and more than likely carving him up or beating him half to death.

My other cellmate was an older black man who was a veteran in the system and was awaiting transfer to begin his fifty-year sentence. He was a down to earth and decent. It amazed me the mixture of inmates I found in these cells, from murderers to petty thieves, all mixed into one tier. A huge conglomerate of societies biggest failures, but not necessarily societies worst people. I met some of the best people, and the worst, inside of those walls.

The next morning, they sent me to my new home at JPRU and directed me to my new dorm. It was a huge open dorm that housed seventy inmates, one of many dorms just like it on the property. The amount of freedom we had within these walls was overwhelming. I got here after nine months of practically maximum-security living, where there was zero contact with fresh air or sunlight, so I was shocked by the amount of trust and space we were given. In this facility, we could roam around freely inside and outside, keep cash on us, smoke cigarettes and cigars, lift weights, shoot pool, and the list goes on. My cot lay in the middle of a long line of cots in the dorm, and it just so happened that I ended up right next to a young black guy named "Dink," who I knew from Edgewood. The "Burper," my cellmate in DOC, ended up just a few bunks away from me.

Dink looked out for me in a major way. He had a set of headphones that he let me use whenever I wanted, and he gave me cigarettes and Black and Mild cigars. I would go out in the yard and lift weights with some older black men I had become friends with. Or I'd lay out on a picnic table and tan while I smoked and listened to music. It was heavenly and felt like a vacation compared to where I had just been. I was certainly still in prison though. There was zero privacy anywhere, not in the sleeping area, bathrooms, or showers. But being outdoors was definitely a step up.

I talked my folks into sending me $40 so I could go to the jail store and buy some essentials. The Burper hadn't gotten his money yet, and he pleaded with me to buy him $20 worth of goods until his cash came in. He assured me that his family was sending him $100 any day. I believed him, and as much as I didn't care for the guy, I felt bad and loaned it to him until the next week.

The Burper and I went up for our boot camp physicals, and they advised us that we would be taken to boot camp in three days. That same day he got the $100 from his family. When he headed for the store, I gave him my list of $20 worth of stuff, and he said he'd be back with it. When he came back from the store with his bags full of goods and set them down on his bunk, I eagerly awaited the candy, cigarettes, and other goods he was to bring me. Instead, I sat there and watched as he unloaded bag after bag into his storage locker. When the last bag was emptied, he didn't even look in my direction. I began fuming. I walked over to him while he sat on his bunk eating a candy bar.

"Where's the stuff on my list?"

"I didn't get it," he replied, matter-of-factly.

"What the fuck? That was the deal," I snapped.

Then he muttered out of the side of his mouth, "You'll get it when I feel like giving it to you, white boy."

I couldn't believe his ignorance. I had honestly misread his character. He had plenty of money to pay me back.

Enraged, I said, "Fuck this, I'm getting mine."

I turned to open his locker. As soon as I did, I felt his big hand on my shoulder. I spun around and punched him in the eye and followed through so hard that we both fell onto his bunk. I landed on top of him, and tried to stand back up, but he was quickly able to wrap his arm around my neck in a headlock as I lie on top of him looking at the ceiling. I struggled to break free so I could throw punches, but he was much too big.

He kept repeating, "Is this what you wanted? Is this what you wanted?" as the correctional officers came flooding onto the tier and broke us up.

Almost immediately, I jumped into character and told them we were just playing around, that it was nothing serious. He too, was awaiting boot camp, and this incident would mess it up for the both of us. So, he chimed in, claiming that it was nothing serious. That wasn't enough though. We begged them not to send us to lock up, that it would ruin our chances at boot camp. They wouldn't budge. It was as if they derived some pleasure from sending us to lock up and making us serve our full time over one squabble, and that's exactly what they did.

Sixty days. I did sixty days on the lockup tier at the Brockridge Correctional Institute, right next door to JPRU. Just like the medical isolation wing in the county I had previously spent time in, it sat way at the end of the hallway of a long line of cells. My cellmate for the first half of the sixty-day stay was a young black guy from East Baltimore known as "Skinny Pimp." We sat there telling war stories day and night, between reading tons of books and flirting with any female guards who came onto the tier. Twenty-four hours in a tiny two-man cell with a toilet right next to the bottom bunk was miserable. We literally ate, slept, and shit within a couple of feet of each other. Only for thirty minutes every other day would they walk us over to another area to let us shower. I probably read every single Stephen King novel while I was in that cell, and many other books.

When my time in lockup was finished, they didn't release me into population at Brockridge. Instead, they took me to the medium security facility called Maryland Correctional Institute at Jessup (MCIJ). I was booked in and taken to a tier in a building called "F West." This facility was huge and held a couple thousand inmates. Being white meant I was a very small minority of the population here, just like at JPRU. The Maryland Hagerstown prisons and Eastern Shore facilities were known to be white-run and have more white inmates. However, Jessup was closer to the cities of Baltimore and DC, and was almost entirely black-staffed, holding about eighty percent black inmates. I was taken to a cell where I met my new roommate, an older black man who was known as "Mr. C." He had been in prison for many years and was on short time now. He had less than sixty days until his release. He begged that I not bring any trouble to his cell. I promised that I wouldn't. Later that night I saw him sniffing a line of dope off of his locker, while I was reading a book in my top bunk. My stomach turned. I wasn't ready for the new territory I had just landed in.

I went out to the yard the next day and walked the track, all the while studying the lay of the land. There were horseshoe pits where the small population of white rednecks hung out. And on the field enclosed by the track, the Latinos played soccer. There was a basketball court, an outdoor weight pit, and an indoor gym full of weights. After I lapped the track a few times, I sat on the bleachers, rolled and smoked a cigarette, and watched the interactions. That's when I realized there was a fully operational dope shop going on out in the yard. I watched as inmates traded money and goods for heroin, and I began to crave the same demon that had put me there.

The next day I convinced Mr. C to see if the guy who was selling dope would take my headphones for a $20 bag of heroin. These were the same beat up old headphones that Dink had given me. It was pathetic that after all of this time, I was willing to trade one of the only things that mattered to me for a high that wouldn't last more than two days. I half-prayed he wouldn't accept the headphones, while the other half of me wished he would. When yard was over, Mr. C came back to the cell and handed me off a small bag of raw heroin.

I waited until after dinner to sniff a line. That night, I sat on the toilet smoking rolled cigarettes and nodding out, when I was startled by ambulance lights outside. I watched out of the window as a body was carried by stretcher out of the lockup unit across from our building and loaded into the ambulance. I assumed that somebody in lockup had killed themselves, but quickly learned the truth the next day when I saw the same man I had gotten my heroin from being marched through the prison in handcuffs and taken to that very same lockup tier.

It turned out that the dope dealer from the prison yard had sold $100 worth of heroin to another inmate. The inmate overdosed and died that night in lockup. The jail was holding someone accountable. They were able to trace the path of the heroin back to the guy who sold it in the yard, and he was charged with murder. He had only eighteen months left on his sentence. His sentence was about to get a lot longer.

This also brought a heroin drought to the jail for a short period of time, which was good for me. The feelings that came rushing back to me after the high wore off were so intense that I wanted to die. After nine months without heroin, I had thrown all my hard work away and quickly caved. It took zero pressure to make me fall victim to the dope again. I lie in my bunk suffering anxiety and depression. At one point the anxiety attacks were so intense that I was rushed to Medical because I thought I was going into cardiac arrest.

They put me on a cocktail of pills that eventually helped numb the anxiety and depression. A high dose of triazadone had me walking around like a zombie at night and helped me to fall asleep. Over time, I became friends with everyone on the tier, and worked out various hustles as I got comfortable there. There was an older white guy who was once an attorney on the streets. He worked several cases for the inmates, and I became his assistant for $25 a week. I would do letter writing and take notes, and copy cases out of law books for him. The money I made from him, or got in the mail, went to cigarettes or heroin.

XXXVII.

It didn't take long for heroin to flood back into the jail. We even had a few dealers on our tier in F West. Half of the tier got high. There were a lot of guys, who had never even tried dope until they got locked up, who now had habits. It was everywhere, and people were shooting it too. Skinny Pimp was on my tier. His homeboy, a young black dude from West Baltimore named Ronnie-J, was selling dope off and on after visits. He also shot dope, but since his cell buddy was a strict Muslim, he didn't want him to know he was shooting. So, they approached me to see if I'd hold the needle in my cell as long as they pieced me off some occasional blow. I eagerly agreed because it not only meant free dope for me, but it also meant I could shoot it now too.

The heroin in that jail was unlike anything I'd ever seen. You got more bang for your buck in prison than you did on the streets. It was so intense that I saw guards come in during count times to buy heroin off of the inmates. I saw female guards selling sex to inmates; some were known to have sex for $100. I had no interest. I didn't have that kind of money, and I was back to being obsessed with getting high.

At one point there was black tar heroin floating around in the jail. It was something I had only heard myths about and wasn't sure even existed. I got my hands on some, and everyone warned me to absolutely not shoot it because it was too potent. Of course, I immediately went into my cell and fired it into my arm. The next two days are a blur. I remember standing on the tier outside of my cell looking up at the TV and falling into a nod so hard that I almost touched my toes in full view of everyone, including the guards. Eventually, the other inmates demanded that I go back to my cell because I was making it "hot," and I'd get the entire tier raided if anyone saw me like that.

When I wasn't getting high, or contemplating suicide after a high wore off, I was playing ping pong or reading mystery novels. One time, Tupac came onto our tier, not the real Tupac, but a guy that looked so identical to him that everyone called him "Pac." He came in loaded with dope to sell, and every time he had a visit, he'd come back with more. Primarily, there were two ways that dope got into the jail, either by kissing a female visitor and swallowing a balloon, or it was brought in by a corrupt guard. This guy was catching visits, and every time he came back from one, I knew he was loaded up with raw dope a few hours later. I ended up running up $100 tab with him and didn't know how I was going to pay it.

I eventually had to bite the bullet and call my family. I rarely talked to them because it was easier for me to leave the outside world alone and live my life on the inside, but now I needed them. I couldn't tell them that I was shooting dope and ran up a tab. So, I told them that while I was playing ping pong, I knocked someone's boombox off a stool and shattered it. The person who it belonged to was a member of the Black Guerrilla Family (BGF), and they were going to make me stab someone to death to pay for it. It was easy for me to concoct this story because it was blended together by parts of stories that almost happened. Nevertheless, I knew it would be more believable to tell my mother that I had to kill someone, than it would be to tell her that I was afraid of being killed, because she knew me better than that. They mailed a $100 money order to his female friend on the streets to clear up my bill. Shortly after, I was caught in a random urine test in jail.

I failed the urine test. They raided my cell and found the syringe and sent me out to the mountains of Hagerstown. Once again, I was at a new jail on a lockup tier. I finished out my days on lockup and was introduced to a new facility called "Roxbury" in Hagerstown. For years to follow, I told everyone I was sent to Roxbury because they found a "shank" in my cell, rather than the truth that it was a needle. I suppose I was embarrassed to admit that I had shared a worn out needle in prison, and the shank story just sounded more tough.

The Hagerstown jail was run by white folks from Western Maryland, and even though it was medium-security like the previous facility, it was run much differently. There was no outside yard for exercise, and we were only taken to a gym for an hour and a half every other day. We spent lots more time locked in our cells. We were made to walk to the chow hall silently and in a single file line, were rushed through our meals, and constantly kept on a strict schedule and regimen. I'll never forget waking up at 4:00am to walk to the chow hall for breakfast, which was about a half-mile walk before daylight in the biting mountain air of winter. The skunks and raccoons that had managed to breach the gate and run around on the prison grounds in the early morning hours were the only things worth seeing.

I lasted about thirty days in that atmosphere before I figured out who had the heroin and who was selling it. I made a couple of purchases and got high a couple of times. When I realized I was close to sixty days away from my release date, I decided to have one last party. I got $50 worth of heroin from an inmate with the promise to pay him that Friday when my check came in the mail from my folks. There was no check coming though. My parents rarely sent anything. My mother had an iron fist on the rest of the family as well, so nobody did anything for me without clearing it with her first. My plan was to get as high as I could, then check into a lockup tier so I didn't have to pay for it, but more importantly, so I could dry out. The last thing I wanted to doing was get out with a full-blown heroin habit. I wanted to try to get out and stay clean, or at least have a fighting chance. I rationalized that I only got high in prison because there was nothing better to do, but on the streets, I stood a chance at sobriety.

That's exactly what I did. I stayed high for about three days. It was right around New Year's Eve, and I was sitting at the cell door high, counting down the minutes until midnight as we all started yelling and beating the doors and walls when the clocks struck twelve. The guards came running onto the tier yelling at us, and threatening to have us ticketed. It seemed absolutely sad to me that we couldn't even celebrate in that small way. When the dope wore off a couple of days later, I stayed back at the end of the line after lunch and pulled a guard to the side and told him that I felt my life was in danger. They pulled me into an office, and I explained that there was a guy on the tier who I had previously robbed, and that it was only a matter of time before he recognized me. I didn't want to get killed or have to kill him. They had to take my lie seriously, this I knew. So, they took me directly to lock up, packed my things, and brought them over behind me.

I sat on that lockup tier exactly fifty-nine days awaiting my release date. I read and worked out every day in my cell. I built up a strong, positive outlook on my life outside of those walls. When the day finally came, I was released directly from my lockup cell and into the outside world. I walked out of the prison gates and down a long road away from the prison in the middle of nowhere hoping to see my mother's car approaching. Instead a truck with two officers in it pulled up with guns drawn on me. They demanded my name and ID. They had received notification from a tower that there may have been an escaped inmate wandering down the road. They eventually lowered their guns, transported me back to the prison parking lot, and told me to wait there for my ride. Under no circumstance was I to wander off again. Finally, my mother arrived, and we drove away from that cold fortress of misery, and I never looked back

XXXVIII.

Two months. For two months on the outside, I made it without a single drug or drink. I went to meetings almost nightly in the beginning and worked waiting tables. I did just enough to barely hang on to the idea of recovery by my fingertips. I gathered enough clean time to get cocky and think I deserved all the things my peers had. The world, and all my friends, had advanced ahead, while for the past several years my world had actually moved backward. Now, I greedily expected to be at the same level as them. They had homes, nice cars, girl-friends, and good jobs, while I was scraping by and living with my parents.

In an addict's mind, they are always a victim and never a product of their own poor choices. It is not until the addict begins to take personal responsibility and accept that the position they are in is a direct result of their own choices that things will change. Then, they may finally begin the path to recovery. I didn't want to consider what I'd done. I only chose to see what I didn't have. Like many times before, I couldn't accept the fact that I couldn't drink, and most of my peers could.

It wasn't long before I was going out to the bars with my friends from the past, who were now functioning, responsible people. For them, the bars were a weekly place of escape, but for me, they were a nightly poison. It wasn't long before I was being thrown out of almost every bar in the area again for fighting and beating people half to death. Those good friends quickly distanced themselves from me.

I also began to crave female attention, and I found a new place to get it. The internet and Instant Messenger became my playground whenever I was stuck home at my parents' house. I met plenty of women online, mostly older women, to fill the void of attention I felt that I needed. I would go over to their houses or have them take me out to the bars with them. They would cater to me and my drinking. As long as I was drunk, I could be attracted to them. My drinking escalated beyond control. I once woke up freezing cold on the dirty concrete in a wooden dumpster enclosure behind the 7-Eleven in Bel Air. I must have gotten so drunk the night before, that I wandered through the streets looking for a safe place to pass out. I remembered nothing, but my watch told me that it was 9:15am. I knew I had to be to work at 10:00, so I stood up, walked a mile into work, and waited tables without ever showering, still drunk from the night before. What I looked like on the outside was no match for how I felt on the inside, though.

Hell was back. It was burning deep inside of me. The only way I could chase the extreme misery of depression and anxiety away was to drink some more. I became familiar with each and every happy hour special at every bar in Bel Air. When I worked a double at the restaurant, I would sneak over and throw back as many beers as I could while on break. If not, I would smuggle bottles of alcohol into work and stash them in secret places. I couldn't live or function without it.

That year, on the week of Easter, I had linked up with a woman on the internet who was much older than me. She had her own place in Edgewood, and we spent the weekend there drinking and going to bars. She paid for my alcohol and cooked for me. In turn I slept with her and gave her affection when I was drunk. I crashed at her house all weekend. It was awkward sharing the house with her son, who was only two years younger than me, but he acted as if it was normal. On Easter Sunday, I had her drop me off at work at 9:30am because I was scheduled to work a double. Halfway through the day, during my break between shifts, I called home to wish my parents a happy Easter. I knew the whole family would be at their house for a gathering. I stood at the payphone located in the bar at work.

When my father picked up and realized it was me, I was greeted with an angry, "Where have you been?"

I played it off, casually trying to downplay his anger. I told him that I had been over at a lady friend's all weekend and at work. I explained to him that I was working a double, and he demanded that I come home and see the family for Easter. I explained to him that I only had a short break, and that I didn't have time to make it home and back. His next words shocked me.

"Either come home and see the family, or don't come home at all!"

I stood there stunned. Was I really just given an ultimatum to either walk out of my job or not be allowed back home? Either way, I had no transportation. I wasn't leaving work and calling a cab home to a family function, all while terribly hungover. So, I went back to work. At the end of the night, I had $220 from working all day, and I had nowhere to go. It was extremely chilly outside, and the rain was coming down heavily. With no place to be, I did what I knew best, I got drunk.

I was dropped off at a local bar called Uncle George's. I figured that once I got a buzz, I could figure out where I was going to stay that night. My hopes were that somebody I knew would be in there drinking, that I could give them my sob story, and they would let me crash at their place for a day or two. It was Easter Sunday though, and the cast of characters in the bar were all strange and unfamiliar. I sat at the bar alone drinking down my fear, when an older brunette lady approached me and asked if I had any blow. I told her I didn't, and she accused me of lying. She said she had bought coke off of me before and knew I sold. I explained to her that I didn't anymore, and she asked me to call someone.

I told her, "Leave me the fuck alone. It's Easter, and nobody I know is around. The only place you can find it is downtown."

She replied, "Oh no, I'm not going all the way down there," as if I was asking her to.

The night carried on, and the rain never let up outside of that dismal bar. I drank cup after cup of draft beer, hoping that a familiar face would wander in from the outside. The same lady came back over and continued to try to make conversation with me, to try to get me to help her find some coke, and I was getting quite annoyed. I told her my story of heroin addiction, and how I wasn't into that shit anymore.

However, as the minutes ticked by toward closing time, my desperation grew, along with my intoxication. When the bartender yelled out last call, I became extremely worried. I had nowhere to go in this cold rain and no semblance of a plan. That's when she showed up again next to me as I was looking down into my last beer of the evening.

"Take me to the city, and we can get high and go to my place."

I agreed. We walked outside and hopped into her Camaro. I was definitely drunk, but I remember the Camaro was warm, and we listened to classic rock on the way down. I became anxious to get high with her. I directed her into the back streets of East Baltimore. We pulled up on a small side street called Register Street where a couple I knew lived. I hoped they were home. It had been years since I had been in the neighborhood, so I had no idea where to cop drugs this late at night. I got out and beat on the old row home door. Sheets hung in the window as drapes. Half of the other houses on the block had plywood in the windows. I lifted my fist to bang on the door again, when I saw Regina's head pop out of the window on the second floor and squint down at me.

"Who the fuck is it? You know what time it is?" she shouted.

"It's me, Danny!" I yelled up at her, "Get down here, I got some money for you!"

She recognized my name right away, "Oh shit, boo! We be right down."

With that, the window shut, and her husband Romey opened the front door. Regina and Romey were old school dope fiends. They had probably been getting high for over thirty years. They lived in a row home with no furniture, and just a mattress or two on the floor, with boxes for end tables, and whatever random scraps they had managed to collect to decorate the place. Cigarette butts and dope paraphernalia lined the counters in the kitchen and the unsteady kitchen table. However, as barren and dirty as this place looked inside, it was a warm safe haven from the streets outside. I had spent many an afternoon in here waiting for them to return with my dope, and been reacquainted with peace and comfort as they brought it back to me, and I introduced it into my bloodstream. I would sit on a mattress or corner of the old wooden floor and smoke cigarettes and nod out with them, laughing and joking about the simplicities of life. With absolutely nothing, they somehow managed to keep their habits alive day in and day out, I almost never saw them sick. I, and the outsiders to the hood like me, were a huge benefit because we would buy them a pill for going out to get whatever we needed when the neighborhood wasn't safe for us. I usually came to them when I had a bunch of money to spend and wanted a place to chill and relax.

This night was the latest I had ever come to see them. Heroin was always a day activity. However, they had gotten cocaine for me to speedball on many occasions, so I knew I could count on them for that. I told Romey what I needed, and he said it was no problem. My lady driver handed me $50 to pass on to him, and we waited in the car while he disappeared around the corner into the night. A few minutes later, he appeared back on the street with four large vials of cocaine and placed them in my hand. The extra $10 was for him. Regina came out to say goodbye to us as we were getting ready to drive off.

She said, "Just so you know, we on now," and held up a gel cap of heroin in front of me.

"What you mean?" I asked.

She told me that they were now selling heroin and had $10 jumbo caps of some of the best stuff around, if I was interested.

I started saying, "Oh okay, I'll keep you in mind…" when I was cut off by my new lady friend.

"Isn't that what you like?" she asked.

I said, "Yeah."

"Let me buy you one."

I didn't argue, but I mentioned that I didn't have a needle. Romey ran into the house and got me one, still in the package. I felt no guilt at all. I was drunk, it was cold and rainy, and I had nowhere to go. We drove off, and I directed her out of the city streets and onto the highway. It had been five months without the drug, counting my time in lock up in prison, but I wasn't thinking about all of that. Instead, I was focused on this rush that I was about to feel. I leaned forward in the passenger seat and cooked up the heroin as she sped up the dark rainy highway. At some point I injected the amber liquid into my bloodstream. I don't know how much of the pill I did, or if I actually did the whole thing. But when the heroin spread out into my veins and capillaries, it did so with the intent of wrestling my soul away from my body, and it did its job well. I died that night, and I honestly have no idea how I ever made it back.

XXXIX.

When I awoke, I was on a stretcher in the upper Chesapeake Hospital. A small crowd of nurses, and techs, and my mother's friend surrounded me. A black lady named Giselle leaned over me, trying to encourage me to stay awake.

"Stay with us, Danny, stay with us," she encouraged me in a soft voice while holding onto my hand.

My body was spastic, and through my foggy mind, I could see and feel it seizing on the bed that I was being wheeled through the hospital on. I was in and out of consciousness, but I vaguely remember being hit with something that shocked me several times back into seizures, and then I was wide-awake. I was conscious enough to see my parents rush into the hospital room with a mixed look of horror and disappointment on their faces, and then I drifted off again.

I awoke in a hospital room later that evening with tubes down my throat to help me breathe and numerous IVs bringing different fluids and medications into my weak body. My breathing was so tight it was painful. *What happened?* I remembered the ride to the city the previous night. I remembered those words, "We on now," and the look on the lady's face as she turned to me with a devilish grin and asked, "Isn't that what you like?" And that's the last thing I remembered. But it was enough to tell me everything I needed to know. I still couldn't believe that one pill of heroin had done all of this. *Had we been in an accident? Am I going to jail?*

My poor parents had been awakened at 6:00am by a police officer banging at their front door. He explained to them that their son had passed away, and they needed to come to the hospital to identify the body. They had arrived just as I was being brought back into this world. Their relief quickly turned to anger and disappointment. I was torturing them with my bad decisions. This was just one stop on a nightmarish road that seemed to never end for them.

Apparently, I overdosed and went unconscious in that woman's passenger seat as we drove up I-95 in the wee morning hours. She drove all the way back to the town of Bel Air, probably high on cocaine and flipping out with paranoia. She pulled up to a church in the middle of the town of Bel Air, drug me around to the big side door, and left me there on the church steps in the rain. I'm sure she had presumed me to be dead. Around 6:00am as the sunlight peeked through the town, two teenagers on their way to work found me. They called the police to report a dead body. At only twenty-two years old, I was taken to the hospital and diagnosed as having had a heart attack and hypothermia.

I laid in that hospital for one week. After the first couple of days, they determined that I could breathe without the oxygen. My family left on the first day and never came back. I only had one visitor, and it was the woman with whom I had just spent Easter weekend. She dropped off flowers, a twenty dollar bill and a pack of cigarettes, which I had pleaded with her to bring to me. She let me know that she also couldn't continue to associate with me, that this incident had scared her and hurt her too much. I barely knew this woman, but it made me sad that I had successfully driven everyone out of my life.

I got accustomed to being in the hospital. I received attention, and I was safe and warm. I didn't want to leave. I dreaded the day I would be released with nowhere to go. Eventually on Friday though, after one full week, I was discharged. I took a shot in the dark and called my parents. I was told that I absolutely could not come home, that I had caused enough damage to the family. I walked out of the hospital with nothing but the clothes on my back, a lighter and cigarettes, and a wad of cash I still had from working Easter Sunday. I walked into town. With time on my hands, I stopped by my work. I was told that the manager was waiting to see me. I explained that I had missed work for hospitalization because I had a heart attack, of course omitting any mention of drugs. In response, they told me I was fired. They were well aware of what I was hospitalized for, and they couldn't have me working there. Somebody in my family must have called them, I figured.

I sauntered out of the building, empty inside. It was 3:00pm, and I had no destination, so I made my way over to Red Lobster for happy hour. They had $1 draft beers from 3:00 to 5:00pm, and I would usually suck down as many as I could in that time frame in order to kick start my evening buzz. As I sat there trying to figure out my next move, I looked over and saw another customer at the bar doing the same thing as me, only he was in a kitchen uniform. I recognized him immediately. It was Hector, a guy I had been locked up with in the Harford County Detention Center. He was Puerto Rican, in his forties, about 280 pounds with a short fade haircut and a gold medallion around his neck at all times. I remembered him and his other Puerto Rican friends being a source of never-ending comedy in the jail. I would never forget that he was in there for five years for putting a smart bomb in his ex-wife's apartment and catching half the building on fire. I knew he spoke very broken English, but I needed a friend.

I went over and re-introduced myself, and we drank some

beers together. I told him about my plight, being on the streets, and having nowhere to go, all the while leaving out any mention of drugs and especially heroin. He had a two-bedroom apartment on the other side of Bel Air with a roommate, another guy I knew. His roommate was an older black guy who went by "J-Roc," who I had also been locked up with. After talking for some time, he agreed to let me crash on his couch for $10 a night. He hinted that things hadn't been going very well with J-Roc, and that I may be able to eventually move into the second bedroom at some point.

We drank and chatted those two hours away. As happy hour ended, he wrote his address down on a napkin and told me that he lived on the bottom floor and that the slider was always open, but not to show up after 10:00pm. We shook hands, and I wandered off into Bel Air searching for the next bar to venture into. As I walked down the Main Street of Bel Air, through the small town shops and law offices, I heard my name shouted from somewhere above. I looked around and then up above me, and saw a familiar face out on the third floor fire escape above an antique store. It was Nick. I hadn't seen him since he overdosed in the McDonald's bathroom on work release.

"What the fuck?" I shouted up at him in bewilderment.

"I live here, bro. Come on up!" he yelled down to me.

I walked through the small white wooden door between the businesses that led to the apartments above. All along Main Street, there were quaint little shops, cafés, offices, and barbers, but above them was another world. It was a world of low-rent apartments filled with drug users and alcoholics. The hallway was thin and smelled like smoke. I climbed the two series of stairs until I reached the third floor. He was standing in the open doorframe waving me in. I entered the cluttered apartment, and he brought me a thirty-two-ounce bottle of beer from the fridge. We reminisced for a while, and he told me that he had gotten married to the manager at McDonald's who he had dated back in work release. They lived together in this Main Street apartment, and he was waiting for her to get off of work so they could ride downtown together. I couldn't believe he had managed to get this innocent girl strung out on heroin, who had never touched drugs before, and then convince her to marry him. I wanted to go downtown too, so I drank and waited with him.

Things were falling into place. I had a couch, and potentially a long-term place, to go home to. I felt like getting high was my reward for spending a week in the hospital. Never mind the fact that heroin was the reason I was in the hospital and homeless in the first place, it would once again serve as the vacation from all of my pain. When his wife arrived home, she was surprised to see me, and I could also sense the worry and embarrassment in her face. She had fallen apart since then, and she knew I could see it. We rushed her to get ready and out the door. We jumped into her car, excited to be reunited and on the way to Baltimore to feel dope wrap its warm arms around us. That was the last time I ever saw Nick or his new wife.

I woke up in the back of an ambulance. Everything is hazy from the time we got into the car in Bel Air that night, but here I was in the back of an ambulance surrounded by police officers and EMTs. I sat up on the gurney, and they urged me to lie back down and relax.

"No!" I snapped, "I'm sorry, but no! I just spent a week in the hospital. I have to get home before 10:00pm. I'm not going back!"

I pleaded with them as I sat up swinging my legs over the side of the gurney. The medical personnel pleaded with me to stay. They explained that they had found me under the payphone in the parking lot of the gas station we were in. I had gone into cardiac arrest. I didn't care—I didn't care what had happened. I didn't care if I lived or died. I didn't care how I got there. The only thing I could focus on was getting to Bel Air by 10:00pm if I wanted a warm couch to sleep on instead of the cold streets.

The pleas of the EMTs fell on deaf ears. They tried to reiterate to me exactly what was happening to me. I had overdosed in the car, and the people I was with had dragged my body out of the backseat and left me under a payphone. Then, they anonymously dialed 9-1-1 from the payphone and reported that my body was lying there and sped off.

An officer arrived on the scene to find me barely holding onto consciousness, followed by an ambulance. I couldn't afford a hospital visit. The previous ones were already going to be astronomical, I thought. I also couldn't miss the opportunity with Hector, because if I blew that, I may not have other opportunities to find a place to stay. The hospital would just prolong the inevitable for a few hours or a day.

I insisted on leaving, and they concurred that they legally couldn't stop me or force treatment. One of the female EMTs tried one last attempt at speaking some common sense into me. Then she placed a consent form in front of me on a clipboard stating that I refused treatment. I scribbled a signature across the line, put my coat on, and hopped out of the back of the ambulance. I stumbled to the curb at the edge of Pulaski highway and extended my thumb as I walked backward up the shoulder hoping to hitch a ride the twenty miles or so back to Bel Air. I remember nothing after that, and have no clue how I got home, but I awoke the next morning on the couch in a warm Bel Air apartment with Hector in the kitchen making eggs. *Maybe, I'll take a break from the heroin for a while*, I thought to myself.

XL.

I didn't have a habit at this point, so it was relatively easy to stop using heroin and replace it with alcohol. Hector was a full-blown alcoholic too. He drank from the time he awoke until he went to sleep, so we got along well. We started hitting the bars together and partying all the time. I got a job at a Friendly's restaurant, two blocks from the apartment community, where I waited tables, drunk every shift. I kept forty-ounce bottles of malt liquor in the walk-in and took swigs out of them between servicing my tables. The management knew about this, but they didn't care as long as the job got done.

A month or two went by, and I was able to pay my rent to Hector a month ahead of time. The rest of my money went straight into a liquor bottle. I rarely ever saw J-Roc. He worked a lot of hours and kept to himself. One thing I learned though, is that Hector liked cocaine. Every other Friday when he got paid, he'd set a little bit of money aside to get some coke to party with. One Friday, we all three arranged to party it up together. That night when the paychecks were cashed, J-Roc talked Hector into giving him $150 to go get an eight ball of coke. We all walked into downtown Bel Air and stopped at a 7-Eleven. J-Roc said the house was up the street, and that he needed the money to go get it. He asked me to go with him while Hector waited at the store. Hector was leery because J-Roc already owed him money for back rent, but really wanted to score some coke, so he handed the money over. Once we got up the street, J-Roc explained that he had no intention of buying an eight ball of coke, that he was ripping Hector off "because he shouldn't be getting high anyway." He said we were going to wait a few minutes, then come running back down the street to Hector acting like the cops were chasing us. He handed me half the money, and after several minutes, we made the dash. We ran down to where Hector was waiting at the 7-Eleven, except when I stopped to talk to Hector, J-Roc kept running. We never saw him for the rest of the night. I tried to keep J-Roc's story going, but it was a bit obvious what had happened.

A couple of days went by, and there was no sign of J-Roc at the house. He didn't come back for any of his things, so Hector hauled them out to the dumpster. They both worked together in the kitchen at Red Lobster, but hadn't seen each other since the incident—until the third morning.Hector had sat up the night before, stewing on his anger and drinking like a maniac, while I slept. I had no idea what was going on until I saw it in the news and got word from the neighborhood. The next afternoon in the middle of the lunch rush, a drunk Hector barged into the front door of his workplace at Red Lobster waving a gun around as diners ducked under their tables. He marched straight back to the kitchen looking for J-Roc with the intention of shooting him. Someone had warned J-Roc, and he slipped out the back-door. Hector busted out of the backdoor of the kitchen into the afternoon sunlight looking for J-Roc and found himself in a busy shopping center parking lot swarming with police. All 280 pounds of him ran in circles through the parked cars in front of the department stores trying to dodge law enforcement until he was finally apprehended. That was the last time I ever heard from or about Hector, yet I continued to stay there in his apartment for quite some time.

I had the apartment to myself, drinking every night and inviting friends over for parties. I was too drunk to show up for a shift at Friendly's one day, so I just never went back. Every day I waited to be evicted from that apartment. One night, I invited some guys to come back for more drinks after the bar. I caught one of them trying to steal my wallet off the kitchen counter, and I beat him so badly in the parking lot that his screams woke up the neighbors at 3:00 in the morning. That wasn't the first or the last time there would be fights in the parking lot, not to mention traffic in and out of the building constantly and at all hours of the night.

I had a daily routine. I would wake up hung over, or still drunk, from the night before and clean the apartment from the previous evening's party. Once the place was fully cleaned, I would watch the clock until noon, when I would allow myself to drink again. That was the one rule that I gave myself to add some semblance of order to my life. The second the clock struck noon, I would go to the refrigerator and grab a forty-ounce bottle of malt liquor and begin the charade all over again. In no time, I downward spiraled into a grueling daily routine. I had gotten to the point that every night I was falling asleep with a bottle of liquor on my nightstand, and I would wake up in the middle of the night and take several swigs out of the bottle and fall back asleep. One morning when I was cleaning the kitchen from a previous night of destruction, I heard keys in the apartment door and my heart sank. *This must be the management coming to evict me,* I thought. The door opened and a Puerto Rican woman, about forty years old came walking in. She looked completely shocked to see me standing there in my "wife-beater" and shorts with a rag in my hand. She could clearly see that I wasn't an intruder. My heart was racing. I knew that I would be going back to the streets. My time here was up. She attempted to ask me questions in her broken English, but we had a hard time communicating. I spoke very little Spanish, but with some effort I managed to convince her that Hector told me I could stay, even while he was in jail.

She let me in on some new information. She was Hector's sister, and the apartment was hers, not his. Hector could never get an apartment due to his previous criminal history, so he had to live there illegally under her name. She was now stuck with the lease, even though he wasn't around to pay her the monthly rent they had agreed upon. She was married and lived with her husband in Edgewood, and worked early mornings doing prep work at Red Lobster. She was the one who had gotten Hector the job there, but now she was done with him.

I did my best to flirt and flatter her and to convince her that I wasn't a criminal. I was just a young guy with no place to go. She warmed up to me quickly, and I knew that she would let me stay. We agreed to stick to my original arrangement with Hector to pay $300 a month to her, and she would continue to pay the rest of the rent as it was. When she left that day, I felt refreshed. I didn't have to worry about being evicted at any given moment. With this newfound hope, I went out into town and found a job. I got hired to wait tables at the TGIFriday's in Bel Air and headed out to celebrate. I went to DuClaw for the first time since I had been fired from there for fighting years ago. It was Wednesday night, and my buddy played acoustic music there. Everyone I had gone to school with went there for the music and beer specials.

It was the first time I had seen most of these people since high school. These were all of the "normal" people, the preps and the jocks, of Bel Air High School that I never really fit in with. It felt like a reunion, as I made my way through the crowds enjoying my buzz, pretending that I was "normal" just like them. Then I saw Braden. I had just been locked up with him. I'd known him off and on my whole life, and he'd always been a bully.

I heard him from across the room asking people, "What the

fuck are you looking at?" He was starting shit with everybody he came across.

He sat down next to me and put his hand on my shoulder, so we started talking. He was hostile though. For once, I was not, and he was bringing down my vibe. He was cordial to me, but while we were talking, he would lash out at people across the bar just for looking at him, or call someone a "bitch" just for brushing up against him.

Finally, I told him, "Chill the fuck out! This isn't that kind of party, and it's embarrassing."

He stood up next to me, swelled up, and popped off, "Who the fuck are you talking to? I'll..."

I hit him fast, twice, and watched him fall to the floor. I had just gotten there, and I was having a good time. I didn't want to get thrown out. I hopped back onto the stool, head down, and sipped my beer as if nothing had happened.

The bouncers noticed his body tangled up underneath the stools on the floor and came over. They were dragging his limp body through the bar when he woke up and started flailing around, screaming and calling them names. I looked down into my beer, trying my best to play nonchalant, just waiting to get thrown out as well, when I felt a hand slap down on my shoulder. I turned around to see the two security guards behind me, and what they said floored me.

"You're good here, bro. He was an asshole. Appreciate ya."

Then they walked away. I don't quite know how I got home that night, but I know I was so drunk that I left without paying my tab. I had to catch a cab back in the morning and pay it off in order to get my ID back from the bartender.

XLI.

Hector's sister started coming around more often now that she knew I was staying there. It became evident that she was coming to see me, and she even showed up with groceries and decorations one time. We stood in the kitchen trying to communicate, and even though she couldn't do so well, she had no problem tracing her hand down my bare chest one morning and saying, "I like you, Papi." I knew I had to use this to my advantage. I was a huge fan of Latina women, but she wasn't very attractive by my standards. However, I was lonely and needed help, and I wasn't about to turn this opportunity down. What started as a surprise encounter when she first met me in her brother's apartment one morning turned into free rent, groceries, and gifts. The only thing I had to do in return was sleep with her once a week in the early morning hours before she went to work. It was a win-win situation.

She would show up at 4:00am while I was still extremely intoxicated from the night before and wake me from my sleep. Sometimes, I wouldn't even remember our encounters. The only time she would stop by was before work because she didn't want her husband getting suspicious. I imagined she was severely lacking in affection at home, and I tried to justify it that way in my mind. She bragged to all of her coworkers about our fling and would sometimes take me to dinner at Red Lobster to show me off. I would play along with it. I was, after all, getting free room and board.

Meanwhile, I chased women my own age and younger than me at night. I'd have groups of people over for drinking parties and mess around with different women nightly. I was always a skilled thief, so I would go into the local liquor stores and steal bottles of Moët, Alize, and other high-end liquors. I always had a full assortment at the house. One afternoon, I had a young black girl over, whom I had just met. We were drinking on the couch and making out when I heard a knock at the backdoor. It was Hector's cousin. I hadn't seen him since the Detention Center. I let him in, and we hung out and chatted for a bit until we realized that we were running out of liquor.

"Take me to the liquor store, and I'll grab a couple bottles of Alize and walk right out with them," I told him.

He said he was on parole and didn't want to be a part of it, but tossed me the keys to his truck and told me to go. I went to the store, did just as I said, and came back. When I walked in the backdoor, not even twenty minutes after I had left, he was on the couch getting a blowjob from the girl I had over. When I realized that he had sent me out on that mission alone, so that he could steal the girl, I lost my mind. I flipped out and ran him out the door. We fought blow for blow in the parking lot for a solid five minutes until I finally left him laying bloody between two parked cars.

Winded and bleeding, I turned to hear a voice shout out, "The police are on their way!"

I quickly got him up and told him to get the hell out of there before the police came, and I went back inside to clean up and throw the girl out. I never did see or speak to the police that day, but the rental office was notified of the incident, and so was Hector's sister. I got a visit from her shortly after saying that if I didn't chill out, she would be evicted from the lease.

My sister's wedding day came, and even though I rarely saw her or my family, I was expected to be at the ceremony and reception. The night before the wedding, I was drinking in Bel Air with a bunch of older guys, and one of them kept mouthing off and testing me all night. The drunker I got, the closer we came to running out of liquor. I was in a drunk, pissy mood. The mouthy guy was the only one who I thought still had any money on him, so when we ran out of beer, I enlisted his help to walk back to my apartment to grab some liquor with me and bring it back. The catch was that I didn't actually have any liquor at my apartment. We walked through the town of Bel Air and cut across the church property that led back to my apartment. Once we were out of sight of the major road, I stopped walking and began my evil plan.

"You wanna run your mouth now?" I snapped at him in the dark.

He spun around full of surprise, mixed with condescension, "What're you talking about?"

"You had so much shit to say back at the house. Say it now!" I barked at him.

We were both drunk, and he obviously wasn't taking me as seriously as I wanted him to.

"Fuck you man!" was all it took coming out of his mouth before I cracked him over the head with the beer bottle I was holding.

I was on top of him the second he fell.

"Empty your pockets and give me your money before I do even worse," I said.

His tough talk turned into cries, "Why are you doing this?" He swore and pleaded that he had no money.

I grabbed his arm and pulled him up off the ground. "Get the fuck out of here! And next time watch who you're talking to."

I watched in the dark as he jogged off into the night, hoping the police weren't being called.

In my drunken state, I was convinced that he deserved every bit of it. The next day, and many days after, I would feel horribly guilty about my actions and many of the things I did under the influence of alcohol. At that time, the guilt would lead me to drink even more in order to bury it. Alcohol was the source of most of my life problems, but also the coping mechanism that allowed me to live with myself and the problems I caused. So, the cycle spiraled out of control. I could have killed him that night, and the drunk me would have justified it. And the next day, the sober me would have been disgusted and sick with remorse.

State law in Maryland said that alcohol couldn't be sold after 2:00am, which was a problem for us alcoholics who could drink until the sun came up. The only place in the area that sold alcohol that late was the local 7-Eleven. I sauntered a few blocks over to one nearby, hoping it was still before 2:00am. I walked into the store inebriated, with $2 in hand, and asked the clerk if they were still selling alcohol. She said no, that it was almost 3:00am. I still needed alcohol to finish up the night though. I couldn't remember the last time I actually laid down with the intention of trying to fall asleep. I was accustomed to drinking until I passed out.

I walked to the back of the store and dropped two forty-ounce bottles of Colt 45 into the leg of my baggy sweatpants, then made my way to the tobacco. They no longer kept cigarettes out in the aisles or on the counters within reach, so I grabbed a couple packs of Swisher Sweets and dropped them into my pants. Next, I lifted a lighter, then without even thinking, I stuck a bag of Doritos and some M&Ms down my pant leg. The older lady behind the counter wasn't paying attention. She was reading a book, and it was 3:00am in an empty store, so I felt free to do as I pleased. I made my way for the exit without purchasing a single thing. With each step I could hear the Doritos bag crinkle in my pant leg, and I winced to myself, hoping she wouldn't look up.

As soon as I pushed the door open, I heard a male voice yell, "Stop!"

I blacked out. It wasn't until I read the statement of charges later that night in jail, or until months later in the courtroom, when I heard the full story that the fire marshal was actually in the 7-Eleven with me making a coffee when he heard the stuff in my pants. I tried to run when he approached me outside of the store, but we ended up wrestling around in the parking lot until officers arrived. At that time, I weighed less than 155 pounds, and I remember the judge's astonishment in court when she read aloud that it took three officers over 200 pounds each to gain control of me. Alcohol made me super-human in all of the wrong ways. Had I been sober, I would have surrendered without a fight.

The total amount of the stolen goods was only $12, so when I was taken to jail, I was issued a bail of only $1,000. I called my parents to let them know that I wouldn't be able to attend the wedding because I was in jail for stealing food because I was hungry and couldn't afford to buy it. Of course, that was a lie, but I was allergic to telling the truth. My sister insisted that even though she was disgusted with me, she still wanted me in her wedding. So, she convinced my mother to put up the $100 for my bail on the morning of her wedding so that I could be there.

A couple of days later, I had a small house party after work. It was mostly a bunch of guys I didn't even know, several black dudes, who were all friends of a friend of mine. I told them I knew some girls in Bel Air who were having a house party that night, and we could all go check it out after we got buzzed up. Once I felt drunk enough, I picked up the phone and called Daphne, the girl who invited me to her house party.

I was talking to her when I heard a voice in the background say, "Bitch, who the fuck you on the phone with? Hang it up!"

"Who the fuck is that? Put that nigga on the phone!" I told her.

I barely knew the girl, but she was gorgeous, and I couldn't believe she had some clown speaking to her like that. He got on the phone and said his name was "G." Words were exchanged. I yelled into the phone, "I'll be right over there, pussy!"

I was charged up, and I had about six guys with me who I barely knew. But they got hyped up to go over there with me, and they were ready to fight too. We piled into two cars and headed over to a neighborhood in Bel Air full of big fancy single family homes. When we pulled up to the house, my adrenaline was pumping. I hopped out of the car and ran to the front door without even looking to see who was behind me. I beat hard on the door.

Right away, Daphne opened the door and said, "Don't do it."

I looked over her shoulder to see somebody holding back this tall black dude. He had a small afro behind his red bandana and a mouth full of gold teeth. His chains were swinging as he tried to wriggle free from the grip around him.

I stepped through the door past Daphne and said, "Let him go."

I noticed in that instant that there were several black dudes there, and I recognized none of them. The rest were rich white Bel Air girls. I squared up and charged him. We traded blows, and I landed hit after hit on him.

Suddenly, I felt a crack across my forehead that lit up my sight for a split second, followed by a voice shouting, "Chill, yo! That's Danny McGhee!"

I felt warm blood stream down my face, but I didn't stop. Within seconds, I was on top of him on a white rug. We were halfway under a dining room table, and I was drilling him, fist after fist, hammering into his face. Blood poured out from my head and face. The crack I heard came from somebody in the crowd with an Alize bottle, which broke across the top of my forehead, the jagged-half raked down my face. Alize bottles are made of thick glass, and this one didn't shatter on impact. It left me scarred. In that moment though, I was unfazed.

I growled insanely as I punched him so many times that it ripped skin off of his face. As I shook my head, the blood in my hair slung on the white walls and on his face below me. I laughed like a madman at my own handiwork. Alcohol and adrenaline made me unstoppable, and that night it made me an animal. I was feeding off of my own energy, and the daze that my survival instinct had put me into when the bottle broke across my face.

When I came back to my senses in that moment and realized where I was, I stood up and stumbled away from the scene. His crowd of homeboys parted to the side and let me through. In the crowd, I saw one familiar face. He was the one who had spoken up in my defense. I nodded to him in gratitude for stopping me from getting jumped. I staggered through the black dudes and all the shocked, rich, white girls and stepped out into the cold night.

The small crowd I had shown up with was still on the front lawn. They had never even come inside the house. When I asked them what happened, they claimed that they had been held off at the front door with a knife. I didn't care whether or not it was true. I was leaking blood bad, but I was proud of what I had just done. The kids with me praised me and said they had never seen anything like it in their life. They went to the store and bought bandages and cleaned me up. I was their hero that night, but inside, and in reality, I knew I was a loser.

Two days after the fight at Daphne's house I was at TGIFriday's, working in the kitchen, when a manager came to inform me that there were detectives there to speak to me. I had no idea which, of the many incidents I had been involved in, that this was in relation to, but I agreed to talk with them. We went out back to the smoking area behind the restaurant, and the detectives introduced themselves and commented on the scars and scabs on my face. I looked terrible, and I was embarrassed to wait tables like that, so I had asked to do prep work in the kitchen instead. I told them about the fight, and they shocked me with their response.

"So that's when you started beating up on women?"

I was confused. I reiterated exactly what had happened. I had nothing to hide. They continued to tell me that on that same night in Daphne's house, three girls had been assaulted with beer bottles thrown in their faces. Two of them were taken to the emergency room, and one was having surgery.

The detective looked right at me and said, "Word on the street is that you did it. You came in there and hit these girls in the face with these bottles. Do you like beating women?"

I was lost. This was crazy. There was no way I could be blamed for this. I repeated my version of the truth from start to finish. I explained that when I walked out of the door there were no girls injured, and that it had to have happened after I left. I told them that the other guys who were there had to have done it.

The detectives said, "Well, 'G' and the other guys said you did it, but we had our doubts."

"Just ask the girls who did it," I said. "Did you ask them?"

They didn't reply. They simply folded up their notes and began to walk out. "We'll be in touch," the more talkative one said. As an afterthought, he added, "Be careful messing with 'G' and them. Those guys are in gangs and carry guns."

I puffed up, "Man, I don't care about those clowns. Talk to the girls, please."

I was honestly worried. *What if the guys had convinced the girls to lie on me, too? Was everybody against me? Maybe Daphne was mad because I had destroyed her parents' house with all the blood everywhere.* I could get strapped with a lot of charges if this went south. I walked over and told the manager what happened. I wasn't sure if she believed me either. I couldn't afford to lose this job already.

Drinking had become even more problematic than heroin was, and somehow at some point, I made the switch back. I started going back to the city. I would accumulate two or three hundred dollars and convince one of my coworkers to run me downtown. I would either give them $50 for the round trip, or buy them cocaine. I would spend the rest on pills of dope and sell as many as I could around Bel Air for double what I paid for them.

One day a young kid named Zane, who I worked with, offered to take me downtown as long as I could score some coke for him and his buddies for a party they were having later. I agreed, and we headed downtown. First, I took him to score myself a handful of dope pills off of Biddle and Luzerne in East Baltimore. Then I went to the usual corners where they sold cocaine, but no one was out. I had him drive up and down the usual streets, until I saw two young guys on a corner of Chester Street standing in front of an abandoned store on a strip of mostly boarded up homes.

We slowed down, and they yelled, "Yo!"

"You got girl?" I inquired.

"Yeah, come on," he waved to me to come over.

I had the nervous young kid, Zane, pull off on the side of the road. I told him I'd be right back, and I ran across the street to the two young guys.

"I need five," I said as we walked across the street to an alley. They weren't saying anything, and I started to worry. "You got it?" I asked.

"Yeah, I'm getting it. It's right up here," he said as we walked further back into the alley.

I knew I was being set up. I had to get back to Zane and make sure he was okay. I turned to leave the alley, and the short stocky one behind me held up his arm and put his hand on my chest to stop me.

"Where you going?" he snapped.

"I'm gone, man. Y'all don't have any coke," I said, trying to hide my fear, although I knew without even looking that there was a gun behind me. I turned around to confirm my suspicions and saw the silver piece in the young boy's hand.

"Empty everything out of your pockets! Everything!" he barked.

I did as I was told, taking no risks. I dropped my cigarettes, needle, lighter, small bundle of heroin pills, and $50 onto the dirt floor of the alley.

"That's everything?" he asked.

When I told him yeah, he told me to bend over and pick up the money and count it out for him. I surveyed my situation quickly. I was about twenty feet out of sight of the main road and about a hundred and fifty feet away from Zane. They had me sandwiched in the alley with one in front of me and one behind me. I leaned forward to pick up the wad of cash laying in the dirt, but instead I scooped up my bundle of pills and my cigarettes and shoulder charged first past the guy in front of me. I moved so fast, that my legs couldn't keep up with the momentum of my upper body, and I slid head first out of the alley into a forward roll across the asphalt and broken glass in the street. I hopped to my feet and sprinted to the passenger door of Zane's car, and we sped off. I didn't even look back to see if the boys from the alley had given chase.

I was bleeding from my arms and shoulders. I had road rash across my upper back and head, but at least I wasn't shot. Zane looked like he was going to cry. His money was gone, and he'd spent his afternoon taking me down and had nothing to show for it. I got the vibe that even with all my injuries, he still felt as if I was lying to him about being robbed. I'm sure he wondered how I managed to keep my heroin, and that would have been my first suspicion as well. He didn't know me well enough to know how many other times I'd risked my life for the drug.

The next day, when I got into work, the detectives came in to see me again. This time they said what they had to say in front of both my manager and me. They had come to apologize for disturbing me at work the previous time and raising suspicions, and for accusing me of beating on women. They said they had spoken to the girls at the party. They girls confirmed my story, that I had beat up 'G' because he was beating on Daphne, and that I had been hit with a bottle and left without touching anyone else. They told police that after I left, the guys at the party took their aggression out on them, throwing bottles in their faces and breaking two of their noses.

Word had already spread that I was a woman-beater and had sustained the injuries to my face by doing so. When the afternoon management team arrived that day, they gathered the employees and made me out to be a hero. They treated me to a cake and a free meal. I was embarrassed, but glad that everyone now knew for sure that I wasn't out assaulting woman at parties.

My temporary heroism at TGIFriday's came to a screeching halt two nights later. I got off of my shift and went to the bar at work to have a couple of drinks. I had a few people lined up to meet me there to buy some pills of dope off of me. I had been selling dope at work, including to a couple of the kitchen workers, so I figured it was easiest just to hang out at the bar and meet people there as well. A young guy sitting a couple stools down from me, drinking alone just like I was, started chatting me up. He quickly moved onto the topic of drugs and asked me if I wanted to buy any pills. I immediately thought this was a narc trying to set me up. This kid was way too forward for a stranger. I told him I didn't deal with cops, and like anybody would, he got defensive. He handed a bag to me under the bar, and I looked down at it and handed it back.

"I've got something better," I said.

Within ten minutes he was in the bathroom, and I was handing him three pills of heroin for $50. I even threw in a needle too. He went into a stall to get high, and I decided to go into the handicap stall next to him and do the same. I sat on the toilet talking through the stall to him as we both performed the ritual. I pushed the syringe in and drifted off.

Not long after, I was startled awake by the sound of police radios in the bathroom, and I could see black boots moving about underneath the stall door. Then I saw it, there was a needle lying on the floor in plain sight. The kid's legs next to me were sprawled out under his door. I woke up fast from my intense nod and dropped the rest of my dope into the toilet and flushed it just as I heard the police bust open the door next to mine. They demanded that I come out of my stall, and I did. We were both taken away in separate squad cars. I had no idea how long we had both been passed out in those bathroom stalls in TGIFriday's, but it was long enough for someone to notify management. Management looked under the stall, and when they saw a foot sticking out and a needle on the floor, they called police. They had no idea that their "hero" employee was also passed out in the stall next door.

The kid was okay, but had left his other two pills of heroin on top of the toilet paper dispenser. So, he was charged for the heroin and the bag of pills in his pocket. I only had a needle on me because I had woken up just in time to flush my dope. So, I was released that night with only a charge for paraphernalia, which carried a maximum $25 fine. Needless to say, I was never going back to work at TGIFriday's. To make matters worse, the story of the police finding us both passed out in the bathroom made the local newspaper, and everyone I knew had seemingly read it.

XLII.

I managed to stay in the apartment a few more months without ever getting another job. My life sank back into the lows of heroin addiction, where my days were a pendulum swing between bliss and illness. I linked up with other addicts in the area, and eventually met a couple who got high, but had nowhere to go, so I let them crash at the apartment with me. Every day was back to the basic struggle for survival, which meant not getting food and water, so I could get heroin instead. It was a primal, all too familiar, way of life. Theft was a daily hustle again, except now we were stealing natural laxatives from the grocery stores to sell to the Russian pawn shops in West Baltimore, who were in turn selling them to the dope boys, who used them to cut the very dope that we were stealing to buy. I also made contacts at the flea markets who would purchase high-end packages of razor blades, pregnancy tests, and over-the-counter medications.

The routine was unchanged: wake up every day, find a ride to the city, make money on the way downtown, score heroin, and chase away the sickness. It was a nasty, miserable way of life. It was empty, unfulfilling, and monotonous. However, it was the only thing I knew. I had ruined everything I ever touched, chased away everyone who ever loved me, hurt every person I came in contact with, and destroyed myself every time I had an opportunity to build myself back up. Heroin was the only thing I couldn't seem to destroy. It was always there, waiting for me, to cradle me in its soft warm arms. I dreamt that one day it would take me for good, and make this never-ending nightmare would come to a soft, easy halt. It would lower me into a casket of satin, into the soft warm womb of the earth, and I would float on its clouds into eternity. I dreamt of the solace of death, of the final reprieve from this life of sickness and withdrawal, from my daily chase, sickness, goose bumps and sweat, and an existence of nothing more than a scourge to society.

The church next door to my apartment complex was huge. It was also the one I had grown up in. It was the church where I attended Bible School as a small child, and where I stood in front of the congregation and was confirmed. It was the same church where my parents shed many tears, and offered up many prayers, held hands with the pastors and pleaded to God for my deliverance. I went into that church every day, several times a day, but not for salvation. I snuck in there because I knew that in a dark back room there was a phone on the wall, and that phone was my only source to call around every day to find a ride downtown.

Hector's sister could tell something had changed in me. I was thinner and had track marks on my arms, and I was always either sick or high. It didn't take a rocket scientist to see that I was strung out. She came in and took the TV and other electronics back to the rental company where she had gotten them. There was nothing left but a couch and my mattress on the floor in the bedroom. One night when I wasn't home, the couple had been locked out of the apartment, so they broke a bedroom window in order to get in. I got angry and threw them out with all of their belongings. Then it was just me, fending for myself, every day. I shot heroin alone one night and got cotton fever. I thought I was certain to die there alone on the floor of that empty apartment. Cotton fever is caused by a microscopic piece of cotton getting into your bloodstream.

The arm I injected swelled up like I had elephantiasis in it. My body got extremely warm, and I broke into a high fever, accompanied by nausea. All night I lay there wondering if I would die. The anxiety and depression that enveloped me carried me away to a hellish place. I shot even more heroin to try to make it go away, or just make me go away permanently, but it only got worse. I walked across town at 3:00am in the cold until I reached the Upper Chesapeake Hospital. I curled up there on a chair in the emergency room until the sun came up, and I felt well enough to leave. That wasn't the last time. I sat in that emergency room on a couple of other occasions alone waiting for death to take me, consumed in anxiety, but never checked myself in. I knew that checking myself in meant no actual treatment and tons of medical bills I couldn't afford. I knew this from previous trips here. Instead, I would sit in the emergency room because I felt safe in the hospital. I felt warm, and if I was going to die, this was the place to do it.

I was awakened one morning in the apartment by the management at the front door. It was time for me to go. They gave me twenty-four hours to get out before they called police. I tried to plead my case, but they insisted that I wasn't the one on the lease, so I had to leave. They had seen the broken window and received numerous complaints, but the final straw was that someone had written "Fuck you Danny" with a sharpie on the brick wall next to my front door. I assumed it was the junkie couple I had thrown out a couple weeks back. Now, I had to either leave the apartment for good or get charged with trespassing, so I packed a bag with my few possessions and headed back out into the streets.

I called my father and asked him if he'd heard from the rehab yet. I had been on their waiting list for over a year. It was a long-term state-run facility called Second Genesis. It was supposed to be an option for me to go there instead of doing my two and a half years in prison, but the waiting list was so long to get in, that I finished my time before a bed had opened up.

I walked into Bel Air, and by a stroke of luck or maybe fate, I ran into my old childhood friends.

My best friend Chris, and a couple of other kids I had grown up with in my parents' neighborhood were all together and high. I couldn't believe it. We'd gone our separate ways and hadn't hung out in almost a decade, and somehow they had all become junkies too. I hopped in the car with them, they gave me some dope to get rid of my ills, and I went back home with them. It was like a warm welcome back into the family and neighborhood I had grown up in. It turned out that Chris' mom had moved out and left Chris in their single-family home alone. It was up to him to pay the mortgage payments or let the bank take it. He had turned it into a shooting gallery right in the middle of suburbia, literally on the same street as my parents' house. I moved in immediately and took the smallest bedroom, which was the only one available. There were already four others living there, and between the four of them, they managed to keep the mortgage afloat and support their full-blown heroin habits. Everybody in the house worked for the same landscaping company, and they got me a job working with them.

I enjoyed waking up and working in the outdoors every day, but it wasn't so enjoyable when I was dopesick. The days seemed to stretch on forever when my bones ached to the core and my body shook with ills. The only light at the end of the tunnel was the ride into the city after work. I lasted a few weeks at that job, riding around to different parts of Baltimore and Harford counties working at office buildings and residential neighborhoods. I would run the trimmer and the leaf blower and do my best to hang in there for the length of those ten and twelve hour days, while feeling the pangs of heroin withdrawal set in as the days grew longer. The two guys who owned the company would tote us around with them, and I often found myself riding in the back of their pickup truck with the equipment. When we would stop at convenience stores for drinks and snacks, I would come out with my waistband and pockets full of stolen merchandise and divvy it up among the crew. At first, they thought it was funny, right up until the day they fired me for it. They thought it had gone too far, and they didn't want their company associated with it. When they fired me, they offered to let me finish out the day. However it was payday, and I took it as a lucky break. It just meant I could get to the city that much faster. I called a female friend who got high to come get me. I was shocked to see that she had her newborn in the back seat. I felt uneasy copping dope and firing it in a vehicle with a baby, but that uneasiness didn't stop me.

The days grew longer without a job. I sat in the house sick most days with no plan or ride to get high. I dug through my roommates' rooms and found their stash of heroin and pilfered out of it at times. Other days, I went through my collection of empty vials and dope baggies, squirting water into them and drawing it up, hoping that there was enough heroin dust in there to take my ills away. It was sickening firing water into scarred, bruised up arms, waiting for a high that never came. Yet, I tried it time and time again.

The strangest thing was that the other guys could go a day, or even a couple of days, without shooting dope and be perfectly fine. It was just like our childhoods, they were bigger than me, matured quicker than me, and had everything that I didn't have. Here we were as adults, and all junkies, yet they could handle it better than me. It was almost as if they weren't addicted at all and only did it recreationally. These were the only people I had ever met who possessed this somewhat magical power. There were many parties at that house, and sometimes I could drink my dopesickness away. Jessie even came around there quite a few times. One night everyone pitched in and got some coke, and I did a couple of shots and freaked out so bad that I almost went to the hospital. I lay in my room alone on the floor all night unable to sleep due to the cocaine. The room was dark and spun around me as I cried and sunk into a vast oblivion of nothingness. It seemed there would never be sleep again, or comfort, just pure hellish misery forever. That's what my life was, it's where it had been, and where it was headed. *Why was I made this way?* I laid in the dark and sawed at my wrists with my driver's license until I broke the skin. *Who am I kidding? I don't have the courage to do it.* The only way I had the courage to kill myself was with heroin, and the many times I tried, it never worked. In that single year, eighteen of my friends and associates had died from accidental heroin overdoses, and I couldn't seem to do it purposefully. Again, who was I kidding? If I really wanted to, I could have. I did just enough to gamble with it, to dump a barely lethal amount into a spoon and take the plunge, and see if I awoke or not. I was leaving it in God's hands, teetering on a ledge between life and death, and He never allowed me to fall.

My father showed up at the house one morning. The rehab finally had a bed available, and he wanted to know if I was going. I was sick of being sick. On top of that, I had additional criminal charges pending, which would not only land me more jail time, but also violate my probation. For that alone, I'd be facing fourteen more years in prison. I had no doubt that after appearing in front of the judge for the third time, he would give me all of my time. My only hope was long-term drug treatment.

The next morning, I got into the car with my father and drove an hour to Annapolis for my intake interview. The problem was that I got high before I went. I wasn't about to enter a new facility dopesick and not have one last celebratory high. When I arrived, I sat on a couch in the lobby of the treatment facility, nodding out as I waited for the intake counselor to see me. I was told at the end of the interview that I had a bed there, but I had to detox before I could enter the program. I had to give them a clean urine test upon intake. Therein lied the problem. Almost every state-run drug treatment center had the same requirement. Only the expensive programs for people with insurance provided in-house detox. We hadn't even explained to the facility that I had open warrants for violation of probation. We figured that we could deal with that after I was accepted.

The public defender I had before had taken a special interest in my cases from the very first time she met me, fragile and dopesick at the Harford County Detention Center years prior. She had seen something in me that I didn't even know existed within myself. When she combined all of my existing cases, she became emotionally invested in defending me and trying to help me. She was my guardian angel. We contacted her in regard to my open violation of probation warrant, and my new charges from the 7-Eleven incident, and about the fact that the Second Genesis facility finally had a bed available for me. She agreed to do her best to get me into the rehab facility instead of jail.

Before she had time to finish working her magic, the police picked me up as a passenger in a vehicle during a traffic stop and took me to jail for the warrant. Something was entirely different in jail this time. I was sick for sure, just like every time before. I was sick and weak, and my first night in jail somebody tried me. I hopped off of the top bunk where I was laying the second he called me "bitch." He was a loud-mouthed older guy who normally would have never crossed me, but he knew I was weak and wanted to take advantage of that. He wanted to show off for the other guys in the dorm. I surprised him when I jumped off the bunk and punched him right under his eye. I reeled back my frail arm and struck him hard, and it barely made an impact. I rushed him, and he was able to overpower me as we wrestled between the bunks. When I broke free from his grip, I was in a position to stomp on his face, but I didn't.

I let up and walked away. I felt like a coward for doing so, but

I was done. I was done with jail. I was done with heroin. I was done with being a worthless piece of shit. Just done. Something had changed. I climbed back into my bunk and writhed and rolled through two days of sickness. I never felt so disrespected by the other inmates in jail.

The tier was mostly black, and all I had to listen to as I lay in my bunk all night and day was things like, "Let's run these white bitches off the tier." Or, "We should start cracking these white bitches heads."

One of them grabbed my bed roll and started walking to the front of the tier with it, telling me I had to leave or I was getting fucked up. I had done nothing wrong. This was just the pack mentality and bully mentality that I had experienced so many times before. Only this time, I was the victim. I honestly didn't care. Something inside of me told me that I just had to wait it out. I was headed somewhere better. I had peace inside. An older black man on the tier, who I had been locked up with many times before, stopped them and stood up for me. He told them to put my bed roll back on my bunk, and they actually listened.

I climbed back up into my bunk with the chaos around me and read the Bible for a week or so. I got lost in it. My body healed quickly, my mind followed, but my spirit was in a place it had never been before. I had an inexplicable sense of peace. In that moment of hell, I had never felt so close to heaven. A sort of surrender and defeat went on inside of me. It happened naturally, and it opened up a floodgate of release within me. I was supposed to be sick and miserable. I was surrounded by evil, and I listened to threats and talk of violence day and night—but inside I smiled. I smiled at every word and every lesson I read in the Bible. I was transported by what I was reading. I felt safer than I ever had before. It was as if I had been stuck in a very deep dark pit for a long time without hope of a way out. I was going to suffer and die in that pit, and just as my life was about to end, I knew that help was on the way. The feeling was akin to looking up at the sunlight way in the distance and knowing that at any moment my ladder would be rolled down and I could climb up into it.

My new attitude and outlook poured out into my phone calls with my father, and I knew he could sense my inner-change and my rising strength. Then on one such call, the good news came. The attorney had contacted the judge, and the rehab still had the bed reserved for me. In just three days, I would go in front of the judge, and he would release me to go directly to the Second Genesis facility. If I completed my long-term treatment there, then I would avoid all jail time and be placed back on probation. If I failed to complete the treatment there, then I would be taken to the Maryland Division of Corrections to complete a fourteen-year sentence. This was my chance—my last chance—and my only way out. I spent my next three days in that jail on top of the clouds, praising and thanking God, and crying tears of happiness. I had finally found a way out, and I was going to make the most of it. At least, those were my intentions.

XLIII.

When they opened the steel door to the dorm and yelled, "McGhee! Bags and baggage!" my heart raced with excitement like it had so many times before, but this time was different. This time felt entirely different because once released from the miserable negativity inside that jail, this time I would be safe. I would be someplace where I couldn't sabotage myself, or my future, as easily as if I were walking out onto the streets.

I also felt completely different inside. I felt warm and hopeful for once. I felt like a warrior, as if the arms of God were wrapped around me and lifting me aloft. I packed my things quickly and stood waiting for the heavy door to the sally port to slide open. Very few inmates paid attention, only a couple lay awake looking at me with jealous hatred in their eyes.

My father drove me back to the Second Genesis facility, which was about an hour drive. It was located on the grounds of the old abandoned Crownsville Mental Institution and wasn't that much more inviting. They processed me in and had me sit on a small bench in the lobby while they sorted out where I would be staying and which counselors they would to assign me to. The men I saw there looked no different than the population I had just left behind. Here though, there would be stricter rules to follow and worse consequences. The population of the facility was mostly black and inner city from Baltimore, Annapolis, and DC. They assigned another young white guy who had been in the facility for a few months to be my chaperone and guide for the first few weeks. I caught on to the inside jokes and the chuckles from everyone seeing him be in charge of someone else because apparently, he had been somewhat of a problem there with a bit of an attitude.

Second Genesis was supposed to be a six to nine month treatment facility that incorporated a thirty-day blackout period of heavy restriction and no contact with the outside world, followed by a couple of months working inside the facility, then on to a job search and work release phase. The facility was incredibly strict, and there were many heavily enforced rules. If someone violated the rules, they were forced to suffer abnormal consequences. For instance, if someone were caught talking in the hallway, he would be forced to stand under an exit sign while his peers yelled at him. One too many infractions and he might have to wear a cardboard sign around his neck that said, "I am a low-down, sneaky dope fiend." Or, "I run my mouth too much." Often a person would have to wear a stocking hat on his head, or a bar of soap on a necklace, or something else that represented his infraction. They were also very strict on accountability, meaning if you saw someone else talking in the hallway, or chewing gum, or some other infraction and didn't hold that person accountable, then you would be punished as well. Breaking rules could also lengthen the amount of time that a person was in the facility or cause him to lose jobs. There were accountability groups a couple of times a week. There was also a weekly meeting where they would sit all of the residents in a circle and have us yell at each other regarding all of the things we didn't like about each other. The program was very intense and taught me how to be verbally confrontational in a different way. As horrible as it may sound, I probably grew the most during the time that I was in there and had some of the best times of my life.

The counselors and residents there were mainly black, which made me more comfortable than if they had all been white. I always felt more at home around black folk. However, the inner politics were completely unfair. There were maybe two white counselors in the whole facility, and they were females who were having relationships with black men inside of the facility. Most of the females who worked there were sleeping with residents. The way a person got into Second Genesis was through the State of Maryland prison system, and a candidate had to convince the legal system that they were an addict and needed treatment in order to beat an otherwise lengthy prison sentence. Half of the inner-city guys that were in the program had never used a hard drug in their life. They had been locked up for dealing, but they lied and said they were addicts in order to get out of serving a long prison sentence. Some of these guys continued selling cocaine even while living in the program. These same guys were sleeping with counselors in the program. These were the same counselors who were holding me accountable and telling me how to stay clean—and that I would never get clean. These same counselors were all recovering addicts, who eventually all relapsed years after I got clean.

There was an obvious disparity on how I was treated by the staff compared to my peers. I got along well with my peers and made a lot of friends, but there were always racial undertones and differences in treatment. Eventually the resident who was my "guide," together with a few others, snuck out in the middle of the night and went on the run. Less than a week later, they were in the newspaper for pulling a string of bank robberies and eventually getting caught. The police had pulled over an innocent man outside of Annapolis one night thinking it was one of them.

The officer shot him in the head and killed him accidentally when the man reached for his seatbelt.

Nevertheless, I remained focused on my recovery and doing the right thing. I attended all of the meetings and participated the best that I could. I met with my counselors and developed treatment plans, as well as plans for my future. I participated in outside meetings when we went, and eventually got a sponsor. Everything was going great, except for one thing. There were women in the program with us. I was obsessed with women, and even though relationships and even being alone with a woman was prohibited, everyone found a way. Almost every woman in that facility was in a relationship with a male resident. Even though it wasn't allowed, the staff turned a blind eye to almost all of it, as long as it wasn't too blatant, and depending on who it was. I met an older black woman who had come into the facility and taken an instant liking to me. We began sneaking around and passing notes and chatting, and eventually meeting up with each other.

It wasn't until another male resident of the facility caught the two of us coming out of a closet after having sex that things changed significantly. This young black male was in his own relationship with a female in the facility that everyone, including the staff, knew about. Still, he went immediately to the staff to tell them what he had just seen us doing. This was counted as a major violation of the rules, and I was taken back in front of the judge to face my fourteen-year sentence. The judge scolded me, gave me one more chance, and said that if she was notified by the facility of anything at all, I would go to prison to finish up my fourteen years.

I had lost focus on my recovery and turned to obtaining emotional fulfillment from the opposite sex, and it had gotten me into trouble. Instead of focusing on myself and what I had done, I focused on how I had been wronged by the people in the facility and how I was being treated differently. I openly expressed my frustration about how everyone was sleeping with each other, including counselors, and I was the only one they tried to send to prison for fourteen years. I knew it was because I was the only white one. I was angry, and the more I confronted people who did me wrong, the more enemies I made in the facility. I grew strong in there, and I had emotional breakdowns. I had plenty of friends in there, mostly black, who saw the unfairness, but the staff was against me. They were trying to put me away for life, and so I walked a thin line.

For two weeks straight they had me scrubbing a brick wall outside of the building with a toothbrush all day long. I cried as I did it. I had no option. It was either that, or go back to jail, so I determined to do what I was told. I played the game, and I learned humility. I scrubbed that wall, and did things nobody else had to do, while other residents sold drugs, went out drinking with counselors, and slept with counselors and with each other. They stood by just watching for me to slip. There was no way I would give them that satisfaction.

Months passed, and I was well past the six-month milestone when I was supposed to be out on work release, but once again, I bit my tongue because I was at their mercy. Finally, after I had flown under their radar long enough, they let me out on a job search. Every day the van would drop me off at Annapolis Mall, and I would catch buses or walk around the city of Annapolis applying for job positions. As a convicted felon, it was no easy task finding a job while living in a rehabilitation facility, but I tried my best. The newfound sense of freedom pushed me, and I was confident.

I landed a job at the Social Services Department, at a mortgage broker, and even at several restaurants. But, nothing was good enough. My job counselor would shoot down every job I came back with, and I couldn't figure out why. It wasn't until a couple of months into my job search, that I learned that my job counselor was sleeping with the same guy who had reported me for my relationship. He was also selling cocaine around Annapolis while living in the facility and sneaking out with her at nights to party. I watched her through the window drop him off at the facility one night. There was nothing I could do though. My hands were tied. If I told anyone, it would surely backfire. They were all in it together, and the few who weren't, believed them over me.

Three months into the job search, after being dropped off every morning and going through the same routine every single day with no hope, something inside of me broke. I caught a bus to the light rail station, then the train to Baltimore City, and walked from downtown to Pennsylvania Avenue. I walked up the avenue and copped a needle and some heroin. If it killed me, it killed me. I didn't care anymore.

It didn't kill me, but I got high as a kite. I came back to the facility wrecked and gave them exactly what they had all hoped for. Everyone could tell I was high, no matter how much I denied it. They gave me a urine test to confirm that I had used, and then contacted the judge. I was barred from leaving the facility or even going to groups and meetings inside of the facility. A couple of days later the judge replied, and I was called to the main office. I was told to sit tight and that within the next week or two, a Bluebird Bus would be there to take me to the Division of Corrections to finish my fourteen-year sentence.

I waited about three days before I couldn't take it anymore. If I was going down, I was going down in flames. I climbed out of a window after count one night and ran up the street to a local bar. I drank enough alcohol to get drunk and then walked back into the front door of the facility, right past the night counselor. I packed my things and walked back to the front lobby, drunk and belligerent, and picked up the phone to call a cab. The older black man who was working that night was one of the crooked counselors who had been gunning for me. He came over and attempted to take the phone from me, and I squared off on him and told him I would "tear his ass up in there." I was nasty-drunk and told him everything I thought about him and the facility and issued a barrage of threats. He ran to another room and called the police. I hoped my cab got there first.

It did. I hopped into the cab and told the driver to get me out of there as quickly as possible and take me into Annapolis. I was trading one futureless hell for another, but I didn't know what else to do. I just couldn't go softly into that dismal night. I found a friend in Annapolis who had recently graduated the program, and he hid me out in his room in a halfway house for a couple of days.

I was back to being a full-time junkie again that quickly. I caught the bus to the light rail and into the city every day and came back high. I would walk to Sandtown and into a project neighborhood referred to as "The Bricks" and cop $6 pills of scramble heroin.

On one particular day, as the hitter handed me three pills of heroin, somebody yelled out "Police!"

Everyone scattered. I ran through the maze of alleys. As I approached the exit of one alley, I saw a squad car and made a U-turn down another alley like a rat in a maze. I ran for my life knowing that if I was caught, it would be the end of my road. I came down another alley onto Pitcher Street and heard the screeching tires of the squad car coming around the corner. I threw the pills onto the floor of the alley and came trotting out the front of the alley into the waiting arms of the police. I waltzed out with my hands up, and they ordered me against the wall. After a pat down I was handcuffed and put on a curb. They asked me what I was doing, and I told them I was trying to buy some dope, but hadn't gotten any yet.

I believe there were angels in that West Baltimore alley that day, either that or corrupt cops. But I prefer to think angels. While one of the cops watched over me as I was seated on the curb, the other one walked into the alley, flashlight in hand, to see if I had thrown anything. I lowered my head in defeat. Not only would I be taken to city jail on my warrant, but I was going to get a new heroin charge as well. It felt like eternity crept by as I sat there wincing on the curb, awaiting my fate.

The officer came out of the alley and said, "If I catch you down here again, I'll arrest you on site." Then he turned to the other officer and said, "Uncuff him."

My heart started to beat again. I was in total shock. What was happening was unbelievable. They let me walk away that day. Not only did I have heroin, but an open warrant as well. He had taken my ID to check for one. I felt the same feeling inside that I had when I was released from jail almost a year prior to go to Second Genesis. It was a comforting feeling, a feeling of hope… but at the same time, it was eerie.

I walked away quickly, rounded the corner, and ducked up an alley. As soon as the police had driven off, I darted into the alley where I had thrown the pills, the same alley the officer had just scoured over with his flashlight. I was determined that they must have rolled up under some leaves or trash and were still there. Nothing of the sort had happened though. I made my way through that alley start-to-finish, checking everywhere. There was nowhere they could have rolled to. They were just gone. The pills had simply disappeared. I knew that someway, somehow, and for some reason that I didn't deserve, God had spared me that day. I had no choice but to change.

XLIV.

The seeds of recovery had been planted at Second Genesis, and I knew I had just made it nine months clean. I couldn't give up that easily. I heard from some addicts on the street that there was a free long-term program on the outskirts of West Baltimore offered by the Salvation Army. I thought if I could get myself in there and stay in there for eighteen months, then I would at least be safe for a little while. I was always told that the police couldn't come into a rehab facility to arrest someone on a warrant. This was my one shot to buy some time without going to prison.

I stood at a payphone out front of a McDonald's in Annapolis with a crinkled piece of paper that I kept all of my contact numbers on. Every time I wanted to call one, I had to bum a quarter off of a passerby to dial it. I went through all of the numbers and came across one I hadn't called in a while. It was Becky, a girl from my neighborhood who I had grown up with. We hung out as little kids at her house every day, but as I grew up and got into trouble, we went our separate ways. She had always believed in me though, I remembered that. She, like a few others during the course of my life, had seen something in me that I hadn't been able to see in myself. She told me I was different than the others that I was running with, that I had more potential. As a child, I felt there was an inkling of truth in her words, but it all went in one ear and out the other. However, as I stood there in Annapolis hanging by a mere thread of hope, and holding onto that crinkled list of numbers, I looked at her name and number and longed to hear those words again. I should have listened. I should have listened to everyone, but my path wasn't meant to be an easy one. I dialed her number, and to my surprise it worked. She was on the other end, shocked to hear who was calling her. I cried into the phone and poured my soul out to her.

Her response was, "Hold tight, I'm coming to get you."

And just like that, a childhood friend who I had rarely seen over the years of adulthood was driving from an hour away to pick up this evil drug-infested failure that was me. I knew that if I couldn't do it for myself, I had to do it for her. I waited at the McDonald's for about two hours, and when she arrived she took me right over to the Salvation Army Adult Rehab Center. We went in together, and they told me that they had a bed for me, but I had to be able to pass a urine screen to get in. I wasn't able to. I had just gotten high the day before. This was always the roadblock. How was an addict fresh off of the streets supposed to get clean in order to get admitted into a rehab? I was going to the rehab so I could get clean. There was only one place in the city that was free that allowed heroin detoxes, and that was at Johns Hopkins Bayview Hospital. Unfortunately, I had already burnt that bridge a while back. My heart sank, and I asked Becky to just take me back to Annapolis, where I would figure things out somehow. She knew better. She knew I would end up dead or in prison. She wasn't letting me go that easily, so she drove me back to the other side of the city to Harford County to find a place for me to dry out for three days so I could pass the urine test.

I found out that my parents were out of town, and my sister was in the house alone. Becky called my parents and sister and got approval for me to sleep there for the next two nights under her watchful eye. I couldn't believe they allowed it, after all of my repeated failures and not being in their lives for so many years. On top of that, all it would take is for the police to show up there over the weekend looking for me, and I was done. There was a warrant with a fourteen-year sentence waiting for me. I was a fugitive. I didn't leave that house for three days. Becky brought me food and a six-pack of beer to take the edge off the first two nights. Then, Monday we drove back down to the Salvation Army with my small bag of belongings and I proudly passed the urinalysis. It was time to start over. Again.

The Salvation Army is located on Patapsco Avenue on the border of West Baltimore. It was a popular prostitution strip at the time because Patapsco Avenue itself was the line separating the city from Anne Arundel County. The rehab sat in a decent area but was flanked by drug-infested neighborhoods on both sides. The sleeping arrangements weren't much different than prison bunking, except there were no bars. We were free to roam within the facility. In the common area, there was a big screen TV with pool tables and plenty of seating. The kitchen staff fed us huge meals, complete with soup and salad bars. Everything from the furniture, to the food, to the clothing we wore were from donations. We were well taken care of. The rehab center was connected to a huge donation warehouse and a Salvation Army store. They took new intakes over to the store to pick out clothing donations that fit us. I was impressed with the whole place. What made the Salvation Army different from other programs I had participated in was its connection to the church. There were several Bible studies through the week, as well as the typical Alcoholics and Narcotics Anonymous meetings, and then a long church-filled Sunday.

During the first thirty days, just like in Second Genesis, I was on a blackout period, which meant I wasn't allowed to leave the facility or have visitors. However, after my initial thirty days was up, I could get a job either working in the kitchen, warehouse, or on one of the donation trucks on routes around the State of Maryland. I made it through my first few weeks with flying colors. I got involved in everything from the meetings to the church. At night I was studying the Bible, reading, planning, and participating in all of the various positive activities they offered. I came out of my shell. I found a fervor for God like I had never had before. I assembled a group of singers, and we sang in front of the church and went to other churches and sang. This was unlike anything I had ever done before. I had never opened myself up and exposed myself to new things. I had always kept up my guard and the tough-guy facade. In the past, it would have eaten me alive inside to sing in front of people or even smile. I felt like I had surrendered and been born again. I had become a new person, who even I was completely unfamiliar with—that was until temptation quickly stole my new persona right back with it.

Just like in jail, as long as I didn't have access to the poison that consumed me, then I was free to let loose and be my true self. But as soon as I was back within its grasp, something inside me would change. I sat in a bathroom stall one night and heard an older guy we called "Chief" twist open a bottle in the stall next to me.

Jokingly, I said, "Hey, pass that over here when you're finished."

"Who's that?" was his mumbled reply.

I told him that it was me, and that we were the only ones in there, and that he didn't have to worry because I wasn't going to tell on him. I meant to leave it at that. I didn't expect him to pass it to me, but maybe I hoped that he would. His hand reached under the stall with a pint of Jim Beam. I took a couple swigs and handed it back. This quickly turned into me slipping him money to bring me back a pint of my own the next time he was out. Then, it became a nightly ritual. I would stew around in the center all day watching the clock, waiting for him to return from work, then I would sit in the stall swigging down the liquor before going to my nightly meetings. Just like always, I loved the way it made me feel. Here I was, in a rehab facility, sitting in Alcoholics Anonymous meetings with a buzz. I couldn't wait until the meetings were over so I could sit in the smoke area and talk trash with the other fellows until lock-in time. The difference now was that I was buzzed and they weren't, so I dominated the conversations, rather than sinking into my normal introverted self.

I managed to keep the drinking under wraps and only let a few of my closest associates know. But, drinking had always been a stepping stone for me, and that hadn't changed. I noticed an old black guy named Dougie, who was a recent graduate of the program. He was with a group of men who lived outside of the program and were paid to come in every day to drive the donation trucks. The thing I noticed immediately about Dougie was that he was high on heroin. I could see it a mile away, and I had no clue how none of the other workers there noticed. I approached him immediately and sparked a conversation, then slipped in the fact that I knew he was high. I then went against my own heart and every single strand of common sense within me and asked Dougie to bring me back some heroin.

I gave him my only $8 and asked him to bring me back half of a pill. Then I waited. I waited the longest night of my life. Like a child anticipating Christmas morning, I waited. Like a man eager to see his long-distance lover for the first time in years, I waited. The next morning, he arrived with my gift. It was just enough to barely get a taste. The fact that I didn't have a syringe and needed to sniff it didn't help. I barely got a buzz from it. I knew though, that my thirty days was up in just two days, and I would be getting a taste of the free world soon. I was past the point of insanity. After time and time again of failing and going back down the same road, with fourteen years in jail facing me, and finally having the chance to fix it all again, here

I was impatiently waiting to sabotage every good thing I could possibly have in life.

I was one of the few men, of over eighty men in the facility, who had a valid driver's license. So, I was signed up to drive a truck around to pick up donations as soon as my probationary thirty days were over. My first day out, I was to go as an assistant with another driver to learn the ropes. I chose Dougie. Dougie lived in Cherry Hill and coincidentally his route ended in Cherry Hill. Cherry Hill Homes is the biggest project neighborhood in Baltimore City. On the outskirts of West Baltimore, it is a huge maze of brick projects. It's equally easy to get killed, buy drugs, or get lost there. We hopped in the truck and started picking up donations all day long.

About half way through the day, we entered the never-ending maze of brick homes. Dougie had set aside certain donations all day that he thought he could sell in the projects. All he had to do was pull up on a busy street corner, open the back of the truck, and start the bidding. People crowded around the back of the truck pointing out the items they wanted, yelling over top of each other, bickering over prices. I was the only white person in the whole mob scene, and probably the entire neighborhood, so I was extra aware of everything going on around me.

Not one item had been sold, when I noticed a car flying up the street. I told Dougie. He quickly pulled the back door down and latched it as the car screeched to a halt right in front of the crowd. Two young black dudes hopped out, hats on backwards, gold chains swinging, as they charged at the crowd. I thought for sure we were getting robbed until they shouted out someone's name. Suddenly, one of the black men from the crowd took off up the street, and we all stood and watched as they gave chase. The two men chasing him weren't there to rob us. They were "knockers," which were plain clothes, undercover police. The skinny guy they were chasing jumped several fences through the backyards, as the two knockers chased after, hopping fence after fence behind him. All fifteen or so of us stood in silent watch as they flicked open their extendable metal police batons and started beating the bushes in one of the backyards. This only lasted a few seconds before the skinny guy emerged from a bush and jetted out into the alley. They caught him in full view of all of us, and started thrashing him with the batons as he lay there on the alley floor screaming. Suddenly, people in the crowd started screaming at the police and claiming they were filming and had cameras. Dougie and I quietly dipped out of sight before the police could come back around and ask questions. No heroin for me that night, but tomorrow was a bright new day. Once I had made up my mind, there was no stopping me and definitely no turning back.

The very next day, they gave me a truck, a list of addresses in Anne Arundel County, and a partner to help with pickups. All day, I drove around picking up donations with only one thing on my mind. I sped through the day so I could get to it as soon as possible. At the end of my shift, with an hour to spare before I had to be back in the facility, I drove way off of my route and into West Baltimore. I drove into Sandtown, right into the area where the police had stopped me and my pills had disappeared in the alley. I parked the truck on that very street and told my helper to sit tight because I had to run an errand. I came back with a needle and a pill of heroin and headed back to the center. I walked into the rehab center, making sure I was seen by everyone while I was still sober, and then I snuck off after dinner and got blasted.

The next morning, I was called into the counselor's office and asked to give a urine test. I had clean urine in my locker just in case this happened, so I retrieved it and when the time was right, I took the test and passed. I was visibly high though. Not only that, but my helper had reported me. He didn't want to tell on me, but he had been in the program much longer, so he had been the first one they confronted the night before when they looked at my GPS and saw that not only had I gone way off route, but I had parked in a drug-infested section of West Baltimore. An hour later they asked me to take another urine test, and I knew I was screwed. I came clean about everything. I took some responsibility, but also played a victim of circumstance. Without dropping Dougie's name, I told them that I had been exposed to a driver who was getting high, and that it was unfair to expect people to get clean in those conditions.

The counselors and people there in charge loved me. I had been so on fire for the Lord, and so involved in my recovery, that they were astonished at this turn of events. I cried and pleaded with them. I would be homeless, but not only that, I was facing significant jail time. It was no one's fault but my own, and rules were rules. They told me to pack up my things and leave, and they promised that if I came back clean in thirty days, I could start over again from square one. I promised that I'd be back, and I left out into the streets lost and broken, knowing that I'd get high some way, whether I wanted to or not.

XLV.

The next few weeks were a blur. I didn't dare tell Becky or my parents or anyone else what had happened. I was tired of letting down the people who had faith in me. I was sick of explaining the unexplainable. How could a person given so many chances continue to fail every single time? I was a living, breathing disappointment. These thoughts helped me justify putting a needle back in my arm day after day. I was back to running the streets of Baltimore, except this time on the Westside. I stayed with black women I'd meet, one for a few days on Poplar Grove right up the street from a dope strip. And there was another more attractive woman who I slept with and stayed with for a couple weeks out in Edmondson Village. She lived with her two young children and didn't get high. I wasn't sure what she wanted from me except for sex. I brought nothing to the table except my own issues. I snuck out one day while she was gone running errands because she started talking crazy about wanting me to give her a baby.

I caught the train, then a bus, back out to Annapolis to try to link up with some people I knew out there. As I was walking through Annapolis, I saw a familiar face. It was a girl I used to get high with, and lived with briefly, years back in Harford County, over an hour away. I had grown accustomed to strange coincidences happening, and I believe they happened for a reason. She was working for a landscaping company and living in Annapolis. She and her boyfriend were both on the methadone program and living a couple miles outside of town. I explained my situation to her and she was determined to help me get clean. She said I could stay with them until I could get back into Salvation Army, but only if I got clean.

This was our plan… She gave me a 100mg bottle of methadone, and I was to take a little sip every day for the next four days to help me with any withdrawals. Then I would be good after that. It worked like a charm. I got through the heroin withdrawal easily with the use of the methadone. I sat in the house alone for four days straight, high as a kite from the methadone, while they worked. On the fourth day I stopped taking it, but floated on through another couple of days as it left my system. I also mixed it with alcohol, which made my time there even foggier.

On my sixth day in their house, I was dying to get to the outside world. I called around to some friends who had graduated Second Genesis and got ahold of this old, white guy named Rick. He came and picked me up, and we went out for a few drinks. Those few drinks turned into a few more, and those turned into us shooting cocaine and heroin all night long in city row homes. I shot so much cocaine and heroin that night, I don't know how I survived. I was hanging out the side of the car vomiting in parking lots in the early morning hours, as they took me back to the house in Annapolis. Rick decided on the way home to swing through one last area and buy some more coke to get "one last high" for the night. As we were driving through some projects in the neighborhood of Brooklyn in West Baltimore, the police got behind us and pulled us over. They ran all of our names through their database while we sat handcuffed on a curb. Rick and the driver were released. I was taken away because I had a warrant.

My run was finally over. I didn't care, it was time to give up. I was destined to spend decades in prison eventually, and I deserved to. Rick didn't fare so well. Less than a year later, he was found dead in an alley in East Baltimore. When police went through his phone, they discovered that the last number he had dialed was to the same guy in Second Genesis who was selling cocaine and sleeping with my job search counselor, the same one who ratted me out for having sex in there. Years later, I found out that the guy was an informant, and that the police let him sell drugs with immunity as long as he gave them other dealers. This was Baltimore City. Normal rules never applied here.

XLVI.

The police took me away that night. I was so high I don't even remember being processed into the jail, but when I awoke the next morning, I was in the Baltimore County Detention Center. I was content though. It was out of my hands. There was no struggle. I understood that I had relinquished all control of my life, and that it was in God's hands. Seeds had been planted in Second Genesis, and even more had been planted at the Salvation Army. I prayed myself to sleep every night in that detention center, not for my will to be done, but for God's will. My way never worked, and I knew that if left to my own devices, my life would fail miserably. I had proven it time and time again. I gave up flailing against the current and instead swam with it. I wrote letters to the Pastors and counselors in the Salvation Army and connected them with my attorney. They wrote letters to my attorney to bring to court, offering me acceptance back into their program, and submitting their own testimony supporting their belief in my ability to succeed. I was taken back and beyond grateful for their willingness to do so after my blatant failure in their program.

The attorney representing me was the husband of the public defender who had taken an interest in all of my cases in Harford County. He had a private practice in Baltimore, and she had pleaded with him to take on my cases outside of Harford. I imagine he begrudgingly did so, but of course, I was extremely grateful. My court date was fast tracked to only thirty days out. Meantime, I laid on a mattress on the floor in the public area of the tier in the detention center. The jail was extremely crowded, with three people to a cell, so the rest of us were forced to sleep on the floor beneath the TV and common area tables. A young guy came to me one day and offered to let me move in and have a bunk in his cell. He said he would sleep on the floor. He thought if I were bunking there, maybe other inmates would be leery of coming in and strong arming them for their food and snacks. I happily agreed, and spent my last days in jail awaiting court, while protecting and teaching these two young guys about God and sobriety. Those were two things that I was eager to embrace for the rest of my life, whether in jail or the free world.

This time, the thirty days awaiting court flew by, and it wasn't long before the day came to face my fate. I was taken to the circuit courthouse in Towson, where my attorney told me that I had one of the most understanding judges in the entire state when it came to drug addiction cases. In spite of that, I had messed up severely, and he would be extremely surprised if I was granted another chance. I wasn't cocky or arrogant, but deep inside I already knew that I was ready. I was finally willing to do whatever it took to succeed. I was confident that things would go my way.

Some might say I felt filled with the Spirit. I was filled with something. It was an inner confidence and peace that everything was going to be just as it should be. I stood in front of the judge. I pleaded my case and expressed my willingness to surrender and change if given the chance to go to the Salvation Army. Fortunately for me, the judge didn't realize I had already been there once and didn't need to know since I had gone there voluntarily and not under a court order. If the judge knew that I had done thirty days in there already and been thrown out for getting high,

I would have never received another opportunity. After some thought and deliberation, he surprised my attorney, and everyone in the courtroom, except me. He released me immediately into the custody of the Salvation Army. My heart danced! I knew things were exactly as they should be. I was moving forward from here and never looking back. I meant it, but I was aware that I had said that time and time again in similar circumstances.

They took me into the holding cell beneath the Baltimore County courthouse, and I ecstatically awaited my release. My legs were shackled, but I stood and shuffled around the floor singing a song I had heard time and time again at the Salvation Army church.

"Take these shackles off my feet so I can dance. I just wanna praise him! I just wanna praise him!"

The guards chuckled watching me, and they encouraged me to get out and do the right thing. My heart was on fire! I didn't deserve all of these chances, I didn't know why I was being released, but I was beyond thankful and ready to prove it.

The first thirty days back in the Salvation Army program flew by. I dove right back into the church and meetings, just as I had before. Most of the same guys were still there. Some had left and relapsed, including my partner on the truck who had told on me that fateful day when I took it to get high. Dougie, the truck driver who got high, and Chief, the guy who had given me the booze, were also gone. All prior temptation was gone. I was given a clean slate, and I kept it that way. I only surrounded myself and associated with those who were as passionate about their sobriety and creating a new life as I was. I made new friends and spent my spare time reading and lifting weights.

When the thirty-day mark was near, I would be expected to begin working. They gave me a job in the kitchen where I would be confined inside the rehab center and away from outside temptation. I hated working in the kitchen, and I fought it. But it was the best thing that could have happened to me. There was a strong lesson in humility there, the first of many. I took orders from a slightly mentally handicapped older man, who was angry all of the time. I cooked, mopped and scrubbed, and served food to all of my associates when they came home from a day's work in the outside world. I looked at them with envy. I understood, however, that in order to stay clean, I had to put my pride to the side. My plan was much different than God's plan. Had I let my ego take charge, I may not even be alive today. Those thoughts were regularly affirmed as I watched people leave for work and not come back, and even one or two of them end up in jail or overdose and die.

After almost thirty more days of working in the kitchen, I had to go to another court date in Baltimore County for a different charge. I went into court uneasy, but more confident than times before. I was strapped with letters of character and how well I had done in the program, documented clean urine tests, and a testimony to give to the judge. What happened baffled both my attorney and me. The judge, against what she claimed to be her better judgment, allowed me to stay out of jail and complete an inpatient drug treatment program. However, she didn't want me to complete it at the Salvation Army, rather she insisted that I complete the state-run program called The Right Turn of Maryland. I was crushed inside.

I loved the Salvation Army. It had become my safe space and my home. I had built a foundation and a trust there, and now I was being unfairly yanked away from it, or so I thought. The same lesson in humility, and God's plans being different from mine, were pressing upon me again. Only through gratitude for where I had come from, could I begin to embrace this change and my uprooting. It was a tough lesson, one that made no sense to me at the time. *Why would I be taken from a place that was obviously working and be moved somewhere new, only to start all over again?*

It wasn't until later, looking back, that I was able to see how these lessons shaped and molded my character—but only because I surrendered my own will and allowed them to.

Right Turn of Maryland was located on the north side of the city far away from the Salvation Army, however the structure was very much the same. I was placed in a room containing metal bunk beds with several other residents. I was on a thirty-day blackout period. The facility was run by the county, and their bunk beds, mattresses, pillows, and meals all came from the Baltimore County Detention Center. Rumor had it that a few of the county judges held ownership in the facility, which is why they were determined to send everyone there, even to go so far to pull me out of another program just to send me here. Unlike the Salvation Army, this program was not free. It was $1,500 a month, and neither my parents nor I could afford it. However, my attorney pulled some strings to get me in on a working scholarship, which meant that I was to work in the laundry room of the facility for forty hours a week in return for letting me stay there.

I plugged in quickly there, just as I had in the other programs. I connected with the guys who were on the right path, got involved in the meetings and the church, started our own Bible study, and worked hard on advancing my recovery plan with my counselors. I was always into writing, so I began writing a lot of poems about God and recovery. The counselors would ask me to stand up front at the meetings and recite them, and I did so happily. Together with my closest friend in there, Kenya from West Baltimore, we wrote hip-hop songs about recovery and performed them in front of the center. They were well-received. Most all of the men in the facility were sentenced there from jail. Many of them had no addiction issues, but much like the population in Second Genesis, they were dealers who were pretending to be addicts in order to beat jail time. For the first time, I left my ego behind and avoided the appeal of the "cool crowd." I didn't hang with the hustlers and troublemakers. Instead, I spent my time with those who were serious about their recovery and living a successful drug-free life. There were women in the facility as well, and for the first time I didn't get caught up in chasing them and trying to fill an emotional void with their attention. I was independent and kept mostly to myself.

When thirty days had passed, I was let out of the front door to go look for a job. I walked the streets of Owings Mills for a few days looking for any job that would help me pay the rent at the facility. Work release residents were charged $600 a month. Once working, I would be eligible for release after sixty days if I remained infraction-free. At the bottom of the hill from the facility was a Pizza Hut. I went in and applied. The manager was a pretty young Indian girl named Preesha. Her parents owned the restaurant. I was honest with her. She was very warm to me, so I flirted with her, and she gave me a chance to wait tables there.

I learned how to do life in the outside world without getting high. This was the first time I held a job and assumed responsibility without being high or drunk in over a decade. The Pizza Hut was in a majority African American area, and I was the only white server there. Most of the black servers didn't want to wait on black customers, so I took all of their customers. I was hungry for money and stayed busy, and stressed, at all times. I learned how to cope with a whole spectrum of emotions without using a chemical to numb myself. The employees and management all knew my story and were fascinated by it. They worked with me, as I dealt with this new way of life. Experiencing feelings of anger, frustration, and disappointment without alcohol or heroin were tricky, but I learned, and Preesha was a huge support. She gave me a second chance when I'd get overwhelmed and snap and threaten to hurt a coworker. I quickly learned how to apologize, and how that wasn't the way to deal with emotions anymore. I was like a kindergartner, learning life all over again, but it worked.

We were required to go to a couple of outside meetings each week near the facility, and bring back signed slips to document our attendance. On many occasions I caught the light rail by myself from Owings Mills into the inner city to go to Narcotics Anonymous meetings. I'd sit on the train and watch junkies nod out or pick at their abscesses. I'd drift by stops where I knew I could get off and cop heroin. I'd see corner boys hustling dope and hear addicts on the buses talking about where they were going to cop. When I got my first paycheck, I bought a set of headphones so I could listen to music and drown out those sounds. I was a sight for sore eyes. I had bleached my hair blonde and had a black woman at a shop in Owings Mills cornrow it for me. I wore baggy, velour sweatsuits as I rode the train listening to the only two CDs I owned at the time: Tyrese and Musiq Soulchild. It got me by. The music sang to my soul. It drowned out the cold winter world around me and the gloomy city flush with junkies and violence.

Being sober while tackling real life responsibilities wasn't the only difference in my life. The biggest change was that I started building self-confidence. I began trusting myself and respecting myself. At work Preesha became extremely interested in me, and after the restaurant closed, we would stay late listening to the radio and talking. Those times turned into me sitting in her car making out with her before she'd drop me off at the facility. She started forging my work times on my paperwork so I could stay out until 2:00 or 3:00 in the morning hanging with her in the empty restaurant. I liked her and she liked me, but she had a child and a boyfriend I never saw. I knew that when my sixty days of work release were up, we'd go our separate ways. We both knew this was temporary. She was helping me, in more ways than she even knew.

The snow started, and it seemed to never end. Beautiful and magnificent to me, the entire world was painted white for two weeks. Just when we thought it would end, another storm would come through. I trudged the half-mile or so back and forth to work every day from the facility listening to my headphones and smiling contently as the snow fell. It was my last week in the facility, my last week before my first taste of complete freedom in a very long time. It was the end of a journey that had taken me all over the State of Maryland through many jails and institutions. I was almost sad that it had to end. I was both eager and intimidated at the idea of my freedom. I wished I could have stayed there forever in the safe comfort of the snow and Preesha. She was one of the temporary angels who held me safe when I was both alone and scared inside. But I knew I had to let her go if I wanted to grow.

My parents had seen the differences in my words and actions. Hopeful that I was finally going to stay clean, they allowed me to return home for the first time in years. I knew it would take years for them to fully trust me again, and maybe they never would, but I was blessed to be given this opportunity. I wasn't foolish enough to expect things to pick up exactly where I wanted them to. I knew it would be a long hard road, and I had no choice but to walk it or die.

On Valentine's Day of 2001, I walked out of the facility. I had successfully completed a drug program, and at twenty-three years old, I may as well have been sixteen again, walking out into the unknown.

I walked in the snow, carrying two black trash bags containing everything I owned, until I reached the Pizza Hut. It was my first day out, and I was supposed to work. However, the snow had been coming down so hard that when I arrived, the restaurant was closed. There was a winter storm advisory for everyone in the northern part of Maryland to stay off the roads. I called my parents, who lived an hour away, to let them know I was out and working on a plan. I knew it would be impossible

for them to travel that far in the deep snow, and I wasn't about
to put them in that position. I called Preesha, who lived up the
street and pleaded with her to help me. I was stuck, sitting in the
doorway of the restaurant with nowhere to go. She came down
to the restaurant an hour later and let me in to use the phone. I
scanned the phonebook for local hotels, but they were all full due
to the weather and Valentine's Day. I had no idea what to do, and
I could feel myself losing hope. There was no way her traditional
Indian family would let me come stay with them, and the facility
definitely wouldn't take me back in. Finally, I got ahold of a hotel
in Pikesville, only a couple of miles away, that had one vacancy,
but they refused to hold it. It was first come, first served.

We hopped in the car and headed south toward the hotel.
Preesha had me driving her car because she was terrified. The
snow was coming down thick, and the car was sliding on the
road, as the visibility declined to nearly nothing. We got within
a half a mile of the hotel and couldn't go an inch more. I couldn't
possibly put her in further danger. She had a child to get home
to. If it hadn't been for being stuck carrying belongings, I may
not have bothered her at all. I made a U-turn on the empty
Reisterstown Road and hopped out with my two trash bags. As
she came around to the driver's side, we embraced for a minute.
I thanked her, and then urged her to head home quickly. I picked
up my bags and trudged south through the snow with tears in
my eyes, stopping only for a moment to watch her red tail lights
get swallowed up in the white storm.

I stumbled into the lobby of the Pikesville hotel half frozen.
I didn't think I was going to make it at times. The snow was up
to my knees in places where my boots punched through, soaking
my jeans, as I dragged my bags through the snow. My face was
bright red and frozen numb, but at last I was safe. I walked up
to the counter and paid $180 for the night. They were charging
double rates for Valentine's Night. Even though my celebration

wasn't about hearts and candy, I was spending my first night out, trapped and alone.

I trudged my way through the snowy courtyard and up the steps to my room on the second floor. Once inside I dropped everything and began peeling my wet clothes off. I needed a hot shower immediately to thaw out. There's nothing like a clean hotel room to yourself, crisp linens, clean towels, and peace after a journey like that one. I let myself sink into it. I rested naked on the edge of the bed with my face in my hands and gathered myself. *So, this is it? This is freedom? This is the world I have longed for?*

I was immediately lonely. I wished Preesha was there with me. I surveyed the room for a phone so I could call and check on her. However, something else caught my eye. There, laying on my pillow, beckoning out to me was a bottle of wine with a big red bow around it. This was my Valentine's Day gift, my reward for coming so far. How perfect it looked, laying there across the pillow, as I sat here in the room alone without a single eye on me. What better time to celebrate? It sang out to me. It called me, promising to keep me warm and take away my loneliness. It invited me to come and play, but I knew better.

I pulled my clothes back on, wanting to walk out front and shatter the bottle across the courtyard. Instead, I cradled it all the way down to the front lobby of the hotel. I walked it straight up to the front desk and handed it to the clerk.

"You can have this back. I don't drink," I said matter-of-factly.

I was beaming inside with pride. I felt good. I felt strong. I knew I had just handed over a lot more than a bottle of wine. I just handed over everything that was bad inside of me. I walked out of that lobby as if I had just rid myself of a curse, thinking *let that bottle be someone else's problem now*, but understanding that for a normal person, it may just be their joy.

Once back in my room, I made a phone call to my parents

to let them know I was safe. My mother said she would attempt to come in the morning to bring me back home so I could start my new life. I proudly told them about the bottle, looking for accolades that I never received. I didn't deserve accolades for doing the right thing. It was something I had to train myself to do naturally if I were to survive this world of temptation. I wasn't normal, and I was going to have to live with that.

I called Preesha, and she ignored my calls intentionally. She ignored my calls over the next couple of days until I got the point. She had no choice but to shut the door on me. She had a boyfriend and a child and a family who wouldn't understand someone with a history like mine. She had played her part and played it well, and she knew that. She walked me through my time at the facility, and now my destiny was in my hands and my hands only. No one else bore my responsibility, and I had finally come to realize that after all these years.

I sat on the bed and looked at the indentation where the wine bottle had previously been, but I didn't entertain myself with thoughts of what might have been. I didn't worry about what tomorrow may bring either. I knew there was only one thing I could control, and that was the very moment I was living in. Thinking about tomorrow would bring me fear, and the past would bring regret, but that moment—the very moment that I was in—could determine everything. I learned to stay in it and handle it the very best way I knew how.

I got down on my knees and thanked God. As I often do when I pray, I cried. Tears of happiness and gratitude streamed down my cheeks as I knelt over the side of that hotel bed. I knew in my heart that amazing things were on the way, if I could stay in the moment and keep doing the next right thing. When my heart was empty of prayers, I climbed into the bed and pulled the cool hotel sheets up to my neck and lay on my side. I hugged a pillow to my chest, feeling as if my heart were going to explode in a warm flood of love and peace. I lay there letting my tears wet the pillow beneath me, struggling with that same old question that I had asked the universe a million times before in nights full of heavy tears.

"Why me? Why me? Why me? Why me?" I didn't understand. Nor did I deserve it. "Why God? Why me?" My tears were happy tears.

This time, I wasn't asking, "Why me? Why am I so cursed?" This time I was asking God, "Why me? Why am I so blessed?"

I knew well what I had done and where I'd been, and I didn't deserve to be there, warm and safe in that room. That hotel was the gateway to a new way of life, and my gratitude was the vehicle that would carry me far off into a future full of my wildest dreams.

THE LAST SEASON

THE ENDLESS SUMMER

*"You can't fight the tears that ain't coming,
or the moment of truth in your lies.
When everything feels like the movies
Yeah, you bleed just to know you're alive."*

~Goo Goo Dolls, "Iris"

THE TEMAZCAL
(10 YEARS LATER)

I felt like silk. My whole body felt smooth from the honey exfoliation that followed the deep tissue massage I had just received. I stood on the stonework of the outdoor shower and let the water from the rain head pour over my relaxed body. The faint smell of essential oil made the whole experience that much more refreshing. I turned off the water and listened to the waves crash in the distance, as I toweled off my honey-scented skin. My tank top and shorts were neatly folded on a wicker chair in the dark room next to the shower, and the music was ethereal with sounds of jungle birds singing in the background.

This was my fourth Mayan spa treatment within the week. I tried them all in my seven-day stay. Tulum was my place. I have come here alone every year for the past three years for Valentine's Day. There is something magical in the air here, and the peacefulness is beyond words. I have my own tiki cabana just feet from the water's edge, and I sit on my small veranda and watch the pelicans circle and dive for fish while drinking my coffee every morning. I walk the beach in the hot sun for miles admiring random female strangers and the Tulum jungle architecture. Then, maybe I'll read a book in the sun on the beach alone, walk into town to shop and explore, or take a tour to one of the area's Mayan ruins. The possibilities are endless when I travel alone, and maybe it was the possibility of adventure that always kept me coming back.

Every night after dinner I would schedule a massage or some other spa service to complete the day. I wanted to try each one: the Thai massage, the crystal massage, the clay massage followed by a rinse in the ocean, the sound massage, all of them. I am always seeking, trying everything, imagining that one day I'll find that which is just right for me, something that will strike the perfect chord within my soul. I have always been a spiritual pilgrim, ever since a child, seeking, exploring, trying to quench a never-ending thirst. Tonight was no different. I was a bit apprehensive and excited at the same time for the journey that lay ahead of me.

Tonight, I would enter the Temazcal. I had seen the Temazcal many times on the property where I was staying. It was in the back next to the stone labyrinth that I just walked earlier this afternoon. The Temazcal, I was told, is an ancient Mayan sort of sweat lodge in which spiritual ceremonies are conducted. I wasn't sure why they were used except for the health benefits of sweating out impurities, but I had to try it. So, I signed up for tonight's ceremony and prepared to experience it in less than an hour.

I walked barefoot along the winding sand path that wove its way among palm trees and huts. This place was like a maze of white sand trails interwoven with one another through various huts and buildings with thatched palm frond roofs. Palm trees crossed over one another everywhere, and dried out coconut shells littered the sides of the trails next to the beautiful foliage. Just walking through the property was dreamy and relaxing.

I arrived early at the Temazcal. There was already a huge fire built next to it that was tended by one of the groundskeepers. I sat on a nearby hammock and gazed into the fire, and shortly thereafter people began to arrive. A young couple came down the path and stood holding hands looking into the fire. I could sense the female's nervousness, as her boyfriend rubbed her shoulders to reassure her. Another older couple came, then a lone woman, then another couple, until finally there were ten of us. A small agile Mexican woman in her thirties arrived and introduced herself as our guide for the evening. She was a Mayan shaman, a true Indian. She was beautiful, and I was intrigued. She had us circle up and introduce ourselves. A couple from Canada, a couple from Australia, then Venezuela, a lone woman from Canada, and a couple and myself from the U.S.

She gave us a brief Mayan history lesson on the Temazcal, and then let us look inside at our prison for the next couple of hours. The outside the building looked tiny, and the inside looked even smaller. It looked like a clay igloo with a small door to crawl in through. In the very center was a fire pit surrounded by a flat dirt floor. I couldn't imagine how eleven of us were going to fit inside. After the introductions and the history lesson, our leader explained that we were going to be in the Temazcal for four, twenty to thirty-minute sessions, and that each session would be separated by a momentary opening of the door to let fresh air in. She described the intensity of the heat and explained the procedure for leaving early if necessary. Then our shaman told us about her history and how she came to be a shaman. She said she was known as The Wolf. She led us in song, singing to the spirits of the fire that were heating the rocks. We followed her lead and sang as she had us form a line at the entrance to the Temazcal.

"If any of you are feeling like a warrior this evening, go in first. The back is where the most heat collects," she told us.

I quickly hopped in the front of the line. I wasn't feeling like a warrior. In fact, I was feeling like a coward who was convincing himself that he was a warrior. I knew that if I put myself in the back of the Temazcal that it would be harder to get out, and thus harder to talk myself into leaving. The tactic proved to be effective.

I crawled into the small enclosure, around the dirt floor

to the other side of the fire pit, and sat cross-legged while the others filed in. Once the eleventh person crawled in and we had all shifted around, we were practically touching arms as we sat in a circle facing one another. *I am going to be okay*, I convinced myself over and over, as the man on the outside shoveled a few huge glowing rocks into the fire pit. Then he sat the shovel down and began layering dried palm fronds over the entrance of the tiny building until every single sliver of sunlight was gone.

The blackness swallowed me whole. There was zero visibility, so I could pretend to be alone if it weren't for the voices. The Wolf welcomed us to the ceremony and spoke a few Indian prayers over us. She cried out to the "Abuela" (grandmother) spirit, then began to sing an ode to her. We all joined in the repetitive verse and sang in an uncanny rhythm together in the dark, inviting the great Abuela to come join us. The singing helped to pass the time and take my mind off the situation I was in. It began to feel fulfilling as we repeated the same line or two over and over in tones that spiraled louder and louder with each round. It seemed as though we sang the verse over and over until we could no longer get any louder and then suddenly stopped. The silence was eerie, and it stayed that way for a few moments until she finally broke it with her soft, liquid voice.

She explained the four parts of the ceremony and the four openings of the "puerto" (door), one time for each of the four directions, and how each time it was closed the heat would intensify. *So far, so good*, I thought. Maybe I was a warrior after all. The heat intensified as we sat there in the dark, but it was bearable, not much worse than a sauna. I beaded up with sweat, and I drove myself crazy with paranoid thoughts of doubt. *What if I overheat? What if I have a heart attack? I hope I don't have to get out of here early and climb over top of everyone else and ruin their experience.* I couldn't quiet my mind, eliminate distractions, and find something else to focus on.

This had been a constant challenge in my life. Self-doubt, worry, anxiety—no matter how much I knew were figments of my own imagination, and no matter how much I was able to bolster my own self confidence—they still crept in and took my thoughts by a stranglehold. Through a lifetime of this constant inner battle I developed techniques. However, inside a small clay sweat lodge in a foreign country surrounded by strangers, these techniques were nothing but wishful thinking. I shifted in the dark many times, nervous about this inner journey, and as I began to sweat profusely, the most rewarding thing happened. The palm fronds at the door were pulled back by the man outside, and the last beams of the setting sun entered the hut along with cooler air. I sucked it in as the temperature around me lowered temporarily. The groundskeeper heaved in a few more glowing hot rocks into our fire pit, and just like that, the door was quickly covered again.

I took a deep breath. *I can do this. I can make it another twenty to thirty minutes in here.* The darkness engulfed me quickly, and so did the rising heat. My body was already warm from the last round, so it didn't take long to start perspiring again. The Wolf spoke in her sweet voice and welcomed us to the second door. She spoke aloud another prayer to the spirits and asked them to be with us through the heat and purge us of any negativity within us. I shifted nervously, but anxious to rid my body of physical and spiritual toxins. I hoped to come out of this physically and emotionally purified and refreshed.

We sat silent for a brief time. The silence was the hardest because it left me alone with my thoughts. My thoughts were always full of self-doubt and fear. The disease of "what ifs" was one that I was all too familiar with. The more I thought, the more I was aware of my own situation. The proximity of the people next to me in the dark heat was giving me claustrophobia. Although I wasn't touching them, I could feel their presence in the darkness. I wondered what they were thinking. I wondered if anyone suffered from anxiety like me. Was anyone wrestling with their own thoughts and inner paranoia? I stretched my arms above and my legs in directions where I thought they wouldn't touch anyone. I kept shifting and fidgeting. Occasionally, I stopped to pray. The door was only six feet away, but it felt more like six miles. I couldn't even think about leaving. The disappointment would be unbearable. The failure, everyone seeing me crawl out in shame, would be too much. I was probably the youngest and the most fit in the group, but inside I was a wreck.

The next twenty minutes felt something like an hour. It consisted of a lot of shifting around from one position to another on the dirt floor. It also consisted of a lot of sweat. I was drenched, and it was pouring off me. My shirt was off, and I had been using it to wipe the annoying beads running down my face every five seconds or so. I was beginning to reel backward into a dark place in my mind, when suddenly the palm fronds were lifted one layer at a time until the night air was able to find its way inside. A small bucket of water was passed around inside, and we each took turns ladling water onto our faces and heads. While we took this brief reprieve, more hot stones were loaded into the pit. The water was passed back outside, and just as quickly, the door was recovered.

Our leader spoke out again in the dark just like the previous times and called out to the great spirits. She then passed out small hand held drums. Eagerly, I clutched one. I jumped at the chance to do anything that might keep my mind occupied while this heat had its way with me. She began singing a song. It was another Mayan verse that was repetitive like a chant, and we were quickly able to join in. The song verses grew louder and louder in a cyclical motion.

For someone who can't sing well, and maybe for anyone, there is something freeing about singing in the dark. No one knows whose voice is whose, and they all blend together so well that there's no picking one out separately and analyzing it. And what's best, there are no eyes on you. I joined in almost immediately once I caught onto the words. Each time the verse came back around to its beginning, we raised our voices a little higher. Someone's hand found their drum and began beating it, and I joined in. Suddenly the inside of the Temazcal became a cacophony of erratic drumbeats and singing. Around and around we went, spiraling higher and higher. The more I beat my drum, the more I became aware of my sweat and my exhaustion, and I started to doubt. I started to doubt my ability to survive in this heat while expending this kind of energy, but I also didn't want to lose focus of the song. If I lost focus of the song and the drum, then I could potentially fall into the abyss of myself. I fought an inner battle between thinking and singing. The heat raked my skin and my lungs, but the words kept coming out. My hands, wet from sweat, beat frantically to the drum. As we got louder, the drumbeats got faster and more erratic. Everyone was losing themselves, even losing their minds, it seemed. The whole inner darkness became a frenzy of hollow drumming and singing.

I wondered what any passerby on the outside might think and laughed to myself. I thought about the groundskeeper stoking the fire just outside and how many times he had heard this same insane chorus of noises standing next to this very Temazcal. Sweat stung my eyes as I frantically beat my drum. I knew I was raising my pulse and my body temperature, but I didn't care. I was lost in the moment. The singing had finally spiraled to a pitch that we could no longer outdo with the next verse. So, when we finished the verse, suddenly the singing stopped. I heard our Wolf leader howl.

She howled loudly into the darkness. More howls joined her, and then I howled too. I howled as loud as I could. Salty sweat ran down my face and into my open mouth. As I howled, I felt free. I laughed to myself in the dark. We howled and howled until the doors opened, and then we breathed. The sky outside was fully dark now and the air that poured in was cooler as it kissed my hot wet skin. My skin breathed it in, my pores were open and sucking at it. I couldn't get enough. I wasn't sure I could do another round without losing my mind, or risk my heart stopping, but I had to find out.

The last of the hot stones were shoveled through the doorway into the fire pit. These rocks looked like the biggest and hottest yet. They glowed temporarily in the dark Temazcal and slowly faded as the palm fronds were lined in front of the door once more. That brief kiss of cool night air was more of a tease than anything, and within one to two minutes my skin was perspiring again.

The Wolf chanted off another prayer, but from five feet away she sounded distant. The only thing I could think about was the heat and wonder if I would survive another round. After about ten minutes, I had shifted my body a hundred times, my breathing had become shallow, and my throat and lungs felt warm. The shallowness of my breath began stirring even more paranoia, and I kept eyeing the door across the fire pit. I had already played the scenario out in my mind a hundred times, but I couldn't help not to do it again. I envisioned myself crawling across everyone's feet and legs around the fire pit, my sweaty body brushing against their sweaty limbs, apologizing to each one of them, as everybody watched me crawl out in shame.

No, I'm a warrior, I thought to myself, but I wasn't in warrior pose. I had curled up on my back in the darkness hugging my legs against my chest, praying. I moved my feet into my hands and got into a baby's pose, wondering if the people around me could see me. The stretches of my body formed a temporary distraction from the turmoil within, but quickly my mind returned to the heat. My mind was lassoed by my beating heart, my tight lungs, and the pool of sweat I rolled around in, trapped in my tight little niche in the dark. *Was anyone else suffering like me?* I doubted it.

I squeezed my eyes tight and continued to silently call out to the Lord. My anxiety further constricted me.

Now on my knees with my face in the dirt, in an Islamic prayer position, I prayed to survive my own mind. I went black. Visions came and went…visions of me falling into a fire, of reaching out and no one being there. In my vision, my girlfriend at the time turned her back on me and left me in the flames. My family was out of reach. I knew it was me, and only me. I fought the flames, I soared through them. It was only God and me. I felt Him there in the fire with me, just there with me watching, but I had to pull myself out. A voice pulled me back into my body. It was The Wolf. She encouraged us to speak aloud, or shout, whatever was on our mind in the dark. A bunch of voices spoke at once. I could pick out words, but not sentences. I instantly joined in.

"I'm a warrior! I'm a fucking warrior!" I felt like I was falling as I yelled it out. I yelled. Was it to convince the universe? Or to convince myself?

As my words rang out into the darkness of the Temazcal, out through the walls and up into the ethers, there was a loud cheer of affirmation from everyone else in the tiny room. They cheered "Whooo!" and "Yeahhhh!"

I could feel my words encourage and motivate them as well. This was my innate ability to lead, even as I doubted myself. *Maybe I am a warrior*, I thought, as my heart raced with anxiety.

I doubted myself and my ability to survive, but it seems I always have. I hoped this was one of those instances. As the voices and the excitement died down, so did the false sense of security that came with it, and my inner warrior retreated. I wasn't sure how there could be any more water left in my body to sweat out. Could my heart bear even a minute longer of this insane heat? I balled up again in the dark and repeated the same short prayer over and over again. I sucked in air and felt like I was getting none at all. I spiraled into the ground and below it, into a hellish place of boiling sweat, and darkness, and strangers laughing at me. My sanity hung by a mere thread now.

The palm fronds rustled at the doorway and shifted as one by one they were lifted away. This was the end. The cool night air eased its way inside the Temazcal and around the fire pit to where I lay. I lay on my side and watched as one by one each person crawled out of the door, and then I mustered my strength to do the same. I crawled out onto the white sand, and even though everyone else was standing, I rolled over onto my back in the cool sand and let the air embrace me.

The sky was black and littered with stars. I imagined I could blow frost from my mouth, but it was seventy degrees out. The air was just so much cooler outside. There were pitchers of water and cups on a wooden shelf. I had to get to them. I slowly made my way to my feet and walked over to the water and downed one cup after another. There were eye contact and nods among the group, but not much speaking. It was as if there was an unspoken rule not to speak right now. It was time to reflect and recover.

I drank tons of water, but was careful not to drink so much to get sick, then helped myself to the mango and pineapple that had been sliced up and left on a plate for us. Puzzled why no one else was interested in the fruit, I sat down and ate a copious amount and enjoyed the refreshment my body responded to. I had nothing to say, just smiles and nods, as the couples each made their way off into the night. Some stayed and talked with our leader. I was very interested in pursuing conversation with her, getting to know her and learning from her, but I didn't have the energy to vie for her attention, so I turned and wandered away from the scene.

My body was extremely weak, and my mind was spinning as I followed the cool white sand pathway into the darkness. A couple of twists and turns along the way, and I was standing alongside my cabana five feet from the ocean's edge. Thousands of stars lit the sky, not a cloud in sight. I could see the moon's reflection in the water clearly, as the small waves lapped and crashed at the shore.

I dropped my wet shorts to my feet and my shirt alongside them and walked naked, slowly into the sea. There was nobody around, not a single sound even in the distance. I could hear the waves, and only the waves, as I walked barefoot between the rocks and into the ocean. The water was extremely cool, but not cold enough to drive me away. It felt perfect on my warm skin, as I continued into the water until I was about stomach deep. I lowered myself to my neck into the ocean and looked into the night. With the cool water came mental clarity, everything seemed crystal clear. I stood back up and looked up at the night sky freckled with stars and realized that once again it was just me and God. My eyes filled with tears, and I thanked Him because at that moment everything was perfect. I smiled in realization that I was right where I was supposed to be and that a journey of a million miles and a million years had brought me here.

The world was spinning, and I was along for the ride, waist deep in a salty ocean that stretched into infinity, looking up into a never-ending sky. And yet, I knew that the Infinite was right there with me, watching me as always. The Temazcal, I realized, was my old life. I was forged by a fire. I was tormented by it, burned by it, and eventually purged by it, but I emerged a warrior. I was alone in that fire, reaching out for everyone, but ultimately left alone. God watched me. He watched His warrior shrieking in the flames because He already knew the outcome. Fear took over and ran my world. It had weakened me while the fiery flames of heroin, alcohol, violence, ego, and pride burned me alive.

The stars gazed upon me, and the water caressed me. I was naked and cool and happy. Tears streamed down my face. The heat didn't take everything, I still had my tears, and they felt good. I couldn't stop smiling. It took everything to walk myself back out of the ocean and pick up my belongings off the beach. I was right where I was supposed to be, and I hoped to find this place again. Not the physical ground where I stood, because I knew I'd be back here again, but the place of understanding my heart had discovered.

I was a warrior, and I had a message to deliver about the fire I had experienced, the fire that started inside of me and destroyed me, then brought me back to life…the fire that haunted me no more. I laid down that night between cool sheets, in a comfortable bed and slept in a soft, quiet place with a smile on my face, as any victorious warrior would. I slept fearlessly and deep.

I had a story to tell.

THE NEW TESTAMENT

I grew up in Baltimore, Maryland, the eye of the heroin storm. Baltimore has been dubbed the "Heroin Capital of the United States" for decades. It is a city rich in junkie lore, and steeped so deeply in a history of heroin that its very foundations were built upon the proceeds of the opium poppy. During the 1800s massive amounts of opium were stored in warehouses in the southeast side of Baltimore before they were smuggled overseas to the city of Canton, China where it had been outlawed. Wars between the Chinese and the smugglers ensued. There was a high demand for the products of the poppy plant in China in the 1800s. It was unforeseen that one day the market in Baltimore would grow into a multimillion-dollar, illegal demand for the same plant. That part of southeast Baltimore was named Canton, in honor of its Chinese counterpart, upon which its financial foundation was built.

There are streets and squares across the city named after the entrepreneurial captains of these opium ships and even after the trade ships themselves. Now, the once blue-collar neighborhood of Canton in Baltimore boasts half a million-dollar condominiums and row homes, clean parks, and high-end retail and restaurants. It's a place where young women walk with yoga mats and lattes to their next Pilates class, and people take their dogs to the dog park, or line up for ice cream on summer nights. All this activity sits just blocks away from an entirely different Baltimore City. Just up the street is the Baltimore that has boasted the highest per capita murder rate in the country many times during the course of my life. It is a sea of dilapidated and boarded up row homes that stretches for miles in any direction.

The same park where young professionals picnic and play wasn't safe just two decades ago during my active addiction. The same row homes that they pay over $250,000 for, were once selling for less than $10,000. In the early 1990's the corner of the park on Eastern Avenue and Patterson Park was the city's central prostitution hub. I remember riding past as a teenager and feeling shocked by the number of young women hanging on that corner. Just like in the movies, they were dressed in heels and short skirts, adorned in jewelry and make up. As heroin made its huge resurgence in the mid to late nineties, the mini-skirts and high heels disappeared, and the prostitutes on the same corners could be seen in pajama pants and bedroom slippers, with scarred faces and visible open sores. By the early 2000s after I had gotten clean, I passed by that same corner only to see young white males lined up sitting on the stone wall of the park looking sickly and half dead. These were addicts, presumably young men, who were more than likely from middle or even upper-class families, waiting on the next customer to come pick them up and give them their fix money to do things they never dreamed they would do. I spoke to a woman I knew from the area who was still involved in prostitution. She said that affluent business men circled the block picking these young boys up and paying them for sex and other sexual acts. These poor young men, who probably swore they'd never do anything like this had been broken by their addiction to heroin, by a drug that knows no bounds.

Heroin has ravaged the city over and over again. One little flower, the opium poppy has destroyed lives, families, and cities.

This flower, from which opium is extracted, is the base for all opiates, not limited to but including morphine, heroin, oxycodone, codeine, dilaudid, and fentanyl. Through science, man has morphed this flower into many different deadly and highly addictive substances. Heroin, the only pharmaceutically unavailable and completely illegal version of this plant, is also the most common on the streets of Baltimore and every major city in the United States. Since the 1940s heroin addiction has been rampant in the city of Baltimore, but after the Vietnam War, it saw a massive increase in demand on the streets. Young soldiers serving in Vietnam who had never touched the drug, found themselves using it to numb themselves to the horrors of battle as an alternative to alcohol, which ironically, they were not legally old enough to purchase. Many of these soldiers returned home with full-blown heroin habits.

The lower-class areas of the inner cities have always had a heavy layer of heroin addiction and a market for dealers. However, something happened in the late nineties to bring it mainstream attention. A new form of heroin was introduced to the Baltimore market. Prior to the nineties, there was only one form of heroin sold on the streets of Baltimore, called "scramble" heroin. Scramble was a white powder that came in clear gel caps and was heavily cut with other agents and commonly used by veteran addicts for injecting. Similarly, in the cities of Philadelphia and New York, they sold what we in Baltimore called 'Morphine Base.' It was sold in folded wax baggies that were often stamped with the brand of heroin that was inside of them. In the mid-nineties however, a new form of heroin started coming in through the Port of Baltimore, which proved to be ten times more potent than any heroin currently on the market. This heroin was referred to as "raw heroin," and was often sold in small vials or plastic baggies as chunky little rocks ranging from shades of brown to gray. The allure of this drug was that it was so potent that it could be sniffed instead of injected, which made it appealing to younger experimental drug users, especially those in suburban communities who had otherwise never seen the likes of heroin.

A huge insurgence of heroin use began to permeate the middle class and affluent suburban areas of Baltimore, and rapidly began to spread to the neighboring states like a contagious disease. It wasn't until the late nineties when children of prominent people within these communities began overdosing that it gained media attention and headlines. Police ramped up their operations, heroin task forces were created, and the war on heroin gained national headlines. Unfortunately, the supply and demand for this new drug was already spreading through the United States like wildfire, and the death toll in Baltimore and surrounding Maryland skyrocketed. There was something about sniffing this purer form of heroin that was causing the users' lungs to collapse, most often while they slept. It was a sneaky, silent killer, and it wasn't just taking the lives of full-blown destitute addicts anymore, it was killing first-time users and high school kids, leaving communities devastated and up in arms. What would often start as sniffing a line for fun at a high school party could quickly lead to a full-blown heroin addiction within months, multiple prison sentences, homelessness, and possibly sitting on the wall at the corner of Patterson Park selling your body for the next fix.

I had fortunately never gone to that extreme. I was versatile and creative, and I was a good thief. That's how I supported my addiction. However, I know that my rock bottom is infinite. "Rock bottom" is often used to describe a place where an addict falls that is the furthest depth of despair that they can reach, in which they have no choice but to rise up or die. People talk about hitting rock bottom, and that everyone's rock bottom is different, but the concept is completely a myth, in my opinion. Rock bottom is infinite. There is no solid bottom. No matter how far we think we wouldn't sink into addiction, our drug can take us there eventually. I have never sold my body to another male. I have never murdered anyone for the drug. I have never done irreparable damage to myself physically. However, I make no mistake in knowing that all these things are possible should I ever go back out and use heroin again. There is no level to which we won't descend, and I see it every day in the news. Addicts crash through rock bottoms. Knowing this and admitting to it are huge pieces in the lesson of humility that we must learn and embrace in order to stay clean. If I go back out there and use again, all my "nevers" will most likely come to pass.

Ultimately, as crazy as it sounds, heroin saved my life. I was a lost soul, a savage who was hellbent on self-destruction, living at animalistic levels, with no respect for others' lives or property, including my own. Heroin eventually broke down every single wall I had erected around myself and brought me to my knees. The very walls I had built, convinced that I was protecting myself, were in reality only closing me in. Heroin made them all crumble and left me bare and naked, with only the breath in my lungs that it almost stole from me as well. With nothing else remaining, I looked into my own soul, and eventually reached out to God to save me. Nothing in my life taught me as many invaluable lessons as heroin did. It taught me empathy, humility, selflessness, integrity, and gratitude, among others.

Few people are as lucky. In Narcotics Anonymous, there's a popular saying that says, "some must die, so that others may live." This is honest and raw. The idea that others died so that I may live gives me a tremendous amount of guilt. I've often thought, *why me?* as I wallowed in my own feelings of guilt and undeserving.

A friend of mine with breast cancer said she was crying out to God in her moment of pain, "Why me?"

And she heard Him answer back, clear as day, "Why not you?"

In the end it's just as valid a question. *Why me?* was the question I asked myself when I suffered. It was the question I asked myself when my life was spared. It is the same question I still ask myself about my life, and it remains the catalyst for me to stay clean and further my personal growth to this day. There will never be a concrete answer to that question for me. There are men and women across America in prison cells for the rest of their days on Earth asking that very same question. There are people permanently brain damaged or disfigured, still using drugs while trapped in their own eternal nightmare. And there are parents and loved ones of addicts crying out the very same question: *Why me?* My story is just one of millions. Like snow-flakes, they are all unique.

That question will more than likely never be answered for any of us. Were we born to go through this fire, and some of us not meant to see the other side? When an eager-eyed mother and father look down on their newborn baby boy or girl for the first time with love spilling from their hearts, the last thing they expect is for that child to grow up and put a needle in their arm. Why do some little babies turn into self-destructive teenagers who crash and burn, leaving only heartache and pain for their families who try everything in their power to teach them right from wrong and love them until they learn to love themselves? Even more of a mystery, why do some live to tell their tales, and others do not? How is it that some die the very first time they shoot heroin, and some live fifty years with full-fledged addiction? How does someone like me get chance after chance, while so many around me fell victim to death's call? I've seen people overdose and not come back on their first relapse, and others who go through relapse after relapse, prison sentence after prison sentence, and countless rehabs, yet keep breathing to continue their reign of terror.

I've met addicts whose mothers or fathers shot them up with their first shot of heroin, and others who came from two-parent homes where the parents were police officers or government officials. There are millions of addicts, like myself, who come from families with no prior history of addiction, and then there are those who have a long lineage of addiction in their family tree. There are those, also like myself, who suffer from anxiety and depression, so they self-medicate with drugs, as well as those who treat their own physical pain with narcotics. Meanwhile there are those who neither suffer mentally nor physically, yet use drugs recreationally only to get caught up in the same whirlwind of addiction. There are millions upon millions asking *Why me?* across this planet.

There is no definitive answer. Guilt weighs heavily upon me every time I talk to someone who lost a family member to drugs. I walk heavy-hearted, feeling undeserving and humbled because I got a second chance at life. However, this same humility is what keeps me doing everything I can to make myself and this world a better place every day. With gratitude comes humility, and with humility comes a willingness to learn, to be shaped and molded, and most importantly to serve. It is my greatest desire to bless others the way that I've been blessed.

Why me? I can only do my best to guess what the answer may be, so I focus on being an example, a light, and a role model for those who stumble down the same path I did. Every time I meet a family member who lost a loved one to addiction, I get uncomfortable with the guilt that I survived it. I'm not used to being the "lucky one." It's not comfortable to me. I plagued my own parents with years of trouble and hardship, and now they have their son back.

The same parents who wanted restraining orders against me and wouldn't speak to me for years, rightfully so, have both been employed at various times within my new businesses. I've been there to extend a hand to them in their times of need, and it's been an amazing feeling. I know that every family member and loved one of an addict deserves this, and the heartbreak of seeing their loss presses me onward. The only thing I can do is light the path and hope that others will follow.

My story is one of pain and suffering, but also one of success. I reached my own level of destitution quickly because of the lack of support I received. I don't say lack of support like it's a bad thing, either. My family cut me off immediately. I was evicted from the house on my eighteenth birthday. I was given multiple chances by them, but it was only when I was showing a genuine interest in getting help. I was never enabled, and my mother made sure that no one else in my family would help me either, including aunts, cousins, or grandparents. This meant not letting me have a place to stay if I was getting high, not giving me money or rides, no visits in jail, and only one phone call a week from jail. At the time, I cursed my family for these things, but in retrospect they saved my life. Their lack of support forced me into homelessness. It forced me to scramble for money, food, and shelter. It brought pain on me much quicker than if I had been enabled throughout my addiction. Unfortunately, as humans, and especially as addicts, pain is our number one motivating factor. It is not until we've had enough pain, that we begin to desire change. I wanted to stop using heroin almost from the time I realized I was addicted to it; however, it would take me several years before I finally was able to walk away from it. Several years of pain, over and over again. I would get clean, feel good about myself and my life, then forget the pain associated with the addiction and fall right back into it.

I've watched time and time again as family members of an addict enable the person to their death. It's a mother's or father's instinct to rescue their child, or a spouse's instinct to support their loved one. The problem comes when their support hinders the addict from feeling the negative effects associated with addiction. So, in reality, their support sustains the drug abuse. If I had family who gave me a place to stay while I was getting high, fed me, paid my bills, and gave me money, or did even one of those things, I may still be out there getting high today. Cutting a child off is one of the hardest things a parent or loved one could ever do, but is instrumental in pushing that person into the negative aspects of addiction, which is required to initiate a desire for change. If we are not careful, we can literally love an addict to death, by enabling them with a lifestyle that doesn't encourage them to stop.

Certainly, this is not a guarantee. The addict may overdose on the streets instead of the comfort of their own home. Or, they may wind up hurt or in jail for a long time because of something they did to get money because their family wouldn't give it to them, however those are the risks associated with addiction. The addict is on fire. We can stand around fanning the flames and hope they go out, or we can push them into the river in hopes that the water will put out the fire, and the addict will find their way safely to shore. It is not our job to fan the flames of an addict who doesn't want to help themselves. It is our job to push them to the water and stand on the shore with an arm extended to pull them out when they're ready. We should be willing to help anyone we love get treatment or stay clean, just not support them during their times of active addiction.

I've been walking the road of recovery for eighteen years now. Through patience and humility, I have been able to acquire not only that which I felt as though I didn't deserve, but also everything I never imagined I could have. I have owned multiple businesses, a home, and vehicles. I have traveled the world, and most importantly, I have started my own non-profit to serve those in need in many different sectors. At no point in the squalor of my addiction did I imagine I would be alive after the age of twenty-five, let alone watch the sun set in Panama, walk the streets of Belgium, or hike in Peru. Most importantly, these and all the opportunities that life has brought me were all paid for and planned by me. It was a long, slow journey to get here, a journey of patience and humility, but still a journey that is possible for any addict who can stay clean.

The most common question I receive from parents and loved ones is, "How?" They want to know how I got clean. "What was the final thing that just made you stop?" they will often ask in anticipation, imagining they can run home and give their son or daughter or husband the secret to kicking heroin once and for all.

I'm asked this question daily, and my heart drops every time. How do you sit in front of someone as a success story and not be able to give them a key to save someone they love? If I point to the sky and say, "It was God," that feels cliché, and is often the last thing they want to hear. If I tell them I did it on my own, that is not entirely true. The answer, if there is one, falls somewhere in between. Every story is different, I've seen people get clean on their first attempt, and others try a thousand times, and ultimately kill themselves trying. I've seen some get clean through going to meetings, and others through religion. I've seen some continue to drink and use other drugs and only stop heroin, but I've seen the majority try the same thing and die in a relapse. Every human being is different, and every single story is different.

One thing I know is that most addicts are highly intelligent, compassionate, and creative human beings. Intellectual depth, intelligence and empathy are wonderful characteristics and signs of a mature soul, but can also be a curse in today's world. Our society is full of overwhelming responsibility, of ignorance and suffering, of perpetual fear, and pressure to race alongside your peers and exceed expectations. To many, drugs seem like a necessity. Heroin simplifies life. It is a numbing agent to the various pains of life: physical pain, emotional pain, mental stress, depression, anxiety, self-doubt, and fear. They all disappear at the end of the syringe. However, it develops into a full-time job and lifestyle to keep the syringe filled and keep those feelings at bay.

The only thing I have to offer is my story. I realize it's easy to say that I believe in God and that God is good when I've lived through so many miracles. However, it is only through my perception that I'm able to recognize those events as miracles. My story could be told in an entirely different way if my perception was different. My life could have been easier if it weren't for my own doing. Most of the negative things that happened to me happened because of my personal decisions and responses to life's challenges. I am mature enough to realize that now. I also realize that there are a lot of people who have been faced with a lot more trauma than I have. I can't speak to why those things happened to them, but I can look back at my own life and pinpoint a lesson in every challenge. I can see God's hand in every hardship I faced, shaping, and molding me. My outlook and responses could have been very different in the end. My life could have turned out quite differently had I made other choices along the way. It was only because I eventually began to recognize God building me through my pain that I was able to change. Had I not shifted my focus from my suffering and victim mentality, my story could have been about nothing but suffering and failure that ended tragically.

I have found that a shift in perception is necessary in order to stay clean. There is an entire shift in the worldview of an addict. It's not momentous, and it doesn't happen instantly. The beginning of this shift happened in me long before I ever got clean. It started, first, once I stopped seeing myself as a victim. I started taking personal responsibility for where I was and everything that happened to me in life. I acknowledged that I had made bad choices. I could pick apart my childhood and teenage years and place blame on my circumstances or on other people, and maybe some of those accusations would be plausible. However, that train of thought never served me or helped me grow. Once I started accepting personal responsibility for everything that happened in my life, and stopped blaming everything and everyone else, something strange happened, I began to grow in self-esteem. My acceptance of personal responsibility made me feel more like a man and less like a victim. As a man, I began to clean up after myself and make changes.

As I got clean and my situations slowly started improving, I became more and more grateful, and through that gratitude I became humble. Being humble meant that I had patience. I stopped getting frustrated at the world around me because things weren't going my way or moving quickly enough for me. All my peers had nice things—careers, cars, homes, wives—and I had nothing. I learned that there was nothing I could do to make things come any faster, than to do my very best each day as I was living it.

I didn't do anything right the first time though. I was egotistical and hardheaded. Just like the many times during active addiction that I tried to return to "only drinking alcohol," which eventually led me right back to heroin, I tested all the other forbidden fruit. There was a hole inside of me, and I desperately tried to fill it. I tried to fill it with many other non-life-threatening addictions. I went through a phase where I chased and juggled as many women as I could. Then, I went through a clothing phase, a gym phase, and a work phase—obsessively trying to fill the hole inside. I dove in over and over again. I made myself busy dressing up my exterior, instead of working on what was on the inside. Eventually my impatience for material success took me back to selling cocaine again, and I almost slipped up and lost everything. The seeds of recovery were sewn deep inside of me, and I caught myself before irreparable damage was done.

Four years into recovery I went to a specialist to have all four of my wisdom teeth removed. I was a different person. I hadn't used a drug in four years. I had worked at the same place all four of those years and had a long-term girlfriend as well. When I had my consult with the oral surgeon, I proudly explained that I was a recovering addict, and that I couldn't take any narcotic drugs. He chuckled as if I were a madman. He insisted that I had to have something. After some back and forth, I remembered the three-day rule.

"Okay," I sighed. "Just give me three days' worth."

My girlfriend was in the room, and although she had never seen me in active addiction, she had heard the stories. The doctor's insistence was making her extremely uneasy. I was given anesthesia intravenously when the teeth were extracted. I remember my words vividly upon waking.

After not touching heroin in four years, my first words to her upon opening my eyes were, "Take me downtown."

I was clearly out of my mind from the anesthesia, but it was eerily foreboding of things to come. The doctor had written a fourteen-day prescription for Percocet, even though we had insisted, and he had agreed, upon three. The temptation had already taken root though. I convinced my girlfriend that I was okay to monitor my own dosage, and that I wouldn't abuse it. Within a few days the whole bottle was gone, and I was back scouring the streets of Baltimore for heroin. This lasted two weeks before I went to the Health Department to see an outpatient detox doctor. The doctor insisted that I take methadone.

"Absolutely not!" I told him. "I've already been down that road, and I'll never go back. I've only been using for a couple weeks this time."

He insisted that methadone was the only solution for me. I'll never forget his exact words that I was "an extreme case, and would never get clean and stay clean without it."

Angry, and having something to prove, I walked out of his office and never looked back. I never touched heroin or methadone again.

In 2011, eleven years since my last drink, I was feeling on top of the world. I had my own home, my own business making six figures, and was back in the dating scene after a long-term relationship had ended. I decided to have a glass of wine at dinner one night on a first date. It had been over a decade. I was successful. I was a new man. *Surely I can drink, right?* About three weeks, three fights, and one incarceration later, I put down alcohol for the last and final time. I cannot drink successfully under any circumstance, no matter how much time has elapsed, this I am sure of. This is one of the hardest concepts to grasp for the recovering addict, and the most common one I see lead to heroin relapse and eventually death. A very minuscule number of addicts are able to drink successfully and live normal lives. The odds are stacked against us. If a person wants to get clean and stay clean, they must be willing to take every single necessary precaution. The allure of drinking is not worth the smallest chance of returning to the pits of addiction and the misery that comes with it. This is something we must constantly keep at the forefronts of our minds.

There is no single way to get clean that works for everyone, but there are tried and tested ways that work for most. The keys to being successful in sobriety are willingness and surrender. It is my humility, which stems from my gratitude for being given a second chance, that gives me the ability to surrender and be willing. Willingness means being open to do whatever it takes to stay clean and preserve my own life, and surrender means checking my ego at the door. I didn't want to go to treatment programs, but I did. I didn't want to go to meetings every single night for the first six months, but I did. I didn't want to hang out with people who I didn't consider "cool," but I did because they knew how to stay clean. I didn't want to take advice from people, or take orders from my boss, but I did. I didn't want to do half of the things that my life of early sobriety demanded of me, but I did because I surrendered. By letting go and surrendering, I was shaped and molded into a much stronger man.

My way of thinking eventually changed, and those who I

once saw as cool suddenly weren't so cool anymore. The hard-core addicts were weak, broken, and in pain. The dealers were feeding on the weakness of the sick, and the gangsters were just lost souls covering up their insecurities with toughness. I began to see the world through the eyes of "normal" people and not through the distorted worldview I had once had. All of those I once thought were strong and tough were quite the opposite. I had been looking up to the wrong people the whole time. It took many years for me to fully open my eyes, and it took a lot of self-honesty and soul searching to get there.

Since a child, I've been chasing the sun. Those hot summers down the eastern shore of Virginia at Cherrystone Campground were some of the best times of my life. When the clouds and rain came, my mood changed with them. Every year when the summer ended, a part of me died with it. As the seasons changed, so did I. Like clockwork, I got into trouble every October. My family became aware of this anomaly and sat with bated breath every fall, wondering if I could make it until winter without issue. As I grew into adulthood, this phenomenon continued. It was every October or early November that I would get locked up, year after year.

It was something my mother would casually bring up with a sigh, "Well, it's October again. Do you think you can make it past your birthday without going to jail this year?"

My birthday was on Halloween, and chances were that I wouldn't make it. I thought it was just a freak occurrence. I never put much thought into it.

As I grew older and got clean, I was still left to battle severe depression and anxiety. Life didn't become perfect, and suffering didn't cease, just because I got clean. There was a lot of internal wreckage to deal with, including the very reasons I drank and drugged to begin with. Years clean, I noticed that my anxiety and depression were much worse in the winter months, and that in the warmer months when the sun was out, they were almost non-existent. In the face of the sun, I become a totally different person.

There is a sense of security I get from the sun. It brings me hope, brightness, energy, and warmth. The soft kiss of the sun upon my skin cradles me. It blankets my body in a sense of comfort, and I spend as much time in it as possible. There was only ever one other thing on Earth that gave me the same comfort, the same warmth, security, and energy—and that was heroin. Heroin was my flawed sun. It burned me every time I got too close. It consumed me in its fire, and by the grace of God, I narrowly escaped with my life.

Our entire life is a chase. If we aren't chasing something, we are dying. We find purpose in the chase. Once we've caught what we are chasing, we are immediately unfulfilled. It is the chase itself that fulfills us. It gives us meaning and focus. It ignites our passion. I found that same fervor in chasing heroin. Every day the chase consumed me, reducing my life to tunnel vision and simplicity. It closed out all the worries and cares of the world. The pursuit was primitive and fulfilling. This is why, throughout all the pain and suffering, it was so hard to leave and so easy to fall back into. I would wake up in darkness and chase the sun all day until I caught it, and then lay in its gentle warmth as it consumed me alive.

There was a faint calling of purpose, a purpose greater than heroin, that lie dormant in the back of my mind, a faint belief in a God who had greater meaning for me, and people who loved me but I was hurting, that inspired me to want to finally stop chasing my flawed sun. Between my belief in greater purpose, the desire to stop hurting others, and the path I was on in the legal system, I was finally able to end the chase once and for all. The longer I have stayed clean, the clearer my belief in God and my higher purpose have become.

I still chase the sun. I chase the real sun—the sun I know I will never catch. I chase the sun inside of me and the sun outside of me. Over the past eighteen years of recovery, I have done my best to build a life that allows me to chase the sun as much as I possibly can. During the cold gloomy winters of Maryland, I often catch flights to any number of Central or Southern American countries, or one of the many Caribbean islands. Travel is one of my new passions, and one of my many outlets for chasing the sun that breathes life into me. I lay in it under palm trees, or splashing about in faraway oceans, and sometimes briefly forget the alleyways and dope holes of Baltimore City.

I also chase the Son. I found a role model Whom I can never catch, but I can spend the rest of my life trying to emulate. I've studied almost all religious and spiritual paths and have found an idol in Jesus of Nazareth, the closest thing to perfection in human form to ever walk this Earth. I've set my eyes on the Son, and strive to be as caring, empathetic, and humble as He was. I know inside that even though reaching that level of perfection isn't possible, my fulfillment is in the chase. This Son, just like the other, keeps me warm. He fulfills me and sustains me. And He is not flawed.

I've heard many statistics about the number of heroin addicts who get clean and stay clean for the rest of their lives after treatment. It seems the most common statistic given is that somewhere around one in thirty-two to thirty-six people actually stop using permanently without relapse and go on to live productive successful lives and eventually die clean. These numbers are painful, and not only disheartening to the families of addicts, but to the users themselves as well. It seems almost hopeless, and yet there are thousands of people right here in the community of Baltimore, and every other community, who have escaped the grip that the drug once had on us.

There is no way I can pinpoint an exact moment that I stopped using, because it didn't happen like that. It was a slow, grueling, and painful process. As I've stated for years, my basic desire to stop using occurred shortly after I started and realized that I was addicted. However, I found that quitting wasn't as easy as it sounds. The mind is a tricky thing, and oftentimes our worst enemy. Getting clean and staying clean, and fighting through the mental and physical withdrawals of heroin use, is by far no easy task. It takes hours and hours, and days and days, of physical, emotional, and mental torture. But it only takes one split-second decision to pick up the drug and make it all go away. It is a task of perseverance, repetition, and failure after failure. I got so used to disappointing myself and those around me that I lost all self-esteem and self-worth, and eventually stopped caring whether or not I lived to see another day.

I wish I had an absolute concrete answer to give those still using, and those in pain because their loved ones are still in active addiction, but the recipe for conquering heroin isn't that simple. From my experience, and from my observation of others, it is a combination of willingness, maturity, humility, perseverance, and complete and utter defeat. It is not until the pain threshold has become unbearable that we are willing to change our circumstance. Only when we admit defeat, and that we cannot successfully use drugs or alcohol anymore, can we begin the process of change. Once we've made this inner-decision, with humility as our guide, we must be willing to do whatever it takes to stay clean and never go back. Doing whatever it takes means removing any objects or sources of temptation from our lives, whether they be people, places, or things. It means following the advice of those who have come down the same path before us. It means doing anything and everything in our power to increase our self-worth and rebuild the parts of ourselves that drugs tore down.

I personally like to look at the places in my life where heroin affected me, then work to build them up every single day. Drugs left me about a decade behind my peers, and even with eighteen years in recovery, I'm still catching up. It is my duty as an addict to work on all of the areas to which drugs and alcohol were cancerous—which for me is almost everywhere. It is commonly said that every day we either live a little or die a little, the decision is ours. I choose to not only live, but to build. Drugs and alcohol damaged my physical body, so I dedicate myself to the gym and clean eating. It numbed my brain and kept me ignorant, so now I read, I do crosswords and other puzzles, and I study and learn daily. It depleted all of my finances, so I work hard, and I learn how to be financially stable, only earning an income through channels that align with my moral character. It destroyed my relationships with those I love, so I practice being a good son, brother, lover, and friend. It numbed my emotions so long, that I have to practice being emotionally responsible. I constantly take an inner-inventory and learn about myself, which is a process that would benefit every one of us and should never stop until we die. Drugs and alcohol also caused me to become selfish and self-consumed, so I devote my time to selfless endeavors, caring for people, and giving back to the same community that I plagued during my addiction. I do my very best to counteract the destruction I caused by contributing in positive ways.

I can't undo the damage I caused during my active addiction, but I can commit to first, forgive myself, and then to make amends by doing the opposite things now that I'm clean. Most of all, no matter how much I do to leave the old me in the past and become a new improved version of myself, I always remain humble and never forget where I came from and how quickly I could go back. No matter how much time we invest in our recovery from the onset, it only takes one poor decision to throw it all away and destroy everything we've built.

I liken the life of a recovering addict to that of a tightrope walker. We start off on the bottom, and the road to recovery is a long climb. The ladder we climb to the tightrope is a long journey of pain and suffering. These are the jails, the treatment facilities, the detoxes, and the counselors we must pass through. When we're ready to walk out into the world, we are terrified. We are standing above the pit on a tiny little platform with the tightrope of life stretched out before us. It is intimidating knowing how carefully we must balance ourselves from here forward, with no platform to brace us anymore, and no ladder to hold onto. Life doesn't stand still. We must step out onto the tightrope with wavering feet and racing hearts.

Slowly and patiently, we must walk the rope of life in front of us; we cannot race ahead. It is because of the intimidation of having to walk this rope for the rest of our lives, or the want to race ahead and catch up to our peers, that the majority of relapses happen in the first twenty-four hours, and ninety percent of the tightrope walkers will relapse within the first year. We can't afford to look at the never-ending rope that stretches ahead. Rather, slowly, and steadily, one foot at a time, we must focus on our current movements. We can look down briefly to remind ourselves how far the drop is. But stare too long, and we'll end up plunging back there again. Our focus must remain singularly on the rope directly in front of us.

Over time, the walk becomes easier as we begin to learn how to maneuver on it. We can look down longer. We can look further forward. We can walk, skip, and even dance on it, as long as we never forget we are on a rope, and that at any moment we can fall back to where we came from. The awareness of our ability to fall is our humility, and the awareness of the rope that we walk is our gratitude. We know if we fall it could mean death, or it could mean permanent damage, but if we survive the fall, we must make it back to the ladder and start all over again.

Eighteen years walking this rope, I've learned to love the rope that I once hated. I've done handstands and cartwheels on this rope, but I have never forgotten it was there. The rope that started in a dark, cold cell has led me through worlds I never dreamed existed. I've walked this rope through the beaches of Costa Rica, through the Amazon jungle, and the red rock mountains of Arizona. This rope has taken me through relationships and friendships with amazing and beautiful people, through heartaches and moments of unparalleled joy. I have walked this rope through the darkness of deep depression and heart-wrenching anxiety, and through years of contentment and eagerness chasing the sun that always comes. This rope has taken me through building businesses and watching my businesses crumble, through watching people pass away and babies be born. I've walked my rope through one funeral after another for addicts who fell from their own ropes. I know that at any moment if I forget the rope, that it could be me too.

Somewhere at the far end of this rope is the sunset of my life. Only then will I not have to balance carefully and worry about the rope beneath me anymore. Until then, I have found a way to enjoy the walk, to embrace the balance that I once despised, and to show others that it is possible to walk this rope as well. The sun is my guide. It gives me the warmth. It kisses my skin like heroin once did. I know that as long as I stay focused on the rope I'm walking, that I'm guaranteed to see the sun rise every day and appreciate its beauty. I no longer have to hide in the shadows. I'm now chasing the one true sun, and one day when I reach the end of my rope, I'll finally set with it.

Until then, God bless.

"I've seen the needle and the damage done,
a little part of it in everyone.
every junkies like a setting sun....
gone, gone, the damage done."

-Neil Young

CONTACT/FOLLOW THE AUTHOR

Daniel McGhee
PO Box 1694
Bel Air, MD 21014

www.chasingaflawedsun.com

www.evolvesohard.com

Facebook: @chasingaflawedsun

Instagram: @officialdannydiamond

CPSIA information can be obtained
at www.ICGtesting.com
Printed in the USA
LVHW051039011020
667507LV00002B/10